D0900994

CHRISTIAN
MYSTICISM
the future of a tradition

Harvey D. Egan, S.J.

CHRISTIAN MYSTICISM
the future of a tradition

PUEBLO PUBLISHING COMPANY / NEW YORK

Scriptural pericopes are quoted from the Revised Standard
Version.

Copyright © 1984 Pueblo Publishing Company, Inc.
All rights reserved.

Design: Br. Aelred-Seton Shanley

ISBN: 0-916134-63-6

Printed in the United States of America.

For Mom, Dad,
Joyce, Jerry,
David, Donna, and Denise—
with special love and blessings.

Contents

ACKNOWLEDGEMENTS

I am especially grateful to Mary Luti, Charles Healey, S.J., and William Read, S.J., for reading the entire manuscript and for their excellent suggestions and constructive criticisms. I also want to thank Boston College for my sabbatical year, the Department of Theology for providing me with help, and my Jesuit community for their support during the writing of this book. Mark Hart and Vincent Masi deserve thanks for their proofreading. I also express my thanks to Sr. Mary Joseph, O.S.B., of *Word and Spirit*, and Victor LaMotte, O.P., editor of *Listening*, for permission to reproduce my articles, "Selected Reflections on the Christocentrism of St. Teresa of Avila" and "The Christian Mystics and Today's Theological Horizon," as parts of chapters 4 and 9. I appreciate the invaluable technical assistance of Joanne Brennan and Charles Connor of Boston College's word-processing center. I also wish to thank Mr. Bernard Benziger and Mr. Kevin McLaughlin of Pueblo Publishing Company. Finally, I am deeply grateful to Father William Johnston, S.J., for his foreword.

Feast of the Presentation of the Lord   Harvey D. Egan, S.J.
February 2, 1983

Foreword

The last two decades have witnessed great progress in
the study of theology. We now look on theology as an
ongoing, developing science asking new questions,
making new discoveries, garnering new insights, penetrating more and more deeply into the deposit of revelation. Theology is a search for an ever-deepening understanding of the mystery of God.

Side by side with this search for God in theology, we
witness a search for God in prayer. Here, too, remarkable development and progress have taken place.
Whereas at one time pride of place was allotted to the
so-called discursive prayer with its activity of the three
powers of the soul, now people are quickly taught affective prayer, the Jesus prayer, prayer with breathing,
prayer of posture, and a variety of rich methods. Today
we become aware of altered states of consciousness and
new levels of awareness. Many people aspire to mystical prayer. This development owes much to dialogue
with modern psychology and with the Orient, but
above all I believe it is the work of the Holy Spirit
leading his people in the ways of mysticism.

So we find ourselves in an age of mysticism. Needless
to say, mysticism has always flourished within Christianity and has formed itself into a great tradition. Until
recently, however, Christian mysticism was for an elite,
for those who lived in monasteries and convents. It was
not for the masses of the people—the butcher, the
baker, the candlestick maker. But things have changed.

One finds ordinary people sitting quietly before the Blessed Sacrament enjoying that obscure sense of God's presence about which Christian mystics love to speak. Moreover, there are indications that many more Christians could enjoy this gift of mystical prayer if only they were taught and had a guide.

Where will they find such a guide? Many people find guidance from books, from the writings of the great teachers. Here they find the advice that helps them listen to the ultimate Guide: the indwelling Holy Spirit. Hence the popularity of the author of *The Cloud of Unknowing*, St. Teresa of Avila, St. John of the Cross, Thomas Merton, and the rest. Here the guides of the past still live in their works and speak to countless men and women who aspire to a life of mystical prayer.

Harvey Egan has written an introduction to and a contemporary transposition of Christian mysticism. This is a crying need for our day, for while certain mystical states of consciousness are common to all religions, Christian mysticism has its own unique and special content. Christian mysticism is an entering into the mystery of Christ, into the Pauline mystery of "the unsearchable riches of Christ . . . hidden for ages in God who created all things" (Eph 3:8–9). As we enter more deeply into this mystery of Christ we enter into a cloud of unknowing, into the void of darkness, into the night of the soul. It is a challenging and beautiful journey, in spite of the suffering inevitably demanded. We know we are on the right path if we can cry out: "Jesus is Lord!" (1 Cor 12:3), and if, one with Jesus and in the Spirit, we cry out: "Abba! Father!" (Gal 4:6).

Christian Mysticism: The Future of a Tradition will be of great value not only to academics interested in mystical theology, but also to Christians who look for guidance in prayer and who aspire to mysticism.

William Johnston, S.J.

Preface

Twenty-four years ago I read for the first time St. John of the Cross' *Dark Night of the Soul.* Although I was an electrical engineer who had read almost nothing religious since my grammar school catechisms, John's book stirred me deeply. I sensed acutely how important this book could be for authentic Christian living and so took it to the local parish priest. With good humor, he urged me to forget about St. John of the Cross and to get back to "normal" Catholic sacramental life and devotions. I obeyed. Still, I never lost my conviction that John of the Cross had put his finger on something of the utmost importance for vital Christian living. I half-saw then what I see clearly now: the Church's pastoral life suffers much for its benign neglect of the enormously rich Christian mystical heritage.

In 1969 I went to Germany to begin doctoral studies in theology under the direction of Karl Rahner. My dissertation attempted to translate the mystical wisdom of St. Ignatius of Loyola into a contemporary framework by using Rahner's transcendental method. Rahner's theological approach had long attracted me for a number of reasons. His theology is anchored solidly to reflection upon a central, yet often hidden, mystical experience that takes place in every human heart. He is also one of the few contemporary theologians with an unabashed interest in the mystics and their writings as a theological source. Moreover, he contends that contemporary Christian spirituality, in order to rejuvenate itself, must be more open to other theological disciplines.

Finally, his own work has done much to heal the rift between mystical experience and academic theology.

During my studies with Rahner, a close friend wisely urged me to study Eastern mysticisms in addition to my other theological studies. He argued that they had much to offer Christianity; he further noted that I would be forced to take them seriously later on for the simple reason that Eastern religions had become such a fad in the United States. My study of contemporary theology and of Eastern mysticisms changed the way I approached the classical Christian mystics. Contemporary theological questions and the challenge from Eastern religions uncovered for me some of the profound wealth in the Christian mystical tradition and the need to retrieve these riches for contemporary Christian theology, spirituality, and mysticism.

Four years later I had the pleasure of becoming friends with William Johnston, the Irish Jesuit at the Sophia University in Tokyo, who has written much on Eastern and Western mysticisms. His gentleness, commitment to his own religious heritage, appreciation of the values in Eastern religions, critical discernment, lucid prose, and insistence upon an East-West dialogue based on mystical experience have long inspired me.

The following year, an American Buddhist community invited me to give a series of talks on Christian spirituality and mysticism. To my astonishment, I discovered that most of the Buddhist membership were former Christians. During the course of the talks it became apparent that they knew absolutely nothing about the profundity of their own Christian mystical heritage. Their questions reminded me that I had never heard a sermon, a homily, a lecture, or a catechism class on the deep and simple prayer of the Christian mystics until I had entered the Society of Jesus.

I began teaching theology at Boston College in 1975. To my delight, I discovered that Bernard Lonergan lived only a few doors away from me. Although I had read all his works, the "implicit" Lonergan I gradually came to know changed the way I read his theological writings. While many legitimately praise him for his cognitional theory and theological method, I learned from him especially that a theologian's call to unrestricted being in love with God can only be distinguished from his theological reflection, but never separated. The proper subject for today's theology is no less than the authentic self that surrenders to its mystical hunger for ultimate truth, meaning, and love.

Convinced by these experiences that Christian mysticism is extremely important for Christianity's present and future, I have taught courses on this tradition for ten years now. This book is born, then, of that personal conviction. The obvious influence of Rahner, Johnston, and Lonergan will be noted by the attentive reader.

I have focused upon four classical and two contemporary Christian mystics or mystical writers for two reasons. First, today's person must become familiar with key figures in the classical tradition to obtain a sense and a knowledge of what genuine Christian mysticism is, especially in view of so many false contemporary opinions. Second, in the light of this tradition's momentum, one must see how significant contemporary figures have transposed this wisdom for the future.

By selecting authors whose mystical authenticity is almost beyond question, this book attempts to summarize them from a contemporary theological viewpoint. The exposition interacts implicitly and explicitly with contemporary issues to translate the Christian mystical heritage into a contemporary frame of reference for its future appreciation.

This book emphasizes Christian mysticism as the fullness of both Christian religious existence and of authentic human living. It centers on the Christian mystics as pioneers of a new, transformed, fully genuine humanity. The mystics amplify and make visible what human life is ultimately about: being loved by a God of unconditional love. Their lives bring into focus the faith, hope, and love which haunt every human heart.

The mystics have surrendered to the deepest aspirations and spontaneities of the human heart. They have actuated the most profound levels of human life, refusing to live only a surface existence. They know who they are because they surrender all to find All. More importantly, they acknowledge this and live differently. Their lives celebrate and praise a God who is madly in love with humanity; they likewise live and celebrate the fact that we are all secretly in love with each other because of God's ever-present love.

Although their common sense, social-political acumen, compassion, and service to humanity show what they do for God, what they *are* for God is more important: icons of agapic love. They are paradigms of every human vocation: the call to exist for God in human authenticity and to exist for others in love, service, compassion, social and political insight, and practical concerns.

This book assumes that because of the purity of their experience of God and the resulting transformation of human existence, the mystics are a source for contemporary theological reflection. And if the dialogue between East and West can be based on mystical experience, Christians must first take seriously their own valuable mystical tradition.

Chapter 1 deals briefly with the word "mysticism," a few key definitions, the essential characteristics of authentic Christian mysticism, popular misconceptions, and biblical mysticism. It stresses mysticism primarily as a way of life in which one explicitly experiences God's purifying, illuminating, and transforming love. By emphasizing Christian mysticism as the full flowering of biblical mysticism, especially an imitation of Jesus' trinitarian mysticism, it rejects the view that mysticism is a craving for experiences or exotic altered states of consciousness, a pathological condition, or even religious experience in the ordinary sense.

Why begin chapter two with an exposition of St. Ignatius of Loyola? After all, the author of *The Cloud of Unknowing* wrote much earlier than Ignatius. But I am beginning with Ignatius because he is the mystic I know best, and the mystic who has most influenced my own life. Moreover, the more I read profitably other mystics, the more fascinated I become with Ignatius.

Also, the very structure of his *Spiritual Exercises* offers an easy way into the mystical journey. That Ignatius does not make the strong ascetical/mystical distinction found among many spiritual writers has many advantages for contemporary spirituality. One finds in Ignatius, then, the ascetical foundations of mysticism and the ascetical dimension of mysticism. For this reason, Ignatius can speak to both those in the premystical and to those in the strictly mystical stages of the mystical journey.

His *Spiritual Exercises*—mystical at heart—have the ability to lead persons at any level of spiritual development into even deeper realms of the spiritual life. And Ignatius' richly incarnational, kataphatic (Greek: *kataphatikos* = affirmative) mysticism found God in all things, all things in God, and never dissociated love of God, neighbor, and world. His profound trinitarian and christocentric mysticism incarnated itself in a community of love for effective apostolic service that included the social and political dimensions of human existence. Thus, I continue to find his mysticism and spirituality remarkably contemporary.

Chapter 3 presents the *Cloud of Unknowing* as a model of Christian apophatic (Greek: *apophatikos* = negative) mysticism. This mystical tradition emphasizes that God cannot be known by the intellect; only dark, silent love can comprehend the ever-greater God. The *Cloud* offers an especially lucid presentation of a mysticism that experiences and speaks about God as known through unknowing, darkness, and naked love.

The fourth chapter turns to another example of kataphatic, sacramental mysticism—St. Teresa of Avila. This Doctor of the Church reached the summit of the mystical life. With her personal, unrestrained, and often homey style of writing, she quickly draws the reader into exceptionally penetrating descriptions of the wide gamut of mystical experiences that she underwent throughout her fascinating life. She is simply my favorite woman mystic. Besides, I have rarely met anyone who did not enjoy reading her.

The fifth chapter returns to apophatic mysticism as taught by St. John of the Cross. It is important to delineate what his mysticism of the "Nothing" can mean for today, especially in view of the relative lack of appreciation among Christians for the apophatic tradition.

Because of his affinities with St. John of the Cross, Thomas Merton is treated in Chapter 6. His blend of monastic, apophatic mysticism with a strong concern for social, political, and economic issues is especially appealing today. He has translated the apophatic and monastic traditions for contemporary Christian living.

Chapter 7 centers upon the kataphatic, evolutionary mysticism of Pierre Teilhard de Chardin. His powerful mysticism of knowing, of finding God in all things, of combining love for God and love for the evolutionary world, is a paradigm of what he himself sought: a "new" mysticism.

Chapters 8 and 9 deal with selected questions of importance today: the relationship of Christian mysticism to secondary mystical phenomena, to charismatic phenomena, to psychedelic drug experiences, to the demonic, to perfection, and to contemporary theology.

Chapter One

Introductory Themes

A BRIEF HISTORY OF THE WORD "MYSTICISM"

The word "mysticism" is not found in the Bible. Historically the word is associated with the Hellenistic mystery religions and cults of the pre-Christian and early Christian era. The "mystics" (Greek: *hoi mystai*), or the "mystical ones" (*hoi mystai,* occasionally: *hoi mystikoi*), were those who had been initiated into the secret rites (*ta mystika*) of these mystery religions and cults. Moreover, the mystics were required to keep secret the rituals of the Greek mystery religions into which they had been initiated. The word "mystical," therefore, originally referred to the cultic or ritual secrets revealed only to the initiated, the mystics. The mystical secret was usually only a secret about the purely material aspects of the rites and rituals of the Greek mystery religions.

Neoplatonic philosophers may have applied the word "mystical" to some of their speculative doctrines because they found certain aspects of these mystery religions conducive to their way of life and thinking. The Greek verb *myo* means to close the eyes, and some of these philosophers urged a deliberate shutting of the eyes to all external reality in order to obtain a secret, or mystical, knowledge fostered by introverted contemplation. Withdrawing from everything external to sink within oneself allowed a person to receive inner, divine illuminations.

The great Jewish religious thinker, Philo of Alexandria (20 B.C.–50 A.D.), welded Jewish beliefs and spirituality with Greek thought. He focused sharply upon the "mystical," or allegorical, interpretation of scripture. For him, "mystical" did not refer to the secret details of a ritual, but to the secret and hidden meaning of God's word. Thus, he was probably the bridge between the Jewish and Greek worlds for the transposed use of the word "mystical" as the later Fathers of the Church used it with respect to scripture.

For many Alexandrian Christians and the early Greek Fathers of the Church, "mystical" signified the allegorical interpretation of scripture, especially the disclosing of Christ as the key in unlocking the secrets of the Old Testament. Origen (185–254 A.D.) is paradigmatic of those Christians who considered exegesis as "mystical and ineffable contemplation" that must combine both scholarly erudition and the experiential knowledge of God. The divine reality ushered in by Christ, the knowledge of divine things, and the spiritual reality present in all genuine worship were likewise considered "mystical." Eventually, Christians used the word "mystical" with respect to the sacraments, especially the eucharist. By the time of Constantine, the word "mystical" had biblical, liturgical, and sacramental connotations and often denoted the hidden presence of Christ in the scriptures, the liturgy, and the sacraments. It often meant his "sacred" or "spiritual" presence.

The word "mystical" entered definitively into Christian vocabulary, however, through the important writings of Pseudo-Dionysius, a sixth-century Syrian monk. Although he still used the word in discussing problems of exegesis, his famous treatise, the *Mystica Theologia*, taught a mystical contemplation that permitted a person to know God as the "Divine Darkness" by way of unknowing. As he says: "But do thou, dear Timothy, in the diligent exercise of mystical contemplation, leave behind the senses and the operations of the intellect,

2

and all things sensible and intellectual, and all things in the world of being and non-being, that thou may arise by unknowing towards the union, as far as is attainable, with Him who transcends all being and all knowledge. For by the unceasing and absolute renunciation of thyself and of all things thou mayest be borne on high, through pure and entire self-abnegation, into the superessential Radiance of the Divine Darkness."[1] John Scotus Eriugena translated his works into Latin in the ninth century, and since then Pseudo-Dionysius has had a considerable influence on the Christian mystical tradition. His writings have long fascinated the Western mind, not only because he claimed to be the convert of St. Paul mentioned in Acts 17:34, but also because many Christians have been nourished by his beautiful cosmic sense and by his insights into the dark, silent, nondiscursive knowledge of God born in the darkness of the mind beyond all thoughts and concepts.

In the Latin Church, however, the word "mysticism" was infrequently used until the late Middle Ages. Broadly speaking, earlier Church Fathers—Augustine, Gregory, and Bernard, for example—used the word "contemplation" for what we call "mysticism." Still, in the Christian mystical tradition "mystical theology" gradually came to mean the knowledge of God attained by direct, immediate, and ineffable contemplation. It was distinguished from both "natural theology" (knowledge of God obtained from creatures) and "dogmatic theology" (knowledge of God received from revelation). It must be emphasized, however, that the best of Christian tradition never reduced mysticism to the psychological level nor dissociated it from its biblical, liturgical, and sacramental basis. As Louis Bouyer writes, Christian mysticism: ". . . is always the experience of an invisible objective world: the world whose coming the Scriptures reveal to us in Jesus Christ, the world into which we enter, ontologically, through the liturgy, through this same Jesus Christ ever present in the Church."[2]

3

For the sake of clarity, it might help to focus our attention immediately upon a few classical and contemporary definitions of "mystical theology" and "mysticism." St. Bonaventure (1217–1274) defined mystical theology as "the raising of the mind to God through the desire of love."[3] For Jean Gerson (1363–1428), mystical theology is "the experimental knowledge of God through the embrace of unitive love."[4] Although somewhat lengthy, St. Teresa of Avila's (1515–1582) definition of mystical theology is worth quoting in full: "The soul is completely suspended in such a way that it seems to be completely outside itself. The will loves; the memory . . . is almost lost; the intellect does not work discursively . . . but is not lost . . . it is as though amazed by all it understands because God desires that it understand, with regard to the things His Majesty represents to it, that it understands nothing."[5] Finally, for St. John of the Cross (1542–1592), "contemplation is the mystical theology which theologians call secret wisdom which St. Thomas says is communicated and infused into the soul through love."[6]

It should be noted that these classical definitions equate mystical theology with mystical experience. Contemporary usage, on the other hand, equates mystical theology with the doctrines and theories of mystical experience. In a way which recalls St. Thomas Aquinas' definition of contemplation as a knowledge of God through experience, St. John of the Cross equates mystical theology with contemplation.

These classical definitions underscore, moreover, an experience of God that is somehow direct, immediate, intuitive, and beyond the normal workings of the intellect and senses. The genuine mystic is united and one with God, and from this loving union flows a special knowledge, a "secret wisdom," which stupefies the intellect and short-circuits the memory. This "secret wisdom" is

4

a loving knowledge transcending abstract, conceptual knowledge. The "infused" quality of this loving knowledge indicates that it is wholly a gift from God and is totally beyond human capability. No strictly human effort can bring it about. Although Teresa's definition highlights the often ecstatic aspect of mystical experience, the aspect of *secret* wisdom must not go unnoticed. Genuine mysticism is rarely showy and spectacular, as is too often assumed today.

One contemporary writer, William Johnston, defines mysticism as the "wisdom or knowledge that is found through love; it is loving knowledge."[7] He further asserts that "mysticism is the core of authentic religious experience"[8] and that all are called to it. Johnston's definition offers several distinct advantages. First, it derives its strength and accuracy from being rooted solidly in the Christian mystical tradition. Second, it is open to the variety of life-styles and great world religions that also foster this loving knowledge. For example, not only a monastic atmosphere of asceticism and formal prayer can nurture mystical loving knowledge, but also the self-surrender required for authentic love in hectic, secular activity. Third, Johnston's definition of mysticism as "the core of authentic religious experience" has the advantage of linking, but not simply identifying, mystical experience with religious experience. By evoking E. Caird's older definition of mysticism as "religion in its most concentrated and exclusive form,"[9] Johnston can satisfy both those scholars who insist that, strictly speaking, only *infused* religious experience is mystical and those who contend, broadly speaking, that all genuine religious experience has a mystical aspect. Finally, his emphasis upon the universal call to mysticism removes it from the realm of the esoteric, from that which is reserved only for an elite.

Another contemporary commentator, Ben-Ami Scharfstein, notes that "very broadly, mysticism is a name for

5

our infinite appetites. Less broadly, it is the assurance that these appetites can be satisfied."[10] This definition highlights indirectly that the human person is by nature mystical. Only the infinite can quench the immense longing that every human person is and lives inherently. The human person will settle for nothing less than the All. The lives of the great mystics guarantee and render transparent, moreover, that our own infinite desires will eventually be fulfilled.

For another contemporary writer, Robert Ellwood: "Mystical experience is experience in a religious context which is immediately or subsequently interpreted by the experiencer as encounter with ultimate divine reality in a direct nonrational way which engenders a deep sense of unity, and of living during the experience on a level of being other than the ordinary."[11] Ellwood's definition brings out several important features of mystical experience. Unlike some recent commentators who argue that "in itself mystical experience is not a religious phenomenon at all,"[12] Ellwood stresses the intrinsic connection between mysticism and religion. For him, moreover, interpretation is an intrinsic part of experience itself. Although he correctly observes that mystical phenomena can and do occur outside of religion, he prefers the more generic term "ecstasy" for such phenomena.[13]

His definition likewise underscores that the mystic considers himself* to be dealing with nothing less than a reality which is both ultimate and divine. Nothing less than the Absolute satisfies the authentic mystic. A mystical encounter with the Absolute occurs in a transconceptual and transrational mode of union and oneness with this Absolute, bringing with it a deeper, richer form of life that transcends daily living. This def-

* In this book, masculine pronouns are used for succinctness only and are meant to refer to both females and males, except in cases where the gender is clear from the context.

inition fails to note, however, that mystical experiences not only become mystical states, but are frequently only the surface manifestation of a deeper, permanent way of life that slowly transforms the mystic's entire being and consciousness.

Still another contemporary commentator, Geoffrey Parrinder, writes: "Theistic mysticism seeks union with God but not identity. Monistic mysticism seeks identity with a universal principle, which may be called divine though that would imply a difference from the human. Non-religious mysticism also seeks union with something, or everything, rather like monism."[14] With other contemporary authors, Parrinder argues correctly for irreducibly plural forms of mysticisms. His definition focuses sharply upon the *union* or *identity* of the mystic with some principle as the essential element in mysticism. He accurately notes that in theistic mysticism, the mystic and God become one, yet remain two. Differentiated unity is the hallmark of theistic mysticism. Monistic mysticism, on the other hand, speaks of a total identity, or an undifferentiated unity, between the mystic and a "universal principle."

My emphases and point of view agree totally with that remarkable scholar of mysticism, Evelyn Underhill, when she writes: ". . . mysticism is no isolated vision, no fugitive glimpse of reality, but a complete system of life carrying its own guarantees and obligations. . . . It is the name of that organic process which involves the perfect consummation of the Love of God: the achievement here and now of the immortal heritage of man . . . It is an ordered movement towards ever higher levels of reality, ever closer identification with the Infinite."[15] What is essential to note is Underhill's treatment of mysticism as a "complete system of life," as a way of living. In so doing, she stands as a strong counterpoint to the contemporary tendency to reduce mysticism to transient experiences, especially moments of ecstatic rapture. She resolutely refuses to identify the mystical as the ecstatic.

Moreover, Underhill places secondary mystical phenomena—such as visions, locutions, ecstasies, raptures, and the like—in a wider context of a mystical life that gradually purifies, illuminates, and transforms the mystic from the very roots of his being. In short, she handles the more extraordinary and well-known mystical experiences as the psychosomatic reverberations, the incarnated expressions, of a deeper and more essential mystical life.

By stressing that mysticism is an "organic process," Underhill disagrees vigorously with those who see it as self-hypnosis, medieval mind-control, brainwashing, or any other form of manipulation of the person. For her, mysticism is primarily the natural unfolding of what is inherently and essentially human: to respond throughout one's life ever more totally to a God who gives himself unconditionally as love and as the final destiny of every person.

Underhill also underscores the "ordered movement" by which the self awakens to, is purified by, illuminated by, and eventually fully united with the God of love. The Christian mystical tradition has long recognized the purgative, illuminative, and unitive phases or stages of mystical ascent.

Mystically married to the very life and love of God himself, moreover, the mystic likewise becomes a real center of this divine life and love from which others may draw. For Underhill, the mystic is a paradigm of human authenticity, an illustration of what it means to be a human being, a clear statement of the meaning of life: eternal union with the God of love.

Finally, of special importance is Underhill's attention to the "object" with which the mystic unites. Some authors correctly emphasize union as an essential feature

8

of mysticism, but overlook that with which the mystic unites. It can be argued that there are mystical traditions and techniques that foster union with God, with nature, with the self as an isolated entity, with diverse "spirits," or even with a variety of archetypes in one's own psyche. For the Christian mystic, however, only One is holy.

CHARACTERISTICS OF AUTHENTIC CHRISTIAN MYSTICISM

In addition to the above aspects, Underhill gives five other significant characteristics of authentic mysticism.[16] First, she accentuates the active and practical features of the mystical life. Mystics, in fact, often describe their way of life as a battle, a pilgrimage, a quest, a search, or a lonely adventure. The mystical way makes demands on the entire person, not merely on the emotions or the intellect. Theoretical knowledge is never a main focus, although some mystics do describe their experiences philosophically. They are really interested only in the experiential knowledge of God that transforms the way they *are*. Being takes total precedence over all forms of theoretical knowledge.

Second, Underhill describes mysticism as a totally spiritual and transcendental activity. This means that the authentic mystic has absolutely no interest in controlling this world by tapping into the unseen world. Unlike magic and the occult, which attempt to acquire and to use so-called spiritual forces, the authentic mystic aims at giving, surrendering, and letting go. Occult knowledge, improving this world, virtue, happiness, and an aesthetic vision are never the essential nor even the secondary motivations in the mystical ascent.[17]

The authentic mystic's direct experiences of God atrophy or redirect all secondary cravings and desires. They also assure him that all he really wants and needs is God and God alone. Once he has surrendered to his primary desire for God, he in fact becomes a powerful

9

force for improving the world, a possessor of a secret knowledge, and perhaps even someone with vast aesthetic abilities. It cannot be overemphasized that genuine mysticism is neither transcendental social work, nor spiritual aesthetics, nor occult practices, nor philosophy, nor magic.

Third, what differentiates mysticism from all other transcendental theory and practice is love. As Underhill says: "The business and method of Mysticism is Love."[18] For her, love is both the self's deepest dynamism and the will's striving. Mysticism, as the science of the heart, concentrates the mystic on God as Beloved. The "object" of the mystical venture is not merely impersonal "reality," but the living, personal reality of divine Love itself. Therefore, the divine Beloved is to be loved, and not explored as some impersonal Absolute. In short, the mystic is in love with an Absolute that is nothing less than self-giving Love.

Fourth, genuine mysticism entails a vital union with the God of love that redirects or kills all lesser relationships. Moreover, this loving union transforms the self for living ever-richer levels of life. United to Holiness itself, the self must become absolutely moral, sanctified, and holy to sustain the "weight" of divine Love and to become eventually this Love by participation. Underhill insists that the mystic must possess extraordinary psychological ability to sustain the concentration and purification required for mystical ascent. The mystic's entire person must become like a lens which gathers, concentrates, and focuses the divine rays into a single point of burning, transforming love.

Fifth, the authentic mystic is never selfish. Disinterested love dominates his life. He is neither consumed with self-interest nor looking for personal happiness. Some mystics have even claimed to be willing to be eternally damned for the sake of love, if God so desired. The contemporary fascination with "peak experiences," al-

10

tered states of consciousness, spiritual power in the mode of Don Juan (the well-known Yaqui Indian shaman found in the writings of Carlos Castañeda), the various "highs" publicized in the mass media, and so on, are absolutely foreign to the wholly un-self-seeking attitude of the authentic mystic, as are the spiritual consumerism and spiritual gluttony characteristic of some in the host of neomystical movements.[19] The irony is that by seeking only God, the mystic usually receives extraordinary experiences, knowledge, happiness, the virtues, and much more. Yet, it must still be emphasized that the mystical path demands the most radical form humanly possible of self-forgetting, self-transcending, and self-surrendering to the all-consuming mystery of Love.

Augustin Poulain lists two primary and ten secondary characteristics of genuine Christian mysticism.[20] The experiential, felt presence of God is the first feature. The mystic is absolutely certain that God is present, claiming to have incontrovertible, subjective evidence of this presence. So powerful is this sense of God's presence that most mystics argue for a qualitatively different type of prayer once mystical prayer begins. Many mystics and mystical theologians distinguish sharply between an "infused," or mystical, form of prayer totally beyond the capabilities of the person and requiring a special grace, and "acquired" contemplation, or the highest form of prayer within the reach of all Christians endowed with "ordinary" grace.

The second primary feature concerns the mode in which the mystic feels God's presence. Mystics speak of a particular type of spiritual sensation. They affirm the existence of "spiritual senses" analogous to the bodily senses.[21] The Christian mystical tradition attests to a spiritual, or mystical, form of touching, hearing, tasting, smelling, and seeing God. Because of the preponderance of the mystic's sense of fusing with, being satu-

11

rated by, or immersed in God, Poulain attaches importance to the spiritual sense of touch. Along with many mystical theologians, he contends that mystics never directly see God, for this is reserved for the beatific vision after death.

The first of Poulain's ten secondary characteristics focuses upon the gift quality of mysticism. Although we can dispose ourselves to receive it, we are absolutely powerless to produce it. This is strictly God's special gift, which is wholly beyond the person's capabilities. In no way can we will to obtain it. God's felt presence arrives unexpectedly. When this occurs, we can do nothing to intensify the experience or to prevent it from ceasing.

A transconceptual, general, vague loving knowledge is mysticism's second secondary feature. An obscure and confused knowledge of God that dazzles the mind accustomed to clear, conceptual knowledge accompanies God's experiential presence.

The third secondary attribute is the incomprehensibility of how God communicates himself to the person. Because God is now operating at the apex of the mystic's spirit, the person understands very little of what is happening at a level so infrequently reached. Perhaps this is why the English mystics often translated the Latin word *mystica* as "hidden."

The fourth secondary note is that God's felt presence cannot be produced by the senses, the imagination, the memory, or the intellect. It occurs at a level beyond these faculties. If acquired contemplation can be compared to study, that is, a process which internalizes something external, infused contemplation, or mysticism, takes place immediately and intuitively at the deepest levels of the mystic's being. God bypasses the normal functions of the senses, imagination, memory, and intellect.

12

The fifth secondary characteristic highlights that God's felt presence occurs with great fluctuations of intensity. The tangibility or perceptibility of mystical experience and states varies widely and rarely remains constant over long periods of time, except at the higher stages.

The sixth secondary feature is that infused contemplation requires much less exertion than acquired contemplation. Even though a person may have to work to dispel distractions in the lower levels of mystical prayer, this prayer still requires more passivity than does acquired contemplation. During mystical ecstasy, of course, contemplation may be irresistible.

The seventh secondary aspect focuses upon experiences of joy, happiness, love, peace, quiet, repose, pain, agony, misery, and suffering which accompany God's felt presence. Tides of consolation and desolation are part of the mystical life. God may make his presence felt either in a delightful or in an excruciating manner. A mystic may experience the whole gamut of consolations and desolations, from delicious raptures to the mystical purgation and death that occur in the well-known "dark nights of the senses and spirit."

The eighth secondary characteristic brings out the importance of virtue in authentic mysticism. The palpable presence of God impels the person towards the virtues. Having experienced Holiness itself, the person wants to become holy. Striving for virtue now seems to be the person's natural penchant.

The ninth secondary note concerns the influence of God's infused presence on the body. Poulain maintains that genuine mystical experience always has manifest psychosomatic effects. Infused contemplation always results in partial or total ecstasy. The mystic is one who lives completely or incompletely outside oneself.

The tenth secondary characteristic is "ligature." To a greater or lesser degree, God's felt presence prevents the mystic's normal inner and outer activity. The mystic may, for example, be able to pray vocally only with great difficulty, or not at all. Use of the memory, imagination, or the intellect may be difficult or even impossible.

One must not misunderstand these last two characteristics. The closer he is to full union with God, the more fully does the mystic share in God's very life. Total ecstasy into God, standing outside oneself in God, means being fully oneself. Mystical transformation shifts the mystic's personal center of gravity from the ego's tiny sphere to the true self. It also effects the transformed and enhanced ability to use the senses, memory, imagination, and intellect. The fully developed mystical life renders the mystic integral: wholly one with God, self, and all creation. The perfect inner life likewise perfects the outer life.

COMMON MISCONCEPTIONS ABOUT MYSTICISM
Unfortunately, the popular, contemporary misunderstandings of mysticism are greatly at odds with the above definitions, descriptions, and characteristics of authentic Christian mysticism. For example, many today identify mysticism with irrationalism, vague speculation, otherworldliness, dreaminess, or a lack of practicality in dealing with daily living. Others incorrectly associate it with parapsychological phenomena, theosophy, the occult, magic, witchcraft, and demonology.

Another common line of current opinion reduces mysticism to moments of ecstatic rapture, or "peak experiences," triggered by music, poetic inspiration, nature, lovemaking, psychedelic drugs, prayer, giving birth, and so on. One line of thought falsely equates mysticism with repressed eroticism, deviant behavior, madness, psychological regression, biological and psychological pathology, or a variety of "altered states of consciousness" usually engendered by sensory deprivation.

14

Some of the most absurd theories view mysticism as a form of "remembrance" of the mystic's biological conception, life in the womb, or early nursing experiences. In this view, mysticism is essentially biology.

Some attempt to dilute mysticism by identifying it with a Christian life of ascetical piety and devotion. According to this line of thinking, mysticism is simply love of God, the interior life, or Christian religious experience in general. Another opinion explains mysticism as a form of experience and life diametrically opposed to an ecclesial life of the sacraments, dogma, and authority. According to this view, the mystic is inherently iconoclastic and heretical.

Walter T. Stace, the English philosopher, has enormously but erroneously influenced contemporary thinking about mysticism. For him, "the core of the experience is thus an undifferentiated unity—a oneness or unity in which there is no internal division, no multiplicity."[22] Undifferentiated unity signifies that the mystic experiences a total fusion with or dissolution into the Absolute. The mystic experiences no difference at all between himself and the Absolute and claims to be this Absolute. This view rules out the possibility of an authentic Christian mysticism, a love mysticism of differentiated unity in which two become one, yet remain two.

Influential theologians, such as Barth, E. Brunner, Heiler, Ritschl, Söderblom, Troeltsch, von Harnack, and others, have also contributed to current misunderstandings about mysticism. These authors sharply distinguish biblical, prophetic religions from Oriental mystical religions, claiming that the two are mutually exclusive and absolutely irreconcilable. Moreover, these theologians reject the long-standing mystical tradition within Christianity as a pagan, Hellenistic infection and deformation of Christianity, as Roman Catholic piety in an extreme form.

From this perspective, Christian mysticism is a contradiction in terms. For these thinkers, genuine Christian faith should reject mysticism as a "work," "law," or "religion" in the most pejorative sense. Barth typifies this view when he considers mysticism as more pernicious than even self-righteous Pharisaism "because it lies so near to the righteousness of God, and it too is *excluded*—at the last moment."[23]

Another common mistake is to equate mysticism with the supernatural suspension of the laws of nature. For many, mysticism denotes the miraculous. This line of thought sees the mystic as someone invaded by God's grace, which produces a host of extraordinary psychosomatic phenomena. In this view, the mystic is essentially someone who receives Christ's wounds on his body (the stigmata), levitates during prayer, sees visions, hears heavenly voices, receives divine communications and revelations, and works various miracles. With the widespread growth of various charismatic movements, moreover, charismatic phenomena, such as prophecy, speaking in tongues (glossolalia), interpreting tongues, faith healing, discernment of spirits, and so on, may be erroneously identified with mysticism.

A close examination of the writings of the Christian mystics, however, favors the definitions and descriptions given by Underhill and Poulain. The Christian mystic claims to experience an immediate contact with God as Beloved that eventually dominates his entire life and being. Christian mysticism is the palpable loving union of the mystic with the God of truth and love. The felt presence of a loving union with this God purifies, illuminates, and eventually transforms the mystic into truth and love themselves.

MYSTICISM IN THE OLD TESTAMENT
Many commentators correctly reject the views that mysticism cannot be reconciled with biblical, prophetic

16

religions and that Christian mysticism is a Hellenistic distortion of genuine biblical Christianity.[24] For example, the writings of the Christian mystics abound with references to the scriptures because they found there paradigms and exemplars of their own lives and experiences, as well as suitable imagery, language, and symbolism to express these. To be sure, the word "mysticism" is not found in the Bible. Still, the reality is there, and not merely by way of exception. Mysticism is a reality connected intimately with the very essence of revealed, biblical religions.

The scriptures record God's "mighty deeds," or what he did for his people, and how this people responded to his initiative. The Jewish religious consciousness was especially sensitive to history as a sacred, saving sign that revealed God's plan for and to Israel. In a sense, history was the sacrament of Israel's religion. The particular, contingent course of historical events revealed to her the reality of the divine-human interaction.

Therefore, the scriptures are not an historical tract in the contemporary sense. The sacred writers grasped the deeper meaning, the salvific significance, the mystical dimension of the events of history. It is in this sense that the Fathers of the Church were correct to search for the spiritual or mystical sense of the Jewish scriptures, for they contain that dimension. That the books of the Old Testament "acquire and show forth their full meaning in the New Testament . . . and in turn shed light on it and explain it"[25] highlights their mystical quality.

The God "who dwells in unapproachable light, whom no man has ever seen or can see" (1 Tm 6:16) created humanity in his very image and likeness. By way of his self-communication, he united humanity with himself through a variety of special covenants. For example, before their sin Adam and Eve enjoyed without interruption God's intimate presence. Many theologians contend that they loved all creatures in God and God in all creatures. Their graced condition endowed them with a mystical faith far beyond normal faith, but still short of the beatific vision. In short, they possessed a mystical knowledge and love of God almost beyond description.

Abraham, Jacob, Moses, Samuel, and other patriarchs of the Old Testament experienced God's intimate call, had their faith tested, wrestled with God, were blessed by him, spoke to him as a personal friend, were often afraid and speechless in his presence, were visibly transformed by their encounters with him, were often ecstatically drawn to him as their greatest good, and were convinced that he was with his people in all they did and underwent. Both Moses and Jacob claimed face-to-face encounters with God, with some qualifications of how directly they gazed into his face (Gn 32:30; Ex 33:11,23). When Job could say to God, "Now my eyes see thee" (Jb 42:5), his agonizing questioning ceased.

With some qualifications, the same can be said of the great Old Testament prophets. For example, Elijah, Isaiah, Jeremiah, Ezekiel, Hosea, and Amos were called in a most intimate way to be God's spokesmen. Often, visions and ecstatic encounters grounded their calling. God's word burning in their hearts rendered them both powerless to speak it and incapable of holding it in. Their authentication to speak God's word often came because they had "stood in the council of the Lord" (Jer 23:18). Their felt knowledge of God resulted in their invincible trust in God's faithfulness, tenderness, compassion, love, and wrath. Having received God's Spirit into their hearts, they prophesied a time when all God's people would definitely receive the Holy Spirit.

The Old Testament prophets were essentially mystics in action.[26] Their profound experience of God in the present sensitized them both to what God had done for his

18

people in the past and to the contemporary religious, social, political, and economic scene. By virtue of their mystical experience of God in the core of their being, they experienced the congruence or incongruence of their times with God's will for his people. In this way did they address the burning questions of their day. And in view of how God had acted in the past when his people had obeyed or disobeyed, the prophets did not hesitate to say what God would do for or to them in the future.

The Old Testament patriarchs and prophets are paradigms of those who experienced God as the Holy, as the tremendous and fascinating mystery.[27] Although absolutely transcendent, wholly other, and darkness itself, he was nonetheless intimately near and the very light of their lives. His awesome presence evoked feelings of fear, dread, powerlessness, openness to annihilation, creaturely nothingness, and sinfulness. Nevertheless, this totally good God also attracted, charmed, intoxicated, ravished, and fascinated those exposed to his presence. The Holy awakened feelings of gratitude, dedication, praise, trust, submission, and love. He was experienced as the object of the deepest human desires, searchings, and yearnings. To be united with this living, vital God was the end and goal of all living. It was life itself. Is this not authentic mysticism?

The patriarchs and prophets taught the Israelites to expect the same gift of faith as they themselves had received. Israel's faithful certainly experienced communion with God, his saving presence, his protecting hand, and his steadfast love. The Old Testament texts indicate a different intensity between the mystical experiences of the patriarchs and prophets and the living faith of the average Israelite, but they say nothing about a qualitative difference. The whole context of salvation history and the general laws of grace point, in fact, to faith as the theological locus of mystical experience.

19

The psalms attest in a special way to Israel's mystical faith. One finds there the mystic's sense of God's infinity, his nearness, and the joys of communion with him. The incredible hunger and thirst for the God who is light, love, and life itself permeate the psalms. The frequency of the words "love" (*ahabah*) and "loving kindness" (*hesed*) underscore the intense intimacy that existed between God and his people.

The felt presence of God which permeated Israel's life completed itself in the blessings and praises found throughout the psalms. They attest that the believer is unconquerable because of God's steadfast love. God can be trusted and must be praised in *all* circumstances.[28] He is praised not only for what he does, but especially for what he is. His beauty, goodness, holiness, and love fill both the created universe and the depths of the human heart. So unselfish is the praise expressed in the psalms that the psalmist wishes to escape death only because in Sheol praise of God is no longer possible. To praise God, according to the psalmist, is life itself.

The Old Testament cries out with intense longings and contains a promise directed toward the future. As Jesus said: ". . . many prophets and righteous men longed to see what you see, and did not see it, and to hear what you hear, and did not hear it" (Mt 13:17). Although God partially satisfied the faith-desires of his people, Israel experienced that it "did not receive what was promised, since God had foreseen something better for us . . ." (Heb 11:39b–40a). That "something better" is, of course, Jesus Christ, who proclaimed to the Jews: "Your father Abraham rejoiced that he was to see my day" (Jn 8:56).

Old Testament mysticism remains a preliminary stage to God's new covenant, which would "give the light of the knowledge of the glory of God in the face of Christ" (2 Cor 4:6). Humanity would be able to gaze at the human face of God and live. The crucified and risen Christ highlights that God is definitively and irreversibly united with his people. "The mediator of a new covenant" (Heb 9:15) established, revealed, and made mysticism accessible in its purest and unsurpassable forms.

MYSTICISM IN THE NEW TESTAMENT

Jesus Christ is the foundation of all Christian mysticism. Because of the permanent union of a human nature with the divine Person of the Word, Jesus Christ possessed not only a divine knowledge, but also an immediate, direct, and unique human knowledge of the Father, of himself as the Son, and of the Holy Spirit.[29] Jesus' trinitarian consciousness can be called a mystical consciousness in the highest sense. Moreover, the hypostatic union of Jesus' human and divine natures is the ground and goal of the mystical life: the ability for perfect, total surrender in love to the God who wishes us to be fully united with him.

Jesus claimed that "no one knows the Son except the Father, and no one knows the Father except the Son and anyone to whom the Son chooses to reveal him" (Mt 11:27). In this and other places in the New Testament (Jn 7:29; 8:55), Jesus spoke of his intimate, full, personal, filial loving knowledge of his Father. He knew that he came from the Father (Jn 5:23) and would return to him (Jn 8:14). The oneness he enjoyed with his Father dominated his consciousness. He heard his word (Jn 8:26), knew his will (Jn 5:30), and had seen him working (Jn 5:19). So intimate was Jesus' relationship with his Father that the Father showed him everything that he did (Jn 5:20).

In short, Jesus "knew" the Father in the fully biblical sense of the word: experiential loving knowledge. Not only did he lovingly know the Father at a level never known before; he could also enable others to share in his experience of the Father (Mt 11:27; Jn 1:18). Be-

21

cause he was God's Word, light, and life in the absolute sense, he could instill wisdom, light, and life in the hearts of those who loved him (Eph 3:17).

To see Christ, moreover, is to see the Father (Jn 14:19). To hear him is to hear the Father (Lk 10:16). To know Christ is to know the Father, and this mystical knowledge of the Father and the Son is eternal life itself (Jn 17:3). To love Christ is to be loved by the Father, a God revealed by Jesus as Love itself (Jn 14:21; 1 Jn 4:8). Jesus promised that those who believed would become one with him and the Father, experience the divine Love that existed between him and the Father, "that they may all be one," just as he and the Father were one (Jn 17:20). As the visibility and tangibility of the Father's unconditional love for humanity, Christ is the sacrament of what mysticism is all about: total union and oneness with the God of love. It must be emphasized, however, that the union and oneness proclaimed by Jesus are not fusion with or dissolution into God, but abiding in and indwelling with him. This is the mystery of mystical love: two or more become one, but never lose their individual identities.

Several commentators have underscored Jesus' use of the word "Abba" ("beloved Father," "Daddy") when he spoke to God.[30] Because of the intimacy of this word, no Jew of Jesus' day would ever address God in this way. To pray to God with such filial affection shocked Jewish religious sensibilities.

Jesus' use of "Abba" when he turned to God was unique. Confidently, reverently, obediently, but with full intimacy and familiarity, Jesus called God his "Daddy." This word captures the mystery of Jesus' identity and mission: a full filial relationship with God. Because of the depths at which he and the Father were one, Jesus experienced himself as his Son, as the authenticated revelation of the Father and his will. Jesus' filial consciousness is the exemplar of the perfect mys-

22

tic's intimate relationship with the Father, God-above-us, loving Transcendence.

During Jesus' time, the Jews were convinced that with the death of the last writing prophets, the Spirit had been quenched because of Israel's sin. Only in the last days would God's Spirit come to satisfy definitively Israel's great longings for God's presence.

On the other hand, Jesus repeatedly made the unusual and explicit claim that he himself possessed the Holy Spirit. The gospels portray Jesus both as driven by the Spirit and as its definitive bearer who would give this Spirit at his death. The gospels depict Jesus as the eschatological prophet who brought final revelation and demanded absolute obedience, because in him the eschatological age had dawned.

John's gospel depicts the Holy Spirit less as the impetus behind Jesus' ministry than as the "Counselor" to continue and complete it. For John, the Holy Spirit is another Jesus (Jn 14:16), or simply Jesus' spirit, the Spirit of truth (Jn 14:17). Jesus proclaimed that only in and through his salvific death would the Holy Spirit be definitively given (Jn 7:39). This Spirit would lead Christians into all truth (Jn 16:13) and enable Jesus to be always present to his people (Mt 28:20). As another Jesus, the Spirit would have the same relationship to Christians throughout the ages that Jesus had to the disciples during his ministry.

Jesus was intimately aware of the presence of the Holy Spirit, God-in-us, loving Immanence. Therefore, Jesus' mystical consciousness is essentially trinitarian. He knew himself to be uniquely Son because of his relationship to his Father and to the Spirit of their love. Jesus experienced the Father ecstatically as God-above-us, the Holy Spirit *en*statically as God-within-us, and himself as the Son, or God-with-us. Because of Jesus' essentially trinitarian consciousness, all authentic Christian mysticism must also be trinitarian.

Jesus' trinitarian consciousness manifested itself indirectly in a number of ways. First, he did not hesitate to forgive sins, an activity that scandalized and astonished his contemporaries. What Jewish leader, king, priest, or prophet had ever dared to forgive sins? What religious founder of any of the world's great religions had ever done so?

Second, Jesus used the word "amen" in an unprecedented way. He employed it, not to endorse or accept the words of another, but to introduce his own words, thereby placing them in a divine context. In a way that parallels the Old Testament prophets', "Thus says the Lord," Jesus did not hesitate to say, "Amen, I say to you."

Third, Jesus spoke with unparalleled confidence and authority. Unlike the religious authorities of his day who gathered together as many proof texts and precedents as possible, Jesus spoke with authority and not like the scribes and Pharisees (Mk 1:22). He even claimed to be greater than the Temple (Mt 12:6), Jonah (Mt 12:41), and Solomon (Mt 12:42), placing himself above the best in the Old Testament tradition. This is especially clear with respect to his position toward Jewish law on murder, divorce, adultery, retaliation, and the taking of oaths. On these matters he claimed more authority than Moses and implicitly set himself up as God's equal when he said: "You have heard that it was said . . . But I say to you" (Mt 5:27f.).

Like many religious founders, Jesus offered counsel on how to live. Moreover, he preached that God's reign was present because he was present. His hearers stood before God's definitive offer of salvation, the irruption of his reign into human history, because Jesus himself was present. He called people to faith, discipleship, and a final decision concerning God's reign in such a way that these decisions could not be separated from their fundamental decision toward him. "I tell you, every one who acknowledges me before men, the Son of man also will acknowledge before the angels of God; but he who denies me before men will be denied before the angels of God" (Lk 12:8–9). No Old Testament figure had ever spoken like that.

It must be emphasized, however, that Jesus did not "come to abolish the law and the prophets . . . but to fulfill them" (Mt 5:17). Jesus was thoroughly the son of a people who lived from the Old Testament. Accepting the social and religious milieu out of which he came, he preached in the language, concepts, and imagery of his day. For the most part, he even interpreted himself and his mission in terms of the Old Testament. In one sense, almost everything he said had already been said in that Testament. One finds in Jesus and the New Testament, therefore, an essential continuity with the Old.

On the other hand, it is clear from what has already been said that there is also a radical discontinuity. Jesus transcended not only his Jewish milieu, but also the wise men, religious founders, enlightened ones, and philosophers of all ages.[31] Jesus' certainty about his relationship to his Father and to the Holy Spirit did not come from philosophical argumentation, a retelling of the ancient traditions of his people, or by meditation techniques. A uniquely intimate experience of the Father and the Holy Spirit permeated everything he did and was. It is no wonder that his disciples came to realize that they were in the presence of much more than another prophet or rabbi and adored him as "my Lord and my God" (Jn 20:28).

Through his ministry, passion, death, the surrendering of his Spirit, and resurrection appearances, Jesus' disciples underwent their own mystical purgation, illumination, and transformation. When they experientially received Jesus' Spirit on Pentecost Sunday (Acts 2:1f.), their mystical transformation and marriage were complete. From now on, with the Spirit's own power, they could and would preach about and witness to what God had done for his people in Christ. This Spirit had transformed them from a small band of disciples into the mystical Body of Christ, a Church with a powerful missionary impetus.

St. Paul himself encountered the risen Christ on the road to Damascus (Gal 1:12; 1 Cor 9:11) and was later ecstatically taken up into the "third heaven" (2 Cor 12:2). From the very depths of his being, Paul experienced and surrendered to the love of God in Christ. For him the Lord was the Spirit (2 Cor 3:17). Pauline mysticism is emphatically Christ-directed; "to live," for Paul, "is Christ" (Phil 1:21).

Paul considered it almost self-evident that all Christians, because of Christ and his Spirit, had relatively easy access to an experience of God in their lives. Although he spoke of the "mature" in faith (1 Cor 2:6) and the "spiritual" (1 Cor 2:15), he expected mature faith of all Christians. The Holy Spirit granted all Christians a "surpassing knowledge" (Eph 3:19), the "fullness of knowledge" (Eph 1:17), and in this way proved to us that we are "sons of God" (Rom 8:14) who can also call God, "Abba, Father" (Rom 8:15). Christ's Spirit would pray in us "with sighs too deep for words" (Rom 8:26).

Linked intimately to a loving knowledge of the crucified and risen Christ is a "secret and hidden wisdom of God" (1 Cor 2:7), a peace beyond all understanding (Phil 4:7), and a supreme consolation (2 Cor 1:15). Those living in Christ's Spirit experience a richer way of life (Eph 1:8–9) filled with love, joy, peace, self-control, gentleness, patience, and kindness (Gal 5:22) that enables them to bear each other's burdens (Gal 6:2). As Paul said: "What no eye has seen, nor ear heard, nor the heart of man conceived, what God has prepared for those who love him, God has revealed to us through the Spirit" (1 Cor 2:9–10).

Therefore, the New Testament contains not only a God-mysticism, but also a Christ-mysticism, and a Spirit-mysticism. John's gospel focuses more upon Jesus as the way to a Father-centered mysticism. Still, according to John, the Spirit is the power behind a Christ-mysticism for Christians throughout the ages. For John, there is a mystical hunger and thirst that only Jesus, as the living bread and the giver of living water, that is, the Spirit, can quench.

Pauline mysticism, on the other hand, centers more upon Christ. Time and again, Paul spoke of being "in Christ." For him, moreover, "it is no longer I who live, but Christ lives in me" (Gal 2:20). Yet neither a Spirit-mysticism nor a God-mysticism is lacking in Paul, as many of the above texts indicate. Christ became a "life-giving Spirit" (1 Cor 15:45), and it is in Christ that the Father appears to us, reveals himself to us, and unites us to himself. Moreover, the Pauline triadic formulae clearly underscore the depths of his trinitarian mysticism.[32] 1 Cor 6:11; 12:4f; 2 Cor 1:21-22; 13:14

Therefore, the real ancestry of Christian mysticism is not to be found in the deforming influence of Greek philosophy, but in the Bible itself. Authentic Christian mysticism looks to the solidly mystical spirituality of the Old Testament, which finds its fulfillment in Jesus' trinitarian mystical consciousness that reached its high point in his salvific death and resurrection.

The Christian sees in Jesus' death and resurrection the very cause and exemplar of the mystical life in all its purity. Jesus' saving death on the cross exemplifies the mystical letting go of everything consoling, tangible, and finite to surrender totally to the mystery of the Father's unconditional love. Jesus' cross reminds Chris-

27

tians that they can and must love to the end, for the Spirit is born in blood, as many Church Fathers noted.

Jesus' bodily resurrection is the ultimate revelation of the Father's acceptance and confirmation of this act of loving surrender to unconditional love. Moreover, it is the seed of the new creation, the sacramental visibility of God's definitive mystical marriage with all creation. Jesus' risen, glorified body is what mysticism is all about: the loving union and transformation of all creation with and into the God of love, that in Christ one can truly be a "new creation" (2 Cor 5:17). As Karl Rahner has written: "Because Jesus Christ redeemed all creation in his love, along with mankind, Christian mysticism is neither a denial of the world nor a meeting with the infinite All, but a taking of the world with one to a loving encounter with the personal God."[33]

In addition to a trinitarian mysticism and one which centers on the crucified and risen Christ, the New Testament also teaches, as briefly indicated above, the ecclesial, social, and sacramental aspects of authentic Christian mysticism. These aspects show themselves especially in the New Testament's focus on the mystical Body of Christ and on the liturgy, especially baptism and the eucharist. In summary, therefore, Christian mystical life and consciousness must be emphatically trinitarian, ecclesial, sacramental, and inextricably bound to the crucified and risen Christ.

It is now time to allow six important figures in the Christian mystical tradition to speak for themselves. Ignatius of Loyola, the author of the *Cloud of Unknowing*, Teresa of Avila, John of the Cross, Thomas Merton, and Pierre Teilhard de Chardin manifested in their lives and/or writings an exceptional appropriation of Christian mystical life and consciousness. Through the transparency and amplification of their Christian lives of faith, hope, and love, they present paradigms of genuine Christian mysticism. The first four mystics—Ignatius, the author of the *Cloud of Unknowing*, Teresa of Avila, and John of the Cross—provide exceptionally clear descriptions of Christian kataphatic and apophatic mysticisms. The last two mystical writers—Thomas Merton and Pierre Teilhard de Chardin—are especially important for showing two significant ways in which the Christian mystical tradition has been transposed into contemporary settings, and what courses this tradition may take in the future.

Chapter Two

The *Spiritual Exercises* of St. Ignatius of Loyola

The *Spiritual Exercises* of St. Ignatius of Loyola (1491–1556) have played a significant role in Catholic spirituality since their composition in the sixteenth century. For over four hundred years, they have fed the spiritual lives of countless Jesuits, religious orders of men and women whose spirituality is Ignatian, and numerous others who for various reasons came into contact with this form of spirituality. In the 1920s, Pope Pius IX confirmed a long line of papal approbations of these *Exercises* by declaring St. Ignatius the "celestial patron of spiritual exercises" and recommending their practice to all.

The Ignatian *Exercises* offer an unusually good starting point for an introduction to Christian mysticism for two important reasons. First, like St. Ignatius, who never abandoned certain ascetical practices even after reaching the heights of mystical contemplation, the *Exercises* do not make the strong ascetical/mystical distinction found among many spiritual writers. They present detailed information which can be used by beginners, intermediates, and proficients of the spiritual life. They have the ability to lead persons at any level of spiritual development into even deeper realms of the spiritual life. In short, they can speak to both those in the pre-mystical stages and to those in the strictly mystical stages of the mystical journey.

The second reason involves the distinction between Christian apophatic and kataphatic mysticisms. The apophatic tradition, the *via negativa*, emphasizes the radical difference between God and creatures. God is best reached, therefore, by negation, forgetting, and unknowing, in a darkness of mind without the support of concepts, images, and symbols. God is "not this, not that." Kataphatic mysticism, the *via affirmativa*, emphasizes the similarity that exists between God and creatures. Because God can be found in all things, the affirmative way recommends the use of concepts, images, and symbols as a way of contemplating God.

According to the Fourth Lateran Council, "between the Creator and the creature no similarity can be expressed without including a greater dissimilarity."[1] It would seem that for psychological and theological reasons, the apophatic mystic experiences, expresses, and emphasizes more the dissimilarity; the kataphatic emphasizes the similarity. Nevertheless, both are orthodox ways of mystically reaching God, and one type of mysticism always contains elements from the other type. Any genuine Christian mysticism must hold the above similarity/dissimilarity distinction together in a creative tension.

Some writers maintain that the Ignatian *Exercises* are devoid of and are an actual barrier to the deepest levels of mystical prayer.[2] More nuanced writers view them basically as "discursive," that is, the prayer of beginners consisting of many acts of reasoning, affections, and resolutions that contrasts radically with the simplified prayer of those more advanced.[3] Some view the *Exercises*, therefore, as "the systematised, *de-mysticised* quintessence of the process of Ignatius's own conversion and purposeful change of life."[4]

It must not be overlooked that the *Exercises* came from a man who was accused frequently of being an Alumbrado, a disciple of a complicated mystical movement that in its exaggerated form led some adherents to claim heretically that they always acted solely under the immediate guidance of the Holy Spirit. Ignatius was not an Alumbrado. To be sure, he was both profoundly orthodox and mystical. During his life he reached the very summit of trinitarian, Christocentric, eucharistic, priestly, and mediator mysticism. Both on the basis of his own mystical experiences and of what he found helpful for others from his extensive pastoral activity, he wrote the *Exercises*.

Many of the first Jesuits reached such mystical heights through the *Exercises* that some demanded longer hours of prayer and a more solitary way of life, which threatened the apostolic orientation of the religious order Ignatius had founded. Many persons who made these same *Exercises* entered contemplative orders. Some of the earliest theological attacks upon the *Exercises* were directed at their allegedly too-mystical tendencies.[5] One of the paradoxes in the history of the *Exercises* is that they were attacked both for being too mystical and at other times for being an obstacle to mystical prayer. Although it may be true that historical circumstances forced Jesuits early in their history to emphasize the ascetical-practical aspect of the *Exercises*, the *Exercises* continued to lead many to the very summit of the mystical life.[6]

Some contemporary writers hold the thesis that "pure" mysticism exists only in the apophatic tradition and relegate the kataphatic tradition to an inferior position.[7] In this book, therefore, the *Spiritual Exercises* are presented to some extent as a counterpoint to today's overemphasis of the apophatic way. The *Exercises* are certainly a paradigm of authentic kataphatic Christian mysticism.

WHAT ARE THE *SPIRITUAL EXERCISES*?

A Great Variety of Methods of Prayer
According to St. Ignatius: ". . . 'Spiritual Exercises' embraces every method of examination of conscience, of

32

meditation, of contemplation, of vocal and mental prayer, and of other spiritual activity that will be mentioned later . . . spiritual exercises are methods of preparing and disposing the soul to free itself of all inordinate attachments, and after accomplishing this, of seeking and discovering the Divine Will regarding the disposition of one's life . . ." (no. 1).[8] In view of the great variety of modes of prayer taught in the *Exercises,* it is somewhat disconcerting to find authors who reduce "Jesuit prayer" to the somewhat mechanical meditation technique taught by John Roothaan (1785–1853), the Jesuit General who rebuilt the Society of Jesus after its suppression.[9] For example, in the "First Method of Prayer" (nos. 238–47) the *Exercises* teach how to ponder in various ways the Ten Commandments, the seven capital sins, the three powers of the soul, and the five bodily senses. The "Second Method of Prayer" (nos. 249–57) centers upon the contemplative tasting of each word's meaning in a chosen prayer. The "Third Method of Prayer" (nos. 258–60) describes the contemplation of the meaning of each word of a chosen prayer using the rhythm of one's breathing.

The "Contemplation to Obtain Divine Love" (nos. 230–37) offers instructions on how to find God in all things; the "General Examination of Conscience" (nos. 32–43) is meant "to help the exercitant purify himself and make better confessions" (no. 32). Ignatian "Meditations" make use of the memory to recall the mysteries of the faith, the understanding to reason about them, and the will to move the emotions. Other meditations are used to reflect upon certain material "from time to time throughout the day" (no. 164). Ignatian "Contemplations," on the other hand, call upon the person to dwell upon a gospel scene "as though I were present there" (no. 114). In the "Reflections," the exercitant must ask how all this concerns him here and now and for the future.

The "Preparatory Prayer" places the person in the presence of God to direct all he does "to the service and praise of His Divine Majesty" (no. 46). The "Mental Image of the Place" fixes in the "mind's eye the physical place where the object that we wish to contemplate is present" (no. 47). The Ignatian "What I Want and Desire" (no. 48) specifies the person's desire in a powerful way by having him ask for a particular grace. The "Colloquies" exhort the exercitant making the *Exercises* to speak to the Father, Christ, Mary, the saints, and so on, "as one friend speaks to another" (no. 54). Ignatius does not hesitate, moreover, to have the exercitant compare himself to God, Christ, Mary, and others in various ways (nos. 55, 59, 248).

The "Repetitions" instruct the exercitant to go back to a previous exercise to "dwell upon the points in which I have felt the greatest consolation or desolation or the greatest spiritual relish" (no. 62). During the "Résumés," "the intellect, without digression, is to recall and review thoroughly the matters contemplated in the previous Exercises" (no. 64). The "Application of the Senses" (no. 124) directs the exercitant to see, hear, touch, taste, and smell in imagination certain aspects of a contemplated mystery. And these are only some of the many approaches Ignatius uses to plunge the exercitant into the mystery of God in Christ and into his own mystery as a human being.

Another example that counters the tendency to see "Jesuit prayer" in simplistic fashion is Ignatius' admonition to the person giving the *Exercises* to adapt them "to the requirements of the persons who wish to make them . . . according to their age, their education, and their aptitudes" (no. 18). He even envisioned persons who have a great desire and aptitude to make the *Exercises*, but are unable to do them full time. In this case, Ignatius recommended making the *Exercises* "by taking an hour and a half for them each day" (no. 19).[10] In short, the *Exercises* allow for much freedom and creativity in the relationship between the written text, the exercitant, and the spiritual director.

Negative and Positive Aspects

Ignatius' description of the *Exercises* explains briefly their negative and positive aspects. Mystics of all traditions and ages call attention to the disorder, evil, sin, falsehood, and brokenness which possess the human heart. One of the aims of the *Exercises* is the restoration of human integrity by removing "inordinate attachments," or false loves. The mystical life demands the removal of all that makes the person false in his relationship to God, to others, and to himself. All genuine Christian mysticism contains a "purgative way."

The positive aspect focuses upon "seeking and discovering the Divine Will." Ignatius expected that God would communicate himself to and work immediately with the exercitant (no. 15). One finds here something unique in the history of spirituality: a mystic who claims to have fashioned a "method" for seeking and finding God's will. He ended many of his letters asking for the grace "to know His most holy will and the strength perfectly to fulfill it."[11]

In a way which undoubtedly goes against the contemporary search for "experience," Ignatius did not seek religious and mystical experiences for their own sake, but for their ability to disclose God's will to him. Even a casual reading of his *Diary* illustrates that in the midst of the profoundest trinitarian and Christocentric mystical experiences, Ignatius was concerned with finding out God's will, for example, on particular points involving poverty in the religious order he had founded.

THE OVERALL STRUCTURE OF THE SPIRITUAL EXERCISES

The "Principle and Foundation"

The retreat director usually begins the Ignatian retreat with the "Principle and Foundation," a meditation designed to impart to the exercitant a vivid sense of the meaning and goal of life and the means to obtain that goal. For Ignatius, "Man is created to praise, reverence, and serve God our Lord" (no. 23). To accomplish this he must either "use" or "rid" himself of "all other things on the face of the earth" insofar as they promote or hinder this goal.

At the very beginning, therefore, Ignatius strives to awaken exercitants to Christian wisdom, to a holistic, total vision wherein everything is seen in its proper perspective. Exercitants must see how they fit into the overall scheme of creation. The "indifference to all created things" (no. 23) sought in this exercise must be seen in the light of a passionate love for the God of love that does not destroy, but properly realigns all lesser cravings and loves. In this proper context of the God of love, "indifference to all created things" is actually an "Ignatian mysticism of joy in the world."[12]

This meditation is perhaps a partial translation of Ignatius' famous enlightenment experience on the banks of the river Cardoner: "The eyes of his understanding began to open; it was not that he beheld any vision, but rather he comprehended and understood many things, about the spiritual life as well as about faith and learning. This took place with an illumination so great that all these things appeared to be something new. He seemed to himself to be another man and to have an understanding different from what he had previously. . . ."[13] In this experience of Christian enlightenment, Ignatius received a mystically infused sense of the unity of the Christian mysteries. Mystically seeing how all things fit together, his outlook was "architechtonic," grasping the root unity of all the truths of the faith. He saw everything from then on in its proper universal perspective, how all things flow from and to the God of love. If contemporary psychology is correct in its affirmation that today's pervading malaise results from a loss of the sense of meaning, the Ignatian "Principle and Foundation" assumes an even greater role in imparting the Christian wisdom necessary for Christian living.

The Four "Weeks"

Ignatius divides the *Exercises* into four "weeks," a designation based not on seven chronological days, but upon the grace granted as a result of each week's exercises. "The time should be set according to the needs of the subject matter" (no. 4), Ignatius writes. The "first week" corresponds to the "purgative way" (no. 10); the "second week," the "illuminative way" (no. 10); the "third week" and the "fourth week" are perhaps a means of deepening, in the light of Christ's passion and resurrection, the "election," or resolution, made at the end of the second week.

The first week centers on the cosmic and historical unity of the mystery of evil. The exercitant must consider the cosmic origin of sin in the fall of the angels (no. 50), the beginnings of sin in human history through the Fall of Adam and Eve (no. 51), "the particular sin of any person who went to hell because of one mortal sin" (no. 52), the history of one's personal sins (nos. 55–61), and finally sin's ultimate consequence: hell (nos. 65–71). By placing the exercitant's sinfulness in this cosmic-historical drama, Ignatius offers an architechtonic view of the mystery of iniquity. A sense of the unity of sin, knowledge of one's disorder and sinfulness, detestation and sorrow, a deep insight into the pains of hell, and a knowledge and "horror" of the world flow from this week.

The real secret to the first week can be found, however, in the "colloquies" to be made with Christ crucified, Mary, and the Father. By reason of the subject matter and the colloquies, the exercitant is presented with a deeply personal view of sin, not an abstract one. For

Ignatius, the mystery of sin must be seen in its relationship to the crucified Christ. Sin led to the murder of "eternal life" itself. When Ignatius asks, "What have I done for Christ?" (no. 53), he links the exercitant's sinfulness to the unity of evil that culminates in the crucifixion of Christ. The first week leads, therefore, to the profound experience of being a *redeemed* sinner, of amazement (no. 60) at God's mercy, of having been spared, "for the great kindness and mercy He [Christ] has always shown to me until this present moment" (no. 71).

"To help the exercitant make the Exercises better and to assist him in finding what he desires" (no. 73) during the first week, Ignatius gives "additional directions" (nos. 73–90) for recollection, interiority, evaluating one's prayer, posture, and penances. These will help the exercitant obtain the specific graces of the first week. It is clear from the text, however, that Ignatius did not expect all to progress beyond the first week. It would be sufficient for some to learn easy methods of prayer, to know how to examine their consciences, to go to confession more regularly, and to receive holy communion more often (no. 18).

Ignatius directed the full thirty-day retreat to those from whom much could be expected in God's service, the ones with the generosity and courage to offer themselves entirely to God's will (no. 5). For these exercitants, the dynamic initiated in the first week, reaching its high point in the question, "What ought I do for Christ?" (no. 53), would provide an easy transition to the second week.

Ignatius calls the second week an exercise in the illuminative way (no. 10). The exercitant must focus upon the biblical mysteries of the incarnation, Christ's birth, his early childhood, or "the life of our Lord Jesus Christ up to and including Palm Sunday" (no. 4). This week also contains several specifically Ignatian exercises which provide the hermeneutical key for understanding the *Exercises* in their entirety.

The first exercise of the second week centers on "the Kingdom of Christ" (nos. 91–98). Ignatius depicts Christ as the "Eternal King" who "calls" each person to distinguished service in the conquering of "the whole world and all My enemies" (no. 95). As loyal and generous soldiers share both in the sufferings and glory of their leader, so too does the exercitant in the service of Christ, the "Eternal King and Universal Lord." The exercitant must not be "deaf to His call, but prompt and diligent to accomplish His most holy will" (no. 91).

This exercise is really the *Exercises* in miniature and a paradigm of Ignatius' radically Christocentric "service mysticism." It is a Christological transposition of the "Principle and Foundation" and is really a second "Principle and Foundation." Because this exercise "helps us to contemplate the life of the Eternal King" (no. 91), it sets the entire Christocentric tone for the second, third, and fourth weeks of the *Exercises.*

The "Two Standards" (nos. 136–48) continues, expands, and forms a tight unity with the "Kingdom" exercise. Once again, the exercitant must focus upon the call of Christ to participate in the worldwide work of redemption. The poverty, scorn, and humiliation of Christ's "standard" is contrasted with the riches, worldly honors, and pride of Satan's "standard." Ignatius' militant spirituality, set in the context of the courtly tradition, views life as a battleground between the forces of good and evil. This exercise is, moreover, a dramatic presentation of Ignatius' well-known rules for the discernment of spirits (nos. 313–36). The exercitant asks for basic discernment: "a knowledge of the deceits of the evil chieftain . . . and a knowledge of the true life" (no. 139).

Within this exercise is the important "triple colloquy" (no. 147), to be made frequently during the second week. The exercitant addresses Mary, Christ, and the Father to beg for the grace to be placed under Christ's standard in perfect spiritual poverty, physical poverty, and humiliations. This colloquy echoes Ignatius' La Storta vision wherein he mystically experienced that "the Father placed him with the Son."

The internal logic of this colloquy leads into the "Three Classes of Men" (nos. 149–55) and the "Three Modes of Humility" (nos. 165–68) exercises. The "Three Classes of Men" tests the readiness of the exercitant to give up inordinate attachments and "to choose what is for the greatest glory of His Divine Majesty and the salvation of my soul" (no. 152). Only exercitants of the "third class" make decisions solely with "the desire of being able to serve God our Lord better" (no. 155).

The exercitant of the first mode of humility will never commit mortal sin, no matter how great the reward. The exercitant of the second mode of humility is in a state of Ignatian "indifference" and would not even commit venial sin for any reason. Those possessing the third mode of humility "choose poverty with Christ poor . . . reproaches with Christ . . . and [are] willing to be considered as worthless and a fool for Christ" (no. 167). Note, however, that the Ignatian condition for so deciding is "the praise and glory of the Divine Majesty being equally served" (no. 167). There were occasions in Ignatius' life when God's greater service demanded a line of action that prevented a literal following of Christ poor, suffering, and humiliated.

The high point of the second week is receiving the "intimate knowledge of our Lord . . . that I may love and follow Him better" (no. 103). For all its pragmatic and "worldly" concerns for God's greater glory on earth, however, Ignatius' mysticism of service finds in Christ poor, suffering, and humiliated the best means to serve the eternal Father. Unless the exercitant has chosen Christ poor, suffering, and humiliated and been placed under Christ's standard in some way, the Ignatian "Election" concerning a way of life or a reformation of life is in jeopardy. The specific, concrete decision to be made during the *Exercises* must flow out of an ever-deeper decision for Christ poor, suffering, and humiliated.

Although a love mysticism, Ignatius' *Exercises* focus explicitly on seeking God's will, not on loving union. Ignatius does not speak about God or Christ as spouse or lover with whom he unites in mystical marriage. This is not a mysticism of introversion, preoccupied with the divine activity at the core of one's being and emphasizing the transforming union leading ever closer to the beatific vision. Neither is it a mysticism which claims that contemplative love is the summit of earthly life, as we shall see in the *Cloud of Unknowing* and in the works of St. John of the Cross.

If the language of the bridal mystics is often that of persons on their honeymoon, Ignatius speaks more like a working man who has been happily married for a number of years. Actually, his attitude is like that of a generous, respectful, courageous, and loving servant who wishes to discern what God wants him to do. His loving service mysticism often centered on visible results for God's greater glory. In its psychological manifestations, God's action on Ignatius united him to God both spiritually and bodily. The divine activity strengthened and nourished not only the deepest dimension of Ignatius' person, his "core," but also his imagination, memory, and senses. In short, those "faculties" of particular significance for apostolic service experienced the influence of the divine influx.

Ignatius gives detailed instructions during the second week for the choice of a way of life or the reformation of life. These instructions focus upon the well-known

Ignatian "Election," or choice, which many commentators consider the primary goal of the *Exercises*.[14] For Ignatius, there are three times during the *Exercises* when the exercitant can make a prudent and good choice. An example of the "first time" (no. 175) is the way in which Christ unquestionably called St. Matthew and St. Paul, and they chose his way of life. The "second time" (no. 176) centers on the clarity that results from discerning the various consolations and desolations experienced during the *Exercises*. The "third time" is a "time of tranquility . . . when the soul is not agitated by diverse spirits and is freely and calmly making use of its natural powers" (no. 177).[15]

In their classical form, the exercises of the third and fourth weeks serve to stabilize, deepen, and confirm the Election of the second week. The third week centers on the Last Supper and the details of Jesus' passion, crucifixion, death, and entombment. The exercitant should give special attention to "what Christ our Lord suffers in His humanity or wills to suffer" (no. 195). He must ask for "sorrow, affliction, and confusion because the Lord is going to His passion on account of [the excercitant's] sins" (no. 193). Once again, the exercitant should ask what he ought to do for Christ.

The fourth week deals with the mysteries of the risen Christ. The exercitant asks to "feel intense joy and gladness for the great glory and joy of Christ our Lord" (no. 221). Special attention should be given to how Christ's "Divinity" manifests itself now that the passion is over. For Ignatius, the risen Christ is mainly one who consoles.

The third and fourth weeks are a time for the most intense empathy, or couvade, with Christ suffering and joyful. The exercitant must enter into the very psychosomatic rhythm of Christ suffering and risen. Perhaps because of the richness of the material, Ignatius allows considerable latitude concerning how these weeks are to be carried out. Once again, the colloquies addressed to Mary, Christ, and the Father play a significant role. These colloquies seem aimed specifically at maintaining a serious seeking of one's needs and the utmost spontaneity in deep prayer.

Additional Material

The *Exercises* end with Ignatius' "Contemplation to Obtain Divine Love" (nos. 230–37), a way of finding God in all things, and a summary of Ignatius' mysticism of loving service. For him, love shows itself in deeds, not words. It consists in the mutual sharing between lover and beloved. During this contemplation, the exercitant must ask for "a deep knowledge of the many benefits I have received, that I may be filled with gratitude for them, and in all things love and serve the Divine Majesty" (no. 233). The exercitant must contemplate the gifts received from creation, redemption, and his own personal uniqueness. Another area to contemplate is how God exists and works in all things for the exercitant. Experiencing everything as gift and reflecting upon himself, the exercitant then offers himself totally to God in loving service (no. 234).

Finally, the *Exercises* contain "Rules to Be Observed in the Future in the Matter of Food" (nos. 210–17), "Rules for the Distribution of Alms" (nos. 337–44), "Notes Concerning Scruples" (nos. 345–51), and "Rules for Thinking with the Church" (nos. 352–70).

It should be noted that these *Exercises* must be made and not merely read. When Thomas Merton tells the amusing story about his taking the *Exercises* into his room, reading them, and nothing happening, the net result is not surprising. The exercitant must do, undergo, live, and experience them.

Neither are the *Exercises* a compendium of the spiritual life nor a manual in ascetical and mystical theology. They are primarily a manual for the retreat director, "the one who is giving the Exercises" (no. 2). The complete text, therefore, should not be given to the exercitant. In fact, the less the exercitant knows in advance about the *Exercises,* the better.

The director-exercitant relationship is one of the pillars of the Ignatian retreat. The retreat director may very well be the key to the success of the *Exercises.* In fact, Ignatius judged only certain Jesuits capable of giving the *Exercises* in their entirety. He likewise preferred certain other Jesuits for giving them to those who would not progress beyond the first week.

THE UNIQUENESS OF THE *SPIRITUAL EXERCISES*

Holistic Emphases
At first glance, the *Exercises* might appear to be nothing more than a series of meditations and contemplations on the life, death, and resurrection of Jesus Christ, interspersed with specifically Ignatian parables, considerations, rules, and directives. Numerous meditation books and spiritual exercises throughout Christian history have contained similar material.

Yet, the *Exercises* are unique in the history of Christian spirituality, not necessarily for their content, but for their structure, dynamism, and explicit goal. Ignatius raised to the level of "the *science* of the saints concerning Christian existence"[16] what had always been implicit in the tradition. Christians have been seeking and finding God's will since the very beginning, but not in the methodical and explicit way proposed by Ignatius. He developed a method that allows a person to seek and find God's will in almost a "scientific," explicit manner.

Many commentators have correctly emphasized as the primary goal of the *Exercises* the systematic, well-regulated, explicit seeking and finding of God's will. Many have overlooked, however, their structure and dynamism, which lead to deeper and progressively more simple ways of praying. The exercitant can discover God's will because the structure of the *Exercises* initiates a dynamic process that makes the exercitant more sensitive to the great Christian mysteries. The *Exercises* are a mystical depth psychology that allows the exercitant to hear more clearly and loudly what he already lives and knows in some way at the deepest levels of his being.

Ignatius redirects the entire person to the truths of salvation history to rid the exercitant of inordinate attachments which hinder the seeking and finding of God's will. The *Exercises* have as one of their many goals the exercitant's intellectual conversion to God's truth. The mystics of the Christian tradition have long recognized that the human intellect also needs purification and illumination. Human wholeness is impossible without a reordering of thinking and intellectual clarity.

Therefore, the retreat director must present the exercitant with the "true essentials" of the faith. This results indirectly in the continuous updating of the *Exercises*, for the retreat director must keep abreast of contemporary exegesis and theology to do his work properly. The exercitant is also expected to use his reason throughout the *Exercises*. Many exercises center on: "to reason more in detail" (no. 50), "knowledge of my sins" (no. 63), "to know more thoroughly the eternal Word Incarnate" (no. 130), "a deeper knowledge" (no. 233), "knowledge" (no. 344), and "the course of our thoughts" (no. 333).

From his own conversion on the banks of the river Cardoner, Ignatius obtained a mystically infused architechtonic, holistic grasp of the Christian mysteries. He had also mystically received "dogmatic discretion" by which he instinctively understood the truths of the faith.[17] Ignatius was convinced of the necessity of facts and intellectual clarity as firm foundations for the affective-volitional life. The truths of salvation history had undoubtedly supported and guided him in his mystical ascent. They served to stabilize his service mysticism. One finds in Ignatius' life and *Exercises*, not a mysticism of wild and uncontrolled enthusiasm, but one of discreet love. In an age so prone to reduce mysticism to ecstatic experience and to deny the intellect its needs and rights in the mystical life, Ignatius stands as an excellent counterbalance.

It would be incorrect, however, to interpret in a rationalistic fashion Ignatius' insistence upon reason and intellectual clarity. He did place much importance upon thoughts, concepts, ideas, and reason, especially the thoughts, concepts, ideas, and reasonings flowing from mystical purgation, illumination, and love. Still, for him, "it is not an abundance of knowledge that fills and satisfies the soul but rather an interior understanding and savoring of things" (no. 2). His emphasis, moreover, is upon interiority, mystical knowledge, loving knowledge—the supraconceptual wisdom that is deeper than discursive-conceptual knowledge, but that does not eliminate it.

The *Exercises* likewise aim at purifying and reorienting all of the exercitant's desires. In the preparatory prayer, for example, the exercitant asks that all his "intentions, actions, and works may be directed purely to the service and praise of His Divine Majesty" (no. 46). The preparatory prayer, in a general way reminiscent of the "Principle and Foundation," drastically changes the direction of all the exercitant's desires.

The second prelude makes this general reorientation concrete, particular, and specific. Exercitants must ask God for what they want and desire. They ask for a particular grace which "must be according to the subject matter" (no. 48). Ignatius recalls salvation history to awaken, channel, and focus the exercitant's desires. He implicitly knew the importance of desires in the mystical life and how the deepest and most genuine human desires come to light in salvation history.

Each exercise attempts, therefore, an emotional-volitional conversion of the exercitant. The "Three Classes of Men," the "Three Modes of Humility," and the "Colloquies" test specifically the exercitant's willingness to choose only what contributes to God's greater praise and service. They are masterful exercises to expose the exercitant's weaknesses, hesitations, and those hidden desires that run counter to genuine desires. They bring to light the exercitant's lack of authenticity and other obstacles to the Ignatian "Election."

The mystical tradition has long recognized the need for purification of the human memory and imagination. Ignatius uses salvation history once again to reintegrate these two troublesome human faculties. Therefore, the first prelude of almost every exercise centers upon remembering the history or the true essentials of a particular Christian mystery (nos. 2, 50, 111, etc.). By means of a lively and methodical use of imagination, the exercitant is urged to examine his conscience twice daily (nos. 25–31).

Exercitants should also review past sins. Previous exercises must be recalled, repeated, reviewed, and summed up to "dwell upon points in which I have felt the greatest consolation or desolation, or the greatest spiritual relish" (no. 62). Ignatius' "mystic memory" frequently did this in his own life in order to relive mystical graces he had received long before.

The first prelude of most exercises is "a mental image of the place" (no. 47). Ignatius would have the exercitant construct in detail the setting of a particular Christian mystery. For many of the contemplations, the exercitant must see, hear, touch, taste, and smell *in imagination* what is taking place (nos. 65–71). Before falling asleep and immediately upon awakening, the imagination and memory must focus upon the assigned exercise in order to prevent mental wandering (nos. 73–74). Ignatius' profoundly incarnational mysticism, a mysticism which seeks union not only with the ever-greater, transcendent God, but also with the God who gave himself in space and time in specific mighty deeds, never allows the exercitant to turn his attention away from the great mysteries of salvation history which are for *his* redemption.

A reading of Ignatius' *Autobiography* and *Diary* reveals a mystic who had experienced a great variety of religious emotions. "Sweet devotions," joy, peace, tranquillity, tears, sorrow, interior and exterior bodily heat, and hair standing on end were all part of Ignatius' mystical life. Frequently throughout the *Exercises*, therefore, the exercitant must request tears, sorrow, shame, pain, confusion, horror, detestation, amazement, affectionate love, joy, gladness, peace, and tranquillity. The exercitant's *felt* needs often control the direction the prayer is to take (no. 109). The "Colloquies" enable the exercitant's spontaneous desires and feelings to surface. The "Third Method of Prayer" (nos. 258–60) helps to integrate strong religious emotions into the exercitant's basic breathing rhythm.

In short, Ignatius knew the importance of religious emotions in the mystical life. His *Exercises* expressly aim at fostering the exercitant's emotional conversion. To find God's will, the exercitant's spontaneous likes and dislikes must be changed. One's entire affective life must be purified, redirected, and transformed. The *Exercises* do not suppress emotions, therefore, but purify, reorient, and transform them in the light of salvation history. An especially potent enemy of inordinate attachments, religious emotions anchor faith, hope, and love more deeply in the exercitant's psychosomatic structure.

Progressive Simplification of Prayer

It should be obvious by now that Ignatius attempts to involve the exercitant totally in the many Christian mysteries. From this process of making the exercitant wholly present to these mysteries, he expected both an interior tasting, or indwelling, of the Christian mysteries and a purification, illumination, and transformation of the exercitant's whole being in its manifold levels of existence. The *Exercises* purify, illuminate, and transform the exercitant both spiritually and psychosomatically.

In view of the lack of writing on this subject, the Ignatian dynamism toward ever-greater interiorization and transparency of the Christian mysteries through more simple, deeper methods of prayer must be underscored. First, even the more laborious "meditations" of the first week demand the exercitant to seek an "interior understanding and savoring of things" (no. 2). The exercitant should linger with those aspects of the meditation that are satisfying (no. 76). He must never rush from point to point, but follow the consolations and the spiritual nourishment.

Second, the exercitant must repeat previously made exercises to dwell especially upon those aspects which brought about the most consolation and desolation. It is as if the exercitant takes mystical "soundings" of his own being to find the nodal points particularly open or resistant to God's grace. The "résumés" likewise recall and review intellectually what happened in the previous exercises. The first week even contains a much underestimated "application of the senses," an exercise which demands much simplicity in prayer. Each exercise ends, moreover, with a colloquy which carries forward, strengthens, and unifies the movement initiated in the preparatory prayer, the preludes, the "what I want and desire," the meditations, the résumés, and the repetitions.

After the first week, the movement toward greater interiority, transparency, and simplicity in prayer is even more apparent. The Ignatian "contemplations" dominate the following weeks. These contemplations make the exercitant present to and dwell in the various Christian mysteries in a richer, more holistic, yet simpler way. The exercitant must see, hear, touch, taste, and smell what is going on as if present (for example, no. 114). As in the first week, the repetitions and the résumés recapitulate, but deepen and simplify, what. went before.

The application of the senses assumes an even more important role after the first week. This exercise is usually made daily before the evening meal.[18] Once again, the exercitant must see, hear, touch, taste, and smell in imagination certain aspects of a particular Christian mystery. This greatly condenses, intensifies, and transforms the prayer begun in the preparatory prayer, the preludes, the contemplation itself, and the repetitions. In fact, some link the Ignatian application of the senses to the deeply mystical way of prayer found in the tradition concerning the "spiritual senses."[19] Augustine offers a paradigm of this deeply mystical prayer when he writes: "What is it then that I love when I love you? Not bodily beauty, and not temporal glory, not the clear sweet melodies of many-moded songs, not the soft smell of flowers and ointments and perfumes, not manna and honey, not limbs made for the body's embrace, not these do I love when I love my God.

"Yet I do love a certain light, a certain voice, a certain odor, a certain food, a certain embrace when I love my God: a light, a voice, an odor, an embrace for the man within me, where his light, which no place can contain, floods into my soul; where he utters words that time does not speed away; where he sends forth an aroma that no wind can scatter; where he provides food that no eating can lessen; where he so clings that satiety does not sunder us. This is what I love when I love my God."[20]

The *Exercises* offer an unusually effective means of simplifying and deepening prayer by way of a gradual interiorization of the Christian mysteries. There is a twofold movement to this process. First, the exercitant interiorizes the Christian mysteries by assimilating them, by bringing them from the outside to the inside, in much the same way that a student assimilates a book or a great work of art.

But the *Exercises* also initiate a movement from the inside to the outside, from the core of the exercitant's being to the more exterior levels of existence. Contemporary theology emphasizes that God has communicated himself as the Mystery which haunts, illuminates, and loves us at the very roots of our being, even before we begin to seek him. His loving word of wisdom at the center of our being, in fact, initiates any genuine search for him. This inner word, the "weight" of this inner love, the inner light of faith, forces us to turn to salvation history to see if and where God's self-communication has reached its irreversible high point. One lives a "seeking Christology," therefore, which promotes an outward movement toward the truths of salvation history. Ignatius uses the outer word of salvation history to awaken, deepen, and set into motion the inner word of God's universal self-communication. Only the inspired outer word of revelation correctly interprets the inner word. But it is only in the light of the inner word that the real salvific meaning and significance of the outer word can be found.[21]

Consolation without Previous Cause

Perhaps the high point of Ignatius' continuously deepening process occurs during the "consolation without previous cause." Ignatius writes: "It belongs to God alone to give consolation to the soul without previous cause, for it belongs to the Creator to enter into the soul, to leave it, and to act upon it, drawing it wholly to the love of His Divine Majesty. I say without previous cause, that is, without any previous perception or knowledge of any object from which such consolation might come to the soul through its own acts of intellect and will" (no. 330). For Ignatius, therefore, there is a special consolation which only God can grant. Only God can cause this type of mystical experience and act in this particular way. Moreover, this experience is an irrefutable sign of God's presence, because "there is no deception in it, since it proceeds only from God our Lord" (no. 336).

This God-given consolation cannot be understood apart from the "consolation with previous cause." As explained above, each exercise points the exercitant toward a specific grace for which he must ask. He must integrate and focus his entire being to dwell on a particular Christian mystery to obtain "what I want and desire." The precise grace sought in each exercise is, therefore, the consolation with previous cause. It is simply the consolation the exercitant works toward and expects if the exercise is successfully made. In short, "such consolation might come to the soul through its own acts of intellect and will" (no. 330).

The consolation without previous cause emerges out of the consolations with previous cause. It is a consolation beyond anything expected from the second prelude, the "what I want and desire." This disproportionate consolation—beyond expectation, not prepared for in the specific way the consolation with previous cause is—brings the exercitant "wholly to the love of the Divine Majesty." For Ignatius, only God can so enter a person, totally integrate him around his love, and then leave.[22]

The radically Christocentric context of the consolation without previous cause should also be emphasized. This consolation arises in, from, out of, and then transcends the Christian mysteries around which and in which the exercitant is totally engaged. This consolation emerges, moreover, from the dynamism that initiates progressively deeper, simpler prayer.

Sacramental Contemplation

As just described, it is clear that the *Exercises* provide a powerful counterpoint to the Christian apophatic mystical tradition. Again, the apophatic tradition emphasizes the *via negativa*, that God is so unlike creatures that *all* created things, even the Christian mysteries, must at some point be forgotten for the higher levels of mystical prayer. Ignatius focuses instead on the progressive simplification and eventual transparency of the Christian mysteries at hand. The *Exercises* never cast them aside in a "cloud of forgetting," but aid the exercitant in experiencing each Christian mystery in its totality.

As will be seen later, the apophatic tradition sometimes has the person use a meaningful word in prayer. The exercitant must not concentrate upon its meaning, but instead use it to control distractions while emptying the mind of all created things. For Ignatius, however, at the higher levels of mystical prayer the Christian mystery itself becomes a highly concentrated "word" with which the exercitant mystically resonates. It is a word that draws attention not to itself nor to its "letters," but to what it is in its essence: a sacrament of the healing, transforming presence of God. The key to Ignatian mysticism, therefore, is the *Exercises'* dynamism, which renders the Christian mysteries increasingly *transparent.* Transparency, not forgetting and unknowing, underpins Ignatius' radical kataphatic mysticism. In and through the increasing transparency of the Christian mystery, the exercitant penetrates to its very depths to experience its salvific valence.

The *Exercises* are, therefore, a paradigm of the sacramental, incarnational contemplation intrinsic to genuine

Christian mysticism. Karl Rahner puts the matter well when he writes: ". . . this basic incarnational structure of the unconfused unity of God and his creatures gives to understand that we can apprehend God in the sign . . . only if we do not cling to the sign . . . as if it were the ultimate reality, God himself. The sign must be welcomed and passed by, grasped and relinquished."[23] Both the revealing and concealing fullnesses of the ever-greater God found in the finite sacramental reality of the mysteries of salvation history manifest themselves in Ignatius' gradual process of simplification and transparency. These mysteries must be welcomed and simplified, grasped and rendered transparent if God will "one day reveal himself even to the pure mystic as the God of the transfigured earth because he is more than pure spirit."[24]

A Linking of Theology, Christology, and Anthropology
Intrinsic to Ignatius' *Exercises* is a mystical transcendental method, a method which implicitly presupposes that theology is Christology is anthropology. The more the exercitant discovers about God and Christ, therefore, the more he discovers what it means to be a human being. The more he discovers what it means to be human, the more he discovers about God and Christ.

Many of the exercises ask the exercitant to meditate on the thoughts that come to mind (no. 53) or to reflect upon himself (no. 234) while contemplating a specific Christian mystery. The exercitant looks at himself, therefore, in the light of salvation history. The outer word of salvation history awakens the inner word of his own God-graced uniqueness and humanity. By dwelling in a specific Christian mystery and then by reflecting upon himself, the exercitant discovers his human, personal, and subjective anticipation of this Christian mystery.

Salvation history and the human person are correlated. To discover anything about one is to discover something about the other. The various mysteries of salvation history are the manifold answers to the one question the human person is and lives. The question "What does it mean to be human?" can be answered only by God. Because the human person is he who has received God's self-communication, which reached its high point in Jesus Christ, the human person must turn to salvation history to uncover the depths of his identity. It is in this sense that "all object-centered meditation is a dwelling of the individual upon his deepest identity, upon the reflection of himself in the mirror of symbolism."[25] Therefore, the mysteries of salvation history are the keys which fit the various locks at all levels of human existence.

God's revelation in history is simultaneously the revelation of the human. By focusing upon salvation history and then reflecting upon himself, the exercitant tastes why this history is *saving*, that is, why a person must be immersed in it with his total being. Thus Ignatian prayer "is a summoning up within oneself of a state of being that is not something to be created but our deepest reality."[26]

Nevertheless, Ignatius' mysticism anchored in salvation history does not deal only with human interiority or only with the "ground of the soul." It forces the person to deal with his entire being and life in relationship to a God who has loved definitively, not only at the fine point of the human spirit, but in space and time as well. This "Ignatian mysticism of joy in the world"[27] does not cut a person off from any aspect of human existence in order to dwell in mystical introversion. The *Exercises* unite the entire person at all levels of being and life and express this unity in a radical service to the world.

The *Exercises* also provide an indirect critical corrective to the contemporary psychological tendency to reduce religion to psychic inwardness and its symbols to projections of inner experience. Christian theology insists, of course, that the human psyche finds its desires fulfilled in the *reality* of salvation history. The psyche's a priori possibilities, its purely formal, contentless archetypes, find their fulfilling and transforming content in the realities of Judeo-Christian salvation history.

Ignatius tacitly assumes that: "In Jesus myth and history meet. Myth reveals the ultimate meaning and significance of life, but it has no hold on history and loses itself in the world of imagination. History of itself, as a mere succession of events, has no meaning. . . . When historical events are seen to reveal the ultimate significance of life, then myth and history meet."[28] The *Exercises* are a method, therefore, that uses the perfect correspondence between the human psyche and salvation history. Neither the demands of the inner psychic life nor the truths of an objective salvation history are short-circuited. Both are maintained in a creative tension.

The psychic "child" still in us, for example, is purified, healed, and transformed by contemplating the divine Child who was born in history. The psychic Christ we crucify within us rises to new life when we contemplate the paschal mysteries of Jesus Christ. In short, the entire gamut of our psychic life needs to be redirected to salvation history. Contemplation of the various mysteries of the life, death, and resurrection of Jesus Christ purify, heal, and transform the human psyche, which is "naturally" Christian.

Mediator Mysticism
In still another way, Ignatius' mysticism opposes itself both to a mysticism of strict interiority and to a mysticism focused exclusively on an all-transcendent God. Mediators played an important role in Ignatius' mystical life. His mysticism is a "mediator mysticism." One finds in his *Diary*, for example, an unusual sensitivity to the

role Christ, Mary, the angels, the holy fathers, the apostles, and the disciples played in his relationship to the eternal Father.[29] He often experienced mystically which mediator to beseech to obtain certain graces. When Ignatius asks exercitants to place themselves "in the presence of Thy glorious Mother and of all the Saints of Thy heavenly court" (no. 98, cf. no. 151), his mediator mysticism is manifesting itself.[30]

He most frequently turned, however, to Christ and Mary to intercede for him. Perhaps the deepest aspect of his Marian mysticism came when "she showed that her flesh was in that of her Son."[31] The exercitant must, of course, pray to Mary for the graces of the first week (no. 63). She appears in the key exercises and important colloquies of the second week. Several mysteries of the third week focus upon her role as the mother of the one who goes to his death for our sins (nos. 297, 298). Ignatius even uses a nonscriptural appearance of the risen Christ to Mary as the first contemplation of the fourth week (no. 218).

Trinitarian Orientation

Of course, Jesus Christ is *the* Ignatian mediator. He not only dominates every week of the *Exercises,* but he also plays the pivotal role in obtaining from the eternal Father the graces proper to these weeks. His *Diary* shows, moreover, that Ignatius had mystically experienced Christ presenting, placing, and uniting him to and with the triune God. Therefore, his deepest mystical experience of Jesus Christ had a clear trinitarian focus. That Ignatius' radical Christocentrism is emphatically trinitarian should be the context of interpretation for many aspects of the *Exercises.*[32] The consolation without previous cause, for example, begins in the exercises on Christ's life, death, and resurrection, but draws the exercitant wholly to the love of the "Divine Majesty." This may very well be a deeply trinitarian experience. In view of the relative lack of trinitarian emphasis today, the implicit trinitarian dimension of the *Exercises* should be made more explicit.

The Ignatian Christ is the "Second Person" of the Trinity who became "man to save the human race" (no. 102). He is also the Creator who became man (no. 53) and the "eternal Word Incarnate" (no. 109). During the third week, the exercitant considers "how the Divinity hides Itself . . . and . . . leaves the most Sacred Humanity to suffer so cruelly" (no. 196). During the fourth week, "the Divinity . . . now appears and manifests itself so miraculously" (no. 223). For Ignatius, therefore, the man Jesus is always the Second Person of the Trinity, and vice versa.

If the *Exercises* are explicitly Christocentric, Ignatius' *Diary* is explicitly Father-centered. Ignatius had many mystical visions of the eternal Father and many of his deepest experiences "terminated" in the First Person. The eternal Father frequently manifested to Ignatius which mediator to employ. Moreover, Ignatius experienced him as the Father of "such a Son" and as the source of the other divine persons.

In the *Exercises,* Christ is sent from the Father to do his will. Christ speaks of "my Father" (no. 95), whom he serves. The "Our Father" prayer concludes almost every exercise. The Father is explicitly implored for the graces proper to each week. In short, the eternal Father is the proper horizon for all that takes place in the *Exercises.* Since this is so, retreat directors should place more emphasis upon the *Exercises'* essential Father-centeredness.

Oddly enough, the *Exercises* contain very few explicit references to the Holy Spirit. A study of the various recensions of the texts of the *Exercises* indicates, moreover, a deliberate attempt to eliminate references to the Holy Spirit. Because of widespread pseudo-mystical movements which claimed direct inspiration from the

Holy Spirit, it is understandable why Ignatius chose to eliminate any hint of this tendency from his already beleaguered *Exercises*.

To be sure, the *Exercises* present Elizabeth being filled with the Holy Spirit (no. 263); the Holy Spirit coming upon Jesus at his baptism (no. 273); the risen Christ giving the apostles the Holy Spirit (no. 304); telling them to baptize in the name of the Father, Son, and Holy Spirit (no. 307); and also telling them to await the coming of the Holy Spirit in Jerusalem (no. 307). He speaks of the one Spirit which guides both the individual and the Church (no. 365), but in the safe context of the "Rules for Thinking with the Church." In short, Ignatius does not explicitly urge the exercitant to seek out the guidance of the Holy Spirit.

Many references to the Holy Spirit do appear, however, in Ignatius' *Diary*. He had received many important mystical experiences of and from the Holy Spirit. In fact, in Ignatius' later years, he remarked that he could experience the Holy Spirit almost at will. His letters indicate that he expected the Holy Spirit to move and to direct people in their spiritual lives. In these letters the Holy Spirit frequently appears in the context of consolation, discretion, decision, and the confirmation of that decision. The *Directories* written or approved by Ignatius to explain certain difficult points in the *Exercises* also speak of the Holy Spirit in the above context.

It would seem fitting, therefore, to interpret and give the *Exercises* in the light of Ignatius' own mystical life, his letters, and the *Directories*. In matters dealing with consolation, discernment, election, and the confirmation of the election, the exercitant will certainly experience the Holy Spirit. Ignatius also explicitly states that God will communicate himself to the exercitant, work directly with him, and draw him totally to his love. The Holy Spirit is God's self-communication, God-in-us, the Father's gift of love poured into our hearts. This is the "good spirit" whose actions run counter to those of the enemy of our human nature (no. 314). Ignatius says of those advancing in the spiritual life that "the action of the good angel is gentle, light, and sweet, as a drop of water entering a sponge" (no. 335). This is clearly the action of the Holy Spirit, whose actions Ignatius attributes to the "good angel" because of the pseudo-mystical controversies of his day. Therefore, the Holy Spirit does assume a position of extreme importance for the proper making of the *Exercises*, although not explicitly. The exercitant will experience the Holy Spirit specifically as the Holy Spirit.

The Trinity permeates the *Exercises* in still other ways. The titles, "His Divine Majesty," "Infinite Goodness," "Divine Justice," and "God," for example, frequently refer to the Trinity. The "Three Divine Persons," moreover, explicitly form the background for the entire second week (no. 102). This contemplation also supplies the pattern for the contemplations of the third and fourth weeks.

Ignatius penetrated to the very core of the Trinity in his own mystical life. He was a trinitarian mystic par excellence. His *Diary, Autobiography*, letters, and the testimony of those who knew him intimately make this clear. When the *Exercises* are given and read in this context, therefore, they too can lead the exercitant into the very depths of the mystery of the triune God.

RULES FOR THE DISCERNMENT OF SPIRITS

Rules More Suitable for the First Week
The *Exercises* aim specifically at removing the exercitant's disorders and making him integral in order to facilitate the seeking and finding of God's will. They accomplish this by fostering the exercitant's intellectual, emotional, psychological, and religious conversion through a dynamic of progressively deeper prayer. Because they interrupt and alter the exercitant's normal

life, he will almost certainly experience "spiritual movements," "tides of consolation and desolation," or spiritual "highs and lows," and be "troubled by different spirits" (no. 6).

On the basis of his own mystical life, Ignatius wrote "Rules for the Discernment of Spirits," or: "Rules for perceiving and understanding to some degree the different movements that are produced in the soul—the good, that they may be accepted; the bad, that they may be rejected" (no. 313). These rules are not a complete course in mystical depth psychology, but offer only "some degree" of awareness.

Ignatius provides fourteen rules for the first week and eight for the second. The rules for the first week are more suited to those "tempted strongly and openly" (no. 9); those of the second week, for those "being attacked and tempted under the appearance of good" (no. 10). The rules for the first week focus more, therefore, on how to cope with the struggles, desolations, and discouragements involved in following Christ's call. Those of the second week, on the other hand, "serve for a greater discernment of spirits" (no. 328) and center more on consolations and the subtle temptations encountered by those more advanced in the mystical life.

Rules 1 and 2 of the first week focus upon the exercitant's existential stance. Ignatius depicts two diametrically opposed postures: one centered upon authenticity, the other, inauthenticity. To mask the inauthenticity of the person's stance, the "enemy" suggests "apparent pleasure," "sensual delights and pleasure" (no. 314). The "good spirit," on the other hand, counters this by harassing the person's conscience "to a sense of remorse through the good judgment of . . . reason" (no. 314).

The action of the two spirits is reversed, however, for those embracing authenticity as an existential stance.

The evil spirit will harass, discourage, and place obstacles in the way of those progressing in the spiritual life. On the other hand, the good spirit consoles, makes everything easy, and bestows joy, courage, and strength. In short, consolation and desolation have both a positive and a negative valence depending upon the person's basic stance toward or away from human authenticity.

Rules 3 and 4 describe consolation and desolation, key realities in Ignatian mysticism. In terms of the two existential stances, consolation "calls and attracts to heavenly things . . . desolation . . . to low and earthly things" (nos. 316, 317). They appear in consciousness as inflaming love, "interior joy," "peace and quiet," or as "darkness of soul" and "turmoil of the mind." They signify, however, an "increase of faith, hope, and charity" or a "loss of faith . . . hope . . . and love." Ignatius sees them in terms of God's praise and service, a point repeatedly made in the *Exercises*. Nevertheless, many Ignatian commentators neglect a most important aspect of Ignatian discernment: *thoughts*. So much attention is given to religious affectivity that they overlook that "thoughts that spring from consolation are the opposite of those that spring from desolation." In short, both our moods and the thoughts resulting from these moods say much about our human authenticity or lack thereof.

Rules 5 to 9 describe the strategy to follow in times of desolation. Of major importance to Ignatius is that "in time of desolation one should never make a change, but stand firm" (no. 318). The exercitant should never make key decisions during this time because "in desolation the evil spirit guides and counsels" (no. 318). The Ignatian exercitant, however, does not remain passive, but must "strive diligently against the desolation" (no. 321) by more prayer, penance, examinations of conscience, and patience. The person must remember, too, that "consolation will soon return" (no. 321).

The exercitant may experience desolation because of personal tepidity, sloth, or negligence (no. 322). God may also be testing his fidelity to authenticity when left without the more manifest signs of the Holy Spirit's presence. Ignatius assures the exercitant, however, that "even though he may not clearly perceive it . . . [God] . . . has nevertheless left him sufficient grace for eternal salvation" (no. 320). Although always to be directly countered, desolation may still be a special grace which brings "true knowledge and understanding" (no. 322). It teaches that authenticity, consolations, and progress in the mystical life are all "a gift and grace of God our Lord."

Rules 10 and 11 center upon the behavior suitable to periods of consolation. Perhaps the brevity of these rules indicates that, for Ignatius, consolation speaks for itself because it comes from God. Following what consolation does is the key to Ignatian prayer. At this point, however, in order to strengthen, deepen, moderate, and extend the effects of the present consolation as much as possible, Ignatius has the exercitant look to the past to "recall how little he is worth in time of desolation" (no. 314) and to the future to "think of how he will conduct himself during the desolation that will follow" (no. 323).

Once again Ignatius reminds the exercitant that in desolation, he should find his strength in God. Both consolation and desolation may effectively initiate the "flight from self-love, self-will, and self-interest" (no. 189) concretely seen in the exercitant's willingness to follow Christ poor, suffering, and humiliated.

Rules 12 to 14 depict the devil's tactics and the exercitant's counterattacks. The enemy is symbolized as a "woman . . . weak in the presence of strength, but strong if he has his will" (no. 325), "a false lover who wishes to remain hidden and does not want to be revealed" (no. 326), and a military commander who studies and then attacks our "weakest side" (no. 327). In the first case, authenticity is obtained only through unwavering courage and fearless faith that "does exactly the opposite to what [the devil] suggests" (no. 325). Thus, one aspect of Ignatian mysticism is to face the opposition head on.

In the second case, the exercitant turns weakness into strength. He must rely upon another by revealing "to a confessor or some other spiritual person who understands [the enemy's] deceits and evil designs" (no. 326). In this way, Ignatius unites a self-assurance with a radical humility that opens up one's most secret temptations to another. In any genuine mystical tradition, the spiritual-guide/disciple relationship is of paramount importance. Certain graces attain their fullness only after they have been revealed to another. In this matter, Ignatius implicitly underscores the social dimension of the mystical life, which must never be abolished in favor of the flight of the "alone to the Alone."

Finally, exercitants must be as shrewd as military commanders in being aware of, evaluating, and fortifying the weaknesses in their spiritual lives. Fearless confidence, a distrust of self, dependence on God and others, shrewd awareness of one's weaknesses, and constant vigilance are absolutely necessary to vanquish the enemy and to be under Christ's standard, the standard of human authenticity.

Rules More Suitable for the Second Week
The eight rules for the second week provide more sensitive discernment for the experienced exercitant in times of subtle temptations. The first rule describes consolation as "true happiness and spiritual joy" (no. 329). God's presence dispels all sadness, for in his presence the exercitant experiences integrity and wholeness. This consolation illuminates the exercitant's real meaning, direction in life, and true self. It is no wonder, there-

fore, that the enemy will "fight against such joy" (no. 329) as deviously and as subtly as possible.

Rules 2 and 8 center upon the "consolation without previous cause." Because only God can give consolation in this specific way, it is the paradigm of all consolations. This unexpected, disproportionate consolation attracts the exercitant "wholly to the love of His Divine Majesty" (no. 330). In this consolation, therefore, the exercitant imitates Christ's total self-emptying and self-surrender to loving Mystery. Some contemporary theologians define the human person as one able to belong totally to God; this consolation perfectly actualizes that potential. Human authenticity and the consolation without previous cause are coterminous and bestow upon the exercitant an experiential certitude of union with God. This consolation also presents evidence for the thesis that anthropology in depth is really Christology, that only from Christ do we know what it means to be human: perfect self-surrender to loving Mystery.

Because this consolation comes entirely from God, "there is no deception in it" (no. 336). It is irrefutable evidence, therefore, of God's presence and a first principle against which all other consolations can be measured. Any experiences which enhance the "wholly" of this consolation may be accepted; experiences which diminish this "wholly" should be rejected.

Even with this consolation, however, Ignatius advises caution. The exercitant "should carefully distinguish the exact time of such consolation from the time that follows it" (no. 336). The experiences in the afterglow of this consolation do not carry the same privileges and may be used by the evil spirit in subtle ways against the exercitant. In the afterglow, it is also difficult to distinguish what comes from God, from the self, and from the "good spirit or the evil one." Ignatius' mystical discretion provides an excellent antidote to the misguided religious enthusiasm that pervades some contemporary circles, which claim to do everything under God's direct inspiration.

Rule 3 speaks of consolations with previous causes in which "both the good angel and the evil one may console the soul but for different purposes" (no. 331). This rule echoes the second rule of the first week, but appeals more to intellectual than to affective criteria. Ignatius makes an invaluable distinction between genuine consolation and pseudo-consolation. The former promotes growth and authenticity; the latter, "the opposite."

Rule 4 states that "it is characteristic of the evil one to transform himself into an angel of light" (no. 332), an echo of 2 Corinthians 11:14. Knowing that a fervent, progressing person cannot be tempted crudely, the evil one offers "good and holy thoughts" that seem congruent with the exercitant's state, but that are really beset with "hidden deceits and perverse designs." Whereas the enemy in the first rule for the first week effectively masked his intentions by offering "apparent pleasures," he now employs intellectual camouflage, that is, "good and holy thoughts." Satan's temptation of Christ in the desert seems to be the paradigmatic dramatization of this rule.

The fifth rule is perhaps the very heart of Ignatian discernment. It complements the thirteenth rule of the first week, which would have the exercitant open up to another by explaining how he can discern for himself and for others. He must carefully examine both the entire scope of his thoughts and the resulting peace, quiet, and tranquillity. Both the intellectual and the affective components must be "directed to what is entirely right" (no. 333). "The beginning, middle, and end" of the thoughts must be "all good and directed to what is entirely right." If these thoughts propose something "less good," "distracting," or "evil," "this is a clear sign that they proceed from the evil spirit" (no. 333). From the affective side, "if these thoughts weaken, disquiet, or disturb the soul by destroying the peace, tranquillity, and quiet which it had before" (no. 333), this, too, signifies the presence of the enemy.

The fifth rule seems intimately related to the second and eighth rules. Rule 8 speaks of "various plans and resolutions" which arise in the aftermath of the consolation without previous cause. These deserve careful scrutiny, for many consider the ideas which arise during religious fervor to be divinely inspired. As Ignatius says, however, they "are not inspired directly by God our Lord" (no. 336). If the thoughts which arise in this period enhance or dilute the consolation without previous cause, this is a sign of the exercitant's congruence or incongruence with God's will. One would seriously misunderstand Ignatius in thinking that he urged the exercitant toward some abstract good. It is always a question of God's will *for the exercitant,* of his own deepest authenticity. The thoughts discussed in this rule must resonate, therefore, with the exercitant's entire life and being.

The sixth rule gives instructions on how to profit from the experience of temptation. Both "his deceptions" and "the bad end to which he leads" (no. 334) eventually unmask the enemy of our human nature. By carefully examining "afterwards the course of the good thoughts that were suggested to him" (no. 334), the exercitant discovers the gradual ("little by little") and subtle process by which the enemy attempts to rob him of genuine consolation. Out of all this should come "experience and knowledge" by which the exercitant "may better guard himself in the future against the customary deceits of the enemy."

Rule 7 proffers a more refined version of rules 1 and 2 of the first week. For those advancing in the spiritual life, "the action of the good angel is gentle, light, and sweet, as a drop of water entering a sponge. The action of the evil spirit is sharp, noisy, and disturbing, like a drop of water falling upon a rock" (no. 335). Because of the present tendency to judge the value of experiences in terms of the extraordinary—by how glamorous they are or whether they are ecstatic—Ignatius' point must be stressed. Genuine progress is delicate, simple, and silent. Only when the person's existential stance is in opposition to that of the "good angel" or the enemy do the good angel and the enemy act "with noise and disturbances that are easily perceived" (no. 335). If the person's and the spirit's stances are congruent, the spirit acts "silently, as one coming into his own house through an open door" (no. 335).

CONCLUDING REFLECTIONS

Strengths and Weaknesses of the Spiritual Exercises
The ways in which the *Exercises* have been given traditionally manifest both weaknesses and strengths, as seen from their history. On the one hand, the tradition has placed too much stress on "retreat resolutions," pragmatic decisions to change one's life to a greater or lesser degree, without proper regard for the intellectual, emotional, psychological, and religious conversions that must underpin these resolutions. Retreat resolutions cannot be "willed." They can only flow out of the deep religious experiences engendered by the *Exercises* when they are properly given.

In the hands of an unskillful director, moreover, the *Exercises'* detailed instructions on prayer can degenerate to a "by-the-book" recipe for prayer devoid of spontaneity and suppressing the emotions. These instructions can also be given the appearance of a "will-asceticism" that emphasizes in semi-Pelagian fashion what the exercitant can supposedly do without grace. An unskilled director can present the mysteries of salvation history like pious holy cards, involving the exercitant in an imaginative game in mythic space and time, instead of in the realities of God's history.

On another note, it is odd that one Jungian writer, Morton Kelsey, criticizes the *Exercises* because they allegedly "sometimes lost touch with the spontaneous images awakened within the individual."[33] Ignatius often emphasized the need for the exercitant to reflect upon oneself and to turn to the spontaneous thoughts, desires, and needs which manifested themselves in the light of the mysteries of the life, death, and resurrection of Jesus Christ (nos. 53, 109, 125, 130, 234, 235, 332, 333). It can be asked if contemporary Jungians, unlike Ignatius, make far too little of the correlation that exists between the exercitant's being and the mysteries of salvation history, between Christ's rhythm and the exercitant's.

The Jungian emphasis upon using the spontaneous images that arise and move in the psyche undoubtedly offers many psychosomatic benefits. It may also be of great value for Christian prayer, if properly transposed. On the other hand, it can be asked how many Jungians simply turn prayer into an intrapsychic event with no genuine self-transcendence, despite Kelsey's assertion that praying by way of spontaneous, inner images gets a person beyond the personal psyche. Will the Jungian emphases produce anything as profound, tested, and true as Ignatius' use of the great mysteries of salvation history to create the proper matrix and milieu for spontaneous images?

Perhaps Ignatius' genius rested in his extraordinary ability to transpose his age's spontaneous ambitions, dreams, ideals, and goals into a creative, dynamic spirituality. It must be admitted, however, that some of the *Exercises'* sixteenth-century cultural trappings hinder a contemporary transposition.

On the other hand, the *Exercises* combine the best ascetical and mystical principles. Although Ignatius does everything in his power to prepare the exercitant to seek and to find God's will, the conviction supporting the *Exercises* is that God will work directly with the exercitant. Both the absolute gratuity of grace and the need for human effort clearly permeate this spiritual classic.

In addition, Ignatius' detailed directives for prayer are a masterful blend of insightful psychology, spirituality, and even physiology. For example, emotions, desires, imagination, memory, reason, understanding, will, and thoughts are all used to integrate the exercitant wholly into the Christian mystery at hand. Ignatius even takes into account the effects that breathing, bodily posture, light, darkness, food, drink, the seasons of the year, and recollection before falling asleep have on prayer.

During his life, Ignatius indirectly, but successfully, healed many people of psychological and emotional dysfunction. Many commentators have underscored the psychotherapeutic value of his *Exercises.* By promoting human authenticity, they can go a long way in transforming and healing the affective pain, lack of meaning, and self-disgust that permeate much of contemporary life. Because of current emphases on the contemplative "technology" of the East and the value of contemplation for psychosomatic integrity, it is ironic that the *Exercises* are not more appreciated in this area.[34]

To caricature the *Exercises,* moreover, as a mechanical, discursive, step-by-step, rigid approach to prayer is a serious misreading both of the Ignatian text and the tradition. These *Exercises* can take a person at almost any level of spiritual maturity or immaturity and lead him to progressively deeper, simpler levels of prayer. Through a dynamic which guides him into the mystery of God in Christ and into his authentic identity, the exercitant may discover God's specific will for him.

The mystical tradition testifies to the great risks and dangers that accompany mystical progress. To descend radically into ever-deeper levels of the psyche should not be done without certain traditional safeguards. The *Exercises* make this vertical descent safer in a number of ways.

First, the exercitant must rely upon an experienced spiritual director who already knows many of the pitfalls involved. This spiritual-director/exercitant relationship indirectly keeps the exercitant in touch with a wiser, more experienced, and more comprehensive mystical tradition. Although it is partially true that the mystic undertakes a lonely journey at the higher stages of mystical ascent, the Christian mystical tradition teaches that even here the tradition and community play a supportive role.

In an age that seems either to embrace authoritarian cult leaders or to reject totally the role of tradition and the need for guidance in the mystical life, Ignatius provides an excellent middle course. Although he emphasizes the role of the spiritual director, he cautions the director to stand "in the middle like the balance of a scale . . . [and] . . . allow the Creator to work directly with the creature, and the creature with its Creator and God" (no. 15). Furthermore, the *Exercises* do not indoctrinate. They allow the exercitant to verify experientially the matter at hand, for human authenticity is self-verifying.

The *Exercises* keep the exercitant in touch with the wider tradition and community in still another way. They direct the exercitant's prayer to mediators, that is, to Christ, Mary, the saints, or the entire heavenly court. Keeping the exercitant's inner eye directed toward reliable persons even at the higher levels of prayer provides strong psychological support. The psychological benefit of even minimal interpersonal contact during crisis situations is well known. For example, prisoners in solitary confinement are strengthened greatly if they catch fleeting glimpses of other prisoners or can communicate with them by tapping on pipes. The psychological stability and assurance provided by praying to mediators during crisis periods of the mystic's own "solitary confinement" must not be overlooked.

Ignatius heightens the interpersonal relationship between the exercitant and the triune God, Christ, Mary, and the saints in yet another way. For example, the many colloquies are highly intimate and personal, "as one friend speaks to another, or as a servant speaks to his master" (no. 54). This intimacy is always held in creative tension with respect, however, an important element in interpersonal relationships perhaps not heeded enough today. Ignatius' *Diary* reveals not only his incredible intimacy with the triune God, Christ, Mary, and the saints, but also an "infused respect," or loving reverence, toward these persons that arose out of love, not fear.[35] The *Exercises* echo this "infused respect" when they teach that: "We should realize that in acts of the will, when we are speaking vocally or mentally with God our Lord or His saints, *more reverence* is required of us . . ." (no. 3, my emphasis).

Perhaps the most secure foundation Ignatius provides for mystical ascent is his strong Christocentrism. Ignatian mysticism is inextricably bound to the person of Jesus Christ and to the events in his life. Ignatius tacitly assumes that one finds in Jesus Christ all the mysteries of God and humanity. Christ holds the key both to the deepest revelation of God and to human authenticity.

On the one hand, the events of the life, death, and resurrection of Jesus contain what they symbolize: the history of God himself. Because Christ is the way, the truth, and the life, salvation history is the proper entrance into the experience of transcendence so desired today. The history of the ever-greater God is the proper launch pad for a genuine mystical experience of the triune God. By approaching mystical ascent by way of the truths of salvation history, there is less danger of confusing an experience of the self, of the unity of the world, or of certain archetypes with authentic experiences of God and Christ. Emphasis upon salvation history ensures a better basis for a genuine Christian mysticism that terminates in a union with the triune God or with the person of Jesus Christ.

On the other hand, Jesus Christ is also the revelation of authentic human existence. He sublates all human history and most archetypal patterns, individual as well as collective. Dwelling in his mysteries is dwelling in authentic human existence. Contemplation of his life, death, and resurrection is an indirect self-contemplation. These mysteries provide, moreover, a sound support system for the dangerous vertical descent into the psyche during mystical prayer. His mysteries enable the exercitant to cope more safely and effectively with the dangers of the dark nights, with the debris that mystical prayer dislodges.

Ignatius' Ecclesial Mysticism

Ignatius' mystical union with Jesus Christ, his "incarnational mysticism,"[36] provides the foundation for his ecclesial mysticism. His mystical experiences united him not only with the triune God and the person of Jesus Christ, but also with "the true Spouse of Christ our Lord, our Holy Mother, the hierarchical Church" (no. 353). What Ignatius emphasized in his "Rules for Thinking with (*sentir con*) the Church" was a mystically felt knowledge, not of the invisible Church of the Reformers, but of the visible, tangible, historical community of Jesus Christ. The Ignatian *sentir* is neither a subjective, pious sense of an invisible Church nor an extrinsic, voluntaristic attachment to an ecclesiastical bureaucracy. It is the genuine Christian experience in the mystical, or spiritual, senses, of full union with every dimension of a Church which is inseparable from the incarnate Christ.

To be sure, these rules must be evaluated in their historical context, for some of them contain an antiquated anti-Lutheran tinge. The following authentic mystical insight is, however, never outdated: ". . . between the Bridegroom, Christ our Lord, and the Bride, His Church, there is but one spirit, which governs and directs us for the salvation of our souls, for the same Spirit and Lord, who gave us the Ten Commandments, guides and governs our Holy Mother Church" (no. 365).

If Christian mysticism is intrinsically incarnational, there cannot be a fundamental contradiction between a Christ-, Spirit-, and ecclesial-mysticism. Congruence between inner and outer life, or between transcendental and historical, tangible, visible experience must exist.

Genuine incarnational mysticism inevitably results in ecclesial mysticism. The deepest, most interior movements in the soul must not only become incarnate, but these incarnations must also be congruent with the mystical Body of Christ, the Church in all its dimensions. Ignatius insisted, for example, that the discernment of spirits should result in, or embody itself in, a concrete decision, the "election." This election, moreover, had to be congruent with "the hierarchical Church" (no. 170). Ignatian mysticism resolutely refused to accept a dichotomy between mystical interiority, the "exteriorization" of this interiority in concrete decisions, and the visible, historical Church.

Inner mystical experiences proved their authenticity for Ignatius if they did not hesitate to become visible, to expose themselves to the light of a living community of faith (no. 326). For him, mystical graces "must always be in harmony with the holy scriptures, the virtues, right reason and edification—in short, with the Church."[37] Therefore, Ignatius' ecclesial mysticism is not something extrinsic to the mystical life, a veneer to protect him from ecclesiastical authority. It is inextricably linked with his mystical experiences of Christ. Jerome Nadal, one of Ignatius' closest disciples, is undoubtedly correct when he writes that when Ignatius began to grow in the discernment of spirits, "the Lord gave him a sublime understanding and very lively feelings in regard to the divine mysteries and the Church."[38]

Despite their anti-Reformation tone, therefore, it is understandable why Ignatius' rules counsel obedience to the hierarchical Church, respect for the Church's sacramental, religious, and liturgical life, respect for Church laws, customs, and precepts, and care in preaching and speaking about predestination, free will, faith, and good works. Some of these rules are outdated, but not the incarnational, ecclesial mysticism behind them. Ignatius' loyalty to Church authority, doctrines, teachings, practices, and customs is an essential feature of all genuinely Christian mysticism, despite the often indiscriminate and naive way Ignatius could apply this in particular cases.[39]

Thus, the Ignatian *sentir con* is a profoundly mystical disposition of spirit, an attitude, an affective intent that provides an especially strong safety net for the dangerous regions of mystical ascent. It is also intimately linked with the Ignatian insight that authentic mysticism must result in the reform of one's life and have pastoral significance.[40] Mystical interiority must result in mystical action that is public, or ecclesial.

For Ignatius, the Church could be an immediate and positive source of mystical inspiration, an ultimate and only negative boundary, or anything in between.[41] For example, Ignatius' own obedience to hierarchical authorities was anything but "blind." Although he would frequently obey "the least sign of a superior's will," his dealings with the popes Paul II, Julius III, and Paul IV indicate clearly that his obedience was not automatic and that he even forced them on occasion to come around to his way of thinking.[42]

Although he was a loyal son of the hierarchical Church, he was a master of ecclesiastical diplomacy and political maneuvering. Ignatius was convinced that in certain cases "Christ himself, through the mediation of his Vicar, would vouchsafe to show them the way to his greater service."[43] But this was tempered with the statement that: "Although the men of the Society are papists, they are this only when they absolutely have to be and in nothing more; and even then, only with an eye to the glory of God and the general good."[44] In short, Ignatius' reverent, but at times critical, obedience to the hierarchical church flowed from his service mysticism, an awareness of how intrinsically linked the universal Church is with the universal good.

Ignatius said that his mystical experiences "were always a striking confirmation of his faith, so much so that he has often thought to himself that if there were no Scriptures to teach us these matters, he was determined to die for them, merely because of what he had seen."[45] This clearly contradicts one contemporary line of thinking that insists genuine mysticism is by nature "anticonventional," "anticollective," and "antidogmatic," that a mysticism in harmony with a teaching Church is necessarily "low-level," or a "redogmatization."[46] In fact, genuine Christian mysticism does not tend toward heresy, iconoclasm, and antiecclesialism.

The Spiritual Exercises *as a Contemporary Counterpoint*
The *Exercises* render a strong counterpoint to several contemporary overemphases. First, Ignatius insists that religious fervor and charismatic phenomena must be rooted solidly in the "true essentials" of the mysteries of salvation history. A short-circuiting of the intellectual life or a mindless, allegedly "charismatic" exegesis of scripture has no place in the *Exercises*. Against the

search for a "transcendence without dogma," Ignatius realized explicitly that only the genuine "outer word" of salvation history can awaken the authentic "inner word" of the experience of being attracted to the God of mystery.

Concentrating on the life, death, and resurrection of Jesus Christ mitigates the overemphasis which some persons in the charismatic movements place upon the Holy Spirit. The Holy Spirit is always the Spirit of Jesus Christ. Whenever one experiences the depths of Jesus' sacred humanity, there is the Spirit of Christ.

It is doubtful that Ignatius would have sanctioned the spiritual sterility that plagues some academic theology. With true fidelity to the demands of the intellectual life, Ignatius still taught that "it is not an abundance of knowledge that fills and satisfies the soul but rather an interior understanding and savoring of things" (no. 2). Properly used, therefore, the *Exercises* can lessen the gap that exists between a living spirituality and academic theology. Ignatius held in high regard "both positive and scholastic theology" (no. 363), or both speculative and affective theology. His genius was in trying to synthesize spiritual, pastoral, and speculative doctrine for the universal good of the Church.[47]

In the light of the mysteries of salvation history, the *Exercises* initiate a process of increasingly deeper prayer by which these mysteries of the divine-human drama become transparent. Creation becomes transparent, reveals itself as a divine milieu, and allows God to be found in all things. This dynamic also helps the exercitant to find God's specific will. This is a mysticism not only of unrestricted love of God, but also of discreet love and service.

Some have criticized the *Exercises* for enforcing a "me-Jesus," "privatized" spirituality. To be sure, Ignatius writes that "in these Exercises, as a general rule, he [the exercitant] will profit all the more if he is separated from all of his friends and from all worldly cares" (no. 20). However, this holds only for the short time during which the *Exercises* are made. The *Exercises* plunge the exercitant into the life of a God who is at work in all things for the world. Service and social involvement stamp this spirituality. In fact, the *Exercises* can easily link up with current trends in liberation theology.[48]

Ignatius' rules for the discernment of spirits should play a greater role in contemporary spirituality. They teach the much-needed lesson that there are qualitative differences in various experiences. They expose pseudo-mystical experiences, or those movements away from genuine human authenticity. What experiences bring genuine consolation and make the exercitant truly congruent with his deepest self? The rules for the discernment of spirits aid a person in seeking out and accepting such experiences and rejecting all others. They also focus upon the importance of thoughts that arise on various occasions. For example, an acquaintance of mine was enlightened when he applied the Ignatian rules to his drinking, and found how devastating his thoughts were when and after he drank. These rules highlight that which causes peace or "noise" in our inner being and why they do so. Some have even transposed these rules for use in group discernment to detect the movements of the various spirits that affect an entire community as a community.[49]

The *Exercises* are especially important today because they purify and transform the universal, human, threefold religious sense. Every human being has an immense longing for transcendence, for belonging totally to the world, and for radical interiority. This threefold religious sense finds its fulfillment only in a genuine trinitarian spirituality centered on the all-transcendent Father, the Son as God in the world, and the Holy Spirit who is true interiority. By focusing upon the Father, the *Exercises* fulfill the need for an ecstatic, vertical experience of the all-transcendent Father, God-*above*-us. By centering on the Son, the need for God-*with*-us, for the horizontal meaning of life to be fulfilled, is satisfied. A Son-centered spirituality is one that loves the earth, sees everything as a sacrament of the divine presence, and sees the resurrection as the pledge of a yet to be fulfilled earth. Finally, the *Exercises* awaken us to God-*in*-us, to an *en*static experience of God's gift of himself to the center of our being that makes us connatural with the Father of love.

Chapter Three

The Cloud of Unknowing

The fourteenth-century mystical classic, the *Cloud of Unknowing*,[1] written anonymously, is an outstanding paradigm of the Christian apophatic mystical tradition. In line with this tradition, the *Cloud* emphatically teaches that love, not knowledge, can reach God. It prefers, therefore, to speak about what God is not. Through mystical love, "there is a negative knowledge which understands God" (chap. 70, p. 139).

It is unfortunate that this solidly Christian mystical tradition is hardly known and appreciated except in fairly limited Christian circles. The *Cloud* could be of the utmost importance for a contemporary mystical spirituality. In presenting a distinctive yet orthodox way of contemplating God, the *Cloud* offers much more than the classical way of negation for speaking about him. Because of this distinctive and, according to many Christians, very strange way of contemplating God, the *Cloud* stands as a strong counterpoint to the kataphatic mysticism of St. Ignatius of Loyola. It will soon become apparent why apophatic contemplation strikes many as odd, and even un-Christian.

Unlike Ignatius, the author of the *Cloud* does not directly concern himself with removing inordinate attachments and seeking God's will. For him "man's highest perfection is union with God in consummate love" (*PC*, chap. 11, p. 169). Thus his central focus is the supremacy of mystical contemplation as entry into loving union with God. In fact, he writes specifically for those somehow attracted to mystical contemplation, for those "who feel the mysterious action of the Spirit in their inmost being stirring them to love" (Foreword, p. 44).

Because the *Cloud* focuses mainly on the dark, silent, mystical contemplation characteristic of the apophatic tradition, its author, unlike Ignatius, says very little about the premystical stages of prayer. He argues that he need not go into such detail since others have written extensively about them. On the other hand, he was impressed greatly by the intrinsic value of these stages for the spiritual lives of countless Christians and for establishing a firm foundation for a later contemplative life.

THE ROLE OF "MEDITATION"

The author of the *Cloud* stresses the necessity of "sweet meditations" upon one's own sins, Christ's passion, and God's goodness for any progress in the spiritual life. It is impossible to advance in prayer without the good and holy thoughts and insights that spring from meditation. Because remembering, thinking, and reasoning are forms of spiritual understanding, he commends them as praiseworthy, unless they are tainted with pride and egoism. "Intelligence," according to our author, "is a reflection of the divine intelligence" (chap. 8, p. 57). It seems clear, therefore, that the *Cloud* has a healthy Christian respect for the role of the intellect in Christian prayer.[2]

The *Cloud* emphasizes, moreover, the interdependence of reading, thinking, and praying. Because God's word is "like a mirror," to hear and to read the scriptures is not merely to learn something about God, but to see in this divine mirror a reflection of oneself as one really is. In short, there can be no authentic prayer without hearing, reading, and thinking. The discursive, step-by-step assimilation of God's word forms the basis for any self-knowledge and knowledge of the mighty deeds of God for his people.

Through discursive meditation upon one's sinfulness, Christ's passion, and God's graciousness, two important things occur. First, meditation gradually heals the disharmony that exists among reason, imagination, will, and feelings. The *Cloud* teaches, as do many in the mystical tradition, that original sin seriously damaged human wholeness and integrity. Meditation begins to restore that wholeness and integrity.

Second, meditation promotes a highly valuable devotion. It helps to engender authentic religious emotions. From meditations flow grief and pity for Christ who suffered, sorrow and remorse because of one's sins, and a joyous, uplifting love of God. In short, meditation assures the emotional conversions necessary for authentic Christian living. Like Ignatius, the *Cloud* advises the contemplative tyro to weigh thoughts and desires as they arise. Meditation helps the novice to become more aware of and to control thoughts and desires that previously had controlled him.

One must pass through the "door" of meditation, therefore, to ascend in the mystical life. Although the author of the *Cloud* had no intention of giving detailed instructions about meditation, he strongly insisted that "it is the safest entry to contemplation in this life" (*PC*, chap. 15, p. 176). Someone who attempts to take more exotic shortcuts to deeper, mystical prayer is, for him, a "day prowler" and a "night thief" who will certainly go astray.

THE PRAYER OF SIMPLICITY

Meditation, or discursive-affective prayer, if faithfully practiced, leads frequently into a deeper form of prayer in which intellectual and/or emotional activity become greatly simplified. One thought, one idea, or one emotion predominates. The person may be able to rest quietly and holistically in a particular gospel scene without looking at the details. Like a few bars from a song once heard, a dominant theme of spirit begins to haunt the person. More of the person seems to be praying and at a much deeper level. The person praying experiences a sense of presence, communion, or a meaningful and eloquent silence.

With various nuances, commentators call this the "prayer of simplicity," the "prayer of simple regard," the "prayer of the heart," "active recollection," "active quiet," or "acquired contemplation." According to these commentators, this is the highest stage of prayer possible without God's special intervention. It is called "active" or "acquired" because it is as far as one can go alone, supported only by God's "ordinary" grace.

The author of the *Cloud* describes this highest stage of premystical prayer when he writes: "If [your daily devotions] are filled with the memory of your own sinfulness, considerations of Christ's Passion, or anything else pertaining to the *ordinary* Christian way of prayer . . . know that the spiritual insight accompanying and following upon this blind desire originates in your *ordinary* grace. And this is a sure sign that God is *not* stirring you . . . to a more intense life of grace as yet" (*PC*, chap. 18, p. 181, my emphasis). The *Cloud* then calls attention to an intellectual ("spiritual insight") and emotional ("blind desire") simplification that occurs during "ordinary" prayer. Extremely important for the author of the *Cloud* is the shift in awareness to a naked form of love that begins to manifest itself. Still, because the "spiritual insight" and the "blind desire" arise out ·of, but do not prevent, daily devotions, it is clear that God has not yet called the person to higher, strictly mystical prayer.

It must be emphasized that to reach this level of prayer is no mean achievement. With the current penchant for seeking instant results and for identifying the most bogus phenomena as genuine mysticism, the virtues, discipline, and fidelity required to pray at this level should not be overlooked. This premystical, "acquired contemplation" manifests a more than ordinary stage of Christian life and maturity.

THE SIGNS WHICH INDICATE
A CALL TO CONTEMPLATION

Of course, the author of the *Cloud* viewed these stages as the essential foundations for higher levels of prayer, for he wrote specifically for those called to mystical prayer in the strict sense. It says much for his universalism that he saw God's grace offering this gift to people from all walks and stations of life. Even habitual and hardened sinners might experience this mysterious, inner attraction to follow Christ more perfectly by way of contemplative prayer. For him, Mary Magdalene was the paradigm of all repentant sinners chosen for mystical prayer.

Thus mystical prayer is such a gift of grace that it is "not given for innocence nor withheld for sin" (chap. 34, p. 91). To be sure, it may be "withdrawn" because of sin. Still, it is so much God's gift that "without God's grace a person would be completely insensitive to the reality of contemplative prayer that he would be unable to desire or long for it" (chap. 34, p. 91). Even the very desire for this mode of prayer is strictly gift.[3]

In line with many in the Christian mystical tradition, the author of the *Cloud* makes a sharp distinction between premystical "meditation" and strictly mystical "contemplation." It must be emphasized, moreover, that the author uses the word "contemplation" like some of the Fathers of the Church before him to designate what is understood today as mysticism in the strict sense. According to many commentators, this sharp distinction offers the advantage of highlighting a qualitatively superior form of prayer that requires a "special" grace from God. However, it blurs the fact that in practice the psychological transition point from meditation to contemplation may not be so clearly indicated. The author of the *Cloud* seems to recognize this when he speaks about contemplatives whose *meditation* "is more like a sudden intuition or obscure certainty" (chap. 36, p. 94). Do these experiences come from special grace or from the ordinary grace mentioned above? On the other hand, there is no doubt that for the author of the *Cloud* contemplation in the strict sense requires God's special grace.

The *Cloud* insists that special signs must be present for a person to move from "ordinary" meditations to contemplative prayer. Put negatively, the contemplative tyro must have sincerely broken with the "world" and left behind the cares of the active life. In accordance with the teachings of the Church and the advice of a spiritual director, the person must purge his conscience of all deliberate sin through the sacrament of penance.

Perhaps the key sign that a person is ascending to contemplative prayer is the habitual attraction to or desire for contemplation. So strong and persistent is this inclination toward mystical prayer that the person finds no peace or joy in meditation or in the good works of the active Christian life. In fact, the deep stirring of mystical love may actually make meditation and other daily devotions impossible. The flame of mystical love begins to intrude upon every aspect of the person's inner and outer life. Like a person in love who cannot forget the beloved, the attraction to contemplation actually haunts such persons. It stays with them morning, noon, and night.

A more exterior sign is apparent when the person experiences joy, the stirrings of love, and enthusiasm whenever reading or listening to anything about contemplation. Reading the *Cloud*, for example, may produce deep resonances within the person. Furthermore, for the person habitually attracted to contemplative prayer, this inner excitement does not come from merely natural curiosity. Thus, a transitory attraction to what is in the *Cloud* does not suffice.

On the other hand, for a variety of reasons, the desire for contemplation may vanish for a while, leaving the person sad and confused. If, once the gift returns, the joy and love felt totally override the previous sorrow, this is one "of the most obvious and clear signs" (chap. 75, p. 145) that a person has a contemplative vocation. If the desire for contemplation is deeper and stronger after its return, this is a powerful confirmation that the person is called to qualitatively richer prayer.

The *Cloud* emphasizes, too, that both the enthusiasm aroused by hearing or reading about contemplation and the inner desire for contemplation should occur together. The exterior sign should confirm the interior sign, and vice versa. At this point the person's greatest joy and happiness come from talking and hearing about contemplation.

THE PASSIVE PRAYER OF QUIET
The deeply interior attraction toward mystical prayer that interferes with so much in the person's interior and exterior life is already the start of the "passive prayer of quiet," the initial phase of mystical prayer in the strict sense. This is passive prayer because, according to the *Cloud*, "God alone is the chief worker and he alone takes the initiative, while man consents and suffers his divine action" (*PC*, chap. 17, p. 179). In all that concerns contemplation, therefore, the *Cloud* insists that God takes the complete initiative. The prayer is called "quiet" because the contemplative becomes aware of a secret, vague, loving knowledge stirring from within which manifests itself without the work required for meditation. Especially at the beginning, this is the easiest and most spontaneous prayer ever experienced by the contemplative.

86

To nurture and deepen contemplative prayer, the author of the *Cloud* recommends a technique that may strike many Christians as rather strange. The contemplative must create a "cloud of forgetting" between himself and all created things. Because thought cannot reach God, the contemplative must forget *everything*, and therefore reject all thoughts, even those of God, Christ, Mary, the saints, and the like. The holiest and most sublime thoughts should be treated and rejected like the vilest temptations. "Firmly reject all clear ideas however pious and delightful," says the *Cloud*, for "they are more hindrance than help" (chap. 9, pp. 60–61).

A "cloud of unknowing" thereby arises between the contemplative and God. Because thinking has stopped, the contemplative must learn to be at home in the darkness caused by the absence of knowledge. In this darkness of unknowing, however, he must direct his "dart of desire," "naked intent," and "blind desire" toward God. This blind contemplation will allow the person to rest quietly in the loving awareness of God as he is. Only a love, intent, or desire shorn of all knowledge (hence, "naked") can penetrate the cloud between God and the contemplative.

To facilitate raising the heart to God in a gentle motion of naked love, the *Cloud* recommends selecting a short, meaningful word such as "God," "love," or "sin." The contemplative fixes this word in his mind, but unlike in the Ignatian second and third methods of prayer, does not ponder its meaning. This monosyllabic word facilitates the binding, emptying, and lulling of the restless imagination and reason to sleep. Perhaps for this reason, the author of the *Cloud* calls this blind, loving contemplation "spiritual sleep." Because the simple, meaningful word keeps the imagination and reason focused but inactive, it also helps to drive away distractions. Most importantly of all, however, at times this word will arise from the contemplative's spiritual center and be a prayer that expresses his or her entire being in love.

CONTEMPLATION AS STRICTLY GOD'S GIFT
No method or technique can awaken contemplative love, according to the author of the *Cloud*. God alone can teach this kind of contemplative prayer. The author cautions the contemplative novice to stay away from any type of secret technique that smacks of the occult.

The *Cloud*'s admonition, vis-à-vis the increasing number of books and exotic meditation centers offering a vast array of methods for altering one's consciousness,[4] raises a number of points. First, the Christian tradition is almost unanimous that authentic mystical prayer is a gift from God beyond method and technique. Second, this tradition emphasizes that one must begin with "lower" forms of prayer and move on to "higher" forms only if certain signs are present and if they have been approved by one's spiritual director. Third, many contemporary techniques assume implicitly that either nescience or nonclinging awareness is sufficient for contemplation.

For example, certain forms of yoga demand a voiding of the mind in a way similar to the *Cloud*. Transcendental meditation (TM) also possesses superficial similarities to the *Cloud*. TM teaches a nonclinging type of awareness, that is, ignoring the thoughts, concepts, and ideas that pass through the mind in much the same way that a person could ignore a film on a screen.[5] The *Cloud*'s distinctive feature, however, is a deep, silent, naked love that directs the entire person to God as he is. Nescience and nonclinging awareness in this type of Christian prayer are valuable only insofar as they allow the living flame of love to take deeper hold of the person's entire life and consciousness.

Although it is absolutely necessary to distinguish the loving contemplation that provides the motive force for

the *Cloud* from other techniques and methods with superficial similarities, it does not seem necessary to con-
demn contemporary meditation techniques as occult
arts, except in special cases. The psychosomatic benefits
that result from them are beyond dispute. If there are
exercises to keep the body healthy, why not mental
gymnastics for psychosomatic health? In fact, Christianity should make this new meditation "technology" its
own in much the same way it has assimilated much of
contemporary secular psychology.

Therefore, simpler, deeper forms of prayer should be
taught earlier to interested Christians. As a minimum,
much of the contemporary meditation technology could
be used as a preparation for Christian prayer as a
means to root this prayer more deeply in the person's
entire psychosomatic structure. Besides, with some
transposition, some of these new techniques could foster genuine Christian prayer.[6]

THE ROLE OF ASCETICISM

Like many writings in the Christian mystical tradition,
the *Cloud* underscores Adam's fall as the reason the
human person is no longer one with God and with
himself. The *Cloud* never emphasizes, however, a body-
soul dichotomy, but does focus upon the basic disharmony of the total body-person with himself. Because of
original sin, the human person experiences disordered
feelings, an unruly imagination, intellectual blindness,
insatiable desires, restlessness, and selfishness. Although baptism and sacramental confession remove
original and personal sins, the author of the *Cloud*
teaches that they do not remove the remnants and the
roots. His solution to human fragmentation is to regain
in Christ what was lost in Adam through the "one-ing"
process of contemplation.

The *Cloud* is aware of the asceticism required to regain
human integrity. The tradition calls that which we can

do on our own in this matter the "active dark night." It is called active because it comes from our effort; it is the dark night because of the pain and hardship involved. The author of the *Cloud* presupposes that this process begins with living a virtuous Christian life of good deeds, the sacraments, and liturgical practices. He has a great esteem for traditional ecclesial practices and sees them as the first line of attack on our divided self. He urges moderation in matters pertaining to eating, drinking, sleeping, and taking care of one's health. Meditation provides the second-stage attack upon our separation from God and self.

Nothing heals the human person so quickly and efficiently, however, as contemplation. Although contemplation is a gift, the contemplative must practice asceticism even here. For example, it requires discipline and patience to curb one's natural curiosity and to give up the desire for learning during the time for contemplation. To cast aside one's traditional devotions and meditations for this more interior work is not an easy task. Perhaps most difficult of all is the effort required to forget all thoughts and to banish distractions in order to remain "continually poised and alert at the highest and most sovereign point of the spirit" (chap. 37, p. 95).

The clouds of unknowing and forgetting may cause the person's intellect and imagination to rebel, because contemplation deprives them of their natural activity. The most dangerous time comes, however, when the person no longer experiences the contemplative desire, yet cannot go back to regular meditations. This in-between state is filled with "great storms" and "temptations." The *Cloud* cautions against both straining to continue the contemplative work and giving up entirely to return to an ignoble life.

THE ROLE OF DESOLATION
The *Cloud* and the *Exercises* converge on several important points concerning desolation. They both point out

90

that God has valuable lessons to teach during periods of desolation. They also remind the one praying that God is still very near and will soon return with his more palpable presence. More pointedly than Ignatius, however, the *Cloud* emphasizes that consolations are only "tokens of grace," not grace itself, and that the senses and the emotions are incapable of experiencing God as he is in himself. Unlike Ignatius, moreover, he urges no vigorous counterattacks during the period of desolation. His tactic during this in-between period of seemingly lost fervor is endurance, patience, and stillness.

Two key points for contemporary spirituality flow from the above teachings. First, against the contemporary tendency to pray only when the feeling is there, both the *Cloud* and Ignatius recommend endurance and patience. Ignatius would even suggest making the prayer period a little longer. Waiting patiently on God is neither giving up prayer nor an unhealthy straining. Despite the painful feeling that nothing is happening, this in-between period actually deepens and simplifies prayer. The Zen tradition emphasizes that the monk "sits" for the universe. This in-between period drives home that just being before God in helplessness is of value, that the desire for prayer is in itself good prayer. It likewise shifts the emphasis from "doing for" God to "being before" or "with" God.

Second, the *Cloud* is undoubtedly correct that the essence of all consolation "is the inner reality of a good will" (chap. 49, p. 111). It is likewise true that a mature contemplative would willingly renounce all delights and consolations, if God so willed. Yet few people, even mature contemplatives, persevere in prayer for long periods of time without an ongoing affective conversion. This means an increasing experience or awareness of deepening psychosomatic unity around a will orientated to God. Surface consolations are certainly not what the

mystical life is all about. On the other hand, too many
spiritual directors have urged a prayer of "substantial
devotion," or a prayer with one's "dry will," that is, a
prayer empty of all feelings and seemingly meaningless,
when other measures are in order.

MYSTICAL PURIFICATION

Active purification is insufficient for removing the very
roots of evil habits, selfishness, and sin. *God alone* can
provide the requisite radical purgation, classically called
the passive dark night, or mystical purification. This occurs in the *Cloud* when the initially consoling, joyful,
living flame of love turns into a deeply purgative flame.
As the blind stirring of love roots itself more deeply, it
causes all past sins to arise and torture the person. If
patient during this hellish experience, the contemplative
comes to realize that this is his purgatory.

Once the naked dart of contemplative love heals the
remnants of personal sins, the contemplative has the
experience of being as a "lump of sin." No longer sins,
but the root unity of one's sinfulness causes the person
great suffering. "This foul, wretched lump called sin is
none other than yourself" (chap. 43, p. 102) writes the
author of the *Cloud.* This profound, holistic tasting of
one's sinfulness is a great gift from God and an intrinsic element of the passive dark night.

The author of the *Cloud* calls attention to an even
deeper form of purgation which comes from the inability to forget oneself in prayer. As he says, "that ele-
mental sense of your own blind being will remain between you and your God" (*PC,* chap. 13, p. 173). According to the *Cloud,* not only sinfulness separates us
from God. Human existence is of its very nature a separation from God. The contemplative experiences great
sorrow when he realizes that the great chasm that exists between God and him cannot be overcome except
by God's special grace and perfect cooperation with

that grace. To be sure, the *Cloud* warns the contemplative against the blasphemous temptation to "un-be." Even separated existence is still God's gift and a great good. One must pray, however, for the special grace to place even the knowledge and experience of oneself into the cloud of forgetting in order to be perfectly united to God.

For the *Cloud,* the converted Mary Magdalene is the paradigm of the most intense kind of contemplative suffering. Mary's greatest pain came not from her sins, but from her inability to love as much as she was loved. At the zenith of the passive dark night, love itself is the contemplative's healing and transforming torture. In short, the more the contemplative experiences love, the greater will be the desire to return this love in full.

In view of the *Cloud*'s description of active and especially passive purification, the contemporary emphasis upon any sort of experience of transcendence without a corresponding emphasis upon purification is highly questionable. One phase of an authentic experience of the Holy is a deepened sense of one's sinfulness and creaturely nothingness. The absence of the latter calls into serious question, therefore, the authenticity of the former.

It is not surprising then that today, some in the contemplative life and others who have undergone religious conversions in the neo-Pentecostal, charismatic, or Jesus-people movements should experience psychosomatic illnesses. Sin is never a purely interior event. There are always incarnational elements that manifest themselves at all levels of the sinner's being. Mystical purgation frequently triggers severe psychosomatic reactions that are an indication of healing and transformation. This is not to say that psychosomatic illnesses are always a sign of God's purifying and healing hand. The lives of almost all the classical Christian mystics contain bouts with mental aberrations, neuroses, and psychoses that cannot be explained away in a purely natural fashion. And one can expect something similar in a contemporary mystical life. How one deals with these things today is another question. Penetrating spiritual discernment might disclose that the afflicted contemplative needs to follow more closely not only the advice of a spiritual director but also to consult an expert psychiatrist. Contemporary mystical purgation may very well involve spiritual direction, psychiatric therapy, and the latest medicines.

The blind stirring of love has two distinctive, yet related, effects. The negative side of this blind love causes a purgative transformation through the experience of one's sins, sinfulness, separated existence, and inability to love enough. Love purges the contemplative in order to remove all obstacles to full union with God. The contemplative, gradually being purified, begins to experience more of God as God. If one compares the contemplative to a pane of glass and God to the sunlight, the dirtier the glass is, the more the sunlight will highlight the dirt. The cleaner the pane, the more apparent is the sunlight.

MYSTICAL BETROTHAL
At this point God's purgation has indeed cleansed the contemplative, although the *Cloud* states that some of the effects of original sin follow a person to the grave. The contemplative has now become mystically betrothed to God and experiences the effects of this quasi-permanent union. Ravishing ecstasies and raptures may occur during this mystical engagement period. These take the contemplative out of himself, obliterating all sense of self and bestowing a taste of God's incredible goodness and love. Lost to self, the contemplative joyfully delights in God.

For the author of the *Cloud*, this quasi-permanent union may manifest itself in still another way. Instead of, or

along with, raptures and ecstasies, the tiny flame of
love may take the form of a subtle, delicate prayer in
the contemplative's spiritual core. It may manifest itself
as a secret, silent, reverent worship of God. This powerful, loving undertow can be present "even in the
midst of their daily routine" (chap. 71, p. 140) as a
haunting presence that does not interfere with often
banal, daily activities, but instead becomes the very life
out of which they flow.

The author of the *Cloud*, therefore, refuses to identify
mystical contemplation with ecstasy, an error committed by many contemporary commentators.[7] For him
contemplation is as simple as offering oneself gently,
totally, and with composure from the depths of a pure
and loving spirit. The genuine contemplative can rest
silently and quietly at the deepest level of being in God
simply as he is, while the other levels are present and
fully attentive to the tasks at hand.

MYSTICAL MARRIAGE
The goal of the contemplative life for the *Cloud* is to be
made spiritually one with God through love. In traditional terminology, this is "transforming union" or
"mystical marriage." God unites the contemplative to
himself in the perfect love of mystical marriage through
the naked love of blind contemplation. According to
the *Cloud*, moreover, God is united with all things,
even sinners, simply because they exist. "He exists in
all things, as their cause and as their being" (*PC*, chap.
1, p. 150). Through God's free gift, the contemplative
way intensifies a union already existing in the natural
order. Through transforming union, the contemplative
actually "becomes God" by participating in his very
own life.

In the order of nature, God is the contemplative's
being, but the contemplative is not God's being. In the
supernatural order, as unified as God is with God's

own being by nature, the contemplative becomes one with God through grace. Still, "though you are truly one with him through grace, you remain less than him by nature" (chap. 67, p. 135). With that, the *Cloud* emphasizes a differentiated unity with God. This is a love union so intense that two actually become one, yet remain two.

The mystery of love is that love unites the lovers, but also clarifies and intensifies their identities in each other. Jesus and his Father are one, but Jesus never became the Father. He spoke more of a mutual indwelling, of one being in the other in radical love. The *Cloud*, in line with much of the Christian mystical tradition, also teaches a mystical union of differentiated unity. This clearly sets this tradition off from some Eastern mystical traditions, which insist upon a mystical dissolution into or fusion with the Absolute, and undifferentiated unity in which only the Absolute survives.[8]

SPIRITUAL FECUNDITY
Contemporary commentators frequently overlook an intrinsic element of transforming union, "spiritual fecundity."[9] Having become God by participation, the contemplative is also Love by participation, and Love gives life. The loving union of mystical marriage makes the contemplative into a parent of divine life. This ability to be spiritually fecund, to impart divine life to others, is perhaps one of the greatest marks of the Christian mystical life.

The *Cloud* calls attention to this spiritual fecundity of the contemplative life. The contemplative becomes like Christ who offered himself to God for the good of all humanity without exception. The naked love through which the contemplative offers himself to God also contains a horizontal dimension that links him with all humanity. The author of the *Cloud* insists that the genuine contemplative looks upon all people as brothers and sisters.

96

For the author of the *Cloud,* contemplation itself is radically apostolic. Contemplative love is the most effective apostolic service, action, or good deed one can do either for the living or the dead. Because the contemplative is united with a God who communicates himself as love, he is already at the source of life that heals and transforms all.

One may agree with those who legitimately criticize the monastic overemphases found in so much of Christian spirituality, and who prefer to stress social justice, social action, and the current theologies of liberation. Still the *Cloud,* in line with some Christian mystics, is correct in stating that for those genuinely called to the contemplative life, contemplation itself is apostolic.

The *Cloud*'s author also does not overlook the more apparent and visible effects of contemplation. He clearly expects the contemplative to be a source of practical love and goodness. The living flame of contemplative love takes such a hold that it vivifies everything the person does. The naked love of blind contemplation transforms the person into a contemplative in action. Contemplative love becomes the very heart of purified and illuminated apostolic service. It breathes the life of God into every aspect of everyday living.

The inner work of contemplation manifests itself even exteriorly. The interior loving repose in God flows exteriorly into a genuine love for others. The inner poise of the contemplative's spirit affects even his bodily disposition. For the author of the *Cloud,* even physically unattractive contemplatives take on an attractive appearance because of the joy and love they radiate. The authentic contemplative possesses a mysterious, attractive charm that influences people from all walks of life. People find the contemplative attractive because of the uncanny contemplative gift to discern their characters and temperaments and to accommodate to them graciously. One needs only to think of Mother Teresa of

97

Calcutta for a contemporary paradigm of the inner and outer spiritual fecundity described by the *Cloud.*

MYSTICAL DISCERNMENT

The blind stirring of contemplative love that purifies, illuminates, and transforms plays a role in the contemplative's life similar to the Ignatian consolation without previous cause. For the *Cloud,* this love teaches discernment. It enables the contemplative "to discern unerringly between good and evil" (chap. 48, p. 110). By penetrating the contemplative's being with such an authoritative divine quality, this naked love establishes itself as the self-evident first principle of mystical discernment. Actions and experiences that deepen and strengthen this basal peace, joy, and love are good, and are to be pursued and accepted. Whatever dilutes or debilitates this touchstone experience is evil, or simply not what God wants for the individual. Therefore, it is to be rejected.

Unlike the Ignatian transient consolation without previous cause, the *Cloud*'s author speaks of this contemplative love as taking such possession that it becomes his basic state in life. In his *Epistle of Discretion of Stirrings,* the *Cloud*'s author says that the dart of love will mystically guide the person's daily life.[10] The dart begins by softly suggesting an action or a particular line of action. Should the person resist or refuse, the flame of love prods the contemplative even more forcefully, until it may feel like a needle in the heart. In this way, mystical love points out God's will for the individual even in the most common events of daily life. Likewise in very subtle matters, the blind stirring provides the basis for an instinctive morality that knows the difference between good and evil without reasoning. When the living flame of love truly possesses the person, it provides the authentic context for understanding Augustine's famous, "Love and do what you will."

In a manner that parallels Ignatius' counsels on the consolations without and with previous cause, the *Cloud* urges the contemplative to be cautious about joys, consolations, and delights that originate from un-identifiable "external" sources. Those experiences that reach the contemplative by way of the senses, or from the outside to the inside, may be caused by either the good or the evil spirit. The *Cloud* says in no uncertain terms that: "Those who set out to work in the spirit thinking that they should see, hear, taste, smell, and feel the spiritual, either interiorly or exteriorly, are greatly deceived and violate the natural order of things" (chap. 70, p. 138). The author warns further that the devil is likely to produce noise, agitation, and bogus experiences in one or more senses, especially in beginning contemplatives.

On the other hand, the contemplative may accept whatever flows from the secret depths outwards in a welling-up of spiritual joy. The *Cloud* considers authen-tic those intensifications of the tiny flame of love situated at the person's deepest and most hidden interior-ity. This point is made consistently in the Christian mystical tradition.

At first glance, the *Cloud*'s statements on experiences occurring in the external and internal senses seem at odds with the Ignatian application of the senses and the Christian mystical tradition concerning the spiritual senses. It seems, however, to be a question of emphasis and not disagreement. Ignatius used the "application of the senses" exercise to initiate a dynamic by which the movement from the outside to the inside would initiate an even more important movement from the inside to the outside. He, too, cautioned that all experiences, ex-cept the consolation without previous cause, must be discerned. For Ignatius, the good and the evil spirit can produce consolation with previous cause. Ignatius also placed more trust in the sacramental dimension of the saving truths of salvation history to awaken the inner movement of God's grace.

The *Cloud* distinguishes the deepest and most subtle stirring of grace from the more superficial "tokens of grace," which may be brought about by either the good or the evil spirit. For the author of the *Cloud*, everything is secondary, as compared with the living flame of contemplative love. That he assigns a secondary place to what is effected in the internal and external senses is not to say that he rejects these experiences outright. In fact, it is clear that he expects the contemplative to receive them. He cautions merely against making too much of them or being too easily deceived by the devil, especially in the beginning of the contemplative life. Although the Christian mystical tradition has spoken of a mystical seeing, touching, tasting, hearing, and smelling of the divine at the mystic's spiritual center, the *Cloud* prefers the language of "stirring" or "attraction" to images derived from the five senses.

Although their emphases differ, both the kataphatic and the apophatic traditions are authentically Christian in this matter. One may emphasize or deemphasize consolations with previous cause, or seeing, hearing, tasting, smelling, and touching in the internal and external senses, as long as the strengthening of authentic prayer is maintained. God does not call everyone to pray in exactly the same way. In any case, both the *Cloud* and Ignatius would agree that the advice of a wise and experienced spiritual director is crucial in this area.

Several years ago, a woman of deep prayer I had taught and advised in prayer began to experience an unusually delicious taste in her mouth whenever she prayed. Having read the *Cloud*, she became deeply disturbed. On the basis of the *Cloud*'s teaching and her profound Christian life, however, I urged her neither to be frightened of this experience nor to seek it out in any way. Since it stayed with her some time and helped to deepen her prayer, I assumed that it was a good thing. She never grew dependent on the tasting. Had the experience distracted her from prayer or had she sought it out in an inordinate way, I would have urged her to treat it like a temptation to be rejected and ignored.

THE ROLE OF VISIONS

The *Cloud*'s balanced understanding of secondary mystical phenomena is apparent from the views presented on visions. The author focuses upon the visions, the "physical revelations" of Christ to St. Martin and St. Stephen (Acts 7:55) to stress that visions are really exceptional gifts of God intended to confirm certain truths of the faith. It is not the literal meaning of the vision but the deeper spiritual meaning that is important for the contemplative. Authentic visions symbolize in an extraordinary way what is already contained in the gospels, and would be unnecessary if the contemplative could have grasped this truth in any other way. They spring from contemplative love. Fantasies and daydreams, on the other hand, arise from excessive curiosity, vanity, and romanticism. The contemplative respects authentic visions because of the great spiritual benefits they bring, and does not ridicule and cast them aside, "as the heretics do" (chap. 58, p. 123).

DISTINGUISHING PSEUDO-CONTEMPLATION FROM GENUINE MYSTICAL PURGATION

Especially in view of the contemporary indiscriminate overemphasis upon mystical experience, the *Cloud* offers valuable insights into "pseudo-contemplation" and the "devil's contemplatives." According to the *Cloud*, pseudo-contemplatives betray themselves by their eccentric, grotesque mannerisms and affectations. They may stare into the heavens vacantly like madmen. Their eyes become like "wounded sheep near death" (chap. 53, p. 116). They may whine, whimper, utter shrill sounds, speak in a "halting coy voice" or a "craven whisper," or gape with their mouths open. They rage against the saints, the sacramental system, and lawful Church authority. Thinking they know God's will for everyone, they harshly and imprudently reprimand others with unchecked and misguided zeal. They affect holiness, but are essentially hypocrites.

Pseudo-contemplatives go astray for several reasons. First, they refuse to heed the advice of an experienced spiritual director and go off on their own. They presume they can begin contemplation without having passed through the purifying and instructive lessons of meditation. Conceit, pride, curiosity, and an interest in the occult spur them on, not the gentle attraction of God's delicate grace.

Most seriously of all, pseudo-contemplatives substitute brute force for the gentle stirring of love. The author of the *Cloud* emphasizes throughout his work the importance of gentleness, lightness, joy, peace, and surrender associated with genuine contemplation. The "slaves of the devil," on the other hand, harshly strain their senses, imaginations, and minds. They fall prey in this way to fantasies, daydreamings, frenzies, exotic pseudo-experiences, morbid introspection, mental aberrations, and physical deterioration. Physical, emotional, mental, and spiritual abuse of oneself leads directly to the calamities of the pseudo-contemplative life. Moreover, such a life will take on as many forms and appearances as there are individual temperaments and dispositions, "just as the real experience assumes many different subjective forms" (chap. 45, p. 106).

Graciousness, gentleness, an attractive bearing, docility, interior freedom, and a critical reverence for ecclesial traditions and life characterize the genuine contemplative. The order, truth, love, peace, and beauty permeating the person's transformed inner life are manifested even exteriorly. Harshness, rudeness, stubbornness, repulsive behavior, inner constraint, and the facile rejection of ecclesial tradition and life characterize the pseudo-contemplative. The disorder, lies, hatred, turmoil, and ugliness permeating his chaotic inner life also manifest themselves exteriorly.

Because there are superficial similarities between the psychosomatic collapses of pseudo-contemplatives and the manifestations of the purgation process associated with authentic contemplation, a difficult problem in discernment arises. As the living flame of love takes deeper possession of the authentic contemplative's life, it assaults the psyche to heal and transform it. In order to rid the contemplative of neuroses, psychoses, and general lack of integration, the tiny flame of love must initially intensify them. The dynamics of the purgative process explain why so many saints suffered periods of mental, psychological, and physical dysfunction. For this reason, not a few psychiatrists and psychologists have simply dismissed the mystical life as pathological. In the context of the saints' lives, however, this "pathology" was the negative sign of a greater future integration. How else does one explain the saints' heroic virtue, their integrity, their prudent decisiveness, their stamina, and their ability to work and love so totally?

An experienced spiritual director can discern the genuine contemplative passing through the dark nights of purgation from the pseudo-contemplative simply undergoing psychosomatic breakdown, as difficult as that may be in individual cases. Just as a medical doctor can tell if a wound is healing or putrefying, a skilled spiritual director can tell if psychosomatic "wounds" are manifesting signs of a healed, transformed life of genuine contemplation or the putrefaction of pseudo-contemplation.

The experienced director should look for love, joy, peace, patience, kindness, goodness, faithfulness, gentleness, self-control, courage, and trust in the midst of psychoses, neuroses, and foibles. It is very easy to over-look the delicate and silent gifts of the Holy Spirit at the epicenter of raging mental, psychological, and physical disorders. The genuine contemplative possesses a remarkable trust in the midst of the breakdown of almost everything in his life. In the midst of so much turmoil and agony, one senses an unusual peace, joy, surrender, and acceptance, a mysterious, recondite, transformed life taking hold in the midst of chaos and decay.

Several years ago I met in Europe an unusually integral, deeply contemplative older woman who as a young woman had spent several years in a mental institution to be cured of schizophrenia. Throughout her sufferings, her spiritual directress told her to persevere, because God's hand was clearly present. From this woman's present bearing, personal integrity, and life-style, I would say that the spiritual directress was absolutely correct in assuming that more was happening than a natural illness.

I have also had first- and second-hand experience with some contemplatives who were written off as "mental cases" and nothing more. Time and their present integral lives have proven this judgment to be hasty. This is not to say that all psychosomatic disorders are manifestations of a mystical dark night, nor that psychiatry and medicine should not be used even in those cases in which God is the primary agent of the contemplative's purification. All human means can and should be applied prudently during this radical purgation process, even though it is God-given.

What must be emphasized, however, is that mystical purgation gets at the very roots of human disorder, brokenness, and sinfulness. Therefore, many contemplatives will manifest quite dramatically the effects of this disorder, brokenness, and sinfulness for a period of time as they are being healed. This process cannot be

104

reduced to merely "natural" causes. On the other hand, many contemplatives never exhibit severe psychosomatic symptoms, but are gradually healed in a less dramatic way. Mystical discernment in these matters is a very difficult art, and not a science.

Despite the awesome purgation process described by the author of the *Cloud*, the interior and exterior transformation he describes attracts most people who read him. In Mother Teresa of Calcutta, for example, the value of contemplative love speaks for itself. Yet for some, the long-term psychosomatic illnesses permeating the lives of St. Catherine of Genoa and St. Margaret Mary Alacoque, to name but a few, seem to call the entire contemplative enterprise into question. William James, for one, underscored the apparent uselessness of St. Margaret Mary Alacoque's life.[11]

Contemporary Christians must be slow to evaluate the lives of some great saints in terms of American pragmatism, doing good to others, self-actualization, holistic health, and the prevalent "beautiful person" syndrome. The Christian tradition has long valued the lives of "victim souls." For the eyes of faith, these persons incarnate in their lives the "absurdity" of Christ's rejection, terrible passion, cruel crucifixion, and lonely entombment. The "victim soul" symbolizes that salvation came to the world through Christ's loneliness, isolation, and shameful death on the cross, and not only through his apostolic service and glorious transformation on Easter Sunday. God has called some to live a mysticism of the "Suffering Servant."

For example, a careful reading with the eyes of faith of the lives of St. Catherine of Genoa and St. Margaret Mary Alacoque discloses the fruits of the Holy Spirit in their lives. Their lives highlight, moreover, the divine power that manifests itself in weakness. Perhaps Pierre Teilhard de Chardin, the Jesuit mystic, scientist, and world traveler, embodies the ideal Christian stance in this matter. Although he emphasized using all human means and abilities to humanize the world and saw the cross of Christ in terms of the upward struggle of evolution, he could still write to his long-time sick sister that accepting her sufferings in faith was perhaps the best means of promoting evolutionary progress.[12]

To be sure, one must applaud some of the contemporary efforts to make Christian life and spirituality more orientated toward human integration, liberation, social justice, and service. Perhaps some of the traditional spirituality was too passive in the face of evil, suffering, and injustice. Yet one may accept liberation theology and various human potential movements only as long as the redemptive value of suffering, helplessness, and powerlessness in Christ is not lost sight of. The Roman centurion who at the end of Mark's gospel recognizes the Son of God in the lonely, abandoned, dead man on the cross is the paradigm of all believers who can discover the divine presence in authentic "victim souls."

THE ROLE OF THE CHURCH

The *Cloud* very carefully situates the contemplative enterprise in its proper ecclesial context. For him, there are two basic forms of life in the Church: the active and the contemplative. He views contemplation as one of the two basic ways in which the *Church* lives her life. The contemplative is not a solitary, but one who participates in an essential form of Church life. Furthermore, the author considers contemplation to be the summit, or full flowering, of authentic ecclesial life.

The *Cloud* fully respects the ecclesial context, matrix, and ambiance of mystical contemplation. The authentic contemplative remains firmly rooted in the Church's doctrine, sacramental practices, and liturgical life. He or she views "Holy Church" as a "well" of grace. Scripture as the Church's book and the tradition of the Fathers as the flowering of scripture provide the "rigorous criteria" for discerning a contemplative vocation. The *Cloud* even compares contemplative ecstasy to the ecstasy of grace that led many early Christians to be martyred for their faith. The spiritual director provides another ecclesial dimension to the contemplative life. The director must be ordained properly for this role or receive the proper charism from the Holy Spirit. Nowhere does the *Cloud* ever suggest, however, that this private charism may contradict what the Church requires.

Although the *Cloud*'s occasional outcries against the "heretics" of the day must be placed in their proper historical context, the contemporary attempt to dissociate mysticism from its ecclesial matrix is misguided. For example, Ira Progoff, a Jungian psychologist, attempts to deracinate the *Cloud*'s contemplation from its ecclesial soil. Dismissing the "transitory significance" of the *Cloud*'s ecclesial Christianity, he seems to defend an abstract, timeless, traditionless essence of contemplation that can be found throughout the world.[13]

Carl Jung himself held the view that in many ways the authentic mystic is really a renegade and an iconoclast. He did concede that the mystic could use the Church's dogma to tone down the awesome power of the original experience. A redogmatized experience made the original experience less dangerous to the mystic's psyche and easier to assimilate psychologically. It also offered the advantage of making the initially heretical experience conform to the teachings of Church authority.[14]

Many contemporary commentators emphasize, on the other hand, that the contemplative's total formative milieu is an intrinsic part of his mystical experience.[15] The person's entire conceptual, social, historical, and linguistic matrix enters into the contemplative consciousness and experience. For these authors, it is obvious that the contemplative's beliefs, goals, motivations, in-

107

tentions, and techniques initiate, shape, and guide the contemplative experience. Another commentator on mysticism, Peter Moore, is correct when he writes that the "mystics of a particular tradition show no more of a tendency to heterodoxy than do the non-mystics within that tradition."[16]

The *Cloud* transcends both the ecclesial conservatism of the far right and the heterodoxy of the far left. By means of his intensive purification by, illumination by, and union with truth and love, the genuine mystic serves both as a living corrective to outdated and narrow Church practices and as one who deepens and strengthens authentic Christian living.

It is evident that ecclesiastical authority suppressed and harassed various mystical movements at certain times because of their pseudo-mystical deformities. But those who contend that the mystic and Church authority are mortal enemies are at a loss to explain why this same authority has always promoted, encouraged, supported, and protected the contemplative way of life.

THE ROLE OF HUMAN KNOWLEDGE
The *Cloud* frequently castigates the intellectually curious with their "scholarly knowledge," those who move in "conceited intellectual circles," and love to quote scripture and the Fathers to defend their positions, "proud scholars," those rushing to the "latest theology," and those who rely too much on their natural intelligence. He urges his disciples to seek experience, not knowledge, for God will not bestow contemplative graces upon those who continue to practice "clever speculation." The contemplative must put his natural faculties to sleep. In fact, when contemplation is born, reason dies. Reading, thinking, and prayer are essential to beginners, but not to those advanced in contemplation. For the "ordinary activities" of life, reason, common sense, good advice, and scripture guide a person. In matters pertaining to contemplation, however, "even

the loftiest human wisdom must be rejected" (*PC*, chap. 17, p. 179). Only God can bring a person to the loving, recondite spiritual knowledge of contemplation that transcends all natural genius and acquired learning.

Still, these views do not make the author of the *Cloud* an antiintellectual obscurant. Although he teaches the primacy of contemplative wisdom over human knowledge, he does not reject the latter. The mind and reason are "marvellous spiritual faculties" that reflect the divine intelligence. They are also essential for the active life, one of the basic modes of ecclesial living. To be sure, he abhorred the way many used their minds to pursue honors, lies, flattery, and pleasure.

He directs his admonition to abandon reason, thinking, and prayer especially to *beginners* in the contemplative life who can easily overlook mystical wisdom because of its simplicity and delicacy. Once the living flame of love firmly anchors itself, the contemplative can then have a balanced perspective on the "ordinary activities" of life, the intellectual life included. Contemplative love may even animate them. The nuanced mystical theology of the *Cloud*'s author is proof that reading, research, scholarship, and thinking continue even for advanced contemplatives.

The *Cloud* represents, therefore, the Catholic position that mystical wisdom may transcend reason, but not contradict it. Transrational knowledge need not, and must not, be irrational. Although scripture, common sense, reason, and good advice are useless *during* the contemplative exercise, they still serve at least as negative norms for its authenticity. The *Cloud* did not hesitate to apply these standards to the antics of the pseudo-contemplatives.

THE ROLE OF JESUS CHRIST
The *Cloud*'s apophatic mysticism poses several problems for a Christianity inextricably bound to the person

of Christ and to the eternal significance of his humanity. Although the *Cloud* emphasizes the absolute necessity of meditations on Christ's passion (the "necessary
door") for a successful transition to the contemplative
enterprise, is not Christ's humanity simply left behind
once this more advanced prayer begins? If all created
things must be placed in a cloud of forgetting for the
tiny flame of contemplative love to take root, must not
Jesus Christ be forgotten?

First, the *Cloud* tacitly assumes that all grace is the
grace of Jesus Christ. This Christic grace calls the contemplative to become what Christ is by his very nature:
perfect union of the human and the divine. By uniting
oneself to Christ, for example, one also unites with all
those "who through the grace of Christ employ every
moment in love" (chap. 4, p. 51). It is the grace of
Christ that sustains both the contemplative work and
the task of contemplation in action.

The contemplative must not pay any attention to
thoughts about Jesus, however, yet he must still turn to
Christ for help during contemplative distractions and
trials. Through contemplation, the person participates in
Christ's perfect and saving sacrifice. Through the self-
surrender in love that is essential to contemplation, the
authentic contemplative lives in his person Christ's total
surrender in trust to his Father's mysterious will.

The contemplative lives the mystery of Christ's passion
and death in still another way. The great sufferings that
arise from the inability to forget self—which prevents
full union with God—teach him the real meaning of
carrying the cross of Christ. The contemplative experiences his very own self as a cross. "The cross of self"
is a terrible burden, but the contemplative can turn to
Christ during this difficult time. If the contemplative receives the special graces for "full and final self-forgetting" (*PC,* chap. 12, p. 172), he will find himself
clothed in Christ as the garment of love.

110

Christ's universal love, which did not concentrate on any one person, offers the *Cloud* the paradigm of blind contemplative love by which the contemplative sacrifices himself for all. However, Christ did have a very special love for John, Peter, and Mary, and defended the contemplative Mary against the complaints of active Martha. For the author of the *Cloud*, therefore, Christ is the model of universal love for all and of warm, intimate, personal friendship with some.

As with many in the apophatic mystical tradition, Christ's ascension plays a special role for the author of the *Cloud*. The return of Christ in his humanity as one person to his Father dramatizes the way the contemplative's homeward-turning love of God in spirit affects the body's "exterior disposition." The depths of this love may even force the contemplative to cry out with the prayer, "Jesus, sweet Jesus." This vocal prayer is the genuine exteriorization of an authentic inner mystical orientation.

The *Cloud* also gives the traditional apophatic interpretation of John 16:7: "It is to your advantage that I go away." Why would Christ ascend before the end of time and thereby deprive those who loved him of his physical presence? Because he wished to give them an even greater grace: "the purely spiritual experience of loving him in his Godhead" (*PC*, chap. 23, p. 187). With St. Augustine, the *Cloud* views the ascension as the theological grounds for shifting the contemplative's attention from bodily eyes fixed on Christ's humanity to "spiritual eyes" and Christ's divinity. On this point the *Cloud* is in line with the mystical tradition on the "spiritual senses."

Especially in her relationship to Jesus Christ, Mary Magdalene, sitting lovingly at Jesus' feet, represents for the *Cloud* the ideal contemplative. Most important of all, she "learned to love him without seeing him in the clear light of reason or feeling his presence in the sensible delight of devotion" (chap. 16, p. 70). Her contemplative love was without thoughts, discursive reasonings, and the "tokens of grace" of emotional consolations. In short, her love was apophatic. She gave no heed whatsoever to any aspects of his humanity, but was "totally absorbed in the highest wisdom of God concealed in the obscurity of his humanity" (chap. 17, p. 71).

It is evident that the *Cloud* is more explicitly theocentric than Christocentric. On the other hand, the author's God-centeredness cannot be separated from his Christ-centeredness, for a number of reasons. First, despite what he says about Mary Magdalene's love being beyond the "sensible delight of devotion," a deeply devotional love for the man Jesus permeates his work. If he describes the love between Mary and Jesus as "sweet," this also describes accurately his love for Christ. His apophatic mysticism remains firmly anchored in the Christocentric liturgical practices, art, and study of an authentic Christian monastic life. A warm devotional love of the man Jesus is the inseparable ambiance and matrix for his dark, silent, mystical love.

Second, as indicated above, meditation upon the human Christ is the sole way to authentic contemplation. The humanity of Christ is *the* "door" to the blind stirring of mystical love. Although the distinction the *Cloud* makes between *meditations* upon Christ's *humanity* and the *contemplation* of his *divinity* may be too tidy and ultimately unacceptable for some, he still makes the former the irreplaceable foundation for the latter.

Third, the genuine contemplative never forgets or casts aside the *person* of Jesus Christ, but rejects only discursive meditations, thoughts about him, and any specific focusing upon his humanity. In fact, nowhere does the *Cloud* teach an intentional forgetting of Christ's humanity. Even Mary Magdalene remains in the presence of Christ's humanity. In fact for her, Christ's humanity has become the cloud of unknowing, "the obscurity of his humanity," in which the divinity can be reached in naked love. As William Johnston notes: ". . . true charity does not terminate at the human nature of Christ but at the person of Christ, which is the person of God."[17] Even in the apophatic tradition, the humanity of Christ remains the sacrament of the encounter with God.

The *Cloud*'s high Christology serves as an excellent experiential criticism of contemporary tendencies to reduce Jesus Christ to just another prophet, wiseman, avatar, or enlightened one. To plumb fully Jesus' human depths is to discover his divine identity. Jesus' full humanity can be understood only to the extent that it discloses Jesus as a divine person.

The *Cloud*'s resurrection Christology, on the other hand, stands out as somewhat deficient. In fact, one finds little appreciation in the *Cloud* for any of the other mysteries of Christ's life, except for his passion. In addition, he speaks of the passion exclusively in terms of meditation. As indicated in chapter 2 on the *Spiritual Exercises*, there are ways of contemplating (and not merely meditating) the life, death, and resurrection of Jesus Christ. Although the method of forgetting and unknowing is an excellent contemplative technique for someone who is called to apophatic prayer, contemplation itself cannot be reduced to forgetting and unknowing.

The *Cloud* speaks of Christ as a man who "consciously mastered time" (chap. 4, p. 51). The author admonishes the contemplative, therefore, to fill the present with contemplative love. He stresses the importance of living in the present. Never does he explicate, however, the importance of the mysteries of salvation *history* for a proper understanding of time. The specific value of the mysteries of Christ's life, death, and resurrection—the exact way Christ as God entered time and related God's time to our time—is never alluded to.

Because the resurrection confirmed all the mysteries of Christ's life and death, it provides one of the theological grounds justifying meditation and contemplation of the full range of these mysteries. However, the eternal significance of Christ's risen humanity transcends thoughts, concepts, and imaginative constructs. Thus, forgetting and unknowing can purify the mysteries of Christ's life, death, and resurrection of the sentimentality, cultural accretions, and false emphases that have developed over the years. On the other hand, just because Christ in his present risen life transcends the empirical does not mean that the only way to experience this presence is through contemplative forgetting and unknowing. Although the way of forgetting and unknowing possesses a special ability to get to the heart of these mysteries, so does the Ignatian method of gradual simplification and transparency. It must also be emphasized that even if the *Cloud*'s theology of the mysteries of Christ's life, death, and resurrection is somewhat deficient, the authentic contemplative lives these mysteries in all their fullness through the purgation, illumination, and union effected by the tiny flame of love.

CONCLUDING REFLECTIONS

In summary, despite protestations to the contrary by some, the *Cloud*'s apophatic mysticism is solidly Christian and orthodox.[18] It presents in a compact and unsystematic way the purgation, illumination, and union caused by the living flame of love nourished in forgetting and unknowing. However, the dark, silent mysticism beyond concepts and images still requires meditation, study, self-knowledge, familiarity with scripture, and tradition for its indispensable foundation. It remains inextricably linked to the fullness of Christian living: community, art, liturgy, traditions, and so on.

Even when the signs indicate that a person is to follow the lead of the tiny flame of love into the very depths of contemplative prayer, kataphatic elements still continue to shape, form, and direct this apophatic mysticism. In fact, the contemplative's transformed being, his daily activities, and even the writing of the *Cloud* indicate that not everything disappears into forgetting and unknowing.

Some commentators assume that Christianity can be squeezed out of apophatic mysticism in much the same way that water can be squeezed out of a sponge. However, a living sponge requires its natural ambiance: seawater. Only when it is dead and dried is it indifferent to what liquid is squeezed into and out of it. To be fully alive and itself, the *Cloud*'s apophatic mysticism must remain in its full Christian ambiance. There are good reasons for defending the thesis that "mysticism" in the abstract does not exist. Only living mysticisms exist.[19]

Thus, both the apophatic and the kataphatic mystical traditions are thoroughly Christian and orthodox. Perhaps personal psychology and the call of grace determine why a person is attracted to one tradition or the other. Both traditions have their strengths as well as their weaknesses.

The *Cloud*'s frequent references to pseudo-contemplatives indicate one of the pitfalls that may lie in this tradition. One may rush into contemplation without heeding the *Cloud*'s sound advice concerning the requisite signs for the authentic contemplative calling. Without adequate preparation and the gentle attraction of grace, the pseudo-contemplative embraces the way of brute force, straining, morbid introspection, facile iconoclasm, or degenerate passivity. He may take the route of forcing the forgetting of all created things and end up with an unhealthy other-worldly fixation leading to physical, emotional, and spiritual deterioration. There is always

115

the danger of assuming that the projection of disordered needs and desires is the naked love demanded by the *Cloud*. Or, misunderstanding the ease and passivity required for the imageless contemplation of the *Cloud*, he may fall into "quietism" wherein nothing really is nothing, wherein laziness and spiritual inertia are hailed as advanced forms of prayer. Moreover, the psychic debris freed by the naked flame of love is not as easily dealt with as it is in the kataphatic tradition.

On the other hand, the *Cloud*'s apophatic mysticism possesses many advantages. This mysticism gets right to the point: only God can satisfy the human heart. By emphasizing the chasm that separates God from all creatures, it also underscores that only God is God, that only One is holy. It undercuts implicitly today's "Jesusism" by shifting a spirituality too centered on the man Jesus to one more Father-centered.

The tiny flame of love nurtured in forgetting and unknowing also effectively destroys the many idols so quickly erected by the human mind, imagination, memory, and emotions. The specific way this naked love manifests itself as "signs" for a contemplative vocation undercuts the contemporary tendency to equate mysticism with religious experience. Mysticism *is* religious experience, but not all religious experience is mysticism in the strict sense. Moreover, the *Cloud* teaches clearly that naked love may show itself as ecstatic or as the gentle, peaceful, silent love permeating all of the contemplative's daily activities.

Because this contemplative love takes on as many forms as there are subjective dispositions, the author urges the contemplative not to make personal experiences the criteria for judging all other contemplative experiences. In most cases, however, he expects this mystical love to heal and integrate the human personality as it graciously, gently, but firmly, directs the person toward God. Furthermore, for the author mystical contemplation is in itself apostolic, a point that needs both nuance and special emphasis today.

Finally, the *Cloud* brings out in no uncertain terms that purifying, illuminating, transforming, and unifying Love is what mysticism is all about. The authentic contemplative forgets all to become this Love by participation. He likewise experiences this Love working in and through him, secretly animating and transforming all creation.

Chapter Four

St. Teresa of Avila (1515–1582)

To attain the title "Doctor of the Church," a person
must possess great sanctity, distinguished learning, and
be proclaimed such by either a Pope or an ecumenical
council. Because this title had been bestowed only on
men and because of its close connection with the
Church's own teaching office, some theologians assumed that a woman could never hold the title. On
September 27, 1970, however, Pope Paul VI solemnly
declared St. Teresa of Avila a Doctor of the Church—
the first woman to be so honored—and a teacher of
"marvelous profundity."

Lacking a formal education, Teresa's eminent learning
was first and foremost an "infused," that is, a God-
given, knowledge. Her mystical erudition flowed from
her mystical love. In many cases, she received during
prayer the grace both to understand and to express various aspects of her inner and her outer life. During
some of her mystical experiences, for example, she discovered that "the soul suddenly finds itself learned,
and the mystery of the Most Holy Trinity, together
with other lofty things, is so clearly explained to it that
there is no theologian with whom it would not have
the boldness to contend in defence of the truth of these
marvels" (*AB*, chap. 27, p. 252).[1]

Teresa wrote mainly because her spiritual directors and
confessors commanded her to write about her extraordinary life of prayer. Still, she did so only with great

118

reluctance. "For the love of God," she once cried out, "let me work at my spinning-wheel and go to choir and perform the duties of the religious life, like the other sisters."[2] She frequently complained that she had neither the time, the ability, the learning, nor the virtue required for writing.[3] Yet, once she actually began to write, so quickly and easily did her thoughts come that she wished she could write "with both hands." It must be emphasized that Teresa lived what she explained in her writing. She maintained that she spoke of "nothing of which I have no experience, either in my own life or in the observation of others, *or which the Lord has not taught me in prayer*" (*WP*, prologue, pp. 34–35).[4]

Although Teresa wrote for a limited audience, her Carmelite sisters, it is easy to understand the incredible influence of her writings, her universal appeal, and why she was proclaimed a Doctor of the Church. Teresa makes the experience of God intelligible through an extraordinarily subtle and psychologically acute description of her own mystical life and through the spiritual authority with which she communicates it. Moreover, one finds in her works a paradigm of the life of faith, hope, and love that all Christians live in a much less dramatic way. To read her works is to be initiated in one's own deepest experience of God. It would be a mistake, therefore, to relegate her works to the "pious" realm just because she did not write academic mystical treatises.[5] Because she "teaches something about mysticism," Karl Rahner says, Teresa "is doing theology."[6] In fact, her writings should be the subject of tomorrow's theology, for academic theology has yet to catch up with her profound grasp of the experience of God.

St. Teresa describes the human soul as an extremely beautiful castle of clear crystal or diamond that contains many rooms, in a way that parallels the many heavenly mansions (*IC*, m. 1, chap. 1, p. 28). God himself dwells in the center of this castle and continually invites the person to come inside and to remain in his truth and love. In fact, Teresa sees the *Song of Songs* as a paradigm of what transpires between God and the soul.[7]

Because we are made in God's image, Teresa stresses the need for self-knowledge. "It is no small pity, and should cause us no little shame," she contends, that, "through our own fault, we do not understand ourselves, or know who we are" (*IC*, m. 1, chap. 1, p. 29). She compares those interested only in the body to someone interested only in a "diamond's rough setting." Real self-knowledge comes only through knowledge of God. To focus on God provides an excellent study in contrasts. Our creatureliness, nothingness, and sinfulness show up even more clearly against the background of the all-holy Creator. Self-knowledge also promotes genuine self-transcendence by strengthening our resolve to know and to embrace whatever is good.

The Teresian mystical journey consists in entering the castle and making one's way through seven stages of "Mansions" containing innumerable rooms in order to encounter the King at the central mansion. No one person will pass through all of the castle's rooms, nor does Teresa attempt to describe them all. As she says: ". . . there are so many that nobody can possibly understand them all" (*IC*, m. 1, chap. 1, p. 29).

THE INDISPENSABLE ROLE OF PRAYER

The castle's main entrance is prayer and meditation. The frequent references to prayer in Teresa's works indicate just how central prayer was for her; for Teresa, Christian life is impossible without prayer. One takes the first step toward amending one's life and acquiring all the virtues through prayer. God reserves his greatest favors for those who pray.

Teresa considered her frequent conversations with people of prayer one of God's most precious gifts. When she found people who liked to pray, she taught them meditation and gave them the proper books. For her, mental prayer is "nothing more than friendly intercourse, and frequent solitary converse, with Him Who we know loves us" (*AB*, chap. 8, p. 110). She also refused to separate vocal from mental prayer. One must pay attention to whom one is praying and to why one is praying, even during vocal prayer.

Out of a sense of false humility, Teresa gave up prayer for over a year. She recognized the abandonment of prayer because of feelings of unworthiness as one of the most serious temptations of her life. As she says: "By far the worst life I ever led was when I abandoned prayer" (*AB*, chap. 19, p. 186). Throughout her writings, Teresa makes frequent references to people who had given up prayer for one reason or another. Repeatedly she stresses that prayer should not be given up for any reason. "Souls without prayer," she maintained, "are like people whose bodies or limbs are paralyzed" (*IC*, m. 1, chap. 1, p. 31). Paralyzed through their excessive concern with worldly affairs, they are unable to enter into themselves to discover the riches of their own person.

In her well-known analogy, Teresa compares the soul to a garden in which God has uprooted weeds and planted many lovely things in their place (*AB*, chap. 11). The person's God-given task is to be a "good gardener" by carefully watering the garden. Watering the garden, that is, prayer, is especially difficult in the beginning. Teresa compares it to the wearisome task of hauling water from a well in buckets.

Prayer intensifies the battle raging within ourselves between God and the world. Because prayer locks us in ourselves and forces us to face our sinfulness, weakness, and misery, it causes much suffering. "I suffered great trials in prayer," Teresa writes, "for the spirit was not master in me, but slave. I could not, therefore, shut myself up within myself . . . without at the same time shutting in a thousand vanities" (*AB*, chap. 7, p. 105). To pray is to place oneself willy-nilly into a psychological pressure cooker. It is not surprising, therefore, to hear Teresa say: "Whenever I entered the oratory I used to feel so depressed that I had to summon up all my courage to make myself pray at all" (*AB*, chap. 8, p. 112). During these periods, Teresa would have preferred performing severe penances to praying.

Teresa's writings bring to light the extraordinary resistances to prayer that plague every human being. It is not surprising that we should deeply oppose what brings about our greatest good. To commit oneself to prayer is essentially to declare war on oneself and on the enemy of our human nature. Because prayer and sin cannot coexist, to focus God's healing and transforming light on the areas of human brokenness produces a threatening situation. One must over the long run either submit to healing or give up prayer.

Another constant Teresian theme follows from this: courage and determination in prayer. Repeatedly Teresa urges her readers to take the first step toward prayer "with firm resolve." Like Ignatius, she views the spiritual life as a type of warfare against oneself and the devil. Because the devil "works like a noiseless file" (*IC*, m. 1, chap. 2, p. 42), she cautions repeatedly against his deceptions. "The wiles of the devil are terrible" (*IC*, m. 5, chap. 3, p. 115), she writes. But with St. Ignatius, she emphasizes the devil's impotence against courageous persons. " 'Oh, the devil, the devil!' we say, when we might be saying 'God! God!' and making the devil tremble" (*AB*, chap. 25, p. 243).

On the other hand, Teresa never confused strength, courage, and resolve with grim determination. The authentic mystical life requires legitimate recreation and a free, joyful, relaxed spirit that believes that all is possible with God. For her, however, "pampered" persons are "most of those who go to hell" (*WP*, chap. 40, p. 266).

THE FIRST MANSIONS

Those who enter the "first Mansions" (*IC*, m. 1, pp. 28–43) find themselves in the first rooms on the "lowest floors." The heat and light from the central mansions hardly reach here. Honors, possessions, business, and the other things of the world preoccupy the person found here. These "dangerous beasts" prevent the person from enjoying even the little heat and light to be found in these mansions. Still, those who enter the first mansions have good desires. They pray and take stock of themselves on occasion. They also have sufficient self-knowledge to realize that they are too preoccupied with the things of this world.

THE SECOND MANSIONS

Paradoxically, the "second Mansions" (*IC*, m. 2., pp. 46–54) contain those who realize just how important it is to leave the first mansions, but who lack the resolve to do so definitively. They have, however, begun to pray. Although they do not have the courage to avoid the occasions of sin, they see at times the wisdom of not sinning. They also hear the King calling them through sermons, the conversations of good people, good books, trials, and illnesses. Because they can hear the Lord from the central mansion, but have not the strength to do his bidding without hesitation, they suffer from being pulled in two different directions. Good desires and perseverance will eventually lead them to discover, however, what a "good Neighbor" this Lord can be.

With striking similarities to some of the Ignatian rules for the discernment of spirits, Teresa warns that at this stage the devil will do everything in his power to keep persons from entering the other mansions, that is, from progressing. His particular ruse is to remind them of everything they have to give up. The devil underscores the almost-eternal nature of earthly pleasures. According to Teresa, reason, memory, understanding, will, and faith can all be employed to make various reflections that penetrate this particular demonic ploy.

Once again, Teresa counsels determination, especially during periods of aridity at prayer. She warns specifically against making consolations and sweetnesses the foundation of one's life of prayer. It is important to show courage in entering our own souls during aridity to see God's greatness and our own weaknesses. Whether prayer is easy or difficult, embracing the cross, preparing oneself for God, and conforming to his will always set the proper foundation.

THE THIRD MANSIONS

A strong desire not to offend God characterizes those in the "third Mansions" (IC, m. 3, pp. 56–69). These people make a strong attempt to avoid all venial sins. Since "one venial sin can do us greater harm than all the forces of hell combined" (AB, chap. 25, p. 243), the desire to refrain from venial sin indicates great progress. Doing penances and spending many hours in recollection give these people great joy. They make good use of their time, comport themselves well in speech and dress, and manifest charity toward all. Their carefully ordered penances manifest discretion and reasonableness. In short, love has not overwhelmed their reason.

Their virtue often makes them impatient with God, especially if they are denied easy access to his consoling presence during prayer. For Teresa, long periods of aridity may indicate a hidden resistance to the way of perfection. The rich young man went away sad after Christ had told him what he must do to be perfect. Aridity may very well manifest an interior sadness because we do not really desire what God wants for us.

Teresa suspects that people who make much of dryness during prayer lack genuine humility. In a way that echoes what Ignatius taught about desolation, she stresses that aridity can teach true humility, that we can do nothing without God. God may test those in the third mansions to show them their weaknesses. If they fret over trifles, it is clear that they have neither mastery over their passions nor freedom of spirit. Teresa urges complete renunciation and perseverance in detachment. Genuine humility grounds the person in peace and resignation, even without the sweetnesses of God's favors. No matter what, therefore, we should consider ourselves "unprofitable servants."

VARIOUS METHODS OF PRAYER

Teresa manifests a great freedom when it comes to particular methods of prayer. She seems to urge whatever method of prayer works for the individual. For example, she spoke highly of meditation books on the life, death, and resurrection of Christ. In fact, for approximately fifteen years she needed meditation books to recollect her spirit (WP, chap. 17, p. 125). For her, "one always walks restfully when the understanding is kept in restraint" (WP, chap. 19, pp. 134–35). Meditation exercises the understanding and reason in a Christian way. It leads to fruitful religious emotions and resolutions concerning one's way of life. As Teresa says: "This method should be the beginning, the middle and the end of prayer for all of us: it is a most excellent and safe road until the Lord leads us to other methods, which are supernatural" (AB, chap. 13, p. 144).

Teresa's views on the role of reason during prayer show great balance. She counsels those able to reason extensively in prayer not to spend all their time so doing. They should take periods of rest in which they simply remain in Christ's presence. This prayer of presence does not fatigue the mind and is extremely fruitful.

On the other hand, there is a great danger in not being able to meditate. Without the understanding, the will has nothing to love. One loses a great deal in reflectionless prayer because the understanding does not enkindle the will in love. Still, one may profit greatly from prayer without thought, *if* God has first ignited the will in love. This happens in the higher stages of prayer and will be discussed later.

Again, for those unable to meditate in the usual way, Teresa recommends the use of a meditation book for reading or mental prayer. She found these books useful for helping her to center her attention and to become more recollected. A simple reading of the gospels frequently sparked great recollection. She also emphasized attentive vocal prayer, that is, "faithfully recited with a realization of Who it is that we are addressing" (*WP,* chap. 24, p. 169). Attentive vocal prayer has the power to carry one into the deepest depths of mystical prayer. Teresa had known a nun, for example, "who could never practice anything but vocal prayer, but who kept to this and found she had everything else" (*WP,* chap. 30, p. 199).

Teresa confessed that she had little ability either to reason or to make extensive use of her imagination during prayer. However, she would imagine Christ as present within her. In this way she would dwell especially on those mysteries of his life in which he was most alone. This prayer of inner presence that lingers gently on the various Christic mysteries became one of her preferred methods of prayer and one she used even after she had been given the highest favors.

Under the influence of one of her favorite books, Francisco de Osuna's *The Third Spiritual Alphabet,*[8] Teresa learned how valuable this prayer of recollection was for those especially in the first three sets of mansions. For beginners with distracting thoughts, Teresa recommends that they examine their consciences, confess their sins, and sign themselves with the cross. After this, they should seek out their "Companion" by imagining Christ at their side. They should strive to gaze at the Lord present within their souls. Because God is everywhere, they can and should seek him out especially within. "The Lord is within us," Teresa writes, "and . . . we should be there with Him" (*WP*, chap. 28, p. 185).

By a simple pulling away from external things to look at the self inwardly, one comes to be and to speak with God and Christ as a Father, Brother, Lord, and Spouse. Gathering all his faculties together, a person rises above earthly things and learns of their deception by entering into oneself to be with God.

Teresa underscores the human effort involved in this type of recollection. It is human volition that decides the time and the place for removing the faculties from external things to initiate introversion, that is, having the soul enter into itself. This prayer, therefore, is not "supernatural." God has not initiated the prayer nor silenced the faculties, as he does in the higher prayer of quiet.

This active method of recollection, however, has a deeply contemplative dynamic. Although grounded in an image, the emphasis is upon a real encounter with Christ that surpasses that of meditation. In fact, the actual image may be relatively weak, but still ensure a deeply felt presence of and contact with the living Christ.

Teresa also describes another type of recollection that she calls supernatural.[9] This form of prayer usually begins before the higher prayer of quiet that characterizes those in the "fourth Mansions." With hardly any human effort, a person greatly desires solitude and involuntarily closes his eyes. Not because of its own choice, but solely because the "great King" calls, the soul enters into itself. The person perceives a gradual, yet striking, shrinking into himself, like a hedgehog or a turtle withdrawing into itself (*IC*, m. 4, chap. 3, p. 87). The senses and the external world seem to give way to a newly found power in the soul.

Teresa stresses that God, not the person, initiates this gentle interior shrinking into oneself. He usually grants this interior absorption to those detached from "worldly things" and serious about their inner life. Silence and watchful expectation should predominate at this point, not thinking and activity. There are, moreover, "secret signs" of being in God's presence. It is important neither to strain nor to restrain the intellect forcefully. The person should cease reasoning but remember that he is in God's presence. He should also keep in mind who this God is. Without the understanding knowing how and why, however, the will quietly loves and enjoys being in God's presence.

In this type of recollection, it is not necessary to give up meditation and using the understanding. If God whispers in the deepest depths of the soul, the understanding stops or is stopped from working. Although the understanding now cannot focus upon anything, the will is firmly fixed on God in gentle loving. The person experiences that God is quietly working in the soul to enlarge its capacity to receive him. God's gentle dilation of the soul produces interior freedom, great confidence, and a willingness to suffer for him, and removes the obstacles to a better service of God. The person should lovingly surrender to God, realize his unworthiness to receive such great gifts, and give thanks for what he has received.

THE FOURTH MANSIONS

The "fourth Mansions" (*IC*, m. 4, pp. 72–94) mark the transition from acquired to infused contemplation. For Teresa, the person in the fourth mansions begins supernatural prayer in the strict sense, that is, prayer unattainable from any personal efforts and prayer that is at times irresistible.[10] These mansions are closer to the divine King and really cannot be described to anyone who has not experienced them. One enters these rooms only after having spent a long time in the other mansions. The world's "poisonous creatures" enter these rooms infrequently. If they do so, they merely strengthen the person's resolve to serve God more faithfully.

The prayer of quiet characterizes the fourth mansions. For Teresa, this is the "second degree of prayer," which she compares to obtaining God's living water by means of windlass and buckets. Far less wearisome than drawing water from a well by buckets, this method allows more rest and bestows gifts and favors far superior to those received in the prayer of recollection. If meditation is like bringing water to a fountain by means of conduits, the prayer of quiet is like having the fountain at a spring. During the prayer of quiet, the person drinks directly from the divine source.

This prayer causes great peace and quiet.[11] It arises in the person's deepest core, spreads, causes the soul to dilate, and permeates both the inner and outer person with a delicate, ineffable joy. Although the faculties are not united to God, they are to some extent absorbed in and amazed by what is happening in the will. The memory has no desire to be busy, and the mind will stay with one thing. This quiet has nothing to do with the outer senses. Rather, God has captured the will with love in quiet fruition.

The person who enjoys the prayer of quiet becomes conscious of God's self-communication and of Christ entering the soul to speak with it as a friend. This fills the void in the soul caused by sin and satisfies its inner core in a way beyond description. It is as if a precious ointment permeates the very marrow of one's bones.

The person realizes that the core of his will has been satisfied for the first time, that until now happiness had reached only the will's "rind."

Because the will is well occupied in loving God, quiet, recollection, peace, joy, and repose predominate. The will may even have great control over the imagination and understanding. If the soul is not so absorbed, however, the prayer of quiet may be somewhat arid. Still, during such arid prayer the will may increase in love without knowing it, while the understanding ceases to work and the imagination roams madly about. Teresa urges the person not to stifle this dry quiet either by straining or by giving up prayer altogether. He should remain still, give the other faculties no heed, and not be depressed or afflicted because of the dryness.

On the other hand, the quiet may be so great that it absorbs, engulfs, and plunges the person into a "holy madness" and a "divine intoxication." As she says: "There is no reason strong enough to keep me within the bounds of reason when the Lord takes me out of myself . . . let us all be mad for the love of Him Who was called mad for our sakes" (*AB*, chap. 16, p. 106). It is as if a spark of the Holy Spirit has become a conflagration causing an inner and outer swoon in which the body has no wish of moving. The person may seem outside himself. As quiet and satisfied as an infant at the breast, the person yet understands something of what is going on, especially that God is very near.

In this divine nearness, God communicates great truths to the person in a dazzling light that helps free him from attachments to the world's vanities. At times, this quiet may be so intense that it lasts for several days. During this period, the will remains firmly fixed to God in love, yet abstracted from daily activity. Meanwhile, the other faculties are free to go about their daily routine. During this period, the person is truly a contemplative in action. This experienced union with God that began in the prayer of quiet brings the person more happiness in a moment than a thousand years of earthly happiness. Teresa says that many who follow the religious life reach this stage of prayer, but few pass beyond it. Although most commentators describe the prayer of quiet as the lowest stage of experiential union with God, it is still union with God, and for Teresa, it is the beginning of all blessings.

Not all quiet comes from God, however, according to Teresa. She calls attention to a bogus quiet produced by the devil to lead to the person's ruin. This demonic quiet brings about nothing in the understanding, unsteadies the will, and eventually leads to disquiet. It leaves little humility and influences the person to think that God is obliged to bestow his gifts. Teresa perceptively notes, however, that even this pseudo-quiet may be used to the person's advantage by increasing the eagerness to pray. If the person then directs all desires and sweetnesses to God and humbly accepts the cross, even bogus quiet may do some good.

Teresa also recognizes a quiet produced by the self. With today's interest in introversion techniques, it is obvious that a person can obtain psychosomatic peace by using certain easily learned methods. For Teresa, however, unless this quiet comes from God, it passes very quickly, does not change the person, and leaves aridity in its wake.

A false quiet afflicted some of Teresa's nuns who were in poor health and who spent too much time in prayer, fasts, severe penances, and vigils. Because of their physical weakness, the slightest spiritual consolation plunged them into a languor or sleeplike absorption. Although these nuns called this lassitude "rapture," Teresa called it "foolishness, for they are doing nothing but wasting their time at it and ruining their health" (*IC*, m. 4, chap. 3, p. 93). In these instances, she counseled more food, sleep, and physical activity, and less prayer and fewer penances. For Teresa, although God-given quiet produced some interior and exterior sluggishness, it rarely did so in the person's soul.

In her discussion of the fourth mansions, Teresa makes a valuable distinction between "sweetness in prayer and spiritual consolation" (IC, m. 4, chap. 1, p. 73). Sweetnesses in prayer arise partly from our own nature and partly from the preparation involved in meditation, although they terminate in God. They strongly resemble, therefore, the Ignatian consolation with previous cause. Like the satisfactions felt from well-ordered work, they are purely natural, like earthly joys. Although felt in the heart, they do not enlarge it but oppress it somewhat.

When a person meditates, thoughts about what he inordinately loves also arise. The "impurities" of our nature partially contaminate what is brought in rather noisily from the outside to the inside. The living water brought by meditation is like water that one finds downstream from a spring. Although sweetnesses during meditation do not make a person virtuous, and despite the reservations Teresa has toward them, she prizes them and would never have a person give up meditation. For her, meditation changes a person for the better. She recognizes that "it may even help some whom this sensible devotion entices to spend more time in prayer and thus to make greater progress" (WP, chap. 38, p. 250).

Teresa identifies spiritual consolations with the "perfect contemplation" begun in the prayer of quiet. The source of such consolations is God, not our recollected natures. Still, the person experiences them in a natural way. Silently entering the person's core, they enlarge the spirit and flow from this inner core outwards. In short, spiritual consolations have all the characteristics of the prayer of quiet. They are like drinking water from the source of the spring, and not from down-stream.

In the "fifth Mansions" (*IC*, m. 5, pp. 96–123), Teresa describes the prayer of union. This type of prayer suspends the faculties, produces a semiecstatic state, and has been called the "sleep of the faculties." Teresa maintained that many of her nuns could enter these mansions, but that few would experience everything contained therein. With the exception of St. Paul, she notes, God bestows the gifts and favors of these mansions to those well-prepared to receive them.

During the prayer of union, God suspends the faculties so that they seem dead or asleep. For a brief period of time, rarely exceeding thirty minutes, the soul can neither see, hear, nor understand. Although the memory, imagination, and understanding are not really absorbed in God, they cannot act, except by extreme force. Moreover the soul seems to have withdrawn from the body. Love alone remains awake and vibrant during this sleep of the faculties.

During the prayer of union, in a manner reminiscent of the Ignatian consolation without previous cause, God enters the soul's deepest center and seems to place the soul in its own center. This happens without using the "doors" of the faculties. Moreover, he unites the soul's center with himself so powerfully and deeply that the devil neither understands nor can prevent this "secret union." After recovering from this state, the person is left with an unshakeable certitude that God was there.

For Teresa, the prayer of union is like the activities that take place before two people are betrothed. There is a greater union in this state than in the prayer of quiet, but it is still transient and far from complete. Nevertheless, during this prayer, the soul experiences great delight and seems almost totally engulfed. It no longer needs to "chew and swallow" as it did in meditation and quiet, but only relishes the food as if it had been placed directly into the stomach. Using another image, Teresa says that the pleasures, delights, and sweetnesses of union far surpass those of the prayer of quiet, for now living water is up to the "soul's neck." Because God is doing all the work, the soul realizes that it needs only to consent.

Although this loving union transcends all desires, still the person has not given himself entirely to God's will. He is unable to do so, for what is required surpasses the soul's capability. Because God has more work to do to enlarge the soul, the person experiences some sadness in prayer, and also seems to be living contrary to nature. He no longer lives for himself, but for God.

During the prayer of union, the person is dead to everything in the world. This prayer generates deep virtues, contempt for worldly vanities, solitude, abnegation, a radical desire for penances and for God, and a wish that he may be known by all. Just as the period before this prayer was punctuated with all sorts of trials, these resume again after the prayer. In fact, the prayer of union brings with it a strong desire to suffer. However, suffering neither squanders the person's strength nor consumes energy. It unites with an even deeper desire to serve, and the contemplative now pays more attention to his neighbors' needs.

Most important for Teresa, however, is not delectable semiecstatic union, but the genuine surrender of our wills to God. Just as the silkworm must die to be transformed into a butterfly, so we must die to our own free will for Christ to be "our Mansion." Like Ignatius, Teresa insists that love consists in deeds. For example, care of a sick woman will not harm one's prayer. Indeed, compassion for the woman and fasting so that the woman may eat, "that is true union with His will" (IC, m. 5, chap. 3, p. 116).

General Characteristics

Great trials and graces characterize the "sixth Mansions" (*IC,* m. 6, pp. 126–203). Severe illnesses, ridicule, and persecution often befall a person in this stage. Abandoned by his friends, the person becomes the target of much backbiting. Scrupulous confessors add to his misery, and he fears that no one will be willing to hear his confession. On the other hand, public praise and being well thought of also pain him, for his one desire is that God be honored.

Memory and understanding may violently attack the person, throwing his inner life into turmoil. His interior life feels like a wasteland. It seems as if faith and virtues are suspended or have disappeared. The person is plunged into an affliction, obscurity, and darkness resembling a death agony. Nothing interior or exterior relieves his misery.

Perhaps the high point of Teresa's mystical dark night was her penetrating vision of her place in hell.[12] With the eyes of her soul she saw a very long, narrow passageway filled with mud and snakes. Hollowed out of the wall at the end of this passageway was a very tiny place in which she could just fit. Still worse than this sight, however, was the oppression, agony, and affliction she experienced in her body and soul. It was as if the soul were being ripped from the body to destroy itself little by little. For Teresa, the "interior fire and despair are the worst things of all" (*AB,* chap. 22, p. 301).

The significance of Teresa's vision does not lie in the obvious imagery, but in what this imagery expresses at its deepest level. She experienced fully both the spiritual and the psychosomatic effects of sin. To get rid of sin and its remnants required nothing less than mystical death, the spiritual destruction and rebuilding of her entire person. To express and describe this genuine spiritual death, Teresa uses images of some of the most frightening things she knew. The images suggestive of her natural claustrophobia and fear of snakes and spiders actually express her great spiritual and bodily torture and her feelings of despair, inner darkness, oppression, and spiritual annihilation. Still, Teresa acknowledges that in comparison with what a person might actually undergo, this "suffering is no more than a drop of water in the sea" (*IC*, m. 6, chap. 11, p. 199).

By far, the most significant graces of the sixth mansions are the genuine raptures that confirm the mystical betrothal initiated in these mansions. One word from God enkindles the soul for union with him. The soul seems flooded by the downpour of living water. The person faints and swoons in great delight. God inebriates the faculties with his love and suspends them. The soul's deepest core has the certitude that it now lives only for and in God. In fact, God seems to have taken possession of the entire soul. It is as if he has become the soul's soul. The irony is that "the soul realizes that it has deserved to go to hell, yet its punishment is to taste glory" (*AB*, chap. 19, p. 181).

The soul now seems no longer to give life to the body. The person stops breathing, loses his bodily strength and bodily heat. If the rapture is powerful enough, the body may even levitate. Because of its spiritual and somatic effects, rapture brings the person more benefits than the prayer of union. Rapture is irresistible contemplation. As she says, "Do what we may, He transports the spirit as easily as a giant might take up a straw, and it is useless for us to resist Him. What a strange kind of belief this is, that, when God has willed that a toad should fly, He should wait for it to do so by its own efforts" (*AB*, chap. 22, p. 217). Neither the body nor the soul has any desire to resist God's will. In fact, there is no need for the soul to give its consent, for it has already done so.

During rapture the person forgets himself and the distance that separates him from God. As Teresa notes, he may even think he experiences undifferentiated unity with God: "For the love which it [the soul] knows His Majesty has for it makes it forget itself and it thinks it is in Him, and that He and it are one and the same without any division, and so it talks nonsense" (AB, chap. 34, p. 324). Raptures penetrate right to the spirit's marrow. They show the person his wretchedness, impart a deep realization that he can do nothing without God, yet infuse courage and heroism in God's service. They produce a strong detachment from everything that is not God.

Genuine rapture may plunge a person into deep loneliness because he experiences that his true life is not in this world. Afterwards, the soul awakens only to love and is somewhat distressed at having to return to normal living. On the other hand, great interior security follows in the rapture's aftermath. The person still fears the devil's deceits, but now possesses extraordinary discernment. Raptures leave the person with an increased desire for God, the gift for evaluating everything in God's light, and a deep sensitivity to the least imperfection. Lacking almost all self-interest, it is well-nigh impossible for the person to return to sin. Moreover, for Teresa raptures were frequently accompanied by an uncanny pragmatism in daily living. If the above signs of genuine rapture are absent, Teresa dismisses phenomena that psychosomatically resemble them as "frenzies." Yet, even genuine raptures vary in intensity and quality. They are partial or full, depending upon whether they fully absorb the body and spirit, or do so only to a greater or lesser degree.

The sixth mansions also contain other phenomena. God may act as the potential bridegroom who wishes to show his bride-to-be some of his treasures. During raptures, therefore, he frequently infuses the soul with mystical knowledge. He reveals great mysteries and enables the person to penetrate to the very core of the mysteries of the Christian faith. Then too, with brief raptures he will sometimes penetrate the soul with darts or wounds of love that increase his desire for God.

In the sixth mansions, God may also speak to the person through genuine bodily, imaginary, or intellectual locutions. During bodily locutions, the person hears the divine words with his bodily ears; during imaginary locutions, with the "ears" of his soul; during intellectual locutions, with the spirit's very core. Therefore, authentic divine locutions affect the mystic at various levels of his being. The deeper the level, moreover, the more likely is the locution authentic. It should be noted that Teresa never experienced bodily locutions.

Locutions alert the soul to God's presence and make the understanding attentive. God can make the soul listen, even against its will, although Teresa indicates that it gladly does so. Genuine locutions carry great authority. If God said, for example, "Be at peace," the soul would immediately be so. Depth, clarity, light, joy, and peace characterize divine locutions. They linger in the memory for a long time after they have been given. At times, God and the soul seem to understand each other like two people in love exchanging glances. These locutions always bring great profit to the person and can never contradict scripture.

Demonic locutions, on the other hand, lack the depth and the effects of divine locutions. The person resists them instinctively without knowing why. They produce bewilderment, discontent, affliction, disquiet, and aridity. The self may also conjure up locutions, but with even less effect than those demonically caused. The superior quality of God-given locutions is their hallmark.

The Role of Jesus' Sacred Humanity
The sixth mansions focus upon another very important Teresian theme: meditation upon the sacred humanity

138

of Jesus Christ. Teresa's highly Christocentric, kata-phatic mysticism seems, at first glance, to clash sharply with the theocentric, apophatic emphases of the *Cloud of Unknowing*. For example, references to Christ in the *Cloud* occur rather infrequently. Almost every page in Teresa's collected works, on the other hand, speaks of Christ as: "good Jesus," "our Companion," both "God and man," "Divine Guest" of our souls, "the good Lover, Jesus," "your true Friend and Spouse," "our Teacher," "such a Son" of the Father, the "very Master" who taught the Lord's prayer, the "Pattern" of our lives, and our "Friend."

Furthermore, for Teresa the true contemplative acts like a chess master out to checkmate the "Divine King." He imitates Christ by carrying his cross, not by dragging it along. In a way reminiscent of Ignatius' militant spirituality, Teresa calls genuine contemplatives "soldiers of Christ" who must be ready for spiritual combat. She prefers, however, to call her nuns "brides of this great King" and "brides of such a Spouse" who belong to "Christ's communities." Those in religious life must learn from and have a special reverence for the apostles who belonged to the "College of Christ."

It is most striking that Teresa returns to the topic of meditating upon Christ's sacred humanity in a section that deals with the deeply mystical prayer of union, raptures, mystical wounds of love, visions, and locutions.[13] For example, she takes issue directly with those books on apophatic prayer which teach that corporeal imaginings, thoughts, and even Christ's humanity hinder and impede the higher stages of mystical prayer. Although such authors admit that supernatural prayer can only be given by God, they stress that we can get part way by humbly raising our spirits above all created things to contemplate the divinity.

In her *Autobiography*, Teresa grudgingly conceded, but only with great nuance, that because learned and spiritual people teach this form of prayer, it must be correct. She admitted that God led people along many paths. In her *Interior Castle*, however, she retorted against those who claimed that she did not understand apophatic prayer: ". . . they will never make me admit that this is a good thing" (*IC*, m. 7, chap. 7, p. 172). In fact, she warns her nuns not to believe anyone who tells them anything different.

For experiential, personal, psychological, and theological reasons, Teresa refused to believe that it was ever necessary or acceptable to place everything created, especially Christ's humanity, into a cloud of forgetting in order to seek the naked Godhead after the first stages of prayer. When she first began to enjoy the pleasures and delights of the prayer of quiet, she admitted that no one could have persuaded her to meditate upon Christ's sacred humanity. But with a little more experience, she began to realize the dangers of too much absorption in prayer. She came to think about this period of prayer without Christ as an "act of high treason," even though she acted this way unknowingly. Partially from her contacts with the Jesuits, whom she admired for their way of life and for their Christocentric prayer, Teresa found a new love for Christ's sacred humanity. Hence, she states in a way highly characteristic of her prayer: "I cannot bear the idea that we must withdraw ourselves entirely from Christ and treat that Divine Body of His as though it were on a level with our miseries and with all created things" (*AB*, chap. 22, p. 210).

Teresa grasped implicitly that all graces, especially contemplative ones, are the grace of Jesus Christ. She taught explicitly, moreover, that neglecting his sacred humanity was the principal reason why so many failed to get beyond the prayer of union. No matter how advanced a person considers himself to be, for Teresa, meditation on Christ's humanity will never hurt him. In fact, without Jesus as his "Guide," he will never enter the last two mansions. Concerning the alleged evidence from John 16:7 (". . . it is to your advantage that I go away") for this type of prayer without Christ, Teresa states that these words were not addressed to Mary, who had firm faith in Jesus both as God and man even before Pentecost. Had the apostles been firm enough in their faith, and as firm as we can be now, they also would have seen this. In short, genuine faith in Christ always finds his sacred humanity a great blessing.

Teresa vigorously disagrees, therefore, with those who say that after a certain stage they cannot think about Christ's passion, the saints, Mary, and so on. Precisely because we are corporeal beings and because perfect contemplation is transient, the understanding must be used to fire up the will. Only angels are permanently enkindled in love, Teresa notes. For human beings, however, it is impossible only to love.

She does concede that thinking about the passion on occasion is simply too painful because of what may be going on in our lives. Still, she asks, "what can prevent us from being with Him in His Resurrection Body?" (*AB*, chap. 22, p. 212). The most sacred humanity cannot be bypassed, even if a person reaches the heights of contemplation. In fact, it is only in the seventh mansions that persons do not need to meditate, or only rarely, because now they are *continually* in the presence of the God-man.

Teresa makes the valuable distinction between reasoning with the understanding and having the memory represent the Christian mysteries to the understanding. Although it is not necessary to do the former in the higher stages of prayer, it is always good to dwell simply on these mysteries. Because they are special signs of God's love for us, they act like sparks to enkindle the soul in love. She recommends, therefore, a prayer of simple regard. The understanding gently pictures the mysteries of salvation history to itself so that they may be impressed upon the memory. In this way, the person comes to understand these truths with the substance of his soul. Even the most sublime prayer does not prevent this prayer of simple regard. If God should suspend the faculties, however, Teresa says let it be so.

Teresa makes the banal, but often forgotten, observation that life is so long and so full of trials that it is foolish to think that we could remain in perpetual quiet. Those who refuse to use meditation, devotions, and "corporeal aids" for their prayer will become "dry as sticks." But God may so fill us with love that we do not need these aids, although these periods of perfect contemplation never last. She cautions, too, against leaving the soul in some sort of vacuum in the name of advanced prayer. Her warm, intimate, personal love for Christ plays a key role in her approach to prayer. Christ is simply such good company and so important as a pattern, that the contemplative should not forsake him for any reason.

Teresa's emphatic Christocentrism likewise manifests itself in her experience and discussion of intellectual and imaginary visions in the sixth mansions.[14] Teresa saw Christ at her side, but neither with the eyes of her body nor of her soul. Paradoxically, she was conscious of his presence and the soul somehow "saw" that he was present, yet the soul saw nothing. She explicitly distinguishes this visionless vision from the presence of Christ that she experienced in the prayer of quiet and union.[15] The intellectual visions of the sixth mansions come unexpectedly, throwing the senses and faculties into fear and confusion. But they bestow deep peace, true wisdom, lasting purification, and an irrefutable certitude. Christ speaks in this indelibly stamped vision, which may last for almost a year. Such visions filled Teresa with a total desire to serve God, with great humility, and with greater love for Christ's sacred humanity. It is no wonder that she considered these visions the highest possible and the most profitable.

During imaginary visions, Christ's image is engraved upon the imagination. Yet Teresa insists that this vision is more than an image. Christ appears more alive here than the people we meet in daily life, and he speaks with an irrefutable authority. These ultraclear revelations of Christ's humanity come with the speed of lightning and never last very long. They occur in rapture and terrify the soul. They are accompanied by a soft whiteness like that of a clear stream or crystal. Such visions are so incredibly beautiful and so beyond the power of the imagination that they could never be invented. The eyes of the soul see the consoling presence of the glorified flesh. The most sacred humanity brings health and refreshment to the body and great virtue to the soul. In some ways, imaginary visions are more profitable than intellectual visions, for they are in closer conformity to our nature. Yet Teresa teaches that the two types of visions occur together. It would seem that the imaginary vision is the echo in the imagination of a deeper, intellectual vision.

Although Teresa had many visions of Jesus Christ in his earthly life, she almost always experienced him as the fully risen, glorified Lord. If Christ appeared with his wounds, on the cross, or in the garden, he was usually in his glorified flesh. She mystically tasted that the risen Christ "sublates," that is, confirms by placing on a unique basis and by adding something new and distinctive, all the mysteries of his life and gives them eternal significance. Teresa also saw Christ in heaven rescuing her from her many persecutors and receiving her with love by placing a crown on her head. At times, the very center of her soul would become a bright mirror wherein Christ would appear. Not only did these powerful mystical visions of Christ enable her to speak with him as the full God-man and friend, they also became a source of discernment, a principle against which other experiences could be measured for their authenticity.

The devil can counterfeit imaginary but not intellectual visions. Like bogus imaginary locutions, however, demonically induced imaginary visions are instinctively resisted by the contemplative. They leave him restless, troubled, despondent, and often unable to pray.

To ask God for visions is to ask for trouble. Teresa says that asking for visions signals a lack of humility, for we never deserve these favors from God. By asking, we expose ourselves to the projections of our own imaginations and to the devil's wiles. Moreover, visions never come without great trials. For Teresa, they are great crosses, even when genuine. In short, Teresa counsels willing only what God wills.

THE SEVENTH MANSIONS

The "seventh Mansions" offer a quasi-phenomenological description of mystical marriage, or spiritual transformation.[16] Christ himself brought Teresa into his own mansion and removed the "blindfold" that had covered the eyes of her soul during the prayer of union and rapture. An intellectual vision of the Trinity illuminated and enkindled her soul at its utmost depth. She mystically understood how the three divine Persons are one substance and one power. In addition, the trinitarian self-communication disclosed to her the meaning of the divine indwelling promised in John 14:23. In short, her soul continually experienced the divine presence and realized that the seventh mansions were now its permanent home.

Teresa makes the penetrating distinction between "spirit" and "soul," or between the soul's higher and lower aspects. After transforming union, the person experiences the highest aspect of his soul, "spirit," as permanently united to God and continually enjoying the divine presence. In such a state, nothing can disturb the spirit's peace and joy, for it is anchored firmly in God. The soul's lower aspect, the "soul," however, is free to engage fully in daily activity and to suffer the trials and aridity of daily life. The person now feels like a king at war, absolutely secure in his highly fortified castle despite the war raging outside its walls. The harmony that now exists between "spirit" and "soul," or Mary and Martha, moreover, enables the person to be perfectly contemplative in action.

Imaginary and intellectual visions of Christ also marked Teresa's mystical marriage. Without passing through any of the faculties, Christ appears in the soul's very center, as he appeared to the disciples behind locked doors. Like two people who cannot be separated, God makes the soul one with himself. This hidden union takes place in the soul's core, wherein it always has secret communications with God. At this level, the devil can neither enter, disturb, nor understand what is taking place. Like two wax candles becoming one light, or like rain falling into a stream to form one water, so does the soul become one with God. The contemplative now experientially understands the words of St. Paul: "It is no longer I who live, but Christ who lives in me" (Gal 2:20). Unlike the transient oneness experienced during the prayer of union, this differentiated oneness is permanent. The soul neither moves nor has any desire to move away from its firm anchor in God, although it can still fall.

Transforming union imparts the forceful awareness of being endowed with divine life. The person who experiences this union becomes almost totally self-forgetting in his all-consuming desire to serve God. He loses all fear of death, yet wishes to live a long life in order to serve God better. Lack of desire for consolations and favors, infrequent raptures, profound detachment, and an absence of aridity also characterize one's state after transforming union. Even on those occasions when the Lord seems to leave the person alone, he painlessly sees everything the Lord has taken from him and deepens his resolve to serve God more faithfully. When negligent, God himself gently guides the person from within in a way strongly reminiscent of the *Cloud*'s teaching. These firm, gentle, subtle, penetrating touches of love from the core outward direct the contemplative in daily life.

THE FOUNDATIONS FOR AND RESULTS OF PRAYER

For Teresa, true humility, detachment from all created things, and mutual love form the only lasting foundation for genuine prayer. She calls humility the "whole edifice" of prayer, because only those who know that everything is gift can truly progress in contemplation. "Have humility and again humility!" she urges, because "it is by humility that the Lord allows Himself to be conquered" (*IC*, m. 4, chap. 2, p. 83). As much as she stresses the human effort required to advance in the interior castle, she still teaches that most of the mansions are entered by invitation only. Hence, entry demands special graces.

Teresa emphasizes not the desire for consolations, but for crosses. Evangelical and spiritual poverty also open the way to deep prayer. On the other hand, perfect prayer promotes humility and poverty of spirit, and helps to destroy all attachments. In short, prayer, its foundation, and the attitude necessary for prayer are all interconnected. One promotes or hinders the others. For Teresa, the genuine person of prayer desires martyrdom, and she considered the religious life one long martyrdom. Someone who could write, "We had not so much as a scrap of brushwood to broil a sardine on,"[17] had certainly experienced the martyrdom of daily life in a poor convent. The religious life with its rules and disciplines fosters authentic prayer and the requisite basis for the perfect keeping of God's law.

146

Love for others is an important foundation for true prayer and it is also its result. Teresa equated love for God not with consolations in prayer, but with service, especially to others. Perfection for her is emphatically evangelical: love of God and of neighbor. One cannot exist without the other. Teresa's great love for people, whom she wanted entirely in God's hand, permeates all her writings. She would have been willing to die "a thousand deaths" to rescue someone from mortal sin. For example, to help a person who was suffering from severe temptations, she prayed to God that "these tortures and temptations might be assuaged and the devils be sent to torture me instead. . . . This led me to suffer a month of the severest tortures" (*AB,* chap. 31, p. 291). One of her criteria for determining genuine rapture is the strength it must bestow in helping one's neighbor. Advancement in prayer always produces great benefits for others by making the person compassionate and truly sensitive to the others' needs. The deeper the prayer, the greater will be the compassion and the sensitivity. Thus, one should not overlook the powerful spiritual fecundity of her mysticism. In fact, she devoted almost one-fourth of her autobiography to describing the fruitfulness of her life of service, especially her practical reforms of the Carmelite communities.

For Teresa, authentic prayer and service are intrinsically linked. She warns beginners, therefore, neither to criticize those who have seemingly left the solitary delights of prayer for service nor to leave their own prayer until they are further strengthened for a life of service.[18] Valuing prayer that produced great love in a short time, Teresa taught that it was impossible to be a contemplative without having great love. As she says, "for had they not a great deal [of love] they would not be contemplatives; and so their love shows itself plainly and in many ways" (*WP,* chap. 40, p. 263).

Teresa emphasizes that just because all nuns pray, not all are destined to become contemplatives. God does not lead all the same way. Contemplation, she notes, is not necessary for salvation. Some nuns serve God through contemplation, others by mental prayer, others by taking care of the sick, and still others by serving their sisters in Christ in material ways. What is important for all is humility, detachment, mortification, and carrying the cross, for this is what Christ gave himself to do.

THE ROLE OF CONFESSORS AND SPIRITUAL DIRECTORS

Confessors and spiritual directors play a key role in Teresian spirituality and mysticism. Much like Ignatius' directive to examine one's prayer after it has been made, Teresa urged her nuns to do likewise, no matter how sublime they thought their prayer was.[19] Part of this was prompted by Teresa's great fear of delusion and of being deceived by the devil in the mystical life. As a potent countermeasure, Teresa charged her nuns to speak openly, candidly, and plainly with their confessor or spiritual director about all aspects of their interior life.[20] Especially if one's ordinary confessor was not learned, Teresa recommended occasional consultations with men of learning whom she greatly admired.

She had great respect for men of genuine learning because they had never led her astray.[21] Moreover, these learned men had been the indirect sources for some of her mystical favors and had confirmed their authenticity in the external forum. She was gravely suspicious of vain confessors and vain men of learning, however, and advised her nuns to shun them as much as possible. "I have also experience of timid, half-learned men," she wrote, "whose shortcomings have cost me very dear" (*IC*, m. 5, chap. 1, pp. 100–1). She preferred, therefore, a holy priest with prayer experience and no learning to one with only some learning. The former, she noted, would not be so sure of himself and would be more aware of the possibility of illusion in her life.

To be sure, Teresa saw the ideal confessor or spiritual director as possessing experience in prayer, prudence, and authentic learning. If the priest lacked experience in prayer, however, but was learned, humble, sympathetic to the contemplative way of life, and possessed a "certain something," he could still be an excellent spiritual director. His holiness, attained through a reverent search for the truth, encouraged Teresa to urge her nuns to put their trust in him. This is extraordinary, if one notes how often in Teresa's time (as in our own), so-called "spirituals" looked down on theologians for allegedly not possessing the Spirit.

In "natural" matters, for example, the spiritual director's intelligence could provide exceptional guidance. In supernatural matters, his knowledge of scripture and the spiritual masters could offer more than merely a negative norm against which to measure the contemplative's experience. His intelligence and respect for God's truth could be excellent weapons for uncovering the devil's devices. "In other matters," Teresa urged, however, "he must not worry himself to death, or think he understands what he does not, or quench the spirits . . . He must strive to humble himself, because the Lord is perhaps making some old woman better versed in this science than himself, even though he be a very learned man" (*AB*, chap. 34, p. 326). Teresa exhorted her nuns, therefore, to pray for learned men who gave the Church such light. They were the "picked men" who were decisive for victory in the spiritual battle.

On the other hand, Teresa did not see a great need for learned men to direct beginners in prayer, although she insisted that the spiritual life be firmly grounded in truth. Rather, beginners needed experienced men of prayer as directors. She also had no use for learned men with no prayer experience, if they lacked that "certain something." Because they wanted to be so utterly rational and reduced everything to their understanding of God's mysteries, she criticized them harshly.[22] Only an intelligence that humbly surrendered to and loved God was capable of penetrating the mysteries of the faith, according to Teresa.

Teresa never disobeyed her confessor's directives, even if she felt God was asking her to do something different, because she had experienced in the Lord that she must always obey her confessors. On occasion, she simply switched confessors, not because she did not want to obey, but because the God of her mystical experiences had to be obeyed and she had to get on with her work. If she genuinely reverenced her confessors' learning, she also valued her own experience as much. Obedient she was. Yet, it is instructive to note that if the confessor was truly at odds with what God asked of her, through her prayer the confessor always came around to seeing things her way.

TERESA'S ECCLESIAL MYSTICISM

Like the mystics so far considered, Teresa's mysticism is radically ecclesial. A deep and genuine respect for the Church's sacramental life, liturgical practices, teachings, commandments, and scriptures permeates her writings. She insisted firmly that "in matters of faith no one would ever find me transgressing even the smallest ceremony of the Church, and that for the Church, or for any truth of Holy Scripture I would undertake to die a thousand deaths" (AB, chap. 33, p. 312). But she likewise prayed: "From foolish devotions may God deliver us" (AB, chap. 13, p. 145) and ridiculed anything that smacked of superstition (AB, chap. 6, p. 93).

One aspect of her mysticism is emphatically eucharistic. One of the main reasons she founded the reformed

150

Carmelite communities was to counteract through prayer the Protestant Reformation, especially the way the "heretics" viewed the eucharist.[23] Never did she fail, moreover, to leave any sin unconfessed. During an intellectual vision, she received a mystical taste for scripture wherein she determined to carry out its least demands.[24] One of the greatest trials in her life occurred when the devil so stormed her understanding and imagination that she could not remember the truths of the faith.[25]

Teresa submitted her writings to "learned men" and Church authorities, for a variety of reasons. At that time, it was rather dangerous for a woman to speak out on spiritual matters. Witches were being burned, the *beatas* (loosely organized devout women) were under suspicion, and the many pseudo-mystics gave women who wanted to lead an authentic Christian mystical life a rather difficult time. Of course, the inquisitors were very interested in any unusual manifestations of the mystical life. These facts could not have been far from Teresa's consciousness when she submitted her writings to Church authority. But neither a *pro forma* legal mentality nor a fear of the inquisition were her main motivations. Instead, her mysticism clearly convinced her that the mystical life of any individual Christian must be linked to the history, tradition, and contemporary life of the wider Christian community.

Despite her deference to the learned and those in authority, she always pleaded her cause with firmness, determination, and a subtle sense of civil-ecclesiastical politics. She was a shrewd, pragmatic, self-possessed woman who did not demur in overcoming the hesitations of St. John of the Cross on certain matters, to rein in Jerome Gratian (one of her key collaborators in Teresian reform, who frequently embarrassed her), or to outmaneuver bishops when God's will indicated a certain line of action.[26] On more than one occasion, so

convincingly did she argue her case on matters of reform before those in authority that she could say:
"They did not dare to risk hindering me" (*AB*, chap.
33, p. 315).

Teresa lived the paradox that genuine Christian mystics
have always lived: an authentic willingness to measure
their mystical interiority against the norms of Church
authority along with a will of steel, ready to overcome
any and all obstacles to what they perceived as God's
will. One never finds in Teresa's life a radical opposition between her mystical life and the life of the larger
Church community, even the so-called ecclesiastical es-
tablishment. Like that of St. Ignatius and the *Cloud,*
Teresa's mysticism offers a potent refutation of today's
too-easily accepted dogma that mysticism, Church, and
authority are intrinsically irreconcilable.[27] Teresa not
only found her experiences compatible with the tradition, truths of the faith, dogmas, devotions, life-style,
and authority that fostered them; she also experienced
mystical union with the Church. The genuine mystic
lives from, deepens, purifies, furthers, and gives new
life to his own ecclesial heritage. Teresa offers much
support to those who view mysticism as essentially the
intensification and full-flowering of authentic ecclesial,
religious life.

CONCLUDING REFLECTIONS
It seems obvious from the above exposition that
Teresa's kataphatic mysticism has many affinities with
that of St. Ignatius' and offers a vigorous counterpoint
to the apophatic emphases of the *Cloud of Unknowing*.[28]
Less structured and theological than the *Cloud,* her
writings indicate clearly how mysticism is intricately
woven into the very fabric of ecclesial, religious life.
Her pragmatic approach to spirituality and mysticism
also causes one to place her in closer proximity to St.
Ignatius of Loyola than to the *Cloud.*

Teresa's works refute the modern tendency to reduce mysticism to a transient psychological experience of undifferentiated unity in which all differences between the self and the Absolute disappear.[29] Against this philosophical abstraction stand Teresa's many mansions and the remarkable variety of mystical experience contained therein.

For Teresa, mysticism is much more than passing psychological experiences. Such passing experiences must become states or manifest various stages of mystical progress. They also bring about the mystic's transformation into an icon of agapic love or they express that transformation. Such extraordinary mystical phenomena are usually expressions of a deeper, richer, more hidden divine life taking hold of the person's very roots and slowly permeating, purifying, illuminating, and transforming all levels of his being. Mysticism, then, is essentially a way of life, a way of being, that involves progressive purification by, illumination from, and eventual union with the God of love.

Two important points should be made. First, after reading Teresa's works, it is difficult to subscribe to the thesis that mystical experience the world over is one and the same and that differences arise only as a result of the manifold ways in which this common experience is interpreted.[30] This thesis declares that when the various mystics' doctrines are peeled away, one and the same "common core" of mysticism remains.

Teresa describes, however, a great variety of mystical phenomena and different stages of mystical ascent. Most common-core theorists concentrate mistakenly on mysticism's highest stage exclusively and, even then, only on a few of its essential aspects.[31] On the other hand, Teresa's mysticism supports the position that beliefs, motivations, intentions, techniques, and goals are used not only to interpret pure experience in an extrinsic way, but also form an intrinsic part of the experience itself. In short, the mystic's total spiritual, social, historical, linguistic, conceptual, and traditional matrix helps both to shape and to constitute partially the mystical experience itself.[32] All these factors intrinsically affect the mystical experience before, during, and after it takes place, not merely in some extrinsic way after the experience, as some commentators believe.

The second point concerns the contention that secondary mystical phenomena such as visions, locutions, illuminations, and wounds of love have nothing to do with pure mysticism.[33] If past Catholic studies on mysticism tended to place too much emphasis upon such phenomena, contemporary studies tend to deny their value altogether. Some commentators, who find much support in Teresa's writings, maintain that too sharp a distinction has been made between mysticism's essence as experienced union with the Absolute and the secondary mystical phenomena that accompany it.[34] It makes no more sense to ignore these recurring mystical phenomena than it would for psychologists to ignore dreams just because many consider dreams irrelevant.

Teresa considered secondary mystical phenomena both a great blessing and a great cross. A blessing, because they either helped her to progress or were manifestations of that progress. A cross, because she greatly feared being deceived by these experiences and diverted from her true goal. In today's often indiscriminate quest for experiences of any sort, Teresa's admonition to discern God-given from self- or demon-induced experiences is especially cogent. Teresa and the entire mystical tradition recognize great differences qualitatively in the wide gamut of experiences they undergo. Some experiences promote authenticity; others promote inauthenticity.

When secondary mystical phenomena are God-given, they are the "exteriorized-interiority," or the psychosomatic reverberations, of God's self-communication to

154

the person's deepest core. They indicate clearly that a person is a "plural-unity" with various levels of depth, and they manifest themselves as the divine "echoes" or "vibrations" resonating from the deepest core to these various levels. These phenomena as such are important, but only inasmuch as they bring to pass or express genuine mystical transformation.

Some contemporary commentators equate mystical experiences with exotic, ecstatic experiences.[35] Others view them as another form of "peak experience," or ecstasy, such as those attained by experiencing music, literature, friendship, love, childbirth, nature, and rigorous physical activity.[36] Teresa's emphasis upon mysticism as a way of life with various stages supports the contention of Evelyn Underhill, however, that "no responsible student now identifies the mystic and the ecstatic."[37] Teresa's useful distinction between "sweetnesses" flowing from our own nature and God-given "spiritual consolations" likewise underscores the need for those interested in "experiences" to face up to the difficult problem of discernment and quality in experience.

Even if Teresa's views on what is truly God-given and "supernatural" might be questioned because of contemporary knowledge of the unconscious, her insistence upon discernment cannot. Even if, with Jungian commentators, one broadly defines mystical experience as that which happens when the unconscious breaks into consciousness, the question still remains as to what comes from God, from the devil, and from one's own nature. Even experiences caused by, through, or in the unconscious are not qualitatively equal.

Teresa's insistence that prayer results in transformation and service corrects two other contemporary aberrations. First, the antimystical, anticontemplative, antireligious-life stance of some Christians makes one wonder whether they have taken too seriously the Marxist

155

claim that religion is the opium of the people.[38] Prayer, according to Teresa, brings about a knowledge that flows from mystical love. This felt knowledge, or enlightenment from love, is both general service to the neighbor and the foundation of apostolic service. If in history some prayer movements can accurately be accused of nurturing narcissistic escape, the same can be applied to certain social movements. Without the enlightenment engendered in genuine prayer, even social action can be narcissistic. Unenlightened, unloving, self-seeking action masquerading as Christian service does exist.

On the other hand, thousands of Americans today have dropped their Judeo-Christian tradition to embrace the meditative practices of the Eastern mystical traditions. Motivated by a desire for transcendent experiences, community living, and new forms of authority, many are "turning East"[39] in the hope of finding instant security, freedom from depression, and fast solutions to the problems of contemporary living. For many, however, this Eastern turn is simply a move from material to spiritual gluttony and consumerism.

Teresa never offered prayer as an anodyne to the cross of daily life. "I want no rest," she insisted. "What I need is crosses" (AB, chap. 13, p. 140). She expressly cautioned against spiritual gluttony. Shifting the emphasis away from "experiences," she focused on a transformed life of carrying one's cross and the cross of others, having heroic virtue, compassion, and love of one's neighbor. The words of Karl Rahner definitely apply to Teresian mysticism: "It must be realized that in earthly man this emptying of self will not be accomplished by practicing pure inwardness, but by real activity which is called humility, service, love of our neighbour, the cross and death. One must descend into hell together with Christ; lose one's soul, not directly to the God who is above all names but in the service of one's brethren."[40]

Teresa's description of various methods of prayer and of increasingly simplified, deeper prayer as one progresses has some likeness to the Ignatian *Exercises*. Unlike the *Cloud*, however, Teresa is unwilling to place everything into a cloud of forgetting, unless God so suspends the faculties. By teaching that the understanding may be used until God ignites the will in love, Teresa strikes a good balance between unmystical straining and pseudo-mystical quietism. Her exposition of the prayer of simple regard shows, too, that the understanding may be employed subtly and delicately even at the very summit of mystical prayer. By way of simple regard, which renders the truths of salvation history transparent to their very depths, Teresa's sacramental contemplation grasped the concealed and revealing presence of the ever-greater God.

The traditional distinction between acquired and infused contemplation may seem to be too sharp if one takes seriously Teresa's description of both a volitional ("acquired") recollection and a God-given ("infused") recollection. The highest levels of acquired recollection cannot be distinguished easily from the lowest levels of infused recollection, especially when the recollection is dry and unconsoling. To deny a distinction between acquired and infused contemplation, however, goes against too much solid evidence in the tradition that holds that such a distinction is necessary.[41]

The person advancing in prayer experiences a gradual constraining of the faculties that usually begins by focusing upon the truths of salvation history. The beginner must make an effort to concentrate his faculties on these truths. Both the beginner's activity of concentrating and the "outer word" of salvation history bind his faculties. Gradually, however, the person experiences the faculties being bound from the inside, from the "inner word" of God's grace at the core of his being. The greater the interior binding, the deeper and richer the prayer.

157

In short, as one progresses in prayer, one notices an experiential transition from grasping the "outer word" of God's revelation in salvation history to being grasped by the "inner word" of God's revelation at the various levels of one's being. The beginner implicitly attempts to awaken the inner word by focusing upon the outer word of the truths of salvation history. Gradually, however, the inner word and the outer word blend. Eventually, God's inner word to the person becomes the experiential matrix for mystically tasting the meaning of his outer word. This is like a person becoming aware of the dual figures in a trick silhouette wherein the dominant figure becomes the background, the background the dominant figure, and vice versa.

As mentioned above, Teresa is aware of a dry prayer of quiet wherein nothing seems to be going on. The *Cloud* (*PC*, chap. 20, pp. 183–84) also called attention to a time when the person would cease to feel the consoling presence of the living flame, and be unable either to progress or to return to earlier modes of prayer. It is important to emphasize the possibility, therefore, of a prayer of dry quiet. The *Cloud* urges the contemplative to be still and to suffer the pain of maintaining a dry cloud of forgetting and unknowing. The contemplative must neither strain nor be entirely passive. Teresa would also urge neither fussing about with much interior activity nor a dead passivity. During this state, as seen above, she counsels that one patiently say vocal prayers with attention to whom one is praying, to imagine Christ at one's side, or even to attempt a dry type of prayer of simple regard.

Teresa's exposition of the prayer of quiet, the prayer of semiecstatic union, and the prayer of ecstatic union indicates a weak, medium, or strong intensity of the experience of oneness with God. The infused contemplation described in the fourth mansions is characterized by an effortless, experiential sense of God's presence that in no way comes through the senses, the imagination, or the intellect. "When we begin to pray," she writes, "we shall realize that the bees are coming to the hive and entering it to make the honey, and all without any effort of ours" (WP, chap. 28, p. 186). It is as if the person in the fourth mansions received new "mystical senses" or "spiritual senses" through which to perceive readily God's presence.[42]

Despite its obscurity and incomprehensibility, the divine presence bestows upon the person an unshakeable certitude. Although he may be occasionally distracted during infused contemplation, especially if the quiet is weak, the person can surrender to the divine presence rather easily. Love, affectivity, and desire permeate this infused contemplation. It transforms the person so that all virtues are sought and deepened. Teresa's "perfect contemplation" bears with it all kinds of psychosomatic effects and even a partial or complete curbing of the faculties so that most normal acts cease partially or completely.

Karl Rahner denies that infused contemplation specifically differs from the ordinary Christian's life of faith, hope, and love. For him, the mystics experience in an unusually explicit and extraordinary psychological way what all Christians of faith, hope, and love experience in a more hidden and implicit way. Because of God's universal salvific will and radical self-communication to all persons, *everyone* is called into the immediacy of God's presence, a call which leaves the person free to accept or reject this offer. He writes: "In every human being . . . there is something like an anonymous, unthematic, perhaps repressed, basic experience of being orientated to God, which is constitutive of man in his concrete make-up (of nature and grace), which can be repressed but not destroyed, which is 'mystical' or (if you prefer a more cautious terminology) has its climax in what the older teachers called infused contemplation."[43] Humanity is, therefore, mystical humanity, experientially in touch with a holy, loving Mystery.

For Rahner, the difference between the mystics' unusual infused contemplation and ordinary Christian existence resides in the person's natural endowments. Psychologically speaking, mystical experiences differ from the life of ordinary Christian faith insofar as the former's natural psychological foundation differs from those found in daily life. The specific way in which the mystics deepen, purify, and radicalize the normal life of faith belongs to natural psychology and to the person's natural ability for concentration, ecstasy, self-emptying, and other contemplative techniques usually associated with Eastern religions.[44]

To locate mysticism's essence in the natural order, however, does not diminish its importance. For example, the "natural" act of helping one's neighbor is extremely important for the life of faith and for our eternal salvation. For Rahner, mystical techniques can be of decisive importance in some persons for anchoring the life of faith, hope, and love more deeply. What is most important for Rahner is that every person has a basic mystical experience that is continually present and to which the person must respond. For this reason, Rahner can pointedly state: "But the question then arises as to whether mysticism outside Christianity (which certainly exists) is an 'anonymously' Christian and therefore grace-inspired mysticism. Or, on the other hand, is Christian mysticism a 'natural' mysticism just like non-Christian, although obviously under the influence of grace like all other free, moral actions of a human being, purified and free from baser elements like all that is naturally moral? Or are these two questions aimed after all at the same thing?"[45]

There is little doubt that for Rahner all genuine mysticism, even non-Christian mysticism, is graced and involves the experience of being called into the loving nearness of God's mystery. There are no purely "natural" mysticisms for Rahner. *Theologically* speaking, therefore, all authentic mysticism is supported by and aimed at loving Mystery, even if interpreted in a non-Christian or secular way. Christian mysticism and the normal Christian life of faith, hope, and love, on the other hand, do not differ supernaturally, but naturally. The former is an unusual psychological phenomenon, whereas the latter is common and ordinary.

Teresa's emphasis upon Christ's sacred humanity places her closer to the Ignatian *Exercises* than to the *Cloud of Unknowing*. Her Christocentric mysticism and spirituality are more explicit, satisfying, and acceptable than those of the *Cloud*. To be sure, the orthodoxy of the *Cloud* is not in question here, but its emphases are. Despite his deep love for the human Jesus, the author bypasses in his theocentric emphasis a little too easily the importance of the history of Jesus Christ, especially his bodily resurrection, even for the higher stages of mystical prayer. His unsatisfactory distinction between meditation on Christ's humanity and contemplation of his divinity underscores this.

Teresa undoubtedly shares with the author of the *Cloud* a great love for Jesus Christ. In a hymn celebrating this love, she prayed: "I really believe that, if Thou hadst lived longer, the very love which Thou hadst for us would have healed Thy wounds again and Thou wouldst have needed no other medicine" (*WP*, chap. 16, p. 121). Her mysticism and spirituality never lose sight of the eternal significance of Christ's humanity for our salvation. From the lowest forms of meditation to the highest types of mystical prayer, the presence of Christ's sacred humanity never vanishes, except during transient experiences of suspension. She shows, moreover, how the experience of Jesus' humanity becomes deeper, richer, and more refined as one progresses mystically. Her many and varied imaginary and intellectual visions of Christ also highlight this.

In the risen Christ, Teresa mystically tasted the sublation and the radical confirmation of all the mysteries of his life. It is Christ's bodily resurrection that provides the theological foundation for the continued meditation and contemplation of the mysteries of his pre-Easter life. To some contemporary charismatics who tend to place Jesus' risen body in conflict with his Spirit or to some apophatic emphases on forgetting Christ's sacred humanity altogether, Teresa stands as more than a competent counterbalance.

Most contemporary Christians were initiated into the faith in such a way that they came to believe in the Trinity, Jesus' divinity, Mary's virginity, the real presence, and so on. Somewhere along the line they began to believe in Jesus' bodily resurrection as one truth of the faith among others. That is not the way it ought to be. Because the apostles believed in the risen Christ, they believed everything else about the Christian faith. The bodily resurrection was the reason why, the very ground, the light in which they saw the other truths of the faith. In short, Christianity is essentially Easter.[46] The Christian faith is an Easter faith. Among the classical Christian mystics, perhaps St. Teresa has the best explicit grasp of this key point. The resurrection-centeredness of her mysticism and spirituality needs strong emphasis today.

In conclusion, it is easy to see why Teresa is a Doctor of the Church. Her spirituality and mysticism accomplish what should be an aspect of all contemporary theology: they guide a person into his own hidden, yet ever-present, experience of the God of mystery, revelation, and love. Teresa is unequivocally a mystagogue, that is, a person capable of leading others into the deepest mysteries of the faith. Her experiential focus upon the Trinity, the God-Man, grace, and the eucharist, moreover, places her spirituality and mysticism at Christianity's very heart.

The service and ecclesial dimensions of her spirituality and mysticism anchor the experience of God to all aspects of life. They counter the contemporary tendency to reduce mysticism to exotic, transient, and psychological experiences by highlighting the importance of salvation history, tradition in the wide sense, and service for fostering authentic mysticism as a complete way of life.

Teresa's writings are permeated by concrete, vivid, evocative, and instructive images, analogies, and symbols. But one must read her books to taste this. It must be emphasized also that the concreteness of her writings establishes a point of contact with the contemporary interest in narrative theology, a theology that refuses to detach itself from the great Christian stories, images, poetry, and myths.[47] Her explication of spirituality and mysticism as intrinsically linked with transformation, love of one's neighbor, and the reform of existing ecclesial and social structures also provides an opening for today's interest in liberation theologies.[48] Her writings are also filled with paradigms for conversion experiences, a topic capturing so much of contemporary theological interest.[49]

Teresa's emphases upon humility, the virtues, detachment, and the cross place her spirituality and mysticism in a context which recognizes that all is grace, that the contemporary interest in what one can do solely on one's own is a dead end, and that peak experiences or altered states of consciousness without personal transformation are not what the genuine mystical life is all about. Furthermore, her vigorous personalism, as evinced by a mysticism unquestionably focused on the living person of Jesus Christ and the trinitarian Persons, offers a powerful counterpoint to the contemporary search for an impersonal Absolute that makes no demands on persons in their very essence.

In short, Teresa's writings could provide an excellent source for today's theology. What Karl Rahner did with the Ignatian *Exercises* should be done with Teresa's writings. They await a first-rate theological mind with a "certain something" to transpose her mystical grasp of the God of mystery, revelation, and love into a contemporary framework. Such a work would be extremely significant for contemporary Church life and theology.

Chapter Five

St. John of the Cross (1542-1591)

In 1926, Pope Pius XI proclaimed St. John of the Cross a Doctor of the Church because of his great learning and sanctity. The mystical experiences, poetry, and mystical theology of this great saint offer an extraordinary guide to the life of perfection and have had a decisive influence on the lives of so many people, Christians and non-Christians alike. One senses throughout his writings that John had reached in, through, and beyond ideas, concepts, images, and symbols to experience in naked faith, hope, and love the mystery of the ever-greater God who permeates all things.

The writings of St. John of the Cross present a vigorous complement, yet counterpoint, to the kataphatic emphases of St. Teresa of Avila. We saw in her works a relatively unsystematic treatment of mystical ascent, permeated with digressions, prayers, pious utterances, and earthy turns of phrase. Her keen descriptions of the mystical life and mystical phenomena are almost inseparable from her spiritual autobiography. One encounters there an impulsive person of expansive nature, enormous vitality, courage, humility, and a lively and nimble imagination. She may be compared to an experienced mountain climber who never loses sight of the top, but who wants to show the person she is guiding the beautiful view from all levels of the ascent.

On the other hand, St. John of the Cross may be compared to an experienced, yet uncompromising, mountain climber who has been so impressed with the extraordinarily beautiful view from the top that he refuses to allow the one he is guiding to look around or to rest until they reach that summit. For various reasons, John rejects systematically and unhesitatingly all secondary mystical phenomena. The following quotation sets the tone of his entire mystical enterprise:

"To reach satisfaction in all
desire its possession in nothing
To come to the knowledge of all
desire the knowledge of nothing
To come to possess all
desire the possession of nothing
To arrive at being all
desire to be nothing."[1]

This radical expression of negative theology's approach to God has strong affinities, therefore, to what we have already seen in the *Cloud of Unknowing.* Because God is more unlike than like creatures, the apophatic mystic, St. John of the Cross, places everything in a cloud of forgetting and walks the way of naked faith, naked hope, and naked love.

Although not really a spiritual autobiography, John's works spring from his profoundly mystical life. They evince a person of reserve, discretion, profound prayer, recollection, and love of solitude. They surpass even St. Teresa in their extraordinary analytical ability and psychological perspecuity in describing the goal of the mystical life: perfect union with the God of mystery, revelation, and love. Their real subject is God. John's sacred, mysterious poetry followed by lengthy commentary is systematically and theologically structured, didactic, and evocative. Thus, to read his works in the correct spirit is to be both instructed in mystical theology and initiated into one's own often hidden experience of God that sustains all theological enterprises. Despite John's uniqueness, he is more than simply one mystic in the Christian mystical tradition. To study his works in depth is to discover most of what is in the other Christian mystics, albeit with varying emphases and differing psychological temperaments.

A number of commentators have called attention to the profound unity underlying the major writings of St. John of the Cross.[2] They note the incredible certitude of God's presence that permeates these writings. The writings also underscore a general movement from an entrance into a twilight of the senses, by which one transcends the world of appearances, to a total night of the spirit, by which the self is transcended, to a mystical dawn and journey toward the noonday sun involving spiritual betrothal and marriage. Before examining the main moments of this movement, however, a look at the prologues to John's major works is in order.[3]

MAJOR THEMES OF THE PROLOGUES

St. John of the Cross wrote "to explain the dark night through which a soul journeys toward that divine light of perfect union with God . . . achieved . . . through love" (*AMC*, Pro., no. 1, p. 69).[4] By blending a mystical poetry, which he calls "expressions of love arising from mystical understanding" (*SC*, Pro., no. 1, p. 408),[5] with discursive commentary, John systematically unfolds the classical purgative, illuminative, and unitive stages that culminate in the "highest degree of perfection one can reach in this life (transformation in God)" (*LFL*, Pro., no. 3, p. 578).[6]

Because the mystical journey cannot be undertaken without competent guidance, John wrote especially for those "without suitable and alert directors" (*AMC*, Pro., no. 3, p. 70). He was keenly aware of how much help beginners needed in the contemplative life. Although he granted that God could bypass the director to work with the person directly, without a director the person would progress more slowly, with more trouble, and with less merit. Time and again, therefore, he cautions the contemplative against going it alone.[7] On the other hand, this gentle man's harshest words are reserved for inept, inexperienced, ignorant, and indiscreet directors. They fail in their dispositive role of alerting their charges to God's often subtle lead. They hold them back by attempting to guide them according to their way. Despite the difficulties of finding an experienced, learned, discreet director, however, John insists that a contemplative should always have a director, even one far from ideal.

John wrote his major works with a specific audience in mind, because he had undoubtedly sensed in them a burning love for God. *The Ascent of Mount Carmel* and *The Dark Night* (which together may be considered one work) were written for the religious of the Reformed Carmelites and their lay associates. One should note the great distance that separates the master from his disciples in this work. On the other hand, two very advanced contemplatives requested *The Spiritual Canticle* and *The Living Flame of Love.* The distance between master and disciples in these works is far less.

John explicitly states that he writes only for "some," that is, for those already somewhat detached from the world, which rendered their spirits akin to his own. In a sense, however, he really wrote for all who desire the "Beloved" as he did and who seek the requisite "nakedness of spirit" for which he is noted. Therefore, any sincere Christian may read his works profitably. In fact, those sincerely searching for life's meaning would do well to give their undivided attention to what this great mystic offers. And if one assumes with some contemporary theologians that the mystics experience extraordinarily, dramatically, and explicitly the faith, hope, and love that live in a more ordinary, humdrum, implicit way in the hearts of all Christians, one has all the more reason to listen to this great Doctor of the Church.

168

Again if one assumes with some contemporary theologians that the mystics are paradigms of authentic human living, that they have found the answer to the immense longing that haunts every human heart, that every heart is truly restless unless it rests in God, this is perhaps the most pressing reason for focusing upon the fully healed, transformed, authentic human being—St. John of the Cross.

The prologues in John's writings indicate clearly that he situates his mysticism squarely within the Judeo-Christian tradition. John is absolutely convinced that his mystical life is the full flowering of what the Church lives and the scriptures express. For John and for his specific audience, scripture-in-the-Church is the decisive milieu wherein God manifests himself in space and time. To make genuine contact with one is to make genuine contact with the other.

The prologues emphasize how important it was for John to take scripture as his guide for formulating his mystical life. It is noteworthy that John rarely quotes other mystical writers, except Augustine and Pseudo-Dionysius, although he had certainly read them. Despite the fact that the Valdés Inquisition of 1559 prohibited even a partial use of scripture in the vernacular, John's works are practically a Castilian Bible.

John does more than cite scriptural passages; he seems to breathe the very life of scripture itself. Through his use of scripture he underscores the universal nature of the mystical life he proposes and lives. His references focus less on the history of the people of Israel, however, than on the history of those great individuals in the Old Testament, such as Abraham, Moses, Job, and the prophets, who were haunted and even tortured by their experience of the living God. Although he refers much more to the Old than to the New Testament, his theocentric emphases are rooted solidly in the person of Jesus Christ. The mystical life is the life of Jesus Christ.

It is likewise Jesus Christ who establishes the decisive link to the Old Testament. As John writes: "In giving us His Son, His only Word . . . He spoke everything to us at once in this sole Word . . . and He has no more to say" (*AMC*, II, chap. 22, no. 3, p. 179). As the Father's one Word of love to us, Jesus Christ is the heart and the key to the many words of scripture.

There is no doubt that for John, God is at the center of the Church and the scriptures that are the Church's books. Although he is certain that he is in God and the Church, and that his mystical life does not run counter to the Church's life, the prologues evince his willingness to submit the formulations of his experiences to the universal Church. For John, the mystical life initiates a person into the very life of God and into the life of the community that celebrates the intimate ways in which this God has communicated himself to his people. The genuine mystic lives what scripture and Church are all about. For John, the authentic mystic actually becomes by participation not only God, but also Church.

In the spirituality and mysticism of St. John of the Cross, there is a tension between subjective experience and its objectifications in Church, scripture, and tradition, but there is never an opposition. The third stanza of *The Dark Night* does suggest that John took "no other light or guide than the one that burned in my heart." On the other hand, he insisted that "we must be guided humanly and visibly in all by the law of Christ the man and that of His Church and of His ministers" (*AMC*, II, chap. 22, no. 7, p. 181). For John, there must be an isomorphism between perfect subjectivity and perfect objectivity. Inner experience and its authoritative, traditional, communal expressions in space and time are essentially congruent. One supports, nurtures, and fosters the other. Contact with God, therefore, in no way removes the authentic mystic from

Church and scripture. On the other hand, the night of faith through which mystics pass purifies and transforms their appreciation for and participation in scripture and Church. In fact, both scripture and Church are demythologized, purified, healed, and transformed along with the mystic.

The prologues underscore still another paradox of the mystical life. The mystical life's dynamism tends toward expressing itself outwardly, yet it is essentially ineffable. St. John of the Cross confesses both his need to explain God's mystical ways and the ineffability of these ways. For John, therefore, even a person of great experience may be helpless in formulating these experiences. However, John was confident that God would help him to explain the mysteries of the mystical life, that an explanation was necessary, but that the explanation would be inadequate, hence only "some explanation."

The mystical life normally implies expression in the world, either through action or language. John contends that his mystical life of "burning love" flowed into a poetry that was not fully explainable. John speaks, moreover, of a "mystical theology" as a real knowledge born of love and experience that transcends rational explanation, but flowers into the "figures and similes" of a profound mystical poetry. Although metarational, this mystical poetry was not irrational for John. In fact, he saw the need to unfold it in more rational, discursive commentaries laced with scholastic theology.

John expressed his mysticism through discourse, highly symbolic poetry, and primordial words such as "Oh" and "Ah." One must pay strict attention to all three levels of language in order to appreciate him. The commentaries on the *Ascent-Night* evince a somewhat stilted, theological language. The commentaries on the *Canticle* and *Flame*, on the other hand, are more metadiscursive, mystagogical, and theopoetical. These commentaries are much closer to the poetry they interpret than the discourses of the *Ascent-Night* are to its poetry.

The commentaries seem to indicate, too, that a person must be prepared before entering into the world of the mystical poetry. The discursive commentaries force a person to take the poetry seriously, to read it in the same spirit of faith, interiority, and recollection in which it was written. The mystical movement in the works of St. John of the Cross advances from the discursive commentaries, to the poetry, to the experience of the living God.

John emphasizes both the inability of scholastic theology (part of the "human science" of his day) to understand adequately the mystical life and the inexhaustible meaning to be found in his poetry. Despite this emphasis, he still insists upon using scholastic theology to formulate his experience and to explain his poetry. If scholastic theology, or "science," is incapable of comprehending the mystical life, experience is frequently incapable of expressing it. Thus, for John, both are necessary. Although he recognizes theology's insufficiency, John sees the need for using a technical, reflective, critical knowledge obtained through reason. He distrusts himself somewhat as a theologian, but he does not despise the technical terminology of scholastic theology. In fact, he readily used the scholastic theology he had received without critically evaluating it, which may account for a certain disjunction between his experience and the commentaries.

Ever since William James' classic, *The Varieties of Religious Experience,* ineffability has been especially emphasized as one of the distinguishing marks of mystical experience.[8] To maintain the absolute ineffability of mystical experience is, however, a contradiction. In a banal sense all experience is ineffable, since no one's experience can be directly shared with or communicated to another. Yet John's prologues indicate that language it-self is an intrinsic part of mystical experience, that the mystical life is incomplete until expressed.

The further paradox is that the mystical life both can and cannot be comprehended or conveyed by words. The purgative dark nights not only crucify the mystic, but the mystic's language as well. He experiences the inadequacy of language to express what he has under-gone. On the other hand, these dark nights purify and transform his language. The mystic receives new cre-ative powers to express what has happened. One can-not but sense the invocative and evocative qualities of John's language. We realize that we do not stand to John as the blind do to someone sighted, but rather as those who see much more dimly.

The overused expression concerning mystics, "he who knows does not say; he who says does not know," therefore, does not really stand. Many authentic mys-tics do say much about their mystical life and their ex-periences. One may detect a certain reticence to speak about them and a genuine desire to help others, but the "saying" is a fact. Although it would be naive to sup-pose that the mystics are offering descriptions accept-able to the canons of contemporary clinical psychology, it is equally naive to dismiss their descriptions as worthless. John's phenomenological descriptions, like St. Teresa of Avila's, remain extraordinarily perceptive.

THE FIRST PHASE OF MYSTICAL ASCENT

Preliminary Remarks
As mentioned above, the first phase of the mystical life for John centers on transcending the world of appear-ances. The first stanza of his poem, *The Dark Night*, re-joices in the first steps the contemplative takes to get to the heart of the Real. The commentary explains that this stanza deals with the "dark night" in which the person joyfully abandoned his disordered appetites and

imperfections.[9] John distinguishes the "first night" of beginners who have been introduced to contemplation and purged in their senses from the "second night" of proficients, which involves a profound spiritual purification. John's "beginner" is undoubtedly someone who has been praying and meditating for some time and, hence, is a person far more advanced in prayer than the average Christian.

In this section, John divides the "dark night" into three phases: twilight, midnight, and dawn. The twilight darkness begins when the person starts to wage war against worldly appetites. The midnight phase requires walking the way of faith, which is darkness for the intellect. The person's goal is to arrive at the dawn phase, in which God as Light is experienced as a divine Darkness.

John's apophatic mysticism contends that when compared to God, all creatures are nothing. In fact, "all the goodness of creatures in the world compared with the infinite goodness of God can be called evil" (AMC, I, chap. 4, no. 4, p. 79). The main problem is that our appetites are disordered and frequently misdirected. Therefore, John advocates a radical mortification of the appetites to redirect them toward their true goal, which is God.

Contrary to popular impressions, however, John does not suggest a suppression, repression, or destruction of the sensory appetites. It is a question of reordering all our desires and affections toward God; only then can the proper love for his creatures grow. Our experience teaches us that our entangled appetites weaken, torture, enslave, and cause more misery than we often care to admit. Authentic human living demands, therefore, a radical transformation of desires and the affective life.

In addition, John focuses exclusively upon inordinate voluntary appetites, not the natural ones that cannot and should not be eradicated. The "first movements" of the natural appetites are like questions put to a person for consent or denial. Because of our human nature, these questions cannot be avoided, but we may say yes or no to our natures' demands according to the circumstances. For example, a hungry person has no choice but to be attracted to food. Whether the person eats indiscriminately any available food, however, is another matter. For John, perfect union with God and transformation are impossible without a rejection of all voluntary imperfections, large or small. As he says: "It makes very little difference whether a bird is tied by a thin thread or by a cord" (*AMC*, I, chap. 11, no. 4, p. 97).

The Active Night of the Senses

The second point John makes on the entry into the twilight of purification concerns the active night of the senses.[10] John distinguishes this active night of purgation, which the person can initiate, from a passive night of purification, which only God can initiate. In a way reminiscent of St. Ignatius' third degree of humility, the person commences the active dark night by choosing to imitate Christ as radically as possible. To destroy self-will, John counsels that one lean toward that which is the most difficult, the harshest, the least pleasant, the most unconsoling, the least, the lowest, and the worst. In short, one must "desire to enter into complete nudity, emptiness, and poverty in everything in the world" (*AMC*, I, chap. 13, no. 6, p. 103).

To follow Christ in his total self-emptying dedication to his Father's will, one should also hold oneself in contempt. The psychologically perceptive John realized, however, that an affective vacuum in one's life is very dangerous. To reverse one's inclinations toward the pleasure and satisfactions of this world, therefore, "another, better love (love of one's heavenly Bridegroom) is necessary" (*AMC*, I, chap. 14, no. 2, p. 105). John's mysticism and spirituality are radically bridal, a mysticism and spirituality of love depicted in erotic language that captures the essence of "by grace alone." For John, "if a person is seeking his God, his Beloved is seeking him much more" (*LFL*, III, no. 28, p. 620). The God-initiated mystical movement of love and mystical eroticism toward God must be underscored. John reorders a person's loves in the light of God's prior love. His emphasis upon emptiness, nudity, and total self-stripping must always be seen in the context of being filled with the God of self-giving love.

The Beginner's State

John's third main point on the night's initial phase deals with the beginner's state when the person is deeply within the active night of the senses. "Meditation" characterizes the beginner at prayer. This means a discursive, step-by-step use of reason, memory, imagination, and will. It may be compared with the detailed, analytical study of a great work of art. Meditation is a prime means for helping the beginner to redirect his loves. To be sure, John prefers the simplicity and purity of contemplation similar to a person capturing with one general, pure act a great work of art's overall meaning. Still, he considers meditation the initial step toward eventual union with God.

Beginners frequently find much satisfaction in long hours of prayer, great penances, fasts, and various devotional activities. However, a secret pride, spiritual greed, and complacency often accompany these activities. Such persons desire to appear holy before others, to be the favorite of the confessor, and they are easily disturbed when others are praised. When their prayer is full of consolations and delights, they think they are holier than others and readily criticize their least fault. If their prayer is dry, they become difficult, peevish, and discouraged, and want to give up prayer entirely.

This indicates that such beginners are not seeking God purely. Self-seeking pleasure also motivates them; they

176

seek themselves in consolations and satisfactions. Measuring God by what they are, and not vice versa, they think they are serving God when they are only gratifying themselves. On the other hand, proper meditation begins to purify the senses by controlling what enters them. Through the delights and satisfactions enjoyed in meditation, the person turns away somewhat from worldly things. Meditation strengthens the person spiritually in God. No matter how much the person tries, however, John emphasizes that he cannot completely purify or rid himself of all his faults. The completion of the purification process of the active night requires the dark night, in which God himself will take over and deepen the purgative movement in the mystical life.

The Passive Night of the Senses

The fourth key point in this section deals with the passive night of the senses.[11] Strengthened somewhat by the consolations obtained from meditation, the beginner is now ready for a dramatically new phase of the mystical life. For John, this phase is the start of the mystical life in the strict sense. Mysticism in the strict sense involves the transition from a self-initiated meditation to a God-given contemplation. Whereas the *Cloud* emphasized the positive elements of this transitional stage, John prefers the negative ones. Aridity and a bitterness terrible to the senses characterize this God-given night which, for John, *is contemplation.*

To distinguish the arid prayer brought about by sins, imperfections, tepidity, and ill-health from the God-given sensory night of contemplation, John gives three signs that indicate the beginnings of infused contemplation. First, nothing consoles the person. Neither God nor creatures bring the person any comfort or satisfaction. Second, the person experiences both a painful awareness of God and the dreadful feeling of not serving God well. Third, God forces the person to become more interior by restricting the activity of the intellect,

177

memory, imagination, and will. In short, the person can no longer meditate. Both the aridity and the fear of having gone astray cause the person intense suffering during this period.

This purgative contemplation produces dryness in and a denuding of the senses, because God "transfers His goods and strengths from sense to spirit" (*DN*, I, chap. 9, no. 4, p. 314). Recondite, subtle, dark, and silent, this purgative contemplation renders the person unable to concentrate upon anything in particular. A thirst that seems to kill, a great concern and solicitude for God, and a feeling of being annihilated also characterize this contemplation. Great temptations and trials may afflict the person at this stage, especially those persons destined for the more dreadful night of the spirit that will be discussed later. God may keep weaker persons in this night for a long period of time, lessen its intensity, and console them more frequently. Then too, some never seem to be wholly in or out of this purgative night.

But it is also true that during purgative contemplation the person may delight in remaining alone in a simple, loving awareness of God. This blind stirring of love has great affinities with the *Cloud*'s naked love and may be the fourth and surest sign of entry into this phase. Rest, quietude, sweet idleness, and a loving, peaceful attentiveness toward God characterize in a positive way this secret, hidden contemplation. Because of the "secret and peaceful and loving inflow of God, which, if not hampered, fires the soul in the spirit of love" (*DN*, I, chap. 10, no. 6, p. 318), the person may pray merely by longing for God. This delicate, experiential knowledge flowing from love may not be perceived at first. John advises, therefore, patience and an unconcern with meditation during this surface dryness.

Infused contemplation contains many blessings. By giving the person a genuine self-knowledge, especially of his weaknesses and sinfulness, it shakes the person out of his spiritual complacency. It also fills the individual with requisite respect for the mystery of God. The person begins to do God's will for his sake, and not for the consolations received. Filled with the realization that all comes from God, the person thinks less about himself and more about his neighbors' needs. Although John contends that the way of purgative night of the senses is rather "common," he likewise holds that spiritual cowardess prevents more than half of those who purposely set out on the road to contemplation from achieving it.

THE SECOND PHASE OF MYSTICAL ASCENT

The second phase of the mystical life, for John, is the "night of the spirit" or the "night of faith." God leads the contemplative into a midnight experience, a total night, in which the very self must be transcended. The section on the night of faith contains three main points: the active night of the spirit, the state of "proficients" at the start of the passive dark night of the spirit, and the passive night of the spirit proper.

The Active Night of the Spirit

The active dark night of the spirit consists in the willing and perfect rejection of all understanding, experience, feeling, imaginings, fantasizing, and even supernatural communications.[12] Insofar as possible, the person must place any and all understanding, feeling, imaginings, desires, and opinions into a cloud of forgetting to walk the way of naked faith in unknowing. John emphasizes the way to God as one of pure, naked faith. Only such naked faith does full justice to the infinite difference between the Creator and all creatures. The paradox of faith is that it is an excessive light that the person experiences as a baffling darkness.

The goal of the mystical life for John is the contemplative's perfect union with God. John does not mean the natural, "substantial union" which the creature enjoys with God as creator and conserver of all being, but a supernatural "union of likeness" by which the person becomes "God by participation." The contemplative actually undergoes a "participant transformation" into God. In this union the "soul appears to be God more than a soul" (*AMC*, II, chap. 5, no. 7, p. 117). John insists, on the other hand, that the soul remains distinct from God in its natural being. In short, John's mysticism is one of differentiated unity in which two become one, yet remain two. Love has no meaning when either the lover or the beloved merges into the other.

John gives an extensive exposition of the night of the understanding.[13] The main purpose of this section, and perhaps of all the works of St. John of the Cross, is "to guide the soul in purity of faith through all its natural and supernatural apprehensions, in freedom from every deception and obstacle, to the divine union with God" (*AMC*, II, chap. 28, no. 1, p. 202).

This section also links the contemplative process to Christ's radical poverty of spirit. Like Christ, the contemplative must be stripped both inwardly and outwardly of all things. In order to die completely to self in imitation of Christ's self-sacrificing death, the contemplative must reject all consolations, experiences, and feelings to live the "exterior and interior death of the cross" (*AMC*, II, chap. 7, no. 11, p. 125). In fact, John almost identifies Christ with purgative contemplation. Christ is the way to perfect union with God. One follows Christ most closely, however, by taking "the narrow path of obscure contemplation" (ibid.). For John, the dark, silent, secret contemplation of naked faith is a perfect imitation of Christ's total emptiness of spirit.

Once again John emphasizes the signs required for a person to move from meditation to contemplation. First, the person experiences great dryness and finds meditation impossible. Second, the senses, and especially the imagination, have almost no ability to dwell on anything in particular. The third and surest sign is the simple joy in remaining alone in loving awareness of God.

Beginners meditate by using the two interior bodily senses, the imagination and the fantasy. According to John, these two faculties proceed in a step-by-step, discursive way to construct images and forms. Moreover, John calls meditation "sensory meditation" and contends that it is "wholly sensible." He states, on the other hand, that it may involve reasoning through these images and forms and focusing on particular ideas.

Contemplation is, however, a dark, general, vague knowledge of God through love. It remains a secret even to the intellect into which it is infused. Unlike the particular, discrete acts of meditation, contemplation absorbs the person to a greater or lesser degree in a general, pure act of loving awareness of God. This extremely subtle, delicate, loving knowledge is almost unnoticeable in the beginning. If meditation for John is the way of the senses, contemplation is the way of the spirit.

Although John favors contemplation over meditation, he cautions against leaving meditation too quickly. Besides, until a person attains perfect contemplation, he will need at times to meditate and at times to contemplate. Meditation done with gentleness and moderation is also a great aid for arriving at contemplation.

John contends that every person has the potential for contemplation, because the "pure light" that makes contemplation possible is always present. However, various obstacles and barriers prevent this simple light from being "infused." John makes the remarkable observation that: "As soon as natural things are driven out of the *enamored* soul, the divine are naturally and supernaturally infused, since there can be no void in nature" (*AMC*, II, chap. 15, no. 4, p. 149, my emphasis). Like the *Cloud,* therefore, John teaches that in Christian contemplation, self-emptying, the voiding of all natural things, the ways of forgetting and unknowing, make sense only if the person is first called by God to remove all natural things. Only if the person experiences absorption in God's love, that is, is "enamored," does nescience for a Christian make any sense. With the contemporary emphasis upon transcendental meditation and various contemporary yogas of nescience, it cannot be overemphasized that in the Christian contemplative tradition the call of love must first be present before mental voiding is attempted. The Christian apophatic way, the way of darkness, is lighted by love alone. The would-be apophatic contemplative must pay strict attention to the signs described both by the *Cloud* and by John before moving from meditation to nescience.

To place all created things into a cloud of forgetting is in accord with Christian teaching only in the context of the "enamored soul," which is specifically called to dark, purgative contemplation. But how are *supernatural* communications to the contemplative to be handled?

In the section on secondary mystical phenomena, John takes up a host of supernatural phenomena. He is aware, for example, of God-given communications which are seen, heard, smelled, tasted, or felt by the external senses. The imaginative eyes or the eyes of the soul may see imaginative visions or intellectual apprehensions. A person may receive spiritual visions and revelations of hidden truths, or an infused wisdom, knowledge, faith, prophecy, and discernment of spirits.

When the contemplative is absorbed in spirit, the Holy Spirit may aid the person to form "successive words," or words, concepts, and judgments. Like Ignatius, however, John differentiates between God's true communication and what the contemplative may add unwittingly to it in the after-period. Even when not recollected, the person may receive "formal interior locutions," which are like ideas spoken to the soul. Best of all, God may impart "substantial locutions." God may impress his word so efficaciously in the soul's center that if he said "be good," the person would immediately be so.

And yet, with respect to all supernatural communications, John unambiguously teaches the contemplative to pay them absolutely no heed. The genuine contemplative should reject these phenomena. John urges the person never to feed upon these communications nor to become entangled with them. Like Teresa, however, he calls attention to the qualitative difference between corporeal, imaginative, and spiritual phenomena. The more interior and spiritual the phenomena, the more blessings they carry and the more likely they are to come from God. On the other hand, because God-given communications produce their main effect in the soul passively and instantaneously, the safest and most suitable course is to reject any and all communications.

In short, John makes a real distinction between a non-rejectable, transintellectual and transimaginative element of the divine communication imprinted passively on the soul's very center and the rejectable, secondary psychosomatic effects of this communication that are produced at various levels in the person's being. These latter results of the divine communication, being particular and distinct, can and should be rejected. For John it is a waste of time to try to discern whether these phenomena come from God, from oneself, or from the devil. They can all be rejected safely, because God's main effect influences the soul's center passively. John contends, moreover, that the law of the gospel, natural reason, and the teachings of the Church are sufficient in any case.

Like Teresa, John teaches that genuine communications from the Holy Spirit produce reverence, humility, and love. Self-induced phenomena, on the other hand, effect nothing lasting, and certainly not virtue. Demonically induced phenomena cause dryness, vanity, pride, and self-love. For John, authentic mysticism is evinced in the person by humility, charity, simplicity, silence, and mortification, not by extraordinary phenomena.

Above and beyond the person's transformation, it is also very difficult, according to John, to distinguish between what God really "means" through the divine communication and what we instinctively add to his meaning. Even more parlous is the devil's role in these secondary mystical phenomena. He loves to meddle with them in order to lead the person into curiosity, confusion, pride, and self-love. For all these reasons, John teaches: "I consider it impossible for a person not striving to reject them [secondary phenomena] to go undeceived" (AMC, II, chap. 27, no. 6, p. 202).

Perhaps one exception to the above is "the knowledge of naked truths" (AMC, II, chap. 26, nos. 1–10, pp. 193–96). This occurs when the contemplative receives a knowledge of God and experiences one of his attributes. For John, this is a knowledge from union with God. It is "pure contemplation," and is, in fact, union itself. The person experiences a "touch" of God at the soul's very center that results in a dark, vague knowledge. Like Ignatius' consolation without previous cause, it comes wholly from God and is totally beyond the devil's ability to counterfeit. This naked knowledge contains nothing specific or particular. It is totally beyond images and concepts. It is infused suddenly and passively. Hence, it is not an exception to John's night of the understanding with its radical emphasis upon the rejection of all natural and supernatural forms, images, and concepts in order to walk the way of a dark, naked faith.

John emphatically proposes the absolute dismissal of the phenomenal aspect of all divine communications.

However, the transconceptual aspect cannot be rejected. God imprints this on the soul's center, which receives it passively. The spiritual director plays an *intrinsic* role in this matter.[14] The contemplative must reveal all supernatural communications "integrally" to a competent spiritual director. John insists that God, if he really reveals something to a person, also imparts the penchant to reveal it to a competent guide. An interior communication does not fully grace a person until he also receives it from another person like himself. John stresses that God's mouth does not speak without also using a human mouth. The satisfaction, grace, strength, light, and security flowing from the divine communication will not reach its full maturity unless the communication is revealed to an experienced director. In fact, the divine communication does not completely root itself in the person unless it is fully revealed to a spiritual director.

John's counsels on God-given "formal locutions" illustrate another reason for the importance of spiritual directors. These God-given commands ready the soul to obey and impart an ability to discern clearly what God wants. But one must also contend with demonic locutions. Because it is difficult to distinguish between God-given and demonic locutions, John insists that one must never act upon a locution until it has been revealed to an expert spiritual director. If one cannot be found, John urges the contemplative to ignore the command given by the formal locution.

Because of the sufferings and anxiety usually present with supernatural communications, John counsels spiritual directors to be kind and gentle with those they counsel. He reminds the directors that they secretly fashion the spirits of their charges. If the directors have a subtle taste for accepting supernatural communications, this inclination will be quietly communicated to their charges. Yet, unlike Ignatius, John urges directors

185

not to give them instructions on the discernment of spirits. Yet, the works of St. John of the Cross are certainly a course in discerning the genuine dark way of naked faith.

For John, genuine supernatural communications from God cannot contradict reason and Church. In fact, God's revelations are always incomplete until they receive a human input from the historical community of believers. John stands, therefore, against today's commonly and mistakenly held opinion that mystical experiences have nothing to do with Church, that mystical communications are complete in themselves and always stand in opposition to the traditional beliefs of an historical community of faith.

The third point of the active night of the spirit centers on the night of the memory.[15] John maintains, once again, that his method of stripping the intellect, memory, fantasy, and will of their natural operations is meant only for those advanced in the contemplative life. One must empty oneself totally in order to be filled with the incomparable and incomprehensible God. Whatever John has said about the night of the understanding, therefore, also applies to the memory.

God may so touch the imagination that its operations are suspended. To prepare for this divine stripping of the imagination, the contemplative must forget whatever can be seen, heard, smelled, tasted, or felt. Even God-given imaginative knowledge must be forgotten, because the main effect of the divine communication occurs instantaneously and passively. One must not pay attention to the images, forms, figures, and ideas that accompany the divine communication, although one may advert to the love of God that they cause. To be sure, the contemplative may remember a formless, imageless, spiritual knowledge that brings about love, delight, and light in order to experience that love, delight, and light once again.

Castigating "these pestiferous men" who would eliminate the reverencing of images, John defends the traditional Catholic position on the veneration of images of God and the saints. John praises the use of images both in aiding the movement toward the spiritual and promoting the love for what they represent. He cautions, however, against their becoming an impediment by "excessive use" or by giving them more attention than is necessary. Sometimes, for John, supernatural images and visions seem to offer a greater threat of becoming an obstacle to divine union than the material images reverenced by the faithful.

The fourth point of the active night of the spirit concerns the night of the will.[16] Union with God demands the purification of the appetites and affections of the will through love. The contemplative must rejoice, therefore, only in God's service and glory, hope for nothing else, be sorrowful only in what does not promote this service and glory, and fear God alone. The only reason to rejoice in riches, children, marriage, and status is the extent to which they serve God's honor. For John, these temporal goods do not necessarily cause sin, but the human heart too readily attaches itself to them and not to God. The same applies to beauty, physical gifts, and intelligence. Natural goods frequently become an obstacle to God's service and praise, insofar as a person rejoices in them for their own sake and not for God's.

John concedes that sensible goods seemingly move some people greatly toward rejoicing in God. He contends, however, that this is impossible without great mortification of the senses. His norm in this matter clearly underscores his all-for-God attitude. He writes: "Whenever a person, upon hearing music or other things, seeing agreeable objects, smelling sweet fragrance, or feeling the delight of certain tastes and delicate touches, immediately at the first movement directs his thoughts and the affection of his will to God, receiving more satisfaction in the thought of God than in the sensible object that caused it, and finds no gratification in the senses save for this motive, it is sign that he is profiting by the senses and that the sensory part is a help to the spirit" (*AMC*, III, chap. 24, no. 5, p. 255). Therefore, perfect spiritual nakedness may use sensible goods only as a springboard to God; it never pauses to enjoy them for their own sake. The genuine contemplative uses them to reach God as quickly as possible. For those on the way to complete union with God, the perfect observance of such nakedness is possible only for someone near or through transforming union.

In addition, a Christian must practice the virtues, do works of mercy, obey the commandments, and exercise good manners for the love of God and not for the joy these moral goods contain in themselves. One should not even rejoice in supernatural goods, such as wisdom, miracles, and prophecy, for their own sake. For John, the naked love of God in dark faith is the best testimony to God.

John's position with respect to "motivating goods" such as religious ceremonies, statues, images of the saints, oratories, and pilgrimages is explicitly Catholic. They can be a great aid to the deeper praise and service of God. They direct the person toward what they represent. While John praises these motivating goods as springboards for the spirit, he does not hesitate to criticize the excesses, aberrations, and nonsense that frequently accompany their use. Any traces of affectation, self-seeking, the desire for "experiences," and spiritual gluttony must be purged uncompromisingly when using these goods.

For the sake of love of God above all else, the dark night of the will demands the elimination of affection in all particular things, be they natural or supernatural. To find one's joy in anything except God alone weakens the spirit, causes distractions, and destroys the person's peace. To rejoice in God alone by a radical stripping of affection from every created thing fosters freedom, peace, stability, and, paradoxically, awakens the contemplative to the genuine beauty and depth of all created things, for they are then seen in their proper relationship to their Creator. If Ignatius could find God in all things, St. John of the Cross eventually finds all things in God.

The State of Proficients
The second important point of this section on the total night of the spirit looks at the state of experienced contemplatives as they begin the passive dark night of the spirit.[17] This night does not occur immediately after the night of the senses. It begins only after a contemplative has spent many years achieving inner freedom, joy, and consolation through a very peaceful and profound loving contemplation. The person is not thoroughly purified, however, and so experiences certain desolations in the midst of this contemplation that forecast the dreadful night to come.

For John, even these advanced contemplatives are still like "little children" in the ways of God. They think themselves holier than they are, are easily distracted, prone to the devil's deceptions, and lack a holy fear of God. Because they are not perfectly detached, they fall prey to the very favors that advance them toward union with God. Because their sensory imperfections are rooted in the spirit, the real stripping of the senses was more like a curbing of the appetites than a real purgation. It takes pure, dark, purifying contemplation to get at the very roots of the contemplative's imperfections.

The Passive Night of the Spirit
The third and last important point of this section on the total night of the spirit examines it as a trial, a way,

189

and finally, as a result.[18] This passive dark night *is* infused contemplation, what John calls "mystical theology." This secret inflow from God both purifies and enlightens the contemplative for an eventual union with God produced primarily through love. Because of the divine transcendence and the creature's sinfulness, the pure, simple, general light of infused contemplation is experienced as a painful darkness. With the contemplative doing and understanding nothing, God strips the intellect, memory, and will of all support. Only pain, grief, and the ardent desire of love for God remain.

Several types of bitter experience characterize the passive dark night. The contemplative becomes acutely aware of his sinfulness and misery. Like brilliant sunlight shining through a dirty window, the divine inflow throws into sharp relief the contemplative's least imperfection and fault. Past and present sins stand out in their total perversity to torture the person. A powerful conviction of being unloved by God and unworthy of any love characterizes the experience. The contemplative is certain that God has legitimately rejected him, that no more blessings will come to him, and that his suffering will never end. Nothing satisfies the contemplative, nor can he understand anything of what is going on. He is so full of his own misery that even the consoling words of an expert spiritual director make no impact. All creatures and every one of his friends seem to abandon him during this period. It is as if he were experiencing the very pains of hell, although this is, in fact, an extremely meritorious, earthly purgatory.

The contemplative seems to come close to death through his sufferings. In fact, John calls this night a "cruel, spiritual death." Insofar as sin and imperfection have become an actual part of the contemplative's nature, this nature must be dissolved. To be totally efficacious, moreover, this dark night may last many years. From time to time, God will relieve the contemplative through his consoling gifts. Yet, because something is still lacking in the contemplative, he experiences even in the midst of consolations the haunting presence of a sleeping enemy on the brink of awakening. The fullness of this night is undoubtedly the greatest suffering possible on earth.

This night also offers the contemplative the most secure path to union with God. Knowledge, desires, satisfaction, and imaginings almost always lead the person astray. The passive dark night binds the understanding, memory, and will to free them from all that is not God. This dark contemplation also illuminates and fires the spirit in love, draws the person within, and awakens in him a deep, inner alertness to the things of God.

This infused loving knowledge is also a ladder of love that raises the person to God by lowering him in radical humility. As love for God increases, self-love decreases, and vice versa. The contemplative, madly and miserably in love with God, cares for nothing else but him and his service. As he climbs the ladder of love, the divine touches impel the contemplative with a holy boldness in God's service, and, like Mary Magdalene, he is unwilling to let go of his Beloved. As he reaches the top of the ladder, he becomes Love itself and at death is definitely assimilated to the God of love.

The dark night of contemplation results in a detachment from all things, without which a rejoicing in all things is impossible. Purgative contemplation causes a deep freedom of spirit that allows one to enjoy all created things to the degree one is purified. John insists, too, that there is nothing painful or dark about the divine inflow in itself. The infused divine light and love cause suffering and darkness only to the degree that sins, imperfections, and weaknesses have taken root in the contemplative's being and wage war against the divine gifts.

John compares the contemplative to a wet, green, dirty log thrown into a cleansing fire. As the log takes in the heat, it gives off noise, smoke, and odor. The more heated the log becomes, the less violent and more interior the purification. One's deepest, most subtle, spiritual imperfections require an intimate, subtle, spiritual suffering to produce complete transformation. Therefore, the contemplative will occasionally taste the very dregs of personal imperfection. John insists, however, that it is a God-communicated love that purifies, recollects, integrates, and gathers the contemplative's scattered appetites into this all-consuming love. Occasionally, either the intellect, the will, or both will experience God's presence in a delightful, consoling way. The contemplative may experience light without heat, heat without light, or both heat and light. He becomes aware, moreover, that his greatest good is actually present in his deepest center. Yet, the person still suffers greatly from the fear of being abandoned by God.

God infuses this loving knowledge of his presence so deeply and passively in the contemplative that the contemplation is actually hidden from him as well as from the devil. The devil may become aware, however, of what God is doing because of the incredible peace and silence at the contemplative's core. The evil spirit may cause as much trouble as he can, therefore, in the other levels of the contemplative's being. This merely drives the contemplative more deeply into his center with God.

God visiting the core directly is the highest degree of prayer possible. The person experiences the "substantial touches" of God himself, which have many characteristics of the Ignatian consolation without previous cause. The person experiences all this as happening in his deepest center, in a realm of his spirit that seems to have little relationship to other aspects of his soul. Of course, this mirrors Teresa's distinction between "spirit" and "soul." These divine touches prepare the contemplative in a special way for transforming union.

THE THIRD PHASE OF MYSTICAL ASCENT

Preliminary Remarks
The third and final phase of the mystical journey concerns the contemplative "dawn" and the movement toward noon. This final phase deals, therefore, with mystical betrothal and marriage. The first important point in this section focuses upon what the contemplative experiences as the midnight of the passive dark night dissolves more and more into the dawn experience of transformation and perfect union with God.[19]

Although this section corresponds in part to some of the things already described toward the end of *The Dark Night,* one cannot help but notice the dramatic shift in tone and emphases in *The Spiritual Canticle.* The discursive commentary on the poem, *The Spiritual Canticle,* stays much closer to the language, images, symbols, and tone of the poetry than the commentary of the *Ascent-Night* does to its own poetry. It is obvious that John wrote this commentary on the *Spiritual Canticle* for someone far advanced in the mystical life, namely, Mother Aña de Jesus of the Carmelites at Bea.

The first stanza of the *Canticle* emphasizes that God's wounding love drives the contemplative away from self-love and disordered love of creatures. The divine touches bestow a deep experience of the ever-present, yet hidden, Father, Son, and Holy Spirit within the contemplative's core. These touches also leave him with a painful sense of God's absence, with a yearning and an immense longing for the Beloved. John also stresses that the way of love always necessitates passing beyond what is perceptible and understandable in the divine presence.

True love will seek out all ways to speak with the Beloved. Because of the divine absence, therefore, the second stanza centers on looking to go-betweens and intercessors for help in seeking out the Beloved. The contemplative wishes to get word to "Him I love most" by having his prayer ascend by way of the choir of angels. He desires his Beloved to hear about his deathlike sufferings caused by the nights of the intellect, will, and memory. When the contemplative allows no one and nothing to intimidate his loving service to God, then the words, "Him I love most," are genuine.

The third stanza confesses that prayers and intermediaries have not helped to find the Beloved. The contemplative realizes that he must vigorously set out to search for him, not stopping to "gather flowers" of natural and supernatural delights and satisfactions, but going to the "mountains" of virtue and the "watersides" of mortification and penance. Neither the world, the flesh, the devil, nor the sensory appetites can stop this search.

Stanzas 4 to 8 offer a lovely hymn to creation, recalling the great variety of things created by the Beloved. All creation contains beautiful traces of God's passing through "in haste," for although creation is beautiful, the incarnation and other Christian mysteries reveal much more of his beauty. The knowledge of his Beloved revealed by creation and the mysteries of the faith deeply wound the contemplative. However, the deathlike divine wounds of love cause an even deeper suffering. Nothing can satisfy the person now except God himself, so he cries out: "Now wholly surrender Yourself." The ecstatic flights imparted by these divine wounds of love make life in the body insufferable. The contemplative complains: "How do you endure, O life, not living where you live?" The contemplative has deeply experienced that his true life is in God alone.

Stanzas 9 to 11 speak even more forcefully about the wounds of love. The contemplative experiences them like poisoned arrows for which only the Beloved has the antidote. These wounds produce a sickness that makes the contemplative bitter toward everything except God. Only perfect, total love can "extinguish these miseries." The contemplative laments, therefore: "Why, since You wounded this heart, don't You heal it?" During this period God also imparts to the contemplative a deep "spiritual feeling" or a "certain affective" sense of his presence. These semiclear glimpses of the divine beauty, even when weak and vague, cause the soul to swoon and faint. The contemplative realizes that death alone can bring the fullness of what he desires and so prays: "And may the vision of Your beauty be my death."

Spiritual Betrothal

The second important point of this final phase of the mystical dawn concerns mystical betrothal.[20] At this stage the contemplative's soul is like wax awaiting the divine imprint. It receives a "sketch" of the divine image and truths through God's self-communication. Paradoxically, however, the closer the contemplative feels to God, the more acutely he experiences what is lacking in this intimacy. In short, the person experiences profoundly the alternating rhythm of the divine presence and absence characteristic of mystical betrothal. During the Beloved's painful absence, for example, the dryness drives him even more deeply into himself. He pleads: "South wind come, you that awaken love, breathe through my garden."

Varying degrees of violent God-given ecstatic flights may be common during this period. These spiritual departures from the body indicate an incredible union of love. Still, John insists that ecstasies indicate a lack of integration between soul and body and that the contemplative is still imperfect. Once perfected, he will experience all divine communications in gentle, peaceful love.

The Beloved communicates many secret things about himself at this time. Especially to be prized is the mystical knowledge concerning the incarnation and redemption. The Beloved also reveals the contemplative's own perfections and gifts, which indicate just how much of the Beloved's is now his. God is now everything to the contemplative, who finds God's reflection in the goodness of all created things. His Beloved is the "mountains," the "valley," "strange islands," "resounding rivers," and the "whistling of love-stirring breezes." Despite these images, pantheism is totally foreign to John's works.

God shows himself nakedly, but unclearly, to the contemplative's spirit and may speak substantial words. He may experience God's very subtle touch like a "spark," or be inebriated and fortified by the Holy Spirit's "spiced wine," and rest in peace, tranquillity, and a "sounding solitude." Experiencing God in his innermost center, the contemplative cries out: "Hide Yourself, my Love." Perceiving God at the very center of the soul, he experiences the rest of his soul as an enemy to what is occurring. He begs the "girls of Judea," the lower faculties and appetites, not to spoil any of this communication.

Mystical Marriage

At times, the contemplative is so full of God that nothing else matters.[21] Through "the siren's song," he sleeps the gentle sleep of love forgetful of all created things. Moreover, the Beloved has called the soul "Bride." The total transformation into the Beloved, becoming God by participation, is a greater gift than mystical betrothal. As John's well-known definition of mystical marriage says: "The union wrought between the two natures and the communication of the divine to the human in this state is such that even though neither change their being, both appear to be God" (SC, s. 22, no. 3, p. 497).

196

Mystical marriage means that God and the contemplative have become one in spirit and love, although neither changes in nature. Like a lump of coal transformed into fire, so is the soul transformed into God. This deepest and most intense love ensures that the contemplative's inner core is always united to God, although the soul's faculties may not be.

The contemplative now experiences God's strength as his strength. Nothing can penetrate the peace and strength from this union, not even the devil's ravings. Now perfected, at times he is so full of and lost in love that he does not even understand evil. During these periods, he can say: "I no longer knew anything," that is, anything except divine love.

John contends that "confirmation in grace" frequently accompanies mystical marriage. This gift imparts the knowledge that the contemplative will persevere in God's love. He has the certitude of remaining in God's friendship until death. This very special grace of certitude concerning salvation also includes sinlessness. Serious sin is not only absent; it is impossible. The contemplative is so full of God's love that any course of action that vitiates this love is psychologically impossible. Since Teresa's teachings on mystical marriage do not go this far, one may assume that John's purgation and final transformation were even deeper than Teresa's.

Although the genuine contemplative remembers former sins, he knows that God's "look" has healed and transformed him into something beautiful. As he says to the Beloved: "Your eyes imprinted Your grace in me." This grace makes the soul appear to be God in appearance and glory, although John insists that it remains substantially different from God. Without fusion, God and the contemplative totally and mutually surrender to each other "in the serene night" of dark, yet clear, "sweet and living knowledge" of infused contemplation. Time and again throughout John's works, he emphasizes the loving knowledge that initiates, effects, and confirms the bridal mysticism of love.

Likewise, John stresses the Christocentric dimension of transforming union. The contemplative penetrates the very core of the mystery of the incarnation by becoming the "Son by participation." The divine Word's union with his humanity is the paradigm of the contemplative's union with God. Since the contemplative, along with his humanity, has been transformed into the beauty of the union of the Word with the Word's humanity, the contemplative now wishes to "behold ourselves in Your beauty." He also desires to go to the "high caverns in the rock," for this rock is Christ. Just as Moses took shelter in the rock when God passed and saw God's "back," the contemplative discovers that God's "back" is Christ's humanity.

Mystical marriage involves both affective and effective love. The person's one desire is to love as much as he is loved, but he realizes that this is fully possible only after death in the beatific vision. The contemplative experiences the Holy Spirit now as spirated love from God to the soul and from the soul to God, just as the Father and the Son together spirate the Holy Spirit. In the quietude of this solitary love, which alone guides the contemplative, he finds an incredible spiritual happiness and freedom. Seeing God in all things and all things in God, he hears "the song of the sweet nightingale," or the harmony that exists between God and all creatures and among creatures themselves.

Through this deification, in which he becomes God by participation, the contemplative can genuinely say: "Now that my every act is love." God's loving influx has totally detached the person from all things and wholly reintegrated him around the love which is now his. Even the "first movements" of his appetites are directed by and toward this love. Therefore, the contemplative, consciously, subconsciously, and unconsciously loves God. Even the senses and the lower aspects of the soul are integrated into this love and enjoy an extraordinary harmony with the soul's highest aspect. Love is now total and perfect. Since the contemplative is fully subjected to, integrated into, and transformed by God's love, even the devil has been routed. As John says: "Nor did Aminadab appear." Everything the contemplative does is love of God, for he says, "Now I occupy my soul and all my energy in His service."

This love, however, draws him away from the active life and external preoccupations into a loving, fruitful solitude. "No longer seen or found on the common" (SC, s. 20), the contemplative spends his time in a continual, loving attentiveness to God. John emphasizes that the pure love of total contemplation of God is the most fruitful form of service. Because this is the highest apostolate and brings the Church the greatest benefits possible, nothing must be done to hinder or to distract the contemplative from the bridal sleep of love. Even great apostolic works should be set aside when the love for which we were created takes hold. This "holy idleness" of love is, for John, apostolic service par excellence. John likewise contends that if those engaged in the active apostolate spent more time in prayer, their labor would be more fruitful.

From these remarks and from what we have already seen of Ignatius, it is easy to understand why commentators distinguish between a "bridal" and a "service" mysticism.[22] John emphasizes the bridal sleep of love; Ignatius emphasizes being with Christ to serve. Yet, to distinguish between these two types of mysticisms is not to set them in opposition. Both John and Ignatius loved God above all and everything in God. Both had been purified, illuminated, and transformed by love. Both followed the inner promptings of this burning love alone. Ignatius warned against long hours of prayer, preferred the "mortified man" to the "man of prayer," and stressed contemplation in action. On the other hand, Ignatius himself spent long hours at prayer and knew that in the active apostolate the gifts which unite the contemplative to God are much more important than natural gifts. Although John sang the praises of the bridal sleep of contemplative love, a holy idleness, he spent much of his time reforming Carmel and writing his works.

Both mysticisms have their strengths and their weaknesses. If the mysticism of John *tends* toward quietism and an *un*holy idleness, the service mysticism of Ignatius *tends* toward a self-seeking, unenlightened activism. John's mysticism dramatizes the "one thing necessary," that we must love God with our whole mind, strength, soul, and being. Ignatius' mysticism dramatizes that unless we love the brother or sister whom we can see, we do not really love the invisible God. Both forms of mysticism are, however, deeply Christian. The mysterious call of God selects some to serve the Body of Christ through the contemplative love of bridal sleep and others to serve by contemplation in action.

The Deepening of Mystical Marriage
The poetry and commentary of John's work, *The Living Flame of Love*, develop the fourth and final point of the last stage of the mystical journey: the deepening of transforming union.[23] The first stanza emphasizes that the contemplative is now exceedingly close to beatitude. The only thing which separates him from the beatific vision is "the veil" of this mortal life. Totally purified and transformed by the Holy Spirit, the contemplative feels the "living flame of love" as no longer "oppressive." This love "wounds" the soul in a delightful way "in its deepest center," causing it to melt in love. The contemplative can experientially differentiate this deepest center wherein God dwells and acts from the less profound centers.

John also distinguishes between the two types of union that the contemplative now experiences: the union of love alone and the union with an inflaming of love. In and through transforming union, the contemplative always experiences the former, whereas the latter is transient. The former may be compared to hot, glowing embers; the latter, to the hot flames shooting from these embers. The living flame of love is, therefore, the highest experience of God possible in this life, for the soul acts with the very love of God himself.

In this stage, the contemplative prays: "Now Consummate! if it be Your will." In short, he desires the definitive transformation of the beatific vision. John also makes the fascinating observation that mortal life is not really snatched away from such highly purified and transformed persons. They die gently and sweetly in an ecstasy of love. Having become divine love through participation, they need only to make the final, delicious surrender to the promptings of this homeward-turning love.

The second stanza discusses the trinitarian dimensions of the deepening of transforming union. John praises and calls the Father, "O gentle hand"; the Son, "O delicate touch"; the Holy Spirit, "O sweet cautery." In inflicting a "delightful wound" that transforms the very soul into a wound of love, God brings about for the contemplative a transformation of the very universe into an ocean of love. This inner delightful wound may even manifest itself in the body as the stigmata of Christ's wounds.

When God's substance touches the soul's substance, the contemplative experiences divine life itself. Reminiscent of Teresa's transverberation experience, these divine touches make all the contemplative's former sufferings and trials seem like nothing. God's "delicate touch . . . pays every debt." These touches kill, however, but in a paradoxical way. As John says: "In killing You changed death to life." The living flame of love kills the "old man," brings to life the "new man" of perfect spiritual life effected by a transforming union of love, and completes it in the beatific vision. Once again, John insists that the contemplative becomes God by participation, but not substantially so.

Unlike his teaching in the *Ascent-Night*, John contends in this work that God calls everyone to this perfect union with him. Few reach these heights, however, because they are unwilling to bear even the small trials that God sends to strengthen them. Just as an athlete must train in order to avoid injury in serious competition, God exercises the contemplative through trials and sufferings to render him capable of bearing the weight of divine love. Neither force nor sense activity, however, can ever attain the heights of contemplative love. Still, at this stage the senses frequently enjoy the reverberations or overflow from the divine communications at the contemplative's center.

The profound third stanza speaks of the multiple attributes of God experienced by the contemplative as "lamps of fire." These lamps give off light and heat, or knowledge and love, in the contemplative's deepest center. When the intellect, memory, and will, "the deep caverns of feeling," have been *totally* emptied of all created things, the soul "becomes God from God through participation in Him and in His attributes" (*LFL*, s. 3, no. 8, p. 614). For John, when the soul desires God fully, it possesses him fully. In this state, moreover, the soul is able to "give God to himself in God."

John discusses "three blind men" who may lead the contemplative astray: the soul itself, the devil, and the spiritual director. When God calls the contemplative away from meditation to dark, silent contemplation, the person may not understand what is going on. Kicking like a child carried by its mother, the contemplative

202

may continue to strain against infused contemplation by insisting upon meditation.

The devil will do everything possible to distract the person from infused contemplation. He uses knowledge and sensible satisfactions to drown out the gentle, interior whisperings of the Holy Spirit, which urge the soul away from the senses and into itself. Although only God can touch the contemplative's innermost core, the devil stands poised and alert at the passageway from sense to spirit. At this juncture he takes his strongest stand.

Once again John emphasizes the importance of learned, discreet, experienced directors to free the person for the solitude and idleness of infused contemplation. If Ignatius sees the spiritual director primarily as one who helps the person discern God's will for him, John views the director primarily as one who facilitates the transition from discursive meditation to dark, silent contemplation. Like Ignatius, however, John focuses upon letting God lead the contemplative. Because those in contemplative orders are quickly led from meditation to the quiet, secret, passive loving attention of infused contemplation, John chides those directors who insist upon meditation. He calls them "blacksmiths hammering on the soul." They are like amateurs who clumsily attempt to retouch a masterpiece.

The director needs considerable skill to help the contemplative discern the signs which signal the transition from meditation to contemplation. The contemplative must give up step-by-step, discursive meditation for a more secret, dark, vague, passive loving attention of God. At times, however, even this loving attentiveness may be impossible. God sometimes places the contemplative in solitude, in a state of inner idleness, a state of listening in which he is weary of all created things and is scarcely aware of the recondite breathing of love and life in his spirit. The spiritual director must be very careful not to quench this God-given holy idleness by forcing the contemplative to meditate, just because it seems as if he is doing nothing.

In the final stanza, John sings: "How gently and lovingly You woke in my heart." This awakening takes place when the Word moves within the soul's substance and bestows a knowledge of all created things through God. When this occurs, "it also seems that all the virtues and substances and perfections and graces of every created thing glow and make the same movement all at once" (*LFL*, s. 4, no. 4, p. 644). The contemplative mystically tastes the mystery of divine creation and concursus, how all things live, move, and have their being in God.

God thereby becomes diaphanous in all things and all things become diaphanous in God. Transforming union causes not only a mystical marriage with God but with all creation as well. The mystic becomes one with the very Love which creates and sustains all things. As John says: "And the soul sees what God is in Himself and what He is in His creatures in only one view" (*LFL*, s. 4, no. 7, p. 645).

Finally, John distinguishes between the habitual experience of the Beloved sleeping in the soul effected through transforming union and the recurring awakenings of the Beloved caused through the deepening of this union. During these awakenings, John exclaims: "How tenderly You swell my heart with love." During the ineffable spirations of love, the contemplative experiences that God calls the soul "His brother and His equal."

CONCLUDING REFLECTIONS

John's comparison of the contemplative to a "turtledove" in stanza 34 of *The Spiritual Canticle* is a perfect symbol of his entire spirituality and mysticism. According to John, the turtledove does not land, perch, rest, eat, or drink until it has found its mate. Then and only then will it enjoy everything else. John emphasizes the single-minded pursuit of a Beloved who seeks the contemplative even more. His spirituality and mysticism are paradigms of the gospel injunction to seek first the kingdom of God and to love God with one's whole soul, heart, mind, and strength.

To understand correctly John's somewhat austere single-mindedness, however, it is imperative to read all his works in the context of his *The Living Flame of Love*. Far too many people begin with his rather somber, imposing, and seemingly impossible *Ascent-Night*. The awesomely beautiful transformation and deepening of a union of love described in the *Flame* put the message of the *Ascent-Night* into a clearer perspective. It is highly recommended, therefore, to anyone who has never read anything from John to begin *always* with his *Living Flame of Love*. When John sings the praises of the God of love, of all things created in and through this love, and of his own transformation into and deepened union with this love, his urgent admonition never to stop until one reaches the top makes great sense.

John offers a vigorous and vital theocentric spirituality and mysticism as a way of life centered on the purifying, illuminating, and transforming experience of the ineffable, incomprehensible, ever-greater God. This Father-centered experience of a God infinitely different from all creation flowers into various stages and actual states of purification, illumination, and transformation. Like the mystics already discussed, John stands as a living refutation of the contemporary tendency to equate mysticism with strong religious emotions, altered states of consciousness, or peak, ecstatic, occult, bizarre, or psychedelic experiences. Because purifying, illuminating, and transforming love dominates the mystic's entire being and consciousness, the authentic mystic is distinguished from the great artists, poets, seers, philos-

ophers, and wonder-workers, who may receive their
initial spark from the same fire of love.

John's consistent advice to reject all natural and supernatural visions, locutions, revelations, consolations,
gratifications, and experiences as an enemy to the way
of naked faith offers a corrective to many contemporary
Christians who are overly interested in religious and
charismatic phenomena to justify their own version of
Christianity. John's constant rejection of all secondary
mystical phenomena also counters a former trend in
some Catholic circles to place much emphasis upon private revelations, visions, the stigmata, and levitations.
That many contemporary Christians are more edified
by Mother Teresa's service to the poorest of the poor
than by Padre Pio's stigmata is a valuable sign of
the times.

Ignatius, the *Cloud*, Teresa, and even John recognize,
however, the value of genuine consolations, satisfactions, and secondary mystical phenomena as a means
to wean the person from disordered attachments, as
they recognize the dangers of becoming attached to the
divine gifts which advance the person in the mystical
life. John, from his experienced vantage point, emphasizes the dangers and not the value of the above. But
on the other hand, from their own extraordinary experience Ignatius, Teresa, and to some extent, even the
author of the *Cloud* stress the positive side of divine
favors.

A person will not advance in the mystical life without
these favors, which God always gives to help the mystic make progress. Even a genuine contemplative will at
times cling to the gifts instead of to God. This is part of
the dynamic of the authentic mystical life. Thus, to
overemphasize John's teachings can lead to discourage-
ment and iconoclasm. An overemphasis of his famous
"nothing" could lead to an un-Christian nihilism and
not to the ever-greater God. To overemphasize certain

206

aspects of Ignatius' or Teresa's teachings can lead, on the other hand, to spiritual gluttony. A genuine incarnational, sacramental spirituality and mysticism demand both an acceptance of the symbol of God's presence and passing beyond it to the ever-greater God. To bypass the symbol is to bypass the God who has in fact revealed himself in space and time. To cling to the symbol too long is to idolize what should be a means to the ever-greater God. Ignatius, the author of the *Cloud*, Teresa, and John suppress neither pole of this sacramental dynamic, but all have their own particular emphases. Authentic Christian mysticism must keep both of these poles in a creative tension.

Some commentators have criticized John's spirituality and mysticism because they believe that the way of naked faith is irreconcilable with Christianity's incarnational, sacramental, and historical basis.[24] For over fifteen years, the learned Dom John Chapman disliked St. John of the Cross and called him a "Buddhist."[25] Abbot Marmion claimed that John was like a sponge full of Christianity that could be squeezed out fully and yet leave his mysticism intact.

Nevertheless, an intrinsic dimension of even apophatic mysticism is the ecclesial context out of which it comes and in which it lives. John's "sponge" was a living organism that did not and could not live outside of its natural ambiance. Contemplation by means of emptying the intellect, will, and memory of all contents does not produce, therefore, an alleged "pure," transhistorical, transecclesial mystical consciousness. What Steven Katz says about yoga applies to apophatic contemplation: "[It] is *not* an *un*conditioning or *de*conditioning of consciousness, but rather it is a *re*conditioning of consciousness, i.e., a substituting of one form of conditioned and/or contextual consciousness for another, albeit a new, unusual, and perhaps altogether more interesting form of conditioned-contextual consciousness."[26]

Pure, abstract mystical consciousness is a contemporary fiction.

Therefore, apophatic techniques do not peel away the mystic's beliefs and traditions like the leaves of an artichoke to leave a mystical core common to all religious traditions and only fortuitously and extrinsically linked to them. John's mystical life and consciousness are Christian from beginning to end. To be sure, his ecclesiality passes through the dark night of faith. The living flame of love purifies, illuminates, and transforms all John's feelings, desires, expectations, images, concepts, and projections concerning the sacramental, historical, liturgical, and scriptural dimensions of the Church. This explains why John expresses his spirituality and mysticism in scriptural terms and defends ecclesial life even after transforming union, for he has become Church by participation. The fully transformed John experienced the transparency of all creation, salvation history, and full ecclesial life in God.

The same is true for John's Christocentrism.[27] Although John's dark, silent contemplation leaves no room for meditations on the life, death, and resurrection of Jesus Christ, Jesus himself is the paradigm of the perfect contemplative. Jesus emptied himself to the point of death on the cross. The Father lovingly accepted this self-surrender in death by raising Jesus bodily from the dead. The life, death, and resurrection of Jesus Christ thereby dramatize in an objective, historical, visible way what takes place more subjectively, implicitly, and secretly in the authentic mystical life. The genuine contemplative—through dark, naked faith—experiences, lives, and becomes the mysteries of the life, death, and resurrection of Jesus Christ. After a certain stage, the contemplative does not need to meditate upon, think about, or imagine these various mysteries, but he must live them. In addition, John also insists implicitly that every contemplative's "Jesusism"—that is, his projec-

208

tions, images, desires, and expressions concerning Christ—must also be purified, illuminated, and transformed by dark, loving, infused contemplation.

Extremely important for a correct understanding of mysticism and for a contemporary spirituality and mysticism is John's profound treatment of the dark night of the senses and spirit. Some Christians tend to label every physical and psychological low as a manifestation of the dark night. On the other hand, there is almost no emphasis upon the need for purification in the quest for human authenticity in the many circles in which mysticism has become "trendy." Even in some supposedly orthodox Christian groups, it requires great courage to speak about the need for penance, abnegation, mortification, and the cross.

For example, Walter T. Stace dismisses the dark night as a kind of emotional reaction, a view indicating a profound ignorance of Christian mysticism.[28] Agehananda Bharati holds the absurd position that mystics suffer a dark night because they have no other abilities and interest to fill in the time between ecstatic experiences.[29] Father Andrew Greeley confesses that he does not understand the dark night and says almost nothing about it in his book on mysticism.[30] One psychological researcher on mysticism, Arthur J. Deikman, explains mysticism in terms of a "deautomatization" process.[31] For Deikman, the destruction of automatic perceptual and cognitive structures by contemplative techniques and life-styles would account for the dark night experience. The breakdown of the psychological structures that limit, select, organize, and interpret perceptual stimuli is experienced as darkness and psychological death.

For St. John of the Cross and the Christian tradition, however, the passive dark nights are much more than emotional reactions, the bleak periods between ecstatic experiences, or even psychological breakdown, that is, "deautomatization." They are essentially God's loving inflow, which purifies, illuminates, and transforms the entire person. Although they may include the above, the passive nights represent essentially and primarily the *unmediated*, negative experience of the God of love flowing into the person's inner core, reinforced by all sorts of internal and external causes of suffering. Bad health, natural psychological problems, intellectual and moral weaknesses, accidents, conflicts with friends and family, the death of a loved one—in short, Teilhard de Chardin's well-known "passivities of diminishment"[32]—may all be part of the dark night, but they are not its essence. Any explanation that leaves out God's immediate action in the person's spiritual center is deficient and cheapens John's coin.

The passive dark night is the dark side of love that causes a total, conscious, preconscious, and unconscious purgation of everything in the person contrary to the divine love at work. Reaching the innermost recesses of the human spirit, this purgation process could offer theologians valuable insights for a theology of purgatory. Although John stresses that there is nothing in this divine love that of itself can cause suffering, it must burn out not only all traces of sin, imperfection, and selfishness, but also enlarge the spirit's capacity to become this love by participation.

Hans Urs von Balthasar seems correct, therefore, when he distinguishes the much more profound God-induced dark night from the "natural" and self-induced purgation process accomplished through yoga and other meditation techniques.[33] If there are physical exercises that work wonders for one's physical well-being, there are also psychosomatic techniques of great value for psychological well-being. Although God may lead a dedicated yogin into the dark night, simply to equate the states of consciousness brought about by self-initiated yogic practices with the Christian dark nights is inadequate.

210

Jacques Maritain also seems on target when he distinguishes the God-given nights that eventually transform the person into a model of human authenticity from other nights caused by natural factors. Some philosophers, poets, artists, novelists, and others have experienced nights that led to debauchery, to physical and mental deterioration, and to physical, psychological, or spiritual suicide.[34]

John's way of a dark, naked faith indicates that apophatic mysticism is more than simply a way of speaking about God.[35] Apophatic mysticism is a particular modality of praying to and experiencing the ever-greater God. It is much more, therefore, than negative "God-talk."

Somewhat disappointing is the little use contemporary theologians have made of the mystics and their purified, illuminated, and transformed experience of the God of love. How long can theologians continue to ignore those who claim to have certitude about the experience of God in their lives and for whom this experience produces such a radical transformation?

Theologians should also give more attention to John's teaching on the ecstatic death of the purified mystic for a richer theology of the death of Christ.[36] Furthermore, perhaps John, with his emphasis upon the sleep of bridal love, stands as a counterbalance to those Christians who have accepted too much from the Marxist critique of religions and have elevated "praxis" as the codeword for all Christian living and theology. And if John states that the pure and simple light of contemplation is *always* present to the soul, albeit not always in an infused way (*AMC,* II, chap. 15, no. 4, p. 149), what relevance does this have for a contemporary theology of grace? Perhaps Karl Rahner's highly intrinsicist theory of grace as the *self*-communication of God who is *always* offering himself to the person has a firm basis in Rahner's reading of the mystics.[37] John's requisite signs indicative of the transition from meditation to contemplation seem to have great significance for a contemporary spirituality and mysticism. As a minimum, these signs indicate that, especially with the contemporary fascination surrounding Eastern techniques of meditation and contemplation, more emphasis must be placed upon the proper Christian foundation before utilizing apophatic techniques.

For John, mysticism is primarily a way of life that involves progressive stages of purification, illumination, and transformation by the God of truth and love. He gives support, therefore, to Evelyn Underhill's observation that the object of the mystical quest, namely, the One Holy God, is much more important than the mystic's transformation and apostolic service.[38] Christian mysticism focuses first and foremost on God alone. It does not use God to transform the mystic or the world. To be sure, God does transform the person, bring about human authenticity, turn him into a pioneer and servant of humanity. But all these values are secondary to the Christian mystic's main activity of falling totally in love with God.[39]

Like the other mystics so far considered, John stands as a great barrier to those attempting to reduce spirituality and mysticism to psychology and psychotherapy.[40] Spirituality and mysticism do have great psychological and psychotherapeutic benefits, of course, but they cannot be reduced to this. Christian mysticism is primarily a love affair with the God of love and truth.

Although John can be praised for his criticism of spiritual gluttony concerning the eucharist, his admonitions against frequent communion are deficient when examined in the light of contemporary Church practice and eucharistic theology.[41] Like the *Cloud*, moreover, he distinguishes too sharply between sensory meditation and spiritual contemplation. The long-standing Christian tradition on the spiritual senses and the Christian kata-

212

phatic tradition show that not all meditation is sensory, not all contemplation is spiritual, and not all contemplation needs to be apophatic. In another vein, John's trinitarian perspective is more explicit than that of the author of the *Cloud*, yet still seems underdeveloped, somewhat extrinsic, and highly formal.

John and Teresa may have different psychological perspectives, but their views are not "absolute opposites," as Dom John Chapman contends.[42] Along these lines, a Carmelite nun once told me that John is always to be preferred to Teresa in points of disagreement between them. It must be emphasized against these two views, however, that both John and Teresa are Doctors of the Church. God leads some persons along the kataphatic path, others along the apophatic, and still others along a path that blends both traditions.

It can also be argued that Teresa did not sufficiently appreciate the apophatic tradition, especially the value of *dry* quiet in the contemplative life. It could likewise be argued that John did not fully appreciate the kataphatic tradition. Not all have been called to walk the way of naked faith. Teresa and John, the apophatic tradition and the kataphatic tradition, however, all reach the same goal: a purifying, illuminating, transforming union with the ever-greater God of love. Thus, both Teresa and John should be read, studied, assimilated, and held in a creative tension. Which path one takes in the mystical life depends upon God's call, which usually corresponds to an individual's psychological temperament.[43]

As mentioned in chapter 1,[44] several continental European theologians are responsible for the still widely held, but mistaken, view that Christian mysticism is Greek-infested, heretical Christianity. The four mystics presented so far offer, however, a full flowering of the Christian life, not its deformation. Furthermore, one can make a strong case for finding in these mystics an

213

acceptable Catholic version of the "by grace, faith and scripture alone" of the Reformation.[45]

It would be surprising to learn how few Christians have ever heard a homily or a talk on the deep, silent, imageless contemplation of John. How many have been initiated in any way into the riches of the apophatic way for nurturing a deeper sense of the ever-greater God? The challenge to Christianity from Eastern religions demands more than an emphasis upon dogma, discipline, the sacraments, and preaching. Contemporary Christians must be exposed to the vast riches of their own mystical heritage.

The God who is experienced as purifying, illuminating, and transforming love does not belong to an elite. He belongs to all Christians intent on seeking God with their entire being. He also belongs to all persons intent upon authentic human living.

Chapter Six

Thomas Merton (1915–1968)

The Trappist monk, Thomas Merton, stands as a twentieth-century, American supplement both to St. Teresa
of Avila and to St. John of the Cross. Because he did
not hesitate to use his own words to speak about his
own soul, his writings have a highly Teresian flavor.
Both were not afraid to reveal their most intimate longings, loves, joys, friendships, hopes, and fears. Both
have attractively revealed to us the syntheses, transfor-
mations, paradoxes, and contradictions which filled
their inner and outer lives. On the other hand, by revi-
talizing the Christian apophatic tradition, Merton also
echoes many of the favorite themes of St. John of the
Cross: the divine darkness, the radical emptiness, and
the desert experience that so characterize the apophatic
mystical way.[1]

Merton differs from both John and Teresa, however, in
one highly significant aspect. He blended in his writings the scriptures, the Fathers of the Church, the
Desert Fathers, the great Christian mystics, the Russian
Orthodox mystics, contemporary Catholic and Protestant theology, modern psychology, art, poetry, literature, existentialism, Taoism, and Buddhism with an incredible sensitivity for how all this bears on civil rights,
racial discrimination, the peace movement, nuclear dis-
armament, social justice, urban violence, poverty, ecumenism, and the East-West dialogue. This Trappist
monk, dedicated to silence, asceticism, contemplation,
and at times, a hermit-like existence, had friends and

contacts with people from almost every walk of life and from many different cultures and religions.[2]

By becoming in his person a melting pot for the monastic and mystical traditions as well as contemporary social concerns, Merton has influenced and continues to influence a wide cross-section of people. Simply by placing his finger on the pressure points of his own spiritual life, Merton wrote with passion, conviction, and clarity about the importance of Christian spirituality and mysticism for activist, twentieth-century America. Perhaps no one in this century has written so cogently about the main needs of this turbulent century: a spirituality and mysticism that rip away the facade of so much of contemporary posturing to disclose life's ultimate meaning as individual and social transformation by the God of truth and love.

Unlike Teresa and John, who focused more on the individual's transformation before God, Merton profoundly grasped and emphasized the significance of mysticism for effective social action and social transformation. To be sure, he never lost sight of the need for individual transformation as the basis of authentic social action and social transformation. And like the prophets of the Old Testament, Merton's purifying, illuminating, and transforming experience of God sensitized him in the most radical way to the burning social issues of our day. This experience forced him to speak out on these issues through a large amount of writing, incredible when one considers how little time his monk's life allowed him for this task.

To read his works is to touch Merton the man, monk, friend, writer, poet, scholar, teacher, student, solitary, social critic, part-time hermit, prophet, ecumenist, and voice of authority in the American Church, and far beyond. To an America just on the verge of awakening to its profoundest needs, he opened up and explained the monastic, contemplative, and mystical traditions. To

216

persons in these traditions, he showed how much of the "world" they had renounced was actually present within them. Yet he also showed what had to be used from the "world" for their renewal, transformation, and even survival. One can easily see why one contemporary writer has called him "the West's most influential fashioner of contemporary spirituality."[3]

It is almost impossible to summarize Merton's thought and experience. Most of his notebooks, journals, autobiographical reflections, and private correspondence are not yet available to scholars. Besides, his published works do not present a systematic and thorough treatment of any one theme. They stand rather as evidence of Merton's powerful and attractive personality. Also defying an adequate, systematic summary is his skillful and creative use of metaphor, symbols, images, and a variety of literary forms to convey his thought. For these reasons, therefore, this chapter limits itself to selected reflections on key aspects of Merton's thought.

THE SELF

Merton contends that every person instinctively desires to know and love the God of truth and love. Comparing the human spirit to a crystal left in darkness, Merton emphasizes that to be fully itself, it must receive the divine light outside and above it to transform it into a perfectly lucid crystal, which seemingly has its own nature absorbed in this light.[4] The human person created in God's image and likeness is destined for an intimate sharing in the divine life itself. Although Merton focused some attention on the human spirit's "natural" being, he stresses its "supernatural" destiny.

Because everyone shares in Adam's flight from unity with God, however, all remain in exile not only from God, but also from their own deepest self. Merton distinguishes sharply between a "true self," "deep self," "new self," "a self that is a 'no-self,'" "a hidden identity"; and a "false self," "shadow self," "outer self," "empirical self," "imaginary self," "mask," and "false identity."[5] For the most part, the external, daily self that we seem to be is a fabrication, a mask, and a distortion of our being that is made in God's image and likeness. "This evanescent shadow or shadow person" lives a lie by refusing to recognize its own helplessness and nothingness. Being a "slave of fantasy," this "worldly self" proclaims itself autonomous and a god unto itself. The human person is a living disaster because of the radical falsehood maintained between the person and the Creator and source of his being.

A return to the infinite ground of pure reality that establishes the person's true identity determines life's goal and task. The true self anchors itself only in God, according to Merton. In fact, this "transcendent self" is identified perfectly with God in love and freedom, but is metaphysically distinct from God. Because the true self made in God's image seems the very enemy of the daily, familiar self, the quest for authenticity requires a great battle. Moreover, the struggle for God is at the same time a struggle simply to be oneself, or, "to be what I am."[6]

The recentering of the self around God comes neither quickly nor easily. First, the core of one's personality transcends analytical, introspective analysis. Sharing in God's very mystery, it cannot be seized and fully comprehended like some interior object. Second, only radical silence, detachment, and humility prepare the way for the graced manifestations of this authentic self. For Merton, therefore, one must live a certain way to prepare for the disclosures of the divine image. One of the primary ways of living in genuine expectation is contemplative prayer.

CONTEMPLATIVE PRAYER
Because every person is involved in the struggle between the true and the false self, the human condition

demands a certain interior silence and discipline. Prayer should be an intrinsic part of every human life. As master of novices, Merton undoubtedly must have taught his charges traditional monastic techniques of prayer, meditation, and contemplation. One will search his writings in vain, however, for detailed information with respect to these specific methods.

Still, his writings do disclose the monastic orientation of Merton's views on prayer, meditation, and contemplation. Belonging to a praising community of faith, he underscored the value of the liturgical life, the sacraments, psalmody, Gregorian chant, and the meditative reading of scripture.[7] A few months of daily Mass, he claimed, had produced more self-emptying and being filled with God than many years of ascetical practices. He also saw no real opposition between the official, public prayer of the monastic community and the individual monk's spontaneous, personal prayer. Labeling the alleged dichotomy between liturgical and private prayer a "modern fiction," he viewed social and individual prayer as the systole and diastole of a holistic approach to prayer. Of its very nature, liturgical prayer must lead to private prayer; private prayer, in its turn, prepares the way for even deeper liturgical worship.

Merton saw the necessity of integrating the senses, the body, and the more fleshly dimensions of human life for worship, meditation, and contemplation that involved the entire person. Ritual, psalmody, Gregorian chant, symbols, and images served this purpose well. These methods purified, healed, and transformed the manifold levels of the individual human being. For Merton, the discipline and practices of a traditional monastic community stabilized a beginner in the life of prayer, aided in the consolidation of the novice's identity, imparted confidence, and deepened the realization that the spiritual life has an attainable goal.

For personal prayer, Merton suggests: attentive vocal prayer; the loving, repetitive use of the name of Jesus; the slow, sapiential recitation of a favorite psalm; invoking God by memorizing, interiorizing, and saying from the heart certain biblical words and expressions; and traditional meditation. Although Merton was not opposed to meditative reasoning centered on the truths of salvation history, he favored reasoning that led into a loving intuition of the truth with one deep, piercing gaze.[8] All forms of prayer for Merton, especially mental prayer, should end in love. Genuine religious meditation proceeds from love and looks for the truth emanating from love. Possessing God's truth by way of a loving knowledge, it seeks to live this truth in love. Religious meditation may begin as an intellectual activity that recollects the human spirit, but it must give way to love, reverence, and adoration.

As indicated briefly above, Merton stresses the supernatural destiny of all creation. This means that the human person was created for and invited to something beyond his natural ability: to share the very life of God. Merton's supernatural vision brands as atheism any attitude that assumes the autonomy of the "natural" and the "unspiritual" world.[9] But there is still another side to his supernatural perspective. No natural techniques can cause mystical contact between the person and the living God.[10] As a divine gift, mystical contemplation cannot be obtained through personal initiative. God himself must speak at the very roots of a person's being to initiate the transition from "ordinary" to mystical prayer. For Merton, contemplative prayer remains a free gift and personal vocation expressing the mystery of divine love.

Borrowing from the Christian mystical tradition, Merton gives three signs which indicate the call to mystical prayer.[11] First, the person nakedly and blindly searches for God, despite the seeming aridity, uselessness, and sterility of his prayer. Second, the normal cares and concerns of daily life no longer matter. The person vaguely senses that what is really meaningful will be found at the depth of this dry prayer. Third, despite the surface barrenness of the prayer, the person has no desire to give it up. The attraction to this dry form of prayer may be so strong at times that pain will give way to a delicious peace and solitude. And like those in the Christian mystical tradition before him, Merton urges the patient, simple, generous giving of oneself to ordinary prayer until one is definitively called to infused contemplation. Merton never denigrates the ordinary ways of prayer. They may prepare a person for the higher stages of contemplative prayer and bring about his transformation.

Prayer, meditation, and contemplation must always be more than technique.[12] Merton stresses the person's attitude and outlook, not the technique used. Faith, hope, love, trust, joy, openness, attentiveness, expectation, reverence, and supplication characterize this attitude. The person of genuine prayer shows not a magical trust in techniques, but a poverty, nakedness, and detachment from all that is superfluous. A silent, total surrender to the mysterious and dark presence of God at the center of one's being is the hallmark of authentic prayer.

Merton views contemplative prayer "like a mind awake in the dark, looking for a light, not totally reconciled to being out of bed."[13] Authentic prayer springs from the crises of living and paradoxically may even intensify these conflicts. It makes the person more sensitive both to sinfulness and to God's gracious love. Still, waiting for God in emptiness and silence may not only indicate that our capacity to receive him has been enlarged, but also that we are already resting in a God who seeks us before we seek him.

Contemplative prayer for Merton is very much "prayer of the heart." One must enter the soul's core and transcend it to discover the God who constitutes the true self. This journey to the heart of one's being requires compunction and compassion, not introversion. The inward journey awakens the person to experience God in the inner sanctuary as presence and grace. It likewise awakens the contemplative to the Real in all reality. One who prays with the heart can find God in all things and ignore the rest.[14] This delicate sinking into his true self anchors the person in the totality of life. It bestows a deep "respect for the concrete realities of every-day life, for nature, for the body, for one's work, one's friends, one's surroundings, etc."[15] Authentic prayer roots a person more deeply in God, in one's true self, and in all life itself.

Merton cautions against expecting something spectacular to happen during prayer.[16] The essential feature of prayer occurs at a level beyond emotions, instincts, and "experiences" in the usual sense. To be sure, deep religious emotions prove most useful in weaning beginners from their disordered desires. Overemphasis upon emotions, consolations, and experiences, however, may produce two undesirable effects. Either the person may give up prayer altogether when the prayer becomes dry; or, if the person is emotional by nature, too much emotionality may result. Therefore, Merton emphasizes what happens in the soul's very depths beyond emotion and instinct. Genuine prayer produces an experiential, yet often anonymous, contact between the living God and the person. This contact slowly transforms the person and reverses his values at the unconscious and preconscious levels. In summary, contemplative prayer for Merton: ". . . is, in a way, simply the preference for the desert, for emptiness, for poverty. . . . Only when we are able to 'let go' of everything within us, all desire to see, to know, to taste and to experience the presence of God, do we truly become able to experience that presence with the overwhelming conviction and reality that revolutionize our entire inner life."[17]

THE WAY OF EMPTINESS AND DARKNESS

Like many in the Christian mystical tradition, Merton emphasizes the arid and dark side of the purifying, illuminating, and transforming contemplative experience of the God of truth and love. Firmly rooted in the apophatic tradition, Merton focuses upon mystical contemplation as essentially a self-emptying activity that fills one with God.[18]

There is also a sense in which Merton's theology is essentially a "crisis" mystical theology. God reveals himself to the contemplative only when he has embraced the "wilderness of the human spirit," the inner desert in which he comes face to face with his own nothingness, sinfulness, helplessness, infidelity, ignorance, and total need for God. The contemplative imitates Christ's own kenosis and experiences an emptiness and a seeming loss of faith that actually deepens his faith.

Mystical contemplation forces a person below the surface comforts of his basic narcissism to face the hell that exists because of the self's lived lie. The genuine contemplative soon tastes the bitterness of not being the self he is called to be and the real guilt that flows from not facing up to the split between the true self and the false self. Ripped away from the diversions, distractions, and superficialities of contemporary living, the contemplative experiences the guilt, suspicion, and hatred brewing in the human heart. He awakens to "an awareness of infidelity as unrepented and without grace as *unrepentable.*"[19]

When the artificial props of daily life are pulled away, the contemplative begins to dread and to doubt. Mystical contemplation plunges him into the real emptiness, helplessness, and futility which characterize the human situation without God. Not only does the contemplative

223

awaken to his own nothingness, sinfulness, and meaningless existence separated from God, but he experiences more deeply how paltry his love is when compared to the Love that loves him.

In short, Merton delineates the basic movement of the classical dark nights of the senses and the spirit of the mystical way. Prayer, meditation, and contemplation cause pain by turning the senses, emotions, memory, intellect, and will away from their usual pleasures. They also heighten the awareness of one's past and present sins, radical sinfulness, separated existence, and inability to love. Merton's originality rests in transposing this movement into the language and framework of contemporary existential philosophy, as exemplified in Kierkegaard, Camus, Sartre, Jaspers, Unamuno, Heidegger, and Marcel.

For Merton, emptiness has both a negative and a positive connotation. The contemplative experiences the emptiness of being a finite, sinful creature separated from God. Genuine contemplation, however, also involves a Christ-like self-emptying, or radical detachment from all forms of selfishness. Authentic emptiness cannot be obtained through techniques. Because it renders the person Christ-like, it is a precious gift of God with a radical soteriological function. It is a movement toward divine fullness, not merely the absence and the negativity of a pure void. In fact, like others in the Christian apophatic tradition, Merton calls God himself "Emptiness" or a "Nothingness." In this tradition, emptiness and fullness are equivalent.

Merton studied the mystical traditions of both light and darkness.[20] For him, these were basically different languages to describe an identical mystical process. Striving to reconcile the apophatic and kataphatic mystical traditions, he criticized those who focused exclusively on the former as authentic mysticism. On the other hand, there is no doubt that Merton's writings show a preference for the images, symbols, and emphases of the apophatic tradition.

For example, he spoke of the "infinitely productive darkness of contemplation" and of the monastic life as nurturing "the darkness of contemplation." For him, contemplation is a plunging into the "luminous darkness," the "dark fire," and the "clear darkness." In a general way, therefore, darkness describes contemplative prayer for Merton. Yet as indicated above, darkness both causes and is caused by contemplation. Aridity, suffering, crises, dread, anxiety, and doubt drive the monk to contemplation and are, in turn, intensified by contemplation. Darkness becomes the inner atmosphere of contemplation that prepares us for God. The authentic contemplative waits for God in purposelessness, emptiness, and darkness.

For Merton, however, darkness is more than the asceticism of waiting for God. True union with God takes place in this darkness. God communicates himself in this darkness. The contemplative actually "sees" God in a cloud of darkness. For Merton, "in the deepest spiritual darkness, in the most profound night of unknowing, in the purity of naked faith, God unites the soul to Himself in mystical union."[21] This darkness, however, is light. Because God, in whom there is no darkness, is so overwhelmingly light, he overpowers the human mind and so appears to it as pure darkness. Like the owl looking into the noonday sun, the contemplative looks into the divine light, which brings about his liberation from the lesser lights that fill his mind.[22] In short, there is nothing gloomy about the divine darkness that is pure light.

Although the language of apophatic mysticism seems negative and harsh at first glance, in the way of emptiness and darkness, God intimately embraces the contemplative and produces an ever-deeper reordering of his loves. The contemplative experiences nothing less than the presence of a Someone who is love, who is "God-given and God Himself as Gift. God as All, and God reduced to Nothing: inexhaustible nothingness."[23] Calling the person into the very mystery of love present and working, this Love transforms the contemplative into God by a union of love.

THE WAY OF DIFFERENTIATED UNITY

Merton refused to give in to the contemporary temptation to reduce mystical experiences to "peak experiences."[24] He is unlike the psychologist Abraham Maslow and his followers, for whom music, art, scientific discovery, friendship, love, sex, giving birth, nature, and prayer can trigger joyful, ecstatic moments of rapture wherein people feel most themselves and "self-actualized."[25] Self-validating and seeming to reconcile life's conflicts, peak experiences produce feelings of awe, reverence, surrender, love, and compassion.

Merton correctly points out, however, that mystical experiences are more specific than peak experiences. While it may be true that some mystical experiences fall under the very broad category of peak experiences, not all peak experiences are mystical. Maslow's description of peak experience also overlooks the radical experience of one's sinfulness, nothingness, and helplessness that occurs in genuine contemplation.

Merton explicitly refuses to identify erotic, aesthetic, athletic, moral, nature, and even normal stages of religious and spiritual experiences with mystical experience. Mystical experience brings about a self-transcendence, a going out of and beyond oneself, to be in contact with nothing less than a personal God. This contact may develop into a loving union so intense that God and the contemplative appear to be one and the same, although their separate substances do not actually fuse. With definite echoes from the Christian mystical tradition, Merton speaks of the person becoming God by participation.

226

Furthermore, during contemplative prayer, the division between subject and object disappears. The contemplative discovers his true self in God, one with God, but not simply God. Merton further distinguishes the daily, empirical, selfish ego from a "transcendent Self which . . . is metaphysically distinct from the Self of God and yet perfectly identified with that Self by love and freedom, so that there appears to be but one Self."[26] The contemplative does not fuse with God nor does the mystical experience simply annihilate the person's identity. Merton does distinguish between the contemplative's personal identity and true self, which are not lost, and the isolated, empirical ego, which is. As he says: "In the Christian tradition the focus of this 'experience' is found not in the individual self as a separate, limited and temporal ego, but in Christ, or the Holy Spirit 'within' this Self."[27]

In summary, Merton emphasizes mysticism's high point as a personal experience of a personal God culminating in a loving union of transformation. The contemplative and God become truly one in love, but two in their respective identities. Although one may speak of God and the contemplative mutually dwelling within each other, the fusion or merging of identities does not take place. The genuine Christian mystic experiences and undergoes a differentiated love union with God.

Merton also calls attention to God's transpersonal quality. The Christian mystical tradition has long experienced and recognized that God is only analogously personal. It makes sense, therefore, for Merton to call God "Subject," "Person," "Nothing," and "Emptiness." The Christian mystical tradition has never hesitated to predicate both personal and impersonal names and attributes of God.[28]

Although it is true that mystical experience gives the person a new experiential center of gravity, Merton's distinction between the true self and the empirical ego raises certain problems. During some mystical experiences, the daily, empirical ego is lost in an ecstasy of love. It can be asked, however, if on this point Merton focuses upon mysticism too much as an experience and not enough as a state of being wherein the contemplative always experiences his unity with God in the very depths of his being. The empirical ego in this state does not disappear, although its outlook has been widened. It would seem that Merton could have learned something valuable for his distinction between the true self and the empirical ego from Teresa's distinction between spirit and soul, as discussed above.[29]

Merton correctly rejects the contemporary tendency to view mystical experience as a form of "regression in the service of the ego."[30] Mysticism cannot be explained as a reduction to an unconscious, subconscious, or preconscious experience of a lower biological or psychological stage in the person's development. It is not, for example, a remembrance of the ecstatic fusion of sperm and ovum at one's conception, of the joy of fusion with the mother's breast as an infant, or of the pleasure of fainting. Genuine mystical experience for Merton is a matter of "superconsciousness," a qualitatively higher stage of consciousness than even rational consciousness. Neither irrational nor a lower level of consciousness, mystical consciousness is transrational and the highest state of human consciousness possible.[31] It should likewise be noted that for Merton, mystical consciousness always increases the person's unity with God, with himself, with others, and with all God's creation.

THE PERSON OF JESUS CHRIST
The person of Jesus Christ plays a central role in the life of any Christian community. Merton's Trappist monastery contained a Christocentric foundation, ambiance, and goal. Grounded in the imitation of Christ, the monastic life directs the monk to becoming another

Christ. The liturgical life, the emphasis upon scripture, monastic art, piety, and practices establish firmly the radically Christocentric atmosphere within which the individual monk and the monastic community live their daily and deepest life.

It seems obvious, therefore, that Merton should never really have had any serious problems about the role of Jesus Christ in the monastic and mystical life. The obvious place of Jesus Christ in Christian monastic and mystical life may account for why Merton said relatively little about Christ in his writings. Rarely does one need to discuss the obvious.

To be sure, Merton did have some things to say about Jesus Christ, albeit not with much originality.[32] For example, union with Christ establishes our divine sonship and the possibility of eternal life. Not merely a wise man with a new doctrine, Christ effected the mystical transformation of humanity through his incarnation. One can become oneself only in Christ, therefore, for the true self is rooted in Christ. In fact, Christ's image is in all of us, and part of the Christian's task is to find that image in others as well as in the self. Merton's view of all life as sacramental flowed from his appreciation of the incarnation. His deeply Christian humanism was emphatically incarnational and was totally committed to the presence of Christ in the world. Even his great love for many things in the Eastern mystical religions and his famous journey to the East radicalized his faith and his sense of the inner presence of Christ.[33]

The solitary prayer that so attracted Merton found its paradigm in the solitary prayer of Christ at night on the mountain.[34] Contemplation in general, moreover, "is a deep participation in the Christ-life, a spiritual sharing in the union of God and Man which is the hypostatic union."[35] Without solving all the problems on this matter, Merton was aware of the difficulty of reconciling his apophatic mysticism, which demands the forget-

ting of all thoughts and images, with a Christianity
rooted inextricably in the person of Jesus Christ. He
viewed contemplative prayer in its self-emptying aspect
as a necessary particpation in Christ's own kenosis. The
true goal of all Christian prayer, meditation, and contemplation is to bring about a loving union with Christ,
the incarnate Word. Christ's resurrection and ascension
are likewise the source of the person's divinization. For
this reason, contemplation is not only possible, but all
mystical graces are solidly Christocentric. Much like the
Cloud, Merton's apophatic way of emptiness and darkness retains a special love for the man Jesus and links
the contemplative process itself to Christ's own self-
emptying. Without giving the last word on this difficult
problem, Merton writes: "No one can dismiss the Man
Christ from his interior life on the pretext that he has
now entered by higher contemplation into direct communication with the Word."[36]

THE MONASTIC WAY

Merton highly praised the transforming and life-giving
effects of the monastic tradition. First and foremost, the
monastic life creates a favorable atmosphere in which
the monk's sense of the supernatural may awaken. Free
of family, ambition, social climbing, job, and even an
active apostolate, the monk seeks to live solely for God
and for others, with an increasing sensitivity to the call
of the God of truth and love.[37]

Without the time-consuming cares of a more active
worldly life, the monastic life centers upon conversion
and change of heart. The physical labors, the humiliations, the annoyances of common life, the tedium of
the daily routine, the rhythm of the liturgy, the asceticism in general—all these elements of the monastic life
serve to destroy the escape routes from God and one's
true self. These seemingly negative elements create an
atmosphere of emptiness to be filled with prayer, meditation, and contemplation. The monastic discipline

strives to foster an atmosphere favorable to the mystical experience of God. "The climate in which monastic prayer flowers," Merton writes, "is that of the desert, where the comfort of man is absent, where the routine securities of man's city offer no support, and where prayer must be sustained by God in the purity of faith."[38] The monastic life blends the penance of Lazarus and the physical activity of Martha to nourish the contemplation of Mary.[39]

In this way, Merton underscored the monastic life as the implicit and explicit ambiance for apophatic mystical ascent. For him, there was a reciprocal relationship between a thorough and mature monastic culture and growth in apophatic contemplation. Like the psychologist, Carl Jung, who protected himself during his perilous journeys into the psyche by increasing his family and social life, Merton grasped the necessity of the monastic tradition, life, and community for stabilizing the contemplative's own mystical ascent.[40] Even the apophatic mystical life is not a flight of the "alone to the Alone," but the sharing in a traditional, historical, and communal life that implicitly and explicitly fosters, nurtures, and protects it. Even Merton's attraction to a more hermit-like existence never lost sight of the social grounding for physical and spiritual solitude.[41]

The monastic life and apophatic prayer interpenetrated in still another way for Merton.[42] He saw that all genuine mystical traditions bring about psychosomatic integration, awaken the individual's spiritual senses, and deepen his aesthetic sense, all in the service of opening the way to the dark, silent, loving contemplation of unknowing. Poetic and theological gifts frequently accompanied a deepening of apophatic contemplation, especially if this grace was to be shared with others. And despite Merton's emphasis upon love and unknowing during the contemplative process, he called attention to the necessity of good theology to foster authentic mysticism. Never, in fact, did Merton see theology and mysticism as necessarily in competition.

Although the early Merton romantically viewed the monastic life as a superior form of existence, the more mature Merton wrote: "My task is only to be what I am, a man seeking God in silence and solitude, with deep respect for the demand and realities of his own vocation, and fully aware that others too are seeking the truth in their own way."[43] To be sure, the monastic life renounces the "world" and dramatically calls into question the values of secular life. For Merton, however, this means that the monk quickly awakens to that part of the "world" that lives within him. In a sense, the monk becomes more interested in the "world" than his secular counterparts because his way of life sensitizes him to the deepest and most hidden things that those in the world refuse to face about it. Therefore, the monk has an important worldly function which is "this silence, this listening, this questioning, this humble and courageous exposure to what the world ignores about itself—both good and evil."[44] By plunging into the "world" in his own naked humanity, the monk discloses the two basic facets of human existence: his own and society's lived untruth, and the mercy, healing, and transformation offered by the God of truth and love.

THE DEAD END OF PSEUDO-MYSTICISM
As indicated above, Merton stressed genuine emptiness and finding one's true self by way of God's healing and transforming gift of grace. It is not surprising, therefore, to find in Merton's writings strong warnings against narcissism, self-preoccupation, and a comfortable flight from the world.[45] For example, he condemned the false mysticism that permeates so much of contemporary life, with its excessive self-preoccupation and its frequent substitution of drugs and sex for love. By seeking a selfish, subjective peace and interior comfort by means of a bourgeois, bogus spirituality that

avoids responsibility and cares little for others, the pseudo-mystic lives worlds apart from the true self sought by Merton.

Even monastic practices and asceticism can develop into an obstacle to radical conversion, if the monk becomes morbidly obsessed with his own psychological processes and reactions. The self can become a vicious trap if prayer, meditation, and contemplation turn a person in upon his own thoughts, ideas, emotions, and experiences in general. When prayer, meditation, and contemplation become merely techniques for producing a false peace or an anodyne against the experience of our own radical poverty and nakedness, they harden the monk in the lies and illusions of the false self. "Far from establishing one in unassailable narcissistic security," Merton writes, "the way of prayer brings us face to face with the sham and indignity of the false self that seeks to live for itself alone and to enjoy the 'consolation of prayer' for its own sake."[46] There is, therefore, a bogus interiority that refuses to go beyond what is immediately pleasant and comfortable. A monk may even fall victim to the comfort afforded him by his reputation for piety, asceticism, and holiness.

Merton was only too well aware of a self-controlled spiritual voiding of the self that fills the person with spiritual pride.[47] In agreement with many in the classical Christian apophatic tradition, Merton distinguishes between a self-emptying caused by God's grace and a willful, almost suprahuman, effort to void the self which culminates in a deadening void. As Merton says: ". . . to become a Yogi and to be able to commit moral and intellectual suicide whenever you please, without the necessity of actually dying, to be able to black out your mind by the incantation of half articulate charms and to enter into a state of annihilation, in which all the faculties are inactive and the soul is as inert as if it were dead—all this may well appeal to certain minds

233

as a refined and rather pleasant way of getting even with the world and with society, and with God Himself for that matter."[48]

Pseudo-mysticism may produce a willful annihilation of certain mental activities, therefore, but not the genuine spiritual death needed for transformed life. Certain self-voiding techniques may mimic the ways of authentic forgetting and unknowing, but they result in a spiritual vacuum, a blank, a dead state of soul. Artificial voiding of the self traps the person in the unregenerated darkness of his own trivial self. This bogus darkness is not the illuminated, fecund darkness of apophatic mysticism, but the gloom of the absence of wisdom. Walled up in the narcissistic seclusion of his own inner darkness, the pseudo-mystic creates the emptiness of a hell that is paradoxically full of self. Even in mysticism, nothing is sometimes only nothing.

THE WAY OF SERVICE
If Merton castigated the pseudo-mystical currents swelling in contemporary life, he likewise harshly condemned the pseudo-spirituality of activism.[49] Hyperactivism dangerously eschews the need for prayer, meditation, and contemplation. Today's Christian faces the serious temptation of worshiping political pressure groups, causes, movements, slogans, and ideologies. Without authentic inner freedom, contemplative peace, spiritual insight, the love born from prayer, integration, and inner transformation, social involvement degenerates into "pseudo-activism."

If pseudo-mysticism escapes into subjective peace without caring for others, pseudo-activism for Merton is also a flight from the truly human. Without saints, mystics, and prophets, an authentic social order is an impossibility. An unregenerate activist can cause serious harm to himself, to others, and to society. By throwing himself into action, he will only infect others with his sinfulness, brokenness, egoism, delusions, illusions, obsessions, violence, and hatreds. Even Merton had to confess that occasionally his desire to help others and to be open had led him into real delusion.[50]

Prayer, meditation, and contemplation provide not an escape from the world, but the best means for seeing it in God's light.[51] Merton saw little temptation today to neglect apostolic service and external activity. The chief danger facing contemporary Christians is their tendency to neglect the inner life that is the very heart and soul of genuine Christian service.

Merton's own life provides an example of how radical solitude and service can temper and transform the monk's occasional self-righteous flight from the world. Real solitude and silence caused in Merton a kindness, compassion, and strong identification with the sinful, suffering world that God heals and forgives.[52]

Merton refused to reduce contemplation to another phase of the active life, to activity accompanied by prayer.[53] Although contemplation is a resting in God, a taste of the "heavenly life," it is still the cleaving to the God who creates, redeems, heals, and divinizes the world. By living in his heart with God, the monk touches the very center where all persons and all created things actually are one. In this way, the contemplative truly enters into the world's very heart to bring about its transformation. Contemplative love is by its nature healing, redemptive, and divinizing; it participates in that love with which God so loved the world.

According to Merton, the monk must get to the roots of the world's good and evil, not by action and analysis, but by simplicity, silence, and solitude. Still, the monk must avoid being a "guilty by-stander." "Even he must to some extent," Merton writes, "participate 'actively' in the Church's work, not only by prayer and holiness, but by understanding and concern."[54] Precisely because of Merton's informed contemplation, he was able to speak prophetically from the desert of his monastery on many of the burning social issues of our day.

Merton rejected the reduction of contemplation to a means for social action, but did see it flowing into powerful social action for some who have the proper vocation.[55] In fact, contemplative prayer is frequently deepened when accompanied by graces that cause the sharing of its fruits with others.

Merton contended that genuine mystical prayer is impossible without a genuine love of and openness to others. One cannot enter one's heart and transcend it into God without being able to forget oneself for the sake of others. For Merton, the true self is found not only in God but also in others. The contemplative cannot really trust and love God without a corresponding trust and love of others.

THE WAY OF THE ORDINARY AND HIDDEN CONTEMPLATION

Jesus Christ lived a rather commonplace existence for most of his life and is the paradigm of the dignity of ordinary human existence lived in truth, love, and authenticity.[56] For Merton, the incarnation in general had the effect of sanctifying the most ordinary human life. Merton placed great emphasis upon the value of the ordinary in human living. Contemplative prayer must be concerned with, interested in, and permeate every single aspect of human life. Far from elevating the contemplative above ordinary Christian life, authentic contemplation has the opposite effect. The genuine contemplative is plunged even more deeply into the ordinary trials and sufferings of human existence. The seeming emptiness, meaninglessness, and monotony of daily life characterize authentic contemplative prayer, not extraordinary experiences, a privileged state, or a secret, esoteric knowledge reserved for an elite. Purity of

236

heart, self-forgetfulness in the service of others, and total dedication to God in love and service are the real hallmarks of the mystical life, not the search for extraordinary experiences which sometimes punctuate that life.

Mystics, in the strict sense, will always be few and far between, for the way of infused contemplation requires a special vocation. Yet because mysticism is the normal way to Christian perfection, Merton contends that all Christians are called to the mystical life.[57] All are called to the mystical orientation of the entire life of prayer: the experience of the emptiness, purity, and nakedness involved in genuine self-giving. For Merton, therefore, there is a latent, or implicit, infused dimension to all prayer. He also makes the valuable distinction between explicit and masked contemplation: not only are there those who both experience and realize that they have experienced infused contemplation, but there are others who experience it, but are not aware of it.

The hidden, or masked, contemplative finds God in active service, usually to the poor, despised, and marginal persons of life. By disposition, temperament, and calling, these masked contemplatives cannot turn to the silence, solitude, and leisure of the monastic life to effect their self-emptying. Instead, in the hectic exterior activity for which they are psychologically suited, they identify in a special way with the "least" of Jesus' brethren, and so do unto him as they do unto them. Their purity of heart, obedience, love, compassion, self-sacrifice, and abandonment to God's will in all they do and suffer cause the self-emptying found at the heart of infused contemplation, although they remain unaware of this. Merton deeply valued the implicit, hidden, unspectacular nature of masked contemplation. This is the hallmark of authentic spirituality, for it is a participation in God's very own hiddenness and obscurity.

237

Even in his student days before his conversion at Columbia University, Merton had awakened somewhat to the power latent in the Eastern and Western mystical traditions to combat what he perceived as a growing Western materialism. Aldous Huxley's *End and Means* planted the seed that was to develop into Merton's full-grown appreciation for the values of Oriental mysticisms and religions. Ironically, too, it was his deeply spiritual Hindu monk friend, Bramachari, who had called Merton's attention to the wealth of Christian mystical literature.

After his conversion and entry into the monastic life, however, Merton became somewhat critical of Eastern mysticisms. His autobiography, *The Seven Storey Mountain*, contends that the ways of the East are not mysticism at all.[58] At most, they are natural techniques for producing peace and tranquillity and have no value for the supernatural life. They also tend to mix with magic and superstition and to degenerate into the demonic.

Still, Merton never really lost his awareness of the *universal* striving for purification, illumination, integration, and intuitive union with the Absolute that characterizes the world's great religions. Thus, he not only criticized the continental European Protestants who rejected Christian mysticism as a Greek-infested aberration of a pristine Christianity, but also castigated the activist, secular, antimystical, and overly Marxist orientation of many contemporary Catholic movements.[59]

Rejoicing in Vatican II's openness to Oriental religions, Merton in the 1960s strongly identified with Eastern mysticisms, especially Zen. He wrote strongly against the prevailing view that saw in them only a penchant for psychological and spiritual suicide, selfish navel gazing, pantheism, hatred for the body and matter in general, and escaping life through drug-like trances. On the contrary, these religions were life-affirming and transforming. Their ancient meditation and monastic practices were extremely effective in destroying the illusions of the false self and establishing the true self in its authentic relationship to the whole of reality. In fact, there were good reasons for believing that the outstanding religious figures in the Hindu, Buddhist, and Islamic traditions were mystics in the strictly supernatural sense of the word, that is, those who had experienced purification by, illumination by, and union with the God of truth and love.[60]

Merton confessed that he had much more in common with the Oriental monks—who emphasized silence, meditation, peace, compassion, and reverence for life—than with his fellow Westerners—fixated on money, power, publicity, militarism, practical advantage, and having their own way.[61] Oriental religions could open a Westerner to the depths of his own Christian tradition, qualitatively improve upon it, and might even be necessary for the West's physical and spiritual survival.[62] Not only may Christians faithful to their own tradition learn much from these great religions, says Merton, but they must do so for the sake of the Christian tradition itself. For Merton, as a supernaturally revealed religion, Christianity needs nothing from the East, but it must incarnate itself in specific social and cultural contexts, that is, assimilate elements from the East in the same way that Greek culture and Roman law were so important for Christianity.

In 1968, Merton journeyed to the Far East as a humble pilgrim in search of the special places of Oriental purification, illumination, and transformation. One Merton scholar, Elena Malits, points out that he had already made this trip spiritually.[63] He had read, studied, and even meditated upon many of the Eastern mystical classics and their commentators. He corresponded vigorously with scholars and practitioners of Eastern religions and mysticisms.

239

In his *Asian Journal,* Merton offers a clear glimpse of his attitude toward Oriental religions. He wrote: "I come as a pilgrim who is anxious to obtain not just information, nor just 'facts' about other monastic traditions, but to drink from ancient sources of monastic vision and experience. I seek not only to learn more (quantitatively) about religion and about monastic life, but to become a better and more enlightened monk (qualitatively) myself."[64] Merton was convinced that a genuine ecumenical dialogue with the religions of the East was both possible and necessary. Although insurmountable theological disagreements existed, genuine dialogue and even communion were possible because of a common basis in religious experiences nurtured in the monastic atmosphere of silence, solitude, and reverence. This preverbal and postverbal monastic basis could provide a strong link that their respective theologies were impotent to accomplish.

Although Merton manifested a great openness to all the great Oriental religions, he was especially attracted to Zen.[65] Merton's deep friendship with the Zen writer, D. T. Suzuki, and Suzuki's influence upon Merton's many articles on Zen reveal this attraction. Suzuki embodied for Merton "all the indefinable qualities of the 'Superior Man' of the ancient Asian, Taoist, Confucian and Buddhist traditions."[66] Moreover, Merton found in his study of the Christian Desert Fathers that their solitude, poverty, emptiness, compassion, and unconventional rejection of the world manifested a Zen-like attitude toward life.

Merton found many similarities between the Zen and the Christian experience of life. For example, Zen "illusion" or "ignorance" is much more than intellectual deficiency, and actually akin to Christian "sin," especially "original sin," since it indicates a lived lie with reference to all reality. The "great death" and "emptiness" required in Zen before final enlightenment find their

240

Christian counterparts in the "dark nights" of St. John of the Cross and Cassian's "purity of heart." What Zen finds in "compassion," Christians find in "charity." The Zen ego that must die to become the "no-Self" shows itself in the Christian dying to self to live in Christ. Zen "nirvana" is the "complete realization of love not merely as the emotion of a feeling subject but as the wide openness of Being itself, the realization that Pure Being is Infinite Giving, or that Absolute Emptiness is Absolute Compassion."[67] Zen "nirvana" is, therefore, what Christ meant by "Spirit and Life." To defend Zen against its alleged impersonalism, Merton called attention to Suzuki's emphasis upon love and to the deep personalism of the Zen philosopher, Nishida.[68]

Zen's profound affirmation of life and vigorous repudiation of narcissistic introversion attracted Merton. "Zen is," Merton writes, "the very awareness of life living itself in us."[69] Especially compelling to Merton was its ability to destroy egoism, illusions, and the lies of the false self and generate authentic human living. Merton's remark that he wanted "to become as good a Buddhist as I can," which shocked so many pious Christians, must be understood in the context of Zen's power to destroy inauthentic human living.[70]

Merton found no contradiction between Zen and Christianity. Both Christians and Buddhists could practice it, "if by Zen we mean precisely the quest for direct and pure experience on a metaphysical level, liberated from verbal formulas and linguistic preoccupations."[71] Neither a religion, nor a philosophy, nor an asceticism, nor a way of salvation, nor a mysticism in the Western sense, Zen had no more to do with religion, Merton contended, than the essential teachings of St. John of the Cross had to do with the baroque incidentals in his writings.[72] Zen could no more be compared with Christianity than math with tennis. Neither supernatural revelation nor kerygma, Zen is a type of consciousness and

241

realization. For Merton, "Zen is consciousness unstructured by particular form or particular system, a transcultural, trans-religious, trans-formed consciousness."[73] Zen is a form of pure consciousness and enlightenment immediately aware of the "suchness" and the "thusness" of being itself. As transverbal, attentive, non-clinging awareness, it can permeate any religion.

It must be emphasized, however, that Merton repudiated both a facile syncretism and a concordist view in his approach to Oriental religions.[74] For Merton, mystics the world over do not experience the same thing nor transcend in an elitist way the philosophies and theologies of their respective traditions. In addition, interpretation is never extrinsic to mystical experience, something that can be cast aside once the experience is given.

Yet he did find certain universal elements common to monks of every age and culture. In some ways, the essence of authentic religious experience varied little from religion to religion. Total dedication, ongoing effort, real discipline, guidance from experienced teachers, the combining of wisdom and technique, a critical distance and detachment from secular life, emphasis upon the experiential dimensions of religious beliefs, a concern for inner transformation and the eventual union with an Absolute, a recognition that more than ethical and pious attitudes are required in life—these and other characteristics bind monks together from every age and culture. The following quotation illustrates how nuanced Merton was in his view of the unity-in-diversity found in the world's great religions: "Without asserting that there is complete unity of all religions at the 'top,' the transcendent or mystical level—that they all start from different dogmatic positions to 'meet' at this summit—it is certainly true to say that even where there are irreconcilable differences in doctrine and in formulated beliefs, there may still be great similarities and analogies in the realm of religious experience. . . . Cultural and doctrinal differences must remain, but they do not invalidate the very real quality of existential likeness."[75]

What was important in all religions for Merton was the quest to become the fully integrated, universal man.[76] The cosmic man integrates all the authentic, diverse elements found in various religions, while being faithful to and deepening his own religious tradition. His emptiness and docility to the Spirit give rise to a creative, full inner life that embraces all life, even in its particularities. Transcending these particularities, he still retains the best and the universal in them in a unified vision. The fully integrated, universal man has both his own radical self-identity and yet, in a certain sense, is identified with everyone. Perhaps Merton had reached this goal. He certainly desired it when he wrote: "If I can unite *in myself* the thought and the devotion of Eastern and Western Christendom, the Greek and the Latin Fathers, the Russians with the Spanish mystics, I can prepare in myself the reunion of divided Christians . . . We must contain all divided worlds in ourselves and transcend them in Christ."[77]

CONCLUDING REFLECTIONS

For a variety of reasons, only rather recently have many Christians recognized the importance of the Christian apophatic mystical tradition for a contemporary Christian spirituality and mysticism. For much too long, some of the great twentieth-century continental European Protestant theologians had infected many with their ignorance of, hostility to, and rejection of all forms of mysticism as "esoteric atheism."[78]

On the other hand, Catholicism has always encouraged a variety of contemplative orders dedicated to the mystical life and has viewed such a life as the full-flowering of Christian existence. Still, Church authorities have not been blind to the aberrations and dangers that the mystical life sometimes brings forth. The quietistic *tendency* of the apophatic tradition has been especially troublesome. Heretical quietism rejects asceticism, vocal prayer, the prayer of petition, ordinary meditation, and even concern for one's own salvation. Trapped in an empty inwardness and a perverse resignation, pseudo-mystical quietism claims to unite the person so completely to God that he is above "ordinary Christians," especially in moral matters. It is no wonder that much of Catholic pastoral emphasis has been upon the "safe" route of ordinary prayer, the sacraments, approved devotions, dogma, obedience, and discipline.

The serious neglect of Christianity's apophatic mystical tradition may be one of the many reasons for the contemporary interest in Eastern religions, mysticism, and techniques. A Christianity that ignores its apophatic dimension must become dessicated and truncated. Merton was on the cutting edge of the retrieval of the depths and richness of the Christian apophatic mystical tradition. As one Merton scholar writes: "Merton's primary significance is this revitalization of apophaticism in the present age and his singularity in American religious history."[79] The way of dark, silent, imageless, loving contemplation prevents not only the ever-greater God but also the risen Christ from being reduced to the ideas, concepts, images, and views we have of them. Especially with the contemporary striving for the deeper levels of experience that nourish any great living religion, Merton's emphasis upon the Christian apophatic tradition is of special importance for a vital American spirituality and mysticism.

Some have legitimately criticized Merton's early writings not only for their sweeping generalities about mysticism, but also for his thesis that all Christians are called to infused contemplation.[80] As indicated above, however, Merton did come to make an important dis-

244

tinction between infused contemplation (mysticism in the strict sense) and hidden, or masked, contemplation (mysticism in the broad sense). An extremely hectic, active life, permeated with a radical stance of faith, hope, and love, can be called contemplative in the masked sense. The person's self-emptying attitude and motivation in his activity characterize his hidden contemplation.

One contemporary activist, William Callahan, S.J., has focused attention on what he calls "noisy contemplation."[81] Callahan contends that people can and do experience God in the midst of the pressures, tensions, turmoil, noise, and confusion of an active, contemporary life. Not only an elite, with quiet surroundings and the requisite leisure for traditional contemplation, are capable of deep and genuine prayer. Those with crushing schedules, noisy surroundings, and little time for formal prayer can also pray authentically.

The active person must develop a heightened sense of God in nature, in himself, in others with whom he works and lives, in the events of his daily life, and in the current events and conflicts of society. A deep love for God, oneself, others, and a concern for what is happening in the world at large are the required attitudes for noisy contemplation. In short, Callahan wants a contemporary Christian to be like Christ, "to be a person who moves in the midst of modern noise and tensions both inside and around us, and who remains aware of others in loving, bonding and caring ways. . . ."[82] This would make the Christian's prayer simple, durable, deep, loving, and socially aware.

But Callahan does not neglect the need for periods of formal prayer, or what he calls "prayer apart." Noisy contemplation cannot exist without silent contemplation. "A healthy rhythm of life and prayer," he writes, "also seeks moments of aloneness and apartness."[83] If many contemporary persons have the discipline to schedule physical exercise into their often hectic, daily lives, they should likewise take the time for "prayer apart."

Callahan seems to restate in contemporary form St. Ignatius' position of being able to find God in all things, if a person is genuinely "mortified," that is, dead to self in all things. To be socially conscious and well-informed about current events, sensitive to one's needs and the needs of others, to have the discipline required for interminable meetings, committees, planning, and scheduling—all this can be a contemporary version of authentic mortification, or self-emptying. The dying to self required for hectic activity truly for the sake of God and one's neighbor, and not for self-glorification or escape from the self, nurtures genuine noisy contemplation.

The writings of Karl Rahner provide an excellent theological foundation for Merton's masked and Callahan's noisy contemplation. For Rahner, as indicated above,[84] it is obvious that the human person is essentially a mystical person, that is, one experientially drawn toward the God of mystery, revelation, and love. Whether he explicitly and directly adverts to it or not, whether he opens himself to it or not, his whole life is directed to the God of mystery who has communicated himself as truth and love. His deepest, most radical experience, that which haunts the very roots of his being, is the God who calls him to surrender to his mystery, the Word that enlightens his spirit, and the love that embraces him. This threefold mystical experience forms the implicit, unexpressed ambiance that always encircles, embraces, and upholds all his everyday life.

For Rahner, the human person is essentially spirit-in-world. The world, moreover, contains the incarnation as one of its constitutive elements. Through his incarnation, life, death, and resurrection, Jesus Christ actually entered into the innermost reality of the world.

246

Because of this Christ-constituted world, Rahner contends that *all* persons are present to Christ's incarnation, life, death, and resurrection. This Christic ambiance ensures, therefore, that every human action done in depth contains at least an implicit mystical experience of Christ.

For these reasons, Rahner does not emphasize a mysticism of interiority alone. He unhesitatingly speaks of the mystical dimension of eating, drinking, sleeping, walking, sitting, and other everyday things. Every single facet of human existence contains an implicit experience of the triune God and the crucified and risen Christ. Rahner's mysticism of daily life is a mysticism of joy in the world, therefore, a faith that loves the earth.

Certain experiences, however, manifest more clearly for Rahner the latent mystical dimension in all genuine human living. For example, the experience of utter loneliness; a forgiveness of others that goes unacknowledged or fails to make a person feel good about having forgiven others; radical fidelity to conscience even when the person appears like a fool before others; faith, hope and love that seem to be absurd at the time; a tenacious hope in the face of a seemingly hopeless death; the bitter taste of the difference between what the person truly wants from life and what life actually gives him—these and similar experiences underscore what Rahner means by the mysticism of everyday life.

Genuine love for another contains a powerful mystical dimension, as indicated by Rahner's well-known thesis that love of neighbor is love of God. For Rahner, even an atheistic, secular life lived in courage, moderation, and silent service exhibits a mystical quality. Perhaps *the* mystical experience for Rahner is the courageous, total acceptance of oneself, others, and life itself when everything that supports this self, others, and life seems to be collapsing. Self-surrender to the Mystery that embraces our lives and fills our nothingness is the key to Rahner's mysticism of everyday life. For Rahner, however, self-emptying occurs not through a mysticism of pure interiority, but primarily through service to others.[85] In this self-surrender, a person participates in Christ's self-emptying on the cross. That this emptiness was not in vain was confirmed by Jesus' bodily resurrection, one effect of which is the support given to the mysticism of everyday life.

Therefore, Merton seems to be in agreement with Rahner and other contemporary commentators who speak about mysticism as a deepened form of ordinary human experience.[86] Genuine human living contains a quiet, silent, depth dimension that is clearly mystical. Radical openness and surrender to authentic life is the very heart of both human authenticity and religious experience. Naked faith, silence, emptiness, and the realization of one's own nothingness in the midst of everyday life mean living mystically, living the ordinary extraordinarily. If mysticism is in some sense the knowledge and wisdom flowing from love, any intense Christian life, even when unspectacular, and even an atheistic, secular life that faithfully surrenders to the innate drive to human authenticity is, according to many contemporary authors, definitely mystical.

It might be objected that these authors have reduced mysticism to religious experience or even to life itself, but this is not the case. These authors have called attention to the mystical quality of Christian *faith, hope,* and *love,* and the mystical aspect of all *authentic* human living. In line with this, most of these commentators also make some sort of distinction between mysticism in the strict and wide sense. Rahner, for example, distinguishes the dramatic mysticism of the saints from the mysticism of ordinary Christians. The mysticism of the saints is not qualitatively different from the faith, hope, and love of the ordinary Christian; it is only an unusual psychological manifestation thereof. Likewise, for William Johnston, mysticism in the strict sense involves awakening the deepest levels of psychic life that are usually dormant, or bringing the unconscious dimensions of the person into consciousness. Despite the emphasis upon the unusual psychological manifestations of mysticism in the strict sense, most authors do not equate mysticism with transient, ecstatic moments of rapture.[87]

Merton performed a valuable service for contemporary spirituality and mysticism by calling attention to the possibility of pseudo-mystical narcissism. When coupled with enstatic meditation techniques, improper motivation can produce a state wherein the experience of the self is a trap out of which the would-be contemplative never escapes. One penetrating writer, Yves Raguin, underscores this point in these terms: "The important thing here is to realize that my depth is deeper than I am. But at the same time I may plunge into myself and never find anything more than myself. The self, in fact, is so deep that it can engulf me without my ever realizing there is something further. . . . It is easy to see why so many mystics lose themselves in themselves and never meet God."[88]

The enstatic plunge into the self does not necessarily lead, therefore, to anything more than the self. As pleasant as enstatic experiences may be, they wall the person up narcissistically in his own well-being so that he loses himself in himself and may never meet God. With the contemporary emphasis upon enstatic techniques and mystical experience in general, not enough attention is given to the problem of the transition from the depth of the self to the ground of the self, God.

Still another writer, Martin Buber, describes firsthand his experience with self-entrapment: "Now from my own unforgettable experience I know well that there is a state in which the bonds of the personal nature of life seem to have fallen away from us and we experience an undivided unity. But I do not know—what the soul willingly imagines (mine too once did it)—that in this I had attained to a union with a primal being or the godhead. . . . Responsibly . . . I can elicit from those experiences only that I reached an undifferentiated unity of myself without form or content. I may call this an original pre-biographical unity and suppose that it is hidden unchanged beneath all biographical change, all development and complication of the soul . . . this unity is nothing but the unity of this soul of mine."[89] Buber contends from his "own unforgettable experience" that he had experienced the "pre-biographical unity" of his own spirit and confused it with the experience of God. Another well-known mystical writer, R. C. Zaehner, confirms Buber's thesis with many examples of enstatic narcissism from Hindu, Christian, and Islamic mysticisms.[90] The would-be mystic, according to Zaehner, can produce a state of pure isolation of the human spirit from all that is other than itself and rest in that isolation. Therefore, to plunge into the self may not be the way to God, but a mystical dead end.

Ruysbroeck, a famous Christian mystic, focused upon a "natural rest" which was not God-directed or God-caused.[91] Although Ruysbroeck was aware of the psychosomatic benefits of this natural rest, he maintained that it was contrary to "supernatural rest." Brought about by a "false and self-regarding emptiness," natural rest produces spiritual blindness, ignorance, and indolence. With no reference to God and others, the self ensnares itself in a degenerate passivity, self-complacency, and "spiritual lechery." There can be a self-emptying, therefore, that is never filled with the wisdom and love flowing from the mystical contemplation of God.

Self-emptying may not only fill the person with an even more inflated self but also with a whole variety of good and evil "spirits." Jesus, for one, warned against the return of an "unclean spirit" with seven more spirits more evil than himself, upon finding his former habitat cleaned and put in order.[92] Carl Jung warned throughout his writings of the possibility of certain archetypes from the collective unconscious filling a person's psychic life with an autonomy of their own. Perhaps these "spirit" archetypes from the collective unconscious account for the "spirit wrestling" undertaken by the medicine man, or shaman, in the writings of Carlos Castañeda and the shamanistic tradition in general. It may also account for the state of being possessed by various spirits attested to in many primitive religions, as well as in contemporary voodoo practices.[93]

The genuine Christian mystic will certainly have to do battle with the evil spirits in his mystical ascent. He undertakes his self-emptying, however, neither to explore the vastness of the inner world nor to harness the power of certain spirits, but solely to be filled with the God of truth and love. Disinterested love alone motivates the genuine Christian mystic, not curiosity about the inner world or the power available from tapping its resources.

With Merton's interest in the Christian apophatic tradition and Eastern mysticism, he would have certainly welcomed a recent book by Anthony de Mello, S.J., on Christian prayer in Eastern form.[94] Just as Merton considered thoughts a greater enemy than the body to the contemplative, de Mello provides techniques to move prayer from the head to the heart and to ensure that the entire person prays. De Mello maintains that all one must do to experience God is to become aware of one's inner silence, sensations, or breathing.

These simple meditation techniques undoubtedly have significant psychosomatic value, cause deep peace and tranquillity, and prepare a person for Christian contemplation. It is not necessarily true, however, as de Mello

251

contends, that awareness of one's inner silence, sensations, or breathing is the equivalent of Christian contemplation. These awareness exercises can be called Christian contemplation, in the sense of communication with God, only if they are done in faith, hope, and love. A Christian may implicitly bring a faith, hope, and love stance to awareness exercises, but this need not be the case.[95] Thus, a distinction must be made between those who meditate to actuate their human potential and those who meditate out of a call to self-transcending love in a fully Christian religious context.[96] In the latter case, faith, hope, and love become constitutive elements of the experience resulting from awareness exercises. Still, the distinction between those who meditate with and without faith, hope, and love may be blurred in actual practice. When the results of awareness exercises are joy, peace, patience, kindness, gentleness, love, faithfulness, and self-control, the Spirit of Christ is present.

A number of contemporary authors reduce mysticism to something biological, abnormal, or bizarre.[97] Merton's rejection of this contemporary thesis that mysticism is a form of regression in the service of the ego thus deserves special attention. He would certainly agree with the undeservedly neglected studies on mysticism by the German psychologist and physician, Carl Albrecht.[98] Albrecht's careful phenomenological studies show that mysticism cannot be reduced to intrapsychic processes. Although certain phases of the mystical ascent may involve some regression, neither regression nor pathology explains it. For Albrecht, the mystical consciousness is a "phenomenological ultimate." This means that it cannot be reduced to anything else, because it contains an irreducible essence that must be studied in its own right. Although science can and must study this irreducible essence, it demands of its very nature a theological and religious explanation as well. In short, scientific investigation alone cannot do sufficient justice to the mystical consciousness.

Merton can be faulted for saying very little about the great variety of mystical experiences and the various states and stages of mystical ascent. Still, his emphasis upon the transrational or "supraconscious" dimension of the mystical consciousness is important. Too many contemporary commentators tend to place mystical consciousness at the lowest end of the consciousness spectrum, that is, to identify it with unconsciousness. Merton and others correctly emphasize the other end of the spectrum, however, where the heightening of consciousness occurs. One Jungian psychologist, Erich Neumann, distinguishes the mysticism effected by the *intensification* of consciousness from that of pseudo-mysticism and its concomitant dissolution of consciousness.[99] The disintegrated consciousness obtained from sniffing glue, for example, is not the same as the unified and integrated consciousness resulting from Zen exercises.

In line with this point, it seems important to stress the distinction made by William Johnston between altered states of consciousness and meditative states of consciousness.[100] The latter have only superficial similarities with the former. For example, contemporary psychologists have studied the changes in consciousness experienced by someone driving for too long and "hypnotized" by the road, by a high-altitude jet pilot on a very long flying mission, by an Eskimo confined to his kayak for long periods of time on the Arctic seas, by someone in a polio respirator, or by someone in solitary confinement. In short, sensory deprivation does produce a disturbed time sense, a loss of psychosomatic control, a changed body image, a loss of memory, difficulty in making judgments, hypersuggestibility, and even feelings of ineffability and rejuvenation.

On the other hand, meditative states of consciousness promote psychosomatic healing, deep peace, tranquillity, integration, and psychosynthesis. Love and wisdom predominate in this type of consciousness. This state of loving wisdom contains nothing bizarre or abnormal, and even produces different brain waves recognized for their life-enhancing quality. Even the secondary mystical phenomena, such as visions and locutions, that result from genuine mysticism differ significantly from the hallucinations of altered states of consciousness. Meditative consciousness both produces and is produced by a self structured by judgment and decision. This self has surrendered to the call of unrestricted and unconditional love. Genuine meditative states result in human authenticity and promote the surrender to the deepest dynamisms of what it means to be genuinely human.

Merton seems to strike a good balance between those who underscore either the "heavenly" or the "earthly" side of contemplation. As noted above, St. John of the Cross saw in contemplative love, even apart from any apostolic labor, the most valuable task a person can perform for the Church and the world. St. Ignatius of Loyola emphasized a contemplation in action, a service mysticism of joy in the world. Many aspects of Merton's Trappist life are bridal—for example, his love for solitude, even if never sustained. But his writings, his prophetic crying out on pressing social issues, and his Asian journey have more of the flavor of service mysticism.

Although Merton was keenly aware of the power of contemplation for social action, he resolutely refused to reduce contemplation to merely a means to this action. Long before political and liberation theology were in vogue, Merton had captured their essential insight: sin has a *social* impact upon the human situation, and social structures must be redeemed if humanity is to be redeemed. Yet he had also grasped that love for oneself and others is possible only in God, because only God can forgive, heal, and transform the unlovable sin that

254

constitutes oneself and others. Thus, Merton underscored the need for both individual and social transformation and had grasped their intrinsic relationship. Although he spoke out loudly on pressing social problems, he did not hold the view that all Christians must
be *directly* involved in effecting social change.

Merton had more than implicitly grasped that the contemplative becomes a nodal point wherein all society is
purified, illuminated, and transformed. Because the
contemplative plunges into God—who acted so dramatically for the world in a salvation history that reached
its high point in the life, death, and resurrection of Jesus Christ—contemplation directs the person toward
God's activity for the world. Therefore, genuine Christian contemplation breaks down the alleged dichotomy
between contemplation and action. To be authentically
open to God in contemplation necessitates being open
to all for whom God in Christ lived, died, and rose. For
Merton, the contemplative aims at becoming the universal person who identifies with everyone and who re-
covers the deepest values of society and humanity.
Even for the monastic-solitary, contemplation has a
cosmic significance. It is essentially a social process that
purifies, illuminates, and transforms the world.

Although Merton was open to the great variety of ways
in which both God and the world can be served, as a
contemplative Trappist monk he never lost his distrust
of science, technology, and contemporary life.[101] Perhaps he can be excused for his somewhat romantic
view of agrarian values and of living close to the land.
On the other hand, it is not necessary to agree fully
with one of Merton's friends, correspondents, and crit-
ics, Rosemary Reuther, who contended that the cutting
edge of a genuine, contemporary monastic life should
be in the urban ghetto and not in the countryside.[102]
Reuther seems aware of the dangers of both the flight
to the city and to the countryside, but her sympathies
are clearly with working in the inner city.

It may or may not be true that in the future the form of monasticism with the most powerful eschatological witness will be located in the inner city. It is false to assume, however, that this is the monastic vocation for everyone, or that the cenobitic and eremetic monastic life in the woods or the desert does not in itself humanize technology and contemporary life.

Merton can also be commended for being one of the first American writers to take seriously the importance of Eastern religions for a contemporary Christian spirituality and mysticism. In many ways, he both anticipated and then followed through on Vatican II's positive evaluation of the great religions of the East. That Christianity can learn much from the East, especially in the area of a "technology" for prayer, meditation, and contemplation, is almost a commonplace statement today in many Christian circles. Even serious, contemporary Christian theological reflection must contain an aspect of "turning East," if it is to be faithful to the signs of the times.

It must be asked, however, if Merton's understanding of Zen was not overly influenced by his friend, D. T. Suzuki, a controversial figure even among Zennists.[103] For example, is it beyond dispute that just because Suzuki and Nishida occasionally used words such as "love," "person," and "personalism" that Christian love and Buddhist compassion are the same, or that Buddhists are also interested in a personal God? Linguistic similarities may very well mask profound differences and ultimately irreconcilable world views. Suzuki, for one, saw Christian love mysticism as an eroticism gone wild. If Zen and much of the Eastern tradition consider the ego to be *the* illusion to be removed, what grounds are left for genuine love that takes the uniqueness and individuality of the other seriously? Christians speak mostly of a love union with a personal God and Zen of enlightenment and the experience of undifferentiated unity. Are these really the same experiences masked only by different interpretations, or are they different experiences masked by similar language?

Also open to question is Merton's contention that Zen can be removed from its Eastern matrix. Is it true that there is a Zen consciousness with a nonhistorical, nontraditional, nonreligious essence that can shine through any religion? Although Zen masters concede that Zen exercises done without Buddhist faith have certain benefits, they still call this "bastard" Zen that does not contain Zen's fullness. Has Merton forgotten the unconscious roots of Zen consciousness? Carl Jung warned Westerners about appropriating Eastern religions because Westerners lack the requisite unconscious foundations. On this point, the remarks of Steven Katz bear further repeating.[104] Katz contends that the contemplative's entire formative milieu becomes an intrinsic part of mystical consciousness. Contemplative techniques *re*condition, not *de*condition, the contemplative's consciousness.

Not all scholars agree with Merton that Christianity and Eastern religions have so much in common. R. C. Zaehner points out that the only thing the great religions of the world have in common is the "observed fact of human unhappiness."[105] Although he does not argue that East and West are irreconcilably opposed, he flatly states that "they are simply not starting from the same premises. . . . The great religions are talking at cross purposes."[106] In fact, Zaehner often endeavored to show that even within one religious tradition, religious and mystical experiences are not one and the same.

Hans Urs von Balthasar also underscores the radical differences between East and West.[107] For him, Eastern religions indicate the *human* effort for God; Western religions show *God's initiative* in revealing himself to humanity. The way of the East is one of techniques for storming the heavens; the way of the West is grace. He

257

also maintains that Eastern religions are natural religions waiting to be taken up and transformed into the supernatural religion of Christianity.

Rejecting the Eastern teaching on the illusion of the ego, von Balthasar stresses the dignity of the "I" created out of and for freedom and love. This "I," moreover, was solid enough to become the basis for the incarnation. Christianity teaches the dignity, uniqueness, and goodness of the human person in his relationship with the personal God of love. What does this have in common with the Eastern emphasis upon an ego that must eventually dissolve in loveless annihilation in an impersonal Absolute?

Merton preferred to underscore what Christianity had in common with the East, but he was not blind to important differences. Still, he stands more in line with the many contemporary Christian thinkers who genuinely value Eastern religions and consider them important for Christianity itself. These thinkers do not view the religions of the East as pagan, demonic, or merely "natural."[108] The grace of Christ is actively at work in them. The fruits of the Spirit resulting in authentic human living highlight the supernatural graced dimensions of the world's great non-Christian religions.

Had Merton lived longer, he would undoubtedly have been surprised at the relative powerlessness of Eastern religions to curb the growing materialism, secularism, and consumerism of their own cultures. He would also have been astonished at the increasing interest in Eastern religions and mysticisms evinced by so many Christians and Westerners in general.

The informed, contemporary Christian, therefore, ought to avoid two extreme positions. The position of the far right, which sees nothing but evil, superstition, and the demonic in Eastern religions, ignores both the teachings of Vatican II and the evidence for holiness, wisdom, and enlightenment found in these religions. The position of the far left, which ignores the profound mystical tradition of the West for a whole-hearted, but still selective and Westernized, embrace of Eastern religions, is naive. Thus, critical discernment is still an intrinsic element of genuine Christian openness to the East.

Raymond Bailey, a Merton scholar, has written that Merton's "greatest contribution was the particularity of his person and the synthesizing and contemporizing of ancient and universal truths."[109] It is also true that Merton's writings contain very little in the way of original thought. Still, he was one of the first American writers to emphasize the importance of mysticism for contemporary Christian spirituality. What other American writer has done so much to revive interest in the Christian apophatic tradition? He was also one of the first American writers to have a solid knowledge of and commitment to his Christian identity, combined with an openness to and appreciation of the religions of the East.

Merton's impact upon the American monastic revival is noteworthy. Rejecting both pseudo-mysticism and pseudo-activism, he showed the link between contemplation and enlightened social action. Merton rejected the contemporary tendency to equate mysticism with bizarre and exotic experiences and highlighted its hidden, quiet, ordinary, and depth dimensions. In this way, he showed its vital connection with authentic human living. In line with the writings of Augustine, Pascal, and Teresa of Avila, Merton's often journal style of writing offers a unique, American, theological literary genre.[110] For all these reasons, it is easy to understand why Merton is such an important figure for a contemporary American spirituality and mysticism.

Chapter Seven

Pierre Teilhard de Chardin (1881–1955)

Pierre Teilhard de Chardin was a Jesuit priest, scientist, paleontologist, world traveler, poet, visionary, and mystic who provides in many ways a vigorous counterpoint to the Trappist monk, Thomas Merton. First, Teilhard's mysticism of knowing, especially as it relates to scientific discovery, contrasts sharply with Merton's apophatic mysticism of unknowing.

Second, Merton's monastic, somewhat bucolic outlook, coupled with his ambivalence toward contemporary life, science, and technology, also clashes with Teilhard's outlook. It is difficult to find someone who has lived such an intense spiritual and mystical life as Teilhard and yet felt so passionately with the contemporary age. As Teilhard wrote: "As far as my strength will allow me, *because I am a priest,* I would henceforth be the first to become aware of what the world loves, pursues, suffers. I would be the first to seek, to sympathize, to toil: the first in self-fulfillment, the first in self-denial—I would be more widely human in my sympathies and more nobly terrestrial in my ambitions than any of the world's servants."[1] In short, radical love for the world and its projects filled Teilhard's soul. For Teilhard, moreover, the scientist is a type of priest performing a holy task. Science itself is a mysticism. "The scientist's quest, however positivistic he may claim it to be, is coloured or haloed—or rather is invincibly animated, fundamentally—by a mystical hope,"[2] he says.

Merton was able to unite in himself and reconcile his monastic vocation to solitude and silence with a strong prophetic sense of speaking out on contemporary social issues. For Teilhard, the burning issue was uniting and reconciling in himself the two worlds of Christianity and science. Although many of his contemporaries felt these two worlds to be irreconcilably opposed, Teilhard saw them as complementary. He wrote: "After 30 years devoted to the pursuit of interior unity, I have the feeling that a synthesis is being effected naturally by the two currents that claim my allegiance."[3]

The religions of the earth and of heaven, science and Christianity, came into conjunction in Teilhard's soul. He claimed to have brought about within himself the "transformation . . . of the 'God of the Gospel' into the 'God of Evolution'—a transformation without deformation."[4] What Teilhard wanted was to Christify evolution, to disclose Christ the Evolver at the very heart of the evolutionary process, and thus to unite the mysticism of the earth with the mysticism of heaven to attain a communion with God through the earth and evolution.

As indicated in the previous chapter, Merton often spoke of the inauthenticity of the false self rooted in the lies and illusions of contemporary life. By facing one's nothingness and meaninglessness, especially in contemplation, the true self anchored in God awakens. For Teilhard, the key to authenticity was seeing and surrendering to an evolution that permeated everything and converged on a personal God of love. Teilhard attempted to show to the scientist whose research led to the chaos and meaninglessness of an infinity of galaxies and subatomic particles that the cosmos held together only "from above." He wanted to convince believing Christians how important it was to take seriously the evolution of the cosmos, because in the incarnation God had descended into the very depths of matter to become All in all. Human progress, evolution, a more humane world, and genuine Christianity were possible only by seeing and surrendering to the personal God of love who is the point of convergence for these dynamics.

In short, Merton and Teilhard differ in what they attempted to bring into harmony: Merton focused on monastic silence and prophetic, social criticism; Teilhard stressed science and Christianity. Yet they are alike in attempting to reconcile two worlds popularly thought of as opposites, or hostile to each other. Both had also grasped the importance of spirituality and mysticism for today. In a sense, too, both were "solitary explorers" in these areas.[5] In the healthy monastic sense, for example, Merton had left the "world" to live more deeply for it. He penetrated the desert areas of the human heart by letting go the false securities of conventional life. This left him truly alone with his own meaninglessness to seek God in the empty and uncharted territory of the human spirit.

While living a fully contemporary life, Teilhard's scientific expeditions actually took him to some of the world's most untouched geographical wildernesses. It was especially Teilhard's scientific work that impelled him to explore the "mystical treasures hidden in the effort to know."[6] Because he believed that science and religions are the "two conjugated faces or phases of one and the same complete act of knowledge,"[7] he aroused the suspicion and hostility of scientists and Christian believers alike for calling their conventional wisdom into question.

Like Merton, however, this solitary explorer sought God, but especially in and through science and evolution. He wanted to show Christians how to discover the mystical vibration inherent in genuine scientific discovery, that God can be found in the very act of scientific endeavor. But he also wished to disclose to scientists that the ultimate meaning and coherence of the universe they study is personal and must be loved because of "the science of Christ through all things."[8] For Teilhard, therefore, Ignatius' finding God in all things applied especially to emphasizing the personal God of love who is the source, the motor, and the goal of all scientific work.

All human striving, religious or scientific, must eventually lead to worship, adoration, and ecstasy, according to Teilhard. Science, evolution, religion, and mysticism likewise belong to the one central longing of the human heart: to find a *personal* totality that the person can ultimately love.

For Teilhard, the complete act of knowledge requires two phases. A person must first immerse himself into the phenomena to obtain the "outer" vision of science. When fully surrendered to, however, this outer vision gives way to an inner vision, a mysterious sense of the Other, whereby the act of knowledge becomes complete. The inner vision is one of religion, adoration, and mysticism. In short, Teilhard demands that scientific thought and religious faith conjoin to form a coherent view of reality.

THE TEMPTATION OF MATTER
The immensity, beauty, and oneness of the natural world deeply attracted Teilhard throughout his life. Permeating many of his experiences and writings is a radical sense of the cosmos, the earth, and of plenitude that runs counter to the daily experience of change, flux, and multiplicity. He had discovered at the very core of the "ocean of matter" a "Great Stability."[9] Throughout the immensity of the cosmos and its infinity of phenomena, Teilhard detected an all-embracing unity. Resonating passionately with this All, he himself "had become pure light."[10] "The mystic," according to Teilhard, "is *the man who is born to* give place in his ex-

perience to that aureole."[11] The diaphanous, luminous oneness of all things had both manifested itself to and in Teilhard. It is no wonder that he emphasized that: "Ultimately, our thought cannot comprehend anything but the Whole, nor, when it really comes to the point, can our dreams entertain anything but the Whole."[12]

In a desert in Egypt, matter had tempted Teilhard by means of a powerful experience of cosmic consciousness. He wrote: "And then all my sensibilities became alert, as though at the approach of a god of easy-won happiness and intoxication; for there lay matter and matter was calling me. To me in my turn, as to all the sons of man, it was speaking as every generation hears it speak; it was begging me to surrender myself unreservedly to it, and to worship it."[13] Teilhard's "naturally pantheistic soul"[14] had listened so intently to the sirens of matter that he wrote: "And why, indeed, should I not worship it, the stable, the great, the rich, the mother, the divine? Is not matter, in its own way, eternal and immense?"[15]

Nevertheless, Teilhard did not succumb to the temptation to worship matter. In many ways, nature was a potent drug that lulled the person to sleep. It could only lead to fusion with the impersonal which, in turn, was linked with decay, entropy, fragmentation, and the absence of thought. Although powerfully attracted to worship the divine around him, he realized from his own experience the dead end of all ancient pantheisms. They followed too readily the line of least resistance to fuse and identify with matter.

Paradoxically, the call of matter had revealed to Teilhard that genuine life could be found only in an "upward reversal," that is, in the evolution of life based upon a union that differentiated. Life evolved out of but away from matter and toward spirit and person. Therefore, Teilhard not only repudiated vigorously the call of matter, but also fulfilled his "pagan" and materialistic pantheistic urge by uniting it with a mysticism of love to transform it into a "Christian pantheism,"[16] by which God is All in all.

It would be incorrect to assume, however, that Teilhard experienced only matter's negative side. Although he considered his plunge into matter an "easy road," it did disclose to him, "as though in an ecstasy, that *through all nature I* was immersed in God."[17] For Teilhard, even matter could be the locus for a divine revelation. Yet he sensed something wrong with this "easy road," because *"there is an absolute direction of growth . . . and . . . life advances in that direction."*[18]

Following the "direct road" to "progress in conscious-ness, in freedom and in moral sense,"[19] however, re-quires purification, concentration, and maximum effort. Because Teilhard had heard the authentic, deeper call of nature beneath the surface attractions of a mystical fusion with it, he vowed to ". . . make a vigorous ef-fort, reverse my course and ascend again to the higher levels. The true summons of the cosmos is a call con-sciously to share in the great work that goes on within it; it is not by drifting down the current of things that we shall be united with their one, single soul, but by fighting our way, with them, towards some term still to come."[20]

Teilhard reversed his course because he had sensed evolution's direction away from the amorphousness of matter and toward greater complexity, increased struc-ture, consciousness, and freedom. The true pantheist surrendered, therefore, not to matter itself but to "something" within matter increasing its interiority, complexity, freedom, and consciousness.

"I believe that the universe is an evolution," Teilhard wrote. "I believe that evolution proceeds towards spirit. I believe that *in man*, spirit is fully realized in person. I

265

believe that the supremely personal is the Universal Christ."[21] For Teilhard, therefore, nature's dynamism, direction, and goal are toward spirit, the human person, and Christ. Matter must become living and conscious, self-conscious and reflective, and finally see God through the eyes of Christ.

Central to Teilhard's view is the emphasis upon an ultimate, future synthesis for evolution that comes only "from above." "The Great Stability," Teilhard writes, "is not at the bottom in the infra-elementary sphere, but at the top in the ultra-synthetic sphere."[22] The "reversal" of which Teilhard speaks is essentially the experiential view that spirit will eventually "dethrone" matter, that spirit will become increasingly personal, and that Christ is the ultimate synthesizer, the world's real soul. Only in Christ will all things hold together, not like the fusion unity of matter, but in a differentiated unity that preserves the identity of each and every element.

For Teilhard, Christ is the pattern for the human descent into and ascent from matter. Christ descended into the very heart of the universe to fill all things and ascended to his Father to establish God as All in all. All authentic human living demands, therefore, a breaking out of a narrow individuality by surrendering to one's "cosmic passion," or "passion for the world." One must hearken to the call of matter by becoming one with it, but still "pre-adhere to God." Teilhard contends that immersion into matter transforms the person, because through "matter we are nourished, lifted up, linked to everything else, invaded by life."[23] The Christian receives new energy to ascend to build God's kingdom on earth. In giving himself to the forces of growth and progress, he also begins to sense a mysterious presence, someone "who is some part of ourselves, yet masters us."[24]

266

Or it may happen that "the force that had been drawing the mystic towards the zone in which all things are fused together, now reverses its direction and brings him back to an exact examination of the experimental multiple."[25] In other words, the scientist must not only descend into matter and surrender to experience in order to analyze, he must also ascend to achieve a scientific synthesis.

According to Teilhard, however, even the scientist's surrender to the cosmic sense for the sake of analysis and his ascent to synthesis find their ultimate unity, meaning, and synthesis only in "Christ . . . radiating *physically* over the terrifying totality of things."[26] As St. Paul did long ago, Teilhard insisted that everything holds together only in Christ. Radical fidelity either to God or to the earth demands both a phase of descent into and a phase of ascent from matter to effect a union with God by means of the earth. Teilhard maintains, therefore, that a person cannot be faithful either to God or to the earth without being faithful to both. The Christian cannot really avoid communion with the earth, if he wishes authentic union with God. The unbelieving scientist cannot avoid communion with God, if he really wishes genuine communion with the earth. Teilhard's phases of descent and ascent underscore a *communion with God through the earth.*

TEILHARD'S SCIENTIFIC AND MYSTICAL VIEW OF EVOLUTION

Teilhard wrote mainly to teach others to see what he himself had seen and continued to see.[27] The "outer" vision obtained from his observation of scientific phenomena and the "inner" vision from his mystical faith became the two focal points of his life that gradually conjoined to form a harmonious unity. The synthesis of these scientific and mystical views of an evolutionary world actually becoming the cosmic Christ is, perhaps, the hallmark of this man's abiding genius.

Exactly what did Teilhard see? In the light of his scientific work and Christian faith, Teilhard wrote: "At the heart of the universe, each soul exists for God, in our Lord. But all reality, even material reality, around each one of us, exists for our souls. Hence, all sensible reality, around each one of us, exists, through our souls, for God in our Lord."[28] From science and faith, Teilhard saw the entire evolution of the cosmos (cosmogenesis) as a real becoming of the cosmic Christ (Christogenesis).

At point "Alpha" in the evolutionary process, God began freely to create by unifying a "physical nothingness."[29] For Teilhard, creation is essentially a process of unification, of complexification, and a becoming-more. Unification results in increasing interiority, consciousness, freedom, personality, and tension. Like a coiled helix, separating in ever-decreasing circles with increasing tension, the evolution of the universe (cosmogenesis) embraces the evolution of matter to life (biogenesis), the evolution of life to man (anthropogenesis), the evolution of man to greater socialization and reflective consciousness (noogenesis), and the evolution of social man to the universal Christ at point "Omega," where God becomes All in all.

Essential to Teilhard's vision is the flow of evolution in the direction of ever-greater complexity, order, consciousness, freedom, and personality. Everything that evolves eventually *converges* at point Omega. Although Teilhard considered evolution a "groping," it still had a direction. This groping is a "combination of the play of chance (which is physical) and that of finality (which is psychic)."[30]

Evolution's groping requires two types of energy: tangential and radial. Tangential energy is the energy known to physicists, the energy of the "without," as Teilhard says, which "links the element with all others of the same order (that is to say, of the same complexity and the same centricity) as itself in the universe."[31] The second energy is radial, "axial," the energy of the "within," the spiritual energy of consciousness that works in opposition to entropy. This energy actually carries evolution forward and upward. It is what "personalizes" evolution, for it is the "physico-moral energy of personalization."[32]

Matter and life find their goal in the human person, for Teilhard, in a twofold way. First, the cosmos enfolds *on* the human person to produce the human organism, especially the human brain.[33] Second, the cosmos enfolds *in* the human person to produce human consciousness, especially self-consciousness. In another manner of speaking, evolution leads up to the human person to find its very soul. In the human person, evolution "internalizes" itself, becomes self-conscious, and can reflect upon itself. Teilhard considered the human person the spearhead of evolution, "hominized earth," "hominized nature," or matter "thinking itself." Shaping itself around the human person, evolution discovers the key to its final harmony and meaning. Furthermore, when biogenesis becomes anthropogenesis, noogenesis begins. With thought and self-reflection, the cosmos attains a new layer or skin.

For these reasons, Teilhard objected strongly to the contemporary tendency of some humanists and anthropologists to treat the human person as somehow apart and distinct from evolution and the earth. The human person is the very prolongation of the evolutionary, cosmic process. In fact, for Teilhard, the very matter that constitutes the human person "is the *totality* of the Universe possessed by me *partialiter*."[34] The cosmos is so much a part of the human person and the human person is so much a part of the cosmos that he contended: "In each one of us, through matter, the whole history of the world is in part reflected. And however autonomous our soul, it is indebted to an inheritance worked upon from all sides—before ever it came into being—by the totality of the energies of the earth."[35] God loves, saves, and transforms the entire cosmos partially in and through each human soul.

Anthropogenesis requires much more than the evolution of the individual human person. It causes the heightened interiority, freedom, and consciousness of the human person as a social organism. Evolution aims at producing not only the human individual but also, and especially, "Humanity," "a mega-organism developing a collective soul."[36] Intensified forms of socialization both cause and result in the formation of one hyper-person from the multitude of individual persons. "What is already thinking through man and above man," Teilhard writes, "is mankind."[37] Humanity already lives in the individual's depths as a common substratum of all individuals. For Teilhard, the human race is forming one community. Humanity derives its oneness, moreover, from its common origin and its shared development.

Teilhard's sense of "Humanity" began to take shape "in the two great atmospheres of Asia and the War."[38] He experienced firsthand during World War I just how much war mixed and joined together the various peoples of the world. But it was especially science, for Teilhard, that fused individuals and peoples to each other and gave rise to the new sense of "Humanity."

In the evolution process, "Humanity" is the "within" and science the "without" of a twofold development. If Humanity is the universal *subjective* synthesis in evolution, science is its universal *objective* synthesis, which provides a common language and vision. "The spirit of research and conquest," Teilhard says, "is the permanent soul of evolution."[39] What human enterprise other than science is so transcultural and has done so much to transform the world's individuals and peoples into "Humanity"?

If matter finds its soul in the human person and human persons attain another soul to become "Humanity" through scientific research, it must be emphasized that the science of Christ runs through all things. Cosmogenesis is radically a Christogenesis. Because of his incarnation, his descent into matter, his glorious death, resurrection, and ascension, all things hold together only in Christ. This means that Christ is the soul of souls, a "soul that superanimates all the assembled soul."[40] Christ the Evolver is the very soul of evolution.

The person of Jesus Christ is in Teilhard's view the very form of the world, its ultimate unifying factor, what it is and is becoming. Teilhard's Christo-cosmic vision sees Christ as the cosmic, universal, and supremely personal factor in evolution. "Such has been my experience," Teilhard writes, "in contact with the earth—the diaphany of the Divine at the heart of the universe of fire . . . Christ; his heart; a fire, capable of penetrating everywhere."[41]

It is little wonder that some have called Teilhard's view a "Christian pantheism," a "panchristic monism," a "Christo-monism," or a "panchristism."[42] Teilhard's universe is no less than Christ and, for him, Christ must be loved as a universe. "That is why," he wrote, "after a life of highest effort, a scientist or thinker may end up impoverished and dessicated—disillusioned; his mind but not his personality has worked upon inanimate objects. He has given himself; he has not been able to love."[43] To be sure, science in itself cannot discover Christ, but only a Christic and personal universe can ultimately satisfy the yearnings of those engaged in scientific research. Science's deepest, albeit often only anonymous, aspirations are to find a totality that is supremely personal and lovable.

THE MEANING OF HUMAN ACTIVITY AND PASSIVITY
In an evolving world of Christogenesis, human activity and passivity attain a special significance. The true

meaning of all human action and suffering comes to light only in a world that is genuinely "divine," "Christic," and "mystical." It was especially to show this to "wavering" Christians that Teilhard wrote his well-known book, *The Divine Milieu*. Christians who believed in heaven, renunciation, and the cross must, according to Teilhard, also love the world. Not only must Sunday be hallowed, but all daily life as well through a spirituality and mysticism that reconcile and unite a love of both God and the world.

If Christians believe in more than the immortality of the soul, if they believe in bodily resurrection as well, then human action must be sanctified by more than a good intention. Human action makes us living extensions of the incarnation by fully utilizing all our talents, abilities, and powers to complete any and all worldly tasks. Absolute fidelity to the tasks of daily life, throwing oneself into the making of a better, more humane world—these advance the kingdom of God on earth and promote Christogenesis. Our actions actually form the cosmic Christ. It is in and through our actions that we can become united to God through the earth. It was through Teilhard's incredible labors that he could write: "I have an almost physical sensation of God catching me up and clasping me more closely, as if—with the road ahead disappearing, and men, beside us fading away . . . only God were *ahead* and *around, thickening* . . . as we advance."[44] Teilhard found God in all things because he was a devoted servant of the earth.

Therefore, the contemporary Christian must be truly attached to the world, to progress, and to the development of his talents. Yet authentic Christian attachment to the world also contains a self-correcting detachment. Work, activity, and labor in the service of the world mean forgetting oneself, overcoming inertia, and conquering laziness. To give oneself to the Christic value of action also means transcending ambition, egoism,

272

and the search for worldly honor. Seeing the task in its overall context likewise requires detachment from the task as an end in itself. Genuine attachment requires going to the limits of one's humanity, which likewise necessitates extreme detachment from self.

Teilhard also stressed the value of those things we undergo for the sake of Christogenesis. He had had first-hand experience of human passivities and of how much his very self was a gift. He wrote: ". . . I went down into my inmost self, to the deep abyss whence I feel dimly that my power of action emanates. But as I moved further and further away from the conventional certainties by which social life is superficially illuminated, I became aware that I was losing contact with myself. At each step of the descent a new person was disclosed within me of whose name I was no longer sure, and who no longer obeyed me. And when I had to stop my exploration because the path faded from beneath my steps, I found a bottomless abyss at my feet, and out of it came—arising I know not from where— the current which I dare to call *my* life."[45] In short, it is not only action but also passivity that causes our growth. Much of our life comes from those things done to us for the sake of our own progress. Teilhard saw the entire cosmos and its forces intersecting in a person at the exact time and place to bring about an effect desired by God. Teilhard called attention both to those "friendly forces" that promote our development and to those "passivities of diminishment" that seem to thwart it.

Natural failings, physical defects, moral weakness, disease, old age, ill fortune, obstacles, accidents, the nasty things others do to us, and death are the "passivities of diminishment." Although Teilhard realized that the person could become united to God through these passivities, he abhorred any facile surrender to such evils. "I can only unite myself to the will of God (as passively endured)," he wrote, *"when all my strength is spent,* at the point where my activity, fully extended and straining towards betterment . . . finds itself continually counter-weighted by forces tending to halt me or overwhelm me."[46] Only then does the person attain communion with God through genuine Christian resignation.

Authentic Christian existence, for Teilhard, requires a realistic view of how communion with God is possible both through action and passivity. He further insisted that attachment and detachment were the two natural phases of one complete life. "If man is to be fully himself and fully living," he wrote, "he must, (1) be centered upon himself; (2) be 'de-centered' upon 'the other'; (3) be supercentered upon a being greater than himself."[47] The Christian must fulfill himself as much as possible. In terms of Teilhard's "ultra-physics," by developing the tangential structures of the world, the person progresses axially, that is, increases in interiority, consciousness, and personality. By employing all one's talents and abilities to better oneself and the world, communion with God through action is brought about, for God is at the heart of the creative process. Or, in order to give oneself to God, one must first be oneself.

In addition to action, however, we must allow ourselves to be "de-centered" in still another way. Life's passivities mold us; they also hollow us out to fill us with God. They cause us to lose the tight grip we have on our narrow selves in order to find our true identity by being "super-centered" on something much greater than ourselves. Likewise, by surrendering to the passivities of diminishment, the person actually unites with the creative principle of evolution, the God of love. In fact, Teilhard viewed suffering as a "supremely active principle of universal hominisation and divinisation."[48] Suffering adds radial energy to the universe and reverses the direction of entropy, but it is especially through death that God penetrates all dimensions of the person and produces the greatest hollowing out for the sake of filling him with the divine milieu. For Teilhard, death itself is the great act of communion with God through the earth.[49]

Although Teilhard seems to be better known for his mysticism of action, it would be a serious mistake to overlook his profound mysticism of suffering. Throughout his writings, he rarely failed to underscore the necessity, place, meaning, and value of suffering even in the evolutionary enterprise. For example, he once wrote to his long-time ill sister:

"O Marguerite, my sister, while I, given soul and body to the positive forces of the universe, was wandering over continents and oceans, my whole being passionately taken up in watching the intensification of all the world's tints and shadows, you were lying motionless, stretched out on your bed of sickness, silently, deep within yourself, transforming into light the world's most grievous shadows. In the eyes of the Creator, which of us, tell me, which of us will have had the better part?"[50]

Teilhard sensed profoundly the cosmic value of suffering. It is a way of "transforming into light the world's most grievous shadows." Suffering is nothing less than an evolutionary energy which promotes cosmogenesis and Christogenesis. Has not Teilhard transformed into a contemporary framework the central insight of "victim-soul" mysticism, that is, that suffering is ultimately redemptive, healing, and transformative?

For this reason, Teilhard resolutely refused to consider Christ's cross "as a symbol of sadness, of limitation and repression."[51] It is actually the supreme paradigm of progress, ascent, suprahuman effort, and of this world's transformation, attained only by a graced willingness to transcend what is most immediately tangible. For Teilhard: "Jesus on the Cross is both the symbol and the reality of the immense labor of the centuries which has, little by little, raised up the created spirit and brought it back to the depths of the divine *milieu*. He represents (and in a true sense, he is) creation, as, upheld by God, it reascends the slope of being, sometimes clinging to things for support, sometimes tearing itself away from them in order to pass beyond them, and always compensating, by physical suffering, for the setbacks caused by its moral downfalls."[52]

Like Jesus on the cross and the sick, contemplatives do not seem to act upon the world in any significant way. Teilhard stressed, however, their awesome "passive action"[53] by which the cosmos is healed, directed, and transformed. By virtue of the contemplative's tension of mind toward God, Teilhard writes, "the ascending force of the world is concealed in a very intense form."[54]

Teilhard was fond of a story by Robert Hugh Benson in which a person comes upon an insignificant nun praying in an out of the way chapel.[55] He has a vision of the axis of the universe passing through the chapel with all the cosmic elements reorganizing themselves around it. Because of this nun's contemplative faith, a practical conviction that God continues to form the universe, she was, in fact, an energy center for evolution. Contemplative faith spearheads the evolutionary process. The little nun's efficacious and transformative faith gave life to, or "sur-animated," the universe. Christian contemplation requires an operative, effective faith which, according to Teilhard, is an actual cosmic energy. To paraphrase a well-known Zen saying: the Christian contemplative contemplates for the universe.

The paradox here is that only the person who genuinely *sees* that cosmogenesis is Christogenesis can heal, transform, and direct the evolutionary process in a significant way. For Teilhard, "the man who *dares* to believe reaches a sphere of created reality in which things, while retaining their habitual texture, seem to be made of a different substance . . . at the same time everything becomes luminous, animated, instinct with love. Through the operation of faith Christ appears."[56] Contemplative faith renders the cosmos diaphanous. It discloses the love of Christ that bathes it and the cosmic Christ it is slowly becoming.

THE ROAD OF EASTERN MYSTICISMS

Teilhard's personal experiences, his readings, and his travels caused him to be deeply attracted to the spiritualities and mysticisms of the East. His ecumenical view of humanity disposed him to learn as much as possible from other cultures. Concerning his Eastern journeys he wrote: "The fact remains, however, that the multiplicity of human elements and human points of view revealed by a journey to the Far East is so 'overwhelming' that one cannot conceive of a religious life, a religious organism, assimilating such a mass without being profoundly modified and enriched by it."[57]

It is clear from his many writings that Teilhard expected to be changed, deepened, and "enriched" by his contact with the East. It was especially his cosmic view, however, that prompted him to have such an interest in Eastern mysticisms. Above all, the East's faith in the ultimate unity of the universe, its radical cosmic sense, appealed to Teilhard's "naturally pantheistic soul."

Teilhard traveled to Asia, therefore, with great hopes. In general, however, he was tremendously disappointed. In China he found "nothing but absence of thought, senile thought or infantile thought. . . . Mongolia seemed to me asleep—perhaps dead."[58] Most of Islam, in addition, he simply dismissed as a "backward-looking revival of Judaism" that "offers itself today as a principle of fixation and stagnation."[59] Hinduism and Buddhism, moreover, were impotent. Because of their

277

resolute denial of evolution and their excessive detachment and passivity, they were unable to support the thrust of cosmogenesis.

In short, Teilhard flatly accused the world's great non-Christian religions of being both unwilling and unable to assimilate science, technology, and Western ideas. This meant a failure to mix with the very current of contemporary life. "No one," he writes, "who has been deeply influenced by modern culture and the knowledge that goes with it can sincerely be a Confucian, a Buddhist or Muslim (unless he is prepared to live a double interior life, or profoundly to modify for his own use the terms of his religion)."[60] Hinduism did not escape Teilhard's critical gaze. It offered to him little more than the "numbing and deadening effect of a religion obsessed by material forms and ritualism."[61] The specific weakness of all Eastern religions, however, was what Teilhard had pinpointed in Buddhist detachment. "The Buddhist *denies* himself," he wrote, "in order to kill desire (he *does not believe* in the value of *being*)."[62]

Eastern mysticisms, in Teilhard's view, thwarted the life process and countered the direction of authentic cosmogenesis in two ways. First, instead of seeking a heightened identity, some Eastern types of mysticisms promoted dissolution of personal identity in an impersonal whole by striving for nirvana, "nature's drug." Through nirvana, the person attempts to become a pure object by dissolving into the surrounding phenomena. For Teilhard, this meant that *"in reality everything is materialized. . . . Life is understood and experienced as a function of matter."*[63] A mysticism that surrenders so easily to matter's seductive call could hardly save the West from its alleged materialism.

The second form of Eastern mysticism is excessively otherworldly and essentially denies the existence of matter. It considers all phenomena as *maya,* or illusion, and flees from the multiplicity of phenomena as quickly

278

as possible. Through enstatic introversion, for example, the yogin attempts to preserve the center of his being by preventing the intrusion of the phenomenal world. The genuine yogin tries to become a pure subject without a world of phenomena. For Teilhard, however, this is "the increased loneliness of the reflective Titan,"[64] an egoism and fruitless solipsism.

On the other hand, Teilhard considered authentic mysticism far removed from fusion with the phenomenal world or narcissistic enstasy. For him, the central desire of all mysticism is "*to be united* (that is, to become the other) *while remaining oneself.*"[65] Love, personality, union, and difference constitute genuine mysticism, not fusion, impersonality, identification, and dissolution. Authentic love mysticism differentiates as it unites. It neither fuses nor leaves the elements alone in themselves. It must confirm and deepen the identity of each element in the mystical union, therefore, yet truly make these elements one. Only mysticisms of love lead to heightened interiority, complexity, consciousness, and freedom.

On the other hand, Eastern mysticisms lead to relaxation, simplification through impoverishment, and unity through fusion. Instead of unifying the various elements into a heightened synthesis, they suppress the elements through dissolution. Passivity, world-negation, asceticism, and being out of date characterize these mysticisms. These mysticisms of "identification"[66] take the radical identity of each person, and fuse or dissolve it with an undifferentiated common ground, thereby annihilating all differences. Many simply become one without a difference. Dehumanizing undifferentiated mysticisms born from the fusion of many elements mean a loss of consciousness, dissolution, expansion, depersonalization, and "de-differentiation," that is, instead of a person becoming more himself, he becomes less so.

To be sure, Teilhard distinguished three types of Eastern mysticism: the Hindu, the Chinese, and the Japanese. Hindu mysticism is a mysticism centered on "God." For the Hindu, the invisible ultimate is much more real and tangible than the visible world. This monist mysticism stresses the unreality of all phenomena and cultivates an intoxication with emptiness. The Chinese type, on the other hand, is a mysticism of the individual confronted with the world. Basically naturalistic and humanistic, it emphasizes the visible over the invisible world. The Japanese type is essentially a social mysticism that possesses an incredible sense of the value of the collective.

In line with Japanese collective mysticism, Marxism attracted Teilhard because of its deep sense of collective man, humanity, and the earth. This "youthful form of religion" inspired "a contagious faith in an ideal to which a man's life can be given."[67] Marxism had awakened humanity to the power of politics, science, technology, evolution, and man's own ability to create a more humane world. Extremely important for Teilhard were its faith and hope in the future. On the other hand, because Marxism essentially ignores the person in favor of an abstract collective and because it internationalizes hatred, it demolishes the only basis for a solid humanism: love and compassion. Marxism's rejection of personal immortality and real transcendence dooms humanity to this world, leaves a "feeling of insecurity and incompleteness," and short-circuits the false hopes it raises for some future, earthly utopia.

Genuine mysticism, for Teilhard, is essentially a question of love and of being centered on a personal God. "Love is a unifying energy, in fact it is 'the supreme spiritual energy' linking all elements and persons in their 'irreplaceable and incommunicable essence' in a universal process of unification."[68] Eastern mysticisms destroy love by their focus upon an impersonal absolute. They seek the higher self by way of identification through relaxation and not by convergence through tension, which is characteristic of love mysticisms. To identify with the absolute is to eliminate love.

For this reason, Teilhard refused to identify either the loving devotion of Hindu *bhakti* or Buddhist compassion with Christian love. Hindu *bhakti* and Buddhist compassion do not have an absolute with a real personal center; they presuppose that love, or differentiated unity, must always pass over into identity, or undifferentiated unity. If two become one without remaining two, how can love survive? If the fundamental illusion for many Eastern religions is the reality of the self, how can love exist once every illusory self has vanished into an impersonal absolute?

One Teilhard scholar, Ursula King, maintains that Teilhard had read more widely on various types of mysticisms and had a greater general knowledge of Eastern peoples and cultures than previously thought.[69] But she also contends that he had neither studied Eastern mysticisms in their own right nor had detailed knowledge about them. Concerning his tenacious views, which always placed Eastern mysticisms in opposition to Western, she writes: "Understood literally rather than typologically, they are often inaccurate, harsh, and unjust."[70]

King maintains, moreover, that Teilhard's distinction between the roads of the East and the West is strictly theoretical, typological, evaluative, and not sufficiently nuanced. He included too much under the umbrella term "Eastern mysticisms." Furthermore, he seemed to have underestimated vastly the ability of the great religions of the East to adapt to science, technology, evolution, and contemporary life. It also seems true that he foresaw neither the importance of Eastern religions for the West's contemporary orientation nor the importance of Western religions for the East's change of focus.

Many criticized Teilhard during his own lifetime for many of the above reasons, but he never wavered from his fundamental approach to Eastern mysticisms. Without denying that Christianity still has much to learn from, to be nourished by, and to contribute to Eastern religions, there may still be an abiding truth to Teilhard's view that: ". . . if the religions of India are less negative than I said, that fact does not essentially affect my thesis, the purpose of which is above all to distinguish 'two essential types' of possible mysticisms. It would be quite extraordinary, I admit, for either of these types to be met anywhere in the *pure* state . . . I still believe that, *logically*, Eastern religions and contemplation kill action. . . ."[71]

THE ROAD OF CHRISTIAN MYSTICISM

According to Teilhard, authentic mysticism is a principle of organization and a main axis along which evolution moves. It not only places a person in contact with the inner elan of evolution; it also concomitantly strengthens this elan. Teilhard rejected Eastern mysticisms because he sought one that would sustain and animate the dynamisms of the contemporary world. Eastern mysticisms of "evasion" gave no life to the evolutionary thrust. Only a mysticism that fostered matter's drive to become spirit, spirit's drive to become person, and humanity's drive to find its common soul in the cosmic Christ would suffice. It must be a mysticism of evolution, one of differentiated unity that preserves "the most individual characteristics of beings far beyond themselves,"[72] yet who are radically one in the personal God of love.

Unlike Eastern mysticisms, which suppress the individual elements in mystical union, Teilhard contends that Christian mysticism sublimates them. Christian mysticism brings about a genuine differentiated union through concentration upon the personal God of love, not a dissolution into an impersonal absolute. Christian

282

mysticism preserves, confirms, and fulfills the identity of each individual by its union with a deeper, personal center. Ultimate unity with the God of love is reached via convergence, not by a return to some primordial oneness. This necessitates both attachment and detachment as mystical attitudes.

Authentic Christian mysticism leads to heightened complexity, interiority, differentiation, consciousness, freedom, and personality. Eastern mysticisms go in the opposite direction: simplification, diffusion, unification, unconsciousness, determinism, and impersonality. Eastern mysticisms are essentially pantheisms of diffusion, are not motivated by love, and terminate in an Absolute that is simply the All. Christian mysticism, on the other hand, is a pantheism of convergence and differentiation, effected by love, and terminating with God being All in all.

Because of the convergence of multiple elements through progressive personalization, Christian mysticism helps to form the universe into an organic whole with a transformed and higher form of unity ultimately caused and constituted by the cosmic Christ. This mysticism not only loves God above all things, but more importantly, in and through all things. It is essentially a mysticism of union with a higher, personal center, the God of love.

It would be a mistake, however, to think that Teilhard considered Christian mysticism as it was or as it existed in his day to be the mysticism for the contemporary age. The "Christian path which declares *all earthly differentiation to be in vain*, and discovers a milieu of effort and homogeneous personalization in the *meritorious*, in grace"[73] could not serve science, evolution, and the aspirations of contemporary persons. Therefore, not only in Eastern mysticisms, but also in Christianity, there was an excessively otherworldly communion with God that too quickly bypassed the desires of this world.

283

Teilhard called for a "new mysticism," a future mysticism based not only upon a *"Christianity faithfully extended to its utmost limits,"* but also upon a "Christianity which surpasses itself."[74] Only this new, future, *evolving* mysticism could provide the maximum energy required for the future of cosmogenesis. Moreover, the world's great religions were converging upon and synthesizing around Christianity as the "principal axis" of evolution to bring about this new mysticism.

According to Teilhard, through a concurrent process of differentiation and unification, the world's great religions will converge around Christianity to integrate and transcend their existing differences. This converging process will produce a heightened synthesis, a new mysticism, a Christianity that surpasses itself. Neither syncretism nor the reduction to some preexistent unity will cause this synthesis. In Teilhard's view, this new mysticism of convergence did not exist in "the sterile and conservative ecumenism of a 'common ground' but [in] the creative ecumenism of a 'convergence' . . . on a common ideal."[75] In rejecting both the facile syncretism of so much contemporary thought and the so-called perennial philosophy of Aldous Huxley to which many subscribe, Teilhard emphasized the *evolution* of mysticism, a yet to be accomplished synthesis. A prime mystical illusion, for Teilhard, was one which "pretends to Union and Presence *independently of Time* and Evolution . . . as if the contact with God could be achieved without the Evolution of Consciousness— from the beginning."[76]

TEILHARD'S RADICAL CHRISTOCENTRISM

Teilhard was keenly aware that one of the contemporary person's most pressing psychological needs was to be assured of evolution's successful outcome. Today's person needs the assurance that the progress for which he has assumed responsibility does not eventually end in some form of cosmic death. From a scientific, philosophical, and theological perspective, Teilhard wrote to provide the assurance that evolution does not come to a dead end, but converges into a "theosphere of love" in which God is All in all.

From science, Teilhard's "ultraphysics" tried to show that evolution does in fact converge, that matter finds its true goal in the human spirit wherein it becomes self-conscious. Evolution converges in the human to become evolution conscious of itself. Teilhard's philosophy emphasized that as consciousness becomes more complex and self-consciousness heightens, human socialization also becomes more complex. With deepening forms of love, "amorization," the human person evolves not only individually but socially as well.

From his supernatural faith, Teilhard Christified evolution by identifying the Christ of revelation with the goal, or Omega point, of evolution. The converging universe demands an ultrapersonal center with the power to draw evolution to its ultimate goal by identifying here and now the love energy of the world. He first identifies cosmogenesis with Christogenesis and then shifts the emphasis to Christogenesis, which takes the "place of the vague focus of convergence" which is "the well-defined reality of the Incarnate Word, in whom all things hold together."[77]

It cannot be overemphasized that Teilhard considered cosmogenesis to be a radical Christogenesis, that evolution is actually becoming the cosmic Christ. His foundation, point of departure, and final goal are simply that Jesus of Nazareth forms a "physical" center for both humanity and for the material world. He emphasized time and again Christ's cosmic function, the "physical" influence of Christ over the whole of cosmic reality. As Teilhard trenchantly put it: "Between the Word on the one hand and Jesus the Man on the other, a sort of Christic 'third nature' comes into being . . . that of the total Christ who totalizes, in whom the individual human element born of Mary is transformed by the Resurrection into the state not simply of a cosmic Element (or Milieu or Compass) but of an ultimate psychic Centre for the gathering together of the universe. . . . In the total Christ . . . there is not just Man and God; there is also he who in his 'theandric' being gathers together the whole of creation: *in quo omnia constat* [in whom all things hold together]."[78]

The "total Christ" exercises a "physical" control over the universe by virtue of the organic and physical aspects of the incarnation. Teilhard placed the Christian mystery of God's incarnation into the context of an evolving and converging universe, and he understood each in terms of the other. Through the incarnation, God enters not only humanity but also the very universe as their cosmic and directing principle. Because God has entered the cosmos to take everything to himself, the cosmos contains a Christic dynamic toward which all converges in harmony and love. The incarnation elevates the natural world and gives it a supernatural finality directed by and centered on the cosmic Christ. As Teilhard says: "It is first by the Incarnation and next by the Eucharist that [Christ] organizes us for himself and imposes himself upon us. . . . By his Incarnation he inserted himself not just into humanity but into the universe which supports humanity . . . a directing principle, of a Centre towards which everything converges in harmony and love."[79]

Teilhard's radical incarnationalism equates God the Creater, God the Redeemer, and God the Evolver. Creation, redemption, and evolution in some sense are all part of one cosmic process: the mystical body of Christ being formed through evolution. "The world is still being created," Teilhard wrote, "and it is Christ who brings himself to completion in it."[80]

Teilhard creatively transposed certain texts in St. John and St. Paul that underscore the cosmic supremacy of

Christ over all of creation.[81] Because of the incarnation, Teilhard considered Christ to be an actual world, an organism that united everything to himself, even "physically" and "biologically." By emphasizing Christ as a universal physical element and as the cosmic center of creation, Teilhard wished to counter the juridical and extrinsic theological interpretations of his day with respect to Christ's salvific activity. Christ's "organic" and "physical" influence really means his full body-person, human-divine, personal presence as the Lord who rose bodily from the dead in glory.

In his hauntingly beautiful, "The Mass of the World,"[82] Teilhard, finding himself in the desert without bread and wine to say Mass, offers all his and the world's efforts, toils, accomplishments, sufferings, and setbacks as the elements to be transubstantiated into the body and blood of Christ. For Teilhard, evolution itself is an eons-old Mass slowly consecrating all the elements of the cosmos into the one cosmic Christ. Looking upon the cosmos as one immense Host, he considered the eucharist to be the very axis of evolution through which Christ produced a cosmic transubstantiation of all things into himself. He wrote: "At every moment the Eucharist Christ controls— from the point of view of the organization of the Pleroma . . . the whole movement of the universe. . . . As our humanity assimilates the material world, and as the Host assimilates our humanity, the eucharistic transformation goes beyond and completes the transubstantiation of the bread on the altar. Step by step it irresistibly invades the universe."[83] Only one thing is happening throughout the universe for Teilhard: the incarnation that completes itself in each individual through the eucharist.

For him, Jesus Christ is the "universal Christ," the "total Christ," the "privileged central axis" of evolution, the "super-Christ," the "Soul of the world," the "Evolver," the "Christic nucleus" of an evolving cosmos which is "incommensurable with any prophet or Buddha."[84]

It would be a serious mistake to think, however, that Teilhard's Christ is an idealized abstraction of evolution or humanity. The cosmic Christ is, for Teilhard, always the historical person of Jesus of Nazareth. Moreover, it is Jesus of Nazareth who leads the total life of the universe and through whose resurrection evolution received its central dynamic. It is Jesus of Nazareth who is the historical point of reference or the historical tangibility of the divine milieu being formed by cosmogenesis. Despite his infrequent references to the historical Jesus, Teilhard never separates Christ-Omega from Jesus of Nazareth. For as he says: "The mystical Christ, the universal Christ of St. Paul, has neither meaning nor value in our eyes except as an expansion of the Christ who was born of Mary and who died on the Cross. . . . However far we may be drawn into the divine spaces opened to us by Christian mysticism, we never depart from the Jesus of the Gospels."[85]

Teilhard's emphasis upon the cosmic Christ who is inextricably the revealed Christ of the gospels allowed him to resolve one contemporary burning issue. According to Teilhard, much of contemporary malaise stemmed from the inability to believe in a personal God. People have great interest, however, in the All, in the totality of things, in an impersonal Absolute. Because love dies in the presence of the impersonal, however, Teilhard contended that human progress and evolution itself were in jeopardy. Only love and a focus upon a personal Absolute could sustain human progress and evolution. "Our world denies personality and God," he wrote, "because it believes in the All: Everything depends on convincing it that, on the contrary, it *must* believe in the personal because it believes in the All."[86]

Teilhard confessed that during his entire lifetime he had never had the least bit of difficulty in addressing God as a "Supreme Someone."[87] He had always related the All to the personal and saw them both in an evolutionary and Christocentric perspective. Because cosmogenesis is Christogenesis, there is "a god who makes himself cosmic and an evolution which makes itself a person."[88] The cosmic Christ conjoins the All and the personal, enabling contemporary humanity to love the totality as a person.

In this way, Teilhard contended that the human person's cosmic passion, love for the All or the legitimate tendency toward pantheism, could be taken up, sublimated, and transformed into a profound Christian pantheism in which the personal God of love is All in all. "The essential of Christianity," Teilhard writes, "[is] . . . to positively place the world in relation with the Supreme Personal, that is to say, to name Him."[89] The human person's fundamental passion for the All and love for the world find their fulfillment in a person-centered, Christocentric mysticism of love. It is the cosmic Christ, the total Christ, who brings about the union with God through the earth.

But it must also be emphasized that "we are united to Christ by entering into communion with all men."[90] Genuine Christogenesis requires a radical anthropogenesis. Teilhard maintained that as the human person evolves, deeper forms of human socialization arise. For this process, however, only charity can supply " 'the supreme spiritual energy' linking all elements and persons in their 'irreplaceable and incommunicable essence' in a universal process of unification."[91] Charity is an axial energy for Teilhard, an evolutionary energy by which evolution reaches ever-higher levels of progress.

Teilhard thereby emphasized that it was impossible to love Christ and the universe without loving other persons, and vice versa. Loving others, especially in the ef-

289

fort to effect a more humane universe, unites a person with others, but also with Christ and the universe. Because of Teilhard's emphasis upon the person's evolving social nature and on love as evolution's axial energy, he vigorously rejected the notion of religion as a private affair. Religion, spirituality, and mysticism tap the love reservoir of the human spirit. Love bonds persons to persons, center to center, and brings all together in a living unity that reinforces the personhood of each. Through love, humanity becomes one person, the cosmic Christ. Teilhard writes: "The only subject ultimately capable of mystical transfiguration is the whole group of mankind forming a single body and a single soul in charity."[92] Still, this "mystical transfiguration" strengthens and preserves the unique identity of each person through the differentiated unity of love.

By focusing upon the cosmic Christ, Teilhard's new mysticism synthesizes "three universal components: the Cosmic, the Human, and the Christic."[93] It blends, in effect, Teilhard's so-called Hindu totality, Western technology, and Christian personalism. His radical ecumenism brings together a deep sense of the earth, a faith in humanity, and a radical sense of transcendence. This new mysticism incorporates, sublimates, and transforms the pantheistic tendencies of Eastern mysticisms, the Marxist faith in humanity, and Christianity's traditional faith in a transcendent, personal God into a Christianity that surpasses itself. The legitimate aspirations of pantheistic Eastern mysticism, Marxist humanistic movements, and traditional Christianity are satisfied and fulfilled in the cosmic Christ in whom the All, becoming, and personality converge.[94]

CONCLUDING REFLECTIONS
Teilhard's own personal experience and thought offer a strong rejection of the commonly held contemporary dogma that all mysticism is basically one and the same the world over. According to this contemporary idea,

all fully developed mystical experience is undifferentiated unity. The decisive differences between various
mysticisms rest solely on the way diverse cultures and
religions interpret this core experience.[95]

On the other hand, Teilhard argues clearly for irreducibly plural types of mysticisms. In many respects, his
typology of mysticisms resembles that of R. C. Zaehner.
Zaehner's well-known thesis is: ". . . there appear to
be at least three distinct mystical states which cannot
be identical—the pan-en-henic where all creaturely existence is experienced as one and one as all; the state of
pure isolation of what we may now call the uncreated
soul or spirit from all that is other than itself; and
thirdly, the simultaneous loss of the purely human personality, the 'ego,' and the absorption of the uncreated
spirit, the 'self,' into the essence of God, in Whom both
the individual personality and the whole objective
world seem to be entirely obliterated."[96]

Zaehner's "pan-en-henic" mysticism closely resembles
Teilhard's Hindu totality, a mysticism of fusion with an
impersonal Absolute. From the perspective of Christian
philosophy and theology, it is entirely possible for a
person to experience the unity of all created things or
his fundamental relationship to the cosmos. If the human person is essentially "spirit-in-world," the pantheistic experience may very well highlight the spirit-IN-
WORLD aspect of human existence. Cosmic consciousness, from this point of view, might possibly be an experience of the ground of all created things or even of
the silent God. Still, Evelyn Underhill seems to be correct when she evaluates cosmic consciousness as only
one aspect of full mystical consciousness, as a mysticism that has not gone far enough.[97]

Zaehner's second type, the "state of pure isolation,"
mirrors Teilhard's "Titan," the state of mystical enstasy
in which the yogin cuts himself off from the phenomenal world to dwell in radical interiority. This form of

mysticism seems quite common. The above chapter on Merton called attention to Buber's own experience of the "pre-biographical unity" of his soul and Raguin's warnings of a mystical enstasy in which a person simply "loses himself in himself without ever reaching God."[98] Because the human spirit can "return-to-itself" and possesses an intuitive awareness of itself, enstatic techniques can produce mystical introversion.

Philosophically speaking, therefore, the human spirit has the capability of being present to itself through a type of intellectual intuition shorn of images. It is present to itself in active identity by way of an act that dissolves the normal contrast between subject and object. The known intellect is the knowing intellect. It is not surprising, therefore, that some mystical traditions have made this intellectual intuition the object of their quest and have developed highly sophisticated techniques for cultivating it.

Although Teilhard would never use the language of merging, absorption, and obliteration to explain the differentiated union effected between God and the mystic, Zaehner's third type of mysticism resembles Teilhard's own description of Western theistic mysticism. To be sure, Zaehner's analysis of theistic mysticism distinguishes carefully the differentiated union with God from the nontheistic, undifferentiated unity with an impersonal Absolute.

It must be emphasized, however, that Teilhard did not share Zaehner's sharp nature/grace dichotomy. Although Teilhard preserved the necessary distinction between nature and grace, he emphasized the world's supernatural finality caused by the incarnation. His new mysticism likewise sought to preserve the best in profane, natural pantheism by sublimating it into the experience of the cosmic Christ. He wrote, for example: "It is not enough to refuse or to ridicule Shiva: for *he exists*. What is necessary is to Christify him. Christ would

292

not be complete if he did not integrate Shiva (as a component), whilst transforming him."[99] The cosmic Christ must assimilate and transform into himself even the seemingly indifferent and hostile forces of the universe that frequently destroy humanity.

Teilhard's decisive emphasis upon evolution also separates him from Zaehner's more static approach to mysticism. Teilhard contended that mysticism has not been, is not, and will not always be the same because an evolutionary universe and the religions are converging along the main axis of Christianity. For these reasons, Teilhard also distanced himself from those who sought in mysticism, spirituality, and religion a nostalgic return to an alleged golden age when humanity was supposedly more unified with itself, nature, and God.[100]

As mentioned above, Teilhard's evolutionary view caused him to repudiate the common core approach to religion and mysticism. It may be, however, that he was somewhat too hasty in this assessment. The German scholar Friedrich Heiler has pointed out seven features common to all the great world religions.[101] First, the "reality of realities" is transcendent and distinct from all transient realities. Second, although transcendent, this reality is also immanent in all things, especially the human heart. Third, this reality is every person's greatest good and the ultimate goal of all his strivings. Fourth, the ultimate reality is love. Fifth, the human way to the real is by way of self-emptying, of sacrifice. Sixth, love of neighbor is an essential aspect of the genuine path to the absolute. Finally, despite the great variety of religious experience, the superior path to the real is love. If these elements are really present in all the great religions of the world—a view Teilhard and others would deny—it is difficult to see how they could be absent from his mysticism of the future.[102]

Teilhard's new mysticism calls for transforming the sense of humanity engendered by the unifying power of science and many contemporary Marxist movements. Christian love is, of course, the supreme form of evolutionary energy, which nurtures ever-deepening forms of socialization. Only this love is ultimately capable of saving the best in science and Marxism.

Teilhard stressed the mystical roots of eros and the need for "affective dyad" relationships between men and women.[103] The mysticism of the future would, however, "virginize" mystical friendships between men and women to harness the evolutionary energy in eros and direct it to higher stages of evolution. Celibate relationships will play an ever more important role in the future. Teilhard would have found the experience of mystical friendship in the life of the twelfth-century English mystic, Aelred of Rievaulx, quite appealing. Aelred wrote: "In that multitude of brethren I found no one whom I did not love, and no one by whom, I felt sure, I was not loved. I was filled with such joy that it surpassed all the delights of this world. I felt, indeed, my spirit transfused into all and the affection of all to have passed into me, so that I could say with the Prophet: 'Behold, how good and how pleasant it is for brethren to dwell together in unity.'"[104]

Teilhard maintained that science was ultimately animated by a mystical hope, that its deepest aspirations were in some way mystical. Bernard Lonergan seems to provide the critical groundings for this point of view. Lonergan underscores, for example, that the question of God is intrinsic to all our questioning and that "being in love with God is the basic fulfillment of our conscious intentionality."[105] The very dynamism of the human mind is to be attentive, intelligent, reasonable, responsible, and in love.

Therefore, the deepest yearnings of the human spirit raise the questions of ultimate truth, value, and authenticity. Only when the human person surrenders to the experience of God's mysterious call to unrestricted and unconditional love "within subjectivity as a vector, an undertow, a fateful call to a dreaded holiness"[106] are these drives of the human spirit satisfied. In addition, human authenticity results only when the person surrenders to the "native spontaneities and inevitabilities of our consciousness"[107] to be attentive, intelligent, reasonable, and in love. It would seem, therefore, that Lonergan's cognitional theory could provide the critical foundations for what Teilhard clearly saw: science, religion, and mysticism must be distinguished, but never separated, for they are anchored in a common root.

All authentic Christian mystics emphasize that the center of the true self is not in the limited, finite ego, but in God. Teilhard likewise stressed the necessity of being centered, not on oneself, but on the cosmic Christ. It was his genius, however, not to overlook the importance of developing oneself, of being oneself, in order to give oneself. Genuine Christian spirituality and mysticism demand both attachment and detachment, both activity and passivity. Self-actualization, or the process by which human potential is actualized and employed, must be intrinsically linked to self-realization, or the process by which the person surrenders to what is greater than himself. A person must develop his talents and abilities, and go to the limits of his humanity. Only then can he surrender to the forces which tend to overwhelm him. Diminishment, the process of being emptied out, takes its meaning, for Teilhard, only from being filled with the God of love, of being an integral part of the divine milieu.

Teilhard's Christo-cosmic universe provides a good link between the historical Jesus of Nazareth and the cosmic Christ. Because of the incarnation, in the historical Jesus the universe actually lived, died, and rose to new, divine life. For Teilhard, moreover, death is an evolutionary activity that inserts a person decisively into the universe by confirming and heightening his identity while uniting him definitively to the totality that is personal, the cosmic Christ.

Karl Rahner has also focused attention on how the historical Jesus becomes cosmic. Not only does Rahner place Christ in an evolutionary perspective through the incarnation, but he sees the incarnation reaching its high point in Jesus' death. "When the vessel of his body was shattered in death," Rahner writes, "Christ was poured out over all the cosmos; he became actually, in his very humanity, what he had always been by his dignity, the heart of the universe, the innermost centre of creation."[108] Both Teilhard and Rahner maintain that Christ belongs to the innermost reality of the universe by reason of his incarnation, life, death, and resurrection. For both, the act of dying is a profoundly mystical act of communion by which a person finally belongs totally to the cosmos by being supremely detached from self and attached to God. In and through death, for Rahner, the person becomes "pancosmic" by virtue of his total self-surrender to the God of love.

The entire universe for Teilhard is a divine milieu, a mystical milieu, wherein all things become diaphanous and transparent to reveal the divine presence. Through a mysterious and unexpected grace, the very heart of the universe ignites to disclose the divine fire permeating all things. If St. John of the Cross found all things in God, Teilhard's sacramental view finds God in all things through his passionate love of the world in God.

One writer on mysticism notes that: "The mystic experience ends with the words, 'I live, yet not I, but God in me.' This feeling of identification, which is the term of mystical activity, has a very important significance. In its early stages the mystic consciousness feels the Absolute in opposition to the Self . . . as the mystic activity goes on, it tends to abolish this opposition. . . . When it has reached its term the consciousness finds itself possessed by the sense of a Being at one and the same time greater than the Self and identical with it: great enough to be God, intimate enough to be me."[109] This mystical process describes Teilhard's own experiences. When he had plunged into the very depths of his being, he exclaimed: "It is you yourself whom I find, you who makes me participate in your being, you who moulds me."[110] By surrendering to the forces of life and diminishment throughout his life, he had experienced a "fontal communion" with God. He had come to be like a sponge in the divine ocean or an element in the divine fire. He had experienced himself slowly being transmuted through everything he did and suffered into the one cosmic Christ.

As noted above, through the incarnation Christ descended into the ultimate depths of matter to ascend and bring the entire creation to God so that God may be All in all. Human authenticity, according to Teilhard, therefore requires a parallel descent into matter (especially through scientific experimentation) and an ascent to God. It cannot be overemphasized that Teilhard's mysticism is one of communion with God through the earth.

The Benedictine writer Bede Griffiths, influenced by Teilhard, Sri Aurobindo (a Hindu thinker with strong affinities to Teilhard), and a strong resurrection spirituality, emphasizes both a yoga of ascent and descent. He writes: "There must be a movement of ascent to pure consciousness, a detachment from all the moods of nature, a realization of the Self in its eternal Ground beyond space and time. But then there must also be a movement of descent, by which the spirit enters into the depths of matter and raises it to a new mode of existence, in which it becomes the medium of spiritual consciousness."[111]

Although Teilhard would undoubtedly praise Griffiths' resurrection emphasis and the necessity of matter to be assimilated by Spirit, he would hardly have agreed

297

with his reverse yogic order of ascent-descent. For Teilhard, one must *first* descend into matter and *then* ascend. Nor would Teilhard have approved of a detachment from all moods of nature. He would have repudiated Griffiths' distrust of science and technology and his thesis that the scientific consciousness is a type of fall from unity with the original center, a form of original sin.

Much credit must be given to Teilhard for stressing that one reaches God by sublimation, and not by squandering oneself. Genuine mysticism for Teilhard increases personality, heightens consciousness, deepens freedom, and intensifies evolutionary tension. Pseudo-mysticisms, on the other hand, decrease personality, lessen consciousness, reduce freedom, and waste evolutionary energy. This puts Teilhard in agreement with commentators on mystical consciousness who emphasize that ". . . contrary to the common view . . . the highest form of mysticism is the synthesis of a *heightened* tension between the ego and the self."[112] It seems necessary, therefore, to underscore what nurtures personality, consciousness, freedom, and evolution, and what thwarts these, especially when so many today consider mysticism to be a form of regression in the service of the ego, a return to a primitive or infantile state of consciousness, or similar to the alleged expansion of consciousness induced by alcohol and drugs.

As mentioned above, Teilhard's stress upon a personal God stands as a strong criticism both of Eastern mysticism and of the contemporary interest in an impersonal Absolute. The Christian mystical tradition indicates, however, that personal predicates for God have never been sufficient in themselves to describe the mystic's "oceanic" experience of being transformed into God.[113] The clean pane of glass invisible in the sunlight, two candle flames becoming one, the drop of rain dissolving in the ocean, and the piece of iron becoming like the

298

fire that heats it are images frequently employed by the Christian mystics. God for them is often described as the fire, water, air, brightness, and light into which they seemingly dissolve. Yet even when the personality of God seems absent in an impersonal feeling of dissolution, the mystics still describe transforming union in such a way that "all that we value in personality—love, action, will—remains unimpaired."[114]

Of course, most Christian mystics have combined this impersonal oceanic language with the language of love and person to describe their experience of mystical marriage with the personal God of love. The transpersonal qualities of both God and the deification process that differentiates as it unites require both personal and impersonal images and predicates. Teilhard is highly orthodox and traditional in this regard. He hesitated neither to call God "person" nor to describe God as "fire." Although he frequently prayed to God as though addressing a person, he nevertheless described himself as being in the "divine milieu," the "mystical milieu," wherein all was diaphanous and transparent. It should also be noted how often he refers to God or Christ as being "ultra-," "hyper-," or "supra-Person." In this way he avoided falling into excessive anthropomorphism or sterile monism.

Teilhard can be criticized, however, for his exclusive focus upon Jesus Christ. The Father and the Holy Spirit have no real role in the divine milieu. His lack of trinitarian perspective and framework seriously limits the value of this vision for a genuinely radical, contemporary, Christian mysticism and spirituality. A more Father-centered focus might have also restored a sense of transcendence to his view of the universe as almost swallowed up by divine immanence.

Another area of weakness in Teilhard's writings is his almost benign sense of evil, especially his tendency to impersonalize sin.[115] For someone who so emphasized

God as person and the increased identity of the human person throughout mystical union, it is ironic that he almost entirely overlooks the radically interpersonal quality of sin. He contends that physical and moral evil must occur in an evolving cosmos by virtue of "statistical necessity." He looks at physical and moral evil in cosmic terms, in terms of their effects upon cosmogenesis, as a form of disunion and the squandering of the love-energy required for evolutionary progress.

Because Teilhard contends that the incarnation took place to unite *all* reality into the cosmic Christ, he transposes the traditional emphasis upon "Christ the Redeemer" to "Christ the Evolver." Christ's cross thereby becomes a symbol for the pain and effort of cosmogenesis, but not the symbol of expiation for sin. Christ dies, not to atone for the sins of the world, but to take upon himself fully the burden of evolution's successful outcome. Teilhard's "uncompromising evolutionism,"[116] his assumption that an evolutionary world view is the *only* context for understanding the truths of the faith, undoubtedly blinded him to Christ's expiatory, redemptive role. Oddly enough, although absent, this expiatory aspect of redemption could easily be inserted into his fundamental outlook without distorting it in any way. As one Teilhardian scholar has correctly noted: ". . . Teilhard failed to link reparation for sin with refusal to love (and therefore with evolution's success) because he was dominated by the fear that any emphasis at all on reparation would immediately obscure, if not entirely do away with, the cosmic character of Christ's work of salvation."[117]

Teilhard's Christocentrism has the advantage, therefore, of restoring to Christian focus Jesus Christ as truly Lord of heaven and earth by transposing into contemporary, evolutionary categories the earlier view of him as *Pantokrator*. His emphasis also counterbalances the contemporary tendency to relativize Jesus Christ, to reduce him to one religious founder among many. Those who would call Teilhard a "Christo-fascist" should note that Vatican II insisted that it is Christ "in whom men find the fullness of religious life. . . ."[118] And one need not subscribe to every aspect of Karl Rahner's well-known "anonymous Christian" theory to accept that the *grace of Christ* is at work in individuals, their organized religions, and their mysticism, even outside of explicit Christianity.[119]

On the other hand, although some of Teilhard's criticisms of Eastern mysticisms are undoubtedly correct, his rejection of the East is much too facile. The teachings of Vatican II confirm that a contemporary Christian spirituality and mysticism must respect the truth, holiness, and wisdom found in the great non-Christian religions of the world. The person of compelling holiness, wisdom, integrity, and human authenticity exists not only in Christianity. Without asserting that all religions and mysticisms are the same and without labeling everything Eastern as "pagan," "demonic," or merely "natural," contemporary Christians must look for the fruits of the Spirit of Christ both in Christianity and in non-Christian religions.

Perhaps a contemporary Christian ought to counterbalance Teilhard's views with those of someone like William Johnston, an Irish Jesuit who has lived in Japan for over thirty years.[120] Writing with lucid prose, critical discernment, genuine openness to and appreciation of Eastern values, but not overlooking key differences between East and West, Johnston contends that Christianity has much to learn from the East. If Christianity owes much to the early Church's assimilation of Greek culture, today's Christianity must not overlook the opportunities for mutual enrichment between East and West.

To be sure, much from the East must be tested, washed, and baptized before its incorporation into

Christianity. Still, religious and mystical experience, silence, humility, meditation, compassion, and nonviolence can form the basis for a genuine, contemporary East-West dialogue. Arnold Toynbee may very well have been correct when he claimed that the most significant event of the twentieth century is the meeting of East and West on the level of religious and mystical experience.[121]

Even with the above limitations, Teilhard offers a profound spirituality and mysticism for the contemporary world. His integration of pantheism's cosmic sense, Marxism and science's humanistic sense, and evolution with his Christian personalism go far in meeting the deepest aspirations of the contemporary person. His blending, moreover, of the cosmic sense, evolution, and humanism, especially with the Christian doctrines of creation, incarnation, and a personal God may very well have produced a synthesis that in some ways transcends the differences between East and West. In this sense, it is a "new" mysticism, the mysticism of the future. By stressing both activity and passivity, meaningful and seemingly meaningless suffering, his evolutionary mysticism of the divine milieu has room both for contemplation-in-action and victim-soul mysticism. In summary, "Teilhard's interpretation of mysticism combines in a unique manner the appeal of the transcendent with that of a dynamic, tangible and evolving world, transformed from within through the immanence and presence of the divine."[122]

Chapter Eight

Christian Mysticism and Unusual Phenomena

Previous chapters presented the author of the *Cloud of Unknowing* and St. John of the Cross as two proponents of classical Christian apophatic mysticism. According to their teachings, a person moves from discursive to affective to simple prayer and experiences the tides of consolation and desolation along this prayer spectrum. These premystical stages require, moreover, an emphasis upon asceticism, or active purgation.

Thus, the person called to apophatic mysticism in the strict sense recognizes special signs indicative of the invitation to the higher levels of prayer. The apophatic contemplative progresses through the passive prayer of quiet and the prayer of semiecstatic union, both interlaced with the terrible nights of passive purgations and overwhelming consolations. Forgetting, unknowing, darkness, and naked love lead the mystic to mystical marriage wherein he begets transcendental life.

St. Ignatius of Loyola and St. Teresa of Avila were exemplified as representatives of the classical Christian kataphatic tradition. Instead of a knowing by not knowing, this mystical heritage focuses upon a progressive simplification of prayer, which culminates in the highest levels of sacramental contemplation. The increasing transparency of the mysteries, images, and symbols of salvation history guides the mystic along the contemplative journey to mystical transformation and spiritual fecundity.

303

The views of Thomas Merton and Pierre Teilhard de Chardin were explicated to illustrate a transposition of the negative and affirmative mystical journeys into contemporary language, themes, and world views.

So far, therefore, this book has emphasized mysticism as a way of life initiated by God's living flame of love which purifies, illuminates, and transforms the mystic for total union with God. It has likewise implicitly defined Christian mysticism as the direct and conscious loving union of the person with God by way of contemplative prayer. In becoming God by participation, the Christian mystic also attains integrity and wholeness. The total body-person partakes of God's transforming activity.

It is evident, however, that unusual phenomena also occur frequently during the mystical journey. For example, the classical Christian mystics experienced a great variety of secondary mystical phenomena. Sooner or later, too, they all encountered the devil. In addition to these experiences found in the classical Christian tradition, contemporary charismatic movements give witness to strange occurrences that seem connected in some way to an authentic mystical life. Finally, recent interest in psychedelic drugs has raised the question of the relationship between these drugs and genuine Christian mysticism.

Of course, the scope of this book does not permit a detailed scriptural, psychological, phenomenological, and theological analysis of any or all of the above phenomena. A general description and a few selected reflections about them and their relationship to Christian mysticism must suffice.

SECONDARY MYSTICAL AND CHARISMATIC PHENOMENA

A General Description of Secondary Mystical Phenomena
During mystical ascent, a host of extraordinary, some-

times bizarre, yet secondary, phenomena normally arises that may aid or hinder the mystic's progress. Ecstasies, raptures, visions, locutions, revelations, the stigmata, levitations, and other phenomena frequently occur with the primary phenomenon of *infused contemplation*, or God's experienced loving self-communication. If past studies tended to overemphasize these unusual phenomena at the expense of the essential mystical phenomenon, that is, infused contemplation, contemporary studies seem to dissociate them too sharply.

It must be emphasized, however, that the classical Christian mystics have always recognized the ambiguous nature of these phenomena. Most secondary mystical phenomena can originate either from God, the devil, or the self. The authentic Christian mystic rarely seeks them. In fact, even those phenomena from God should, in most cases and if possible, be ignored, because they are usually only the overflow of his much deeper work that brings about its effect instantaneously. Moreover, the Christian mystics always subjected these unusual events to an intense discernment process; they always considered the possibility that they were being deceived.

Some of these phenomena have already been mentioned briefly in connection with the teachings of some of the mystics discussed in this book. For didactic purposes, however, it seems best to treat them here in a more orderly fashion.

Ecstasy and Rapture

Ecstasy seems to flow naturally or connaturally from the gift of mystical prayer.[1] Because of the intensity of absorption in or entrancement with God, the ecstatic person loses consciousness, to a greater or lesser degree, of everything except God. During ordinary prayer, the mystic recollects himself in a deliberate attempt to forget everything except God. During ecstasy, however, the mystic *must* focus upon God. In short, ecstasy is irresistible contemplation or enforced recollection.

Many commentators divide ecstasy into its physical, psychological,. and mystical elements. The physical aspect of ecstasy comprises the partial or total suspension of the internal and external senses. Breathing, the heartbeat rate, circulation, and body temperature decrease. In one sense, ecstasy denotes a trance condition of abnormal psycho-physical conditions.

Psychologically speaking, ecstasy means that God's infused loving knowledge strongly attracts the person's psychosomatic structure to reintegrate it around the call of divine love. The experience of God at the person's deepest center galvanizes his attention to the exclusion of everything else. In this way, God's loving presence produces a psycho-synthetic effect throughout the various levels of the person's being. Ecstasy implies a passionate concentration on God and a sense that one is outside of oneself for absorption in God.

Mystically speaking, ecstasy denotes entranced infused contemplation, an extraordinarily powerful, yet transitory, experience of union with God. Infused contemplation seems to complete itself in the experience of being ravished. The full flowering of the prayer of union paralyzes the normal workings of the internal and external senses, the imagination, the memory, and the intellect. It forces them to participate in an experience that transcends their capability, yet, paradoxically, eventually transforms and fulfills them in perfect integrity.

Strictly defined, *raptures* are sudden, violent, irresistible ecstasies. Rather than an ecstasy resulting from a period of intense concentration upon God's self-communication, rapture is a coercive, abrupt, uncontrollable ecstasy that may interrupt a person's normal state of consciousness.

Genuine mystical ecstasies likewise leave the mystic humbled, exalted, strengthened, without spiritual greed,

306

and even more ready to embrace the cross on the road
to mystical ascent. Such ecstasies are distinguished
from pathological and diabolical ecstasies by their life-
enhancing quality. Pathological and diabolical ecstasies
fixate the person on ideas, desires, and psychic debris
and lead to moral, psychological, and physical deterioration. On the other hand, genuine ecstasies wean a
person away from everything destructive by bestowing
a deep taste for God which integrates the entire body-
person around this synthesizing experience.

Despite the many beneficial effects from ecstasies and
raptures, most commentators consider them nonessen-
tial to infused contemplation. They occur because the
mystic's psychosomatic structure cannot support the
weight of God's loving influx. For example, powerful
ecstasies may be more indicative of psychosomatic frail-
ties and of a nature too easily prone to entrancement
and absorption than of a high degree of mystical contemplation and holiness. In fact, ecstasies cease with
transforming union. By this time, God has increased
and transformed the person's capacity to receive his
self-communication without abnormal physical and
psychological ramifications.

Because ecstasies really indicate the outward condition
of infused contemplation, or the psychosomatic reverberations from God's deeper presence, it would therefore be a serious mistake to equate the mystic with the
ecstatic.[2] However, all authentic Christian mystics did,
in fact, experience ecstasy. Given the incarnational
structure of grace and the psychosomatic brokenness
found in every person, must not ecstasies occur for
mystical contemplation to purify, illuminate, and transform the entire body-person?

Visions
In *sensible* or *corporeal visions* (also called *apparitions*),
the mystic sees with his bodily eyes a real or apparent

object naturally invisible to others. At Lourdes, for example, Bernadette had an apparition of the Blessed Virgin Mary. It must be emphasized, however, that few mystics have experienced corporeal visions. Most mystics and mystical commentators agree that sensible visions are most likely to be bogus. In this century, for example, the Church has approved only the apparitions of Our Lady at Fatima, Portugal, in 1917; Banneau, Belgium, in 1932; and Beauraing, Belgium, in 1933. The Church has either refused to approve or explicitly condemned a vast number of alleged apparitions of Mary.[3]

In *imaginative visions,* the image takes place in the mystic's creative imagination, or "picturing faculty," with an incredible clarity and sense of reality. Genuine imaginative visions, however, are not imaginative in the pejorative sense of being "imaginary," or hallucinatory. God's authentic action affects the imagination in some way, either by stirring up and synthesizing previously acquired phantasms or by infusing new ones. This action may occur during sleep, or, more commonly, during ecstasy. The mystics attest, moreover, that the object seen with the imagination possesses more reality than anything ever seen with the bodily eyes.

Intellectual visions occur when infused contemplation directly affects the mystic's intellect without the aid of sensible images or the normal use of the internal and external senses. God's self-communication agitates, modifies, and coordinates previously acquired ideas or infuses new ones. The resulting simple, intuitive knowledge imparts a deep sense of immediacy, certitude, and often personal presence. These intellectual visions seem to be infused contemplation itself refracted from the mystic's deepest center into his intellect. Commonly arising with transforming union, this most sublime and exalted type of vision brings peace, great light, and a desire for heavenly things. Although they carry God's indelible stamp, these profound visions must be care-

308

fully distinguished from the aftershocks they often produce in other regions of the mystic's being.

Locutions

The same distinctions and comments also apply to mystical *words,* more often called *locutions* or *auditions.* For example, the mystic may hear with his bodily ears an *auricular* locution, or external word, produced in some way by God. While sleeping or when awake, an *imaginative* locution, or interior word, may come forth with great power from within the mystic's being. Finally, from the deepest recesses of the mystic's being, he may hear with the ears of his soul *intellectual* locutions.

As noted above, St. John of the Cross discusses three types of intellectual locutions: *successive, formal,* and *substantial.*[4] Successive intellectual locutions usually arise only during deep recollection and manifest themselves as a God-directed form of reasoning or a God-controlled concatenation of ideas. Although formal intellectual locutions require no special recollection, they render the mystic passive and unable to prevent them. He experiences them as one or more ideas uttered directly to his spirit and as definitely coming from another source. Moreover, he always understands them. Substantial intellectual locutions, on the other hand, always and immediately bring about what is uttered. For example, if God says substantially to the mystic, "Fear not!," he concomitantly becomes fearless. Teresa meant this when she declared that God's words are his deeds (*AB,* chap. 25, p. 242).

The *exterior* and *interior* loquela experienced by St. Ignatius, however, must be distinguished from the above phenomena.[5] Words and an unusually lovely tonality comprise this divine music, which arose both from the very depths of his soul and from shallower regions of his psyche. Although he chided himself for being less attentive "to the meaning of the words and of the *lo-quela*,"[6] because the sweetness of the tone of the divine musical voice so attracted him, he considered it a miraculous, divine gift that stirred him to a deeper love for God. Although he never questioned the divine origin of the *loquela*, he examined the "relish and sweetness" he derived from it for possible signs of the evil one.

Therefore, in some cases, music rather than words may predominate in locution experiences. The music-loving mystics—Francis of Assisi, Catherine of Siena, Richard Rolle, and Suso, to name just a few—sometimes experienced the divine harmony as heavenly song. Mystical poetry and the dialogue nature of much mystical writing may also indicate that the expression of the communication of divine life requires rhythmical language.[7]

Automatic writing also bears the marks of the inner mystical life expressing itself rhythmically. For example, one of the most important commentators on St. Catherine of Genoa, Friedrich von Hügel, distinguished her genuine utterances from later editorial additions by the presence or absence of melodious language.[8] To be sure, the nature of automatic writing varies in quality and intensity. The mystic's inner life may "merely" inspire him to write, or it may take such control that it seems another person is using his hand and doing the actual writing.

Much of St. Teresa's writings arose during periods of intense recollection, perhaps even ecstasy. The words flowed from her pen almost uncontrollably, without hesitations, and swiftly. The writings of Blake, Madame Guyon, Boehme, and Swedenborg also show signs of being automatic. In such cases, the mystical consciousness seems able to override the usual inhibitions of both the will and the surface intellect. Swedenborg, for example, wrote: "Nay have I written entire pages, and the spirits did not dictate the words, but absolutely

310

guided my hands, so that it may [be assumed to be] they who were doing the writing."[9] It is further instructive to note that he learned to discriminate between writings supposedly guided by evil spirits and those supposedly inspired by the Lord.

Revelations

Along slightly different lines, *revelations* are visions and locutions that expose past, present, or future hidden things, either for the good of the Church or for the individual. Furthermore, most mystical commentators distinguish between *public* and *private* revelations. Public revelation ceased with the formation of the canon of scripture at the close of the apostolic era; it constitutes the deposit of Christian faith.[10] Mystical writers define postapostolic revelations as private, even when they are for the good of the entire Church. These private revelations do not belong to the "treasury" of the Christian faith entrusted to the Church to be preserved faithfully and expounded infallibly.

Private revelations may simply convey to the mystic a deeper knowledge of revealed truths or unveil specifics about God's workings (when the mystic shall die, his future trials, what is in store for an individual or a nation).

Private revelations often presuppose the gift of prophecy. *Prophetic* revelations commission the mystic to address the entire Church, or a significant portion. He must deliver a message, plead for a particular devotion, call for conversion and penance, warn against certain aberrations in Church life and teaching, suggest new styles of life or spiritual doctrine, or foretell the future. These postapostolic, prophetic revelations, therefore, apply the faith in a practical way to daily Christian living.

In many ways, prophetic revelations disclose what is somehow already known, albeit implicitly, from faith,

Church life, and theology. They actually bring forth new commands, not new statements. Prophetic imperatives indicate how Christians should live or what they should do in their specific historical circumstances. In other ways, these revelations do nothing more than provide the initial spark or the final confirmation for something which, for more important reasons, was already recognized as correct, useful, and necessary: for example, consecration of the world to the Sacred Heart of Christ.

It must be stressed that when the Church approves the revelations made to saints, it declares only their *probability* of being true and their essential harmony with scripture and Church teaching. This negative approbation means that Catholics may believe in them with a human faith. In those cases where prophetic revelations foretell the future or make demands upon others not obvious apart from these disclosures, the validity, authenticity, and confirmation of such revelations require a miracle which of itself must not be subject to question.[11]

To be sure, revelations do not usher in a new age of Christianity. How many revelations, for example, simply manifest the individual visionary's disappointments, bitterness, fears, anxieties, superstitions, childishness, and frustrations? It is instructive to note how many of the great saints' revelations were simply false. Even most genuine revelations usually contain some spurious elements.[12]   *Rahner—Visions + Prophecies*

Touches, Tastes, and Smells
The authentic Christian mystical tradition also vouches for experiences of *intellectual, imaginative,* and *sensible touches, tastes,* and *smells.* St. Augustine wrote: "Yet I do love a certain light, a certain voice, a certain odor, a certain food, a certain embrace when I love my God: a light, a voice, an odor, a food, an embrace for the man within me. . . ."[13]

312

Within the history of teaching on the mystical senses, therefore, it is indisputable that many mystics experienced at the root of their being divine touches, divine smells, and divine tastes. They speak about their spirits having "senses" in a way analogous to the bodily senses. As we saw above with St. Ignatius of Loyola, he definitely expected the person making the *Spiritual Exercises* to see, hear, smell, taste, and touch in *imagination* various aspects of the divine self-communication (nos. 121–25).

The question of sensible touches, tastes, and smells is much more ambiguous. It seems that no genuine Christian mystic ever claimed to have received sensible touches, tastes, and smells from God. Mystical sensible touches, tastes, and smells are more commonly associated with demonic obsessions, a topic to be treated later.

The author of the *Cloud*, as indicated above,[14] urges caution with regard to "consolations, sounds, joys, or delights originating from external sources . . . for they may be either good or evil, the work of a good angel or the work of the devil" (chap. 48, p. 110). Because either the good or the evil spirits may influence the bodily senses, he urges careful discernment of sensible mystical favors.

Fragrant odors, or *fragrant effluvia*, may exude from a saint's living or dead body. Sensible odors emanated, for example, from the stigmatic body of St. Francis of Assisi and St. Catherine Ricci. The exhumed corpses of Sts. Helen of Hungary and Teresa of Avila likewise emitted a pleasant smell. Moreover, the saints' tombs and relics have often discharged a delightful fragrance. Miracles seem frequently to be associated with this phenomenon.

However, the highly dubious nature of *sensible* mystical visions, locutions, touches, tastes, and odors must be underscored. Few authentic Christian mystics experienced them; more rarely did they impute any importance to them. The proper orientation of the senses flows not from sensible mystical phenomena, but from the Church's magnificent sacramental system deeply rooted in an incarnational spirituality. Sacred images, statues, sacred gestures, words, blessings, vocal prayer, the rosary, Gregorian chant, sacred music, bread, wine, water, salt, oil, chrism, incense, fire, and the like, directly feed the Christian's sense life and indirectly lead him away from bogus sense religious experience. The Church's concern for an authentically Christian sense life likewise promotes the awakening of the deeper spiritual, or mystical, senses.

Stigmata

The *stigmata*, or the reproduction of the wounds of Christ on the mystic's body, have also been known to give off odoriferous effluvia. The first known Christian stigmatic, St. Francis of Assisi, received the wounds of Christ on his hands, feet, and side during an ecstasy on Mt. Alvernia on September 17, 1222. Although he tried to hide these wounds and greatly desired a less ostentatious way of sharing in Christ's sufferings, these wounds stayed with him for the rest of his life. Since his time, approximately 325 stigmatics have appeared, 62 of whom the Church has canonized.

The wounds of Christ come spontaneously without exterior injury, occur almost always in ecstasy, and are often preceded by great physical and moral sufferings, elements of the dark night of the spirit. The stigmata may occur permanently or only periodically; they may be visible or invisible. St. Catherine of Siena, for example, suffered from invisible wounds of love that became visible on her body only after her death.

Although most stigmatics bear the marks of the crucifixion, some carry only the marks of Christ's crowning with thorns or of his scourging. The wounds bleed afresh periodically, usually on a Friday or during the holy season of Lent. Although the stigmata may last for years, they cannot be cured medically. No matter how long they last, the wounds look as fresh as when they first appeared and exhibit no traces of putrefaction or cicatrization.

Of course, the genuine stigmatics possessed a great love of the suffering Christ, a desire to enter into his martyrdom, and uncommon sanctity. The Church has proclaimed as miraculous the stigmata of St. Francis of Assisi, St. Claire of Montefalco, St. Catherine of Siena, St. Teresa of Avila, St. Veronica of Giuliani, and many others. On the other hand, the Church has been most reluctant to authenticate other known cases. Genuine stigmata must always be carefully distinguished from those diabolically, hysterically, pathologically, or auto-suggestively induced.

Levitation
Another secondary mystical phenomenon closely allied with ecstasy is *levitation*. Many of the ecstatic saints experienced the unsupported lifting up of their bodies off the ground in contradiction to the laws of gravity. Although ecstasies and raptures can certainly induce the subjective feeling of being raised off the ground, eyewitness testimony and documentation of the saints' levitations confirm this as an objectively verified phenomenon. The levitating mystics usually manifest no movement in their limbs and seem as rigid as marble statues.

The first confirmed stigmatic, St. Francis of Assisi, is also the first confirmed case of *ascensional ecstasy,* that is, the slight raising of the mystic off the ground. Documented evidence shows that Sts. Paul of the Cross, Philip Neri, Joseph Cupertino, Peter Alcantara, Francis Xavier, Agnes, and others likewise levitated.

Some mystics experienced *ecstatic flight*, that is, flying to great heights and balancing themselves easily at these heights. On occasion, a few underwent *ecstatic progress*, that is, flying through the air almost as quickly as a bird. All levitations end with a slow and cushioned return to the ground.

Mary of Agreda exhibited such lightness of body after communion that simple breathing upon her could move her body like a feather. On the other hand, these same levitators occasionally possessed an extreme immobility or superhuman heaviness of body. No one, not even a group of people, could lift St. Joseph Cupertino off the ground when he was stretched out in ecstasy. Once again, however, mystical commentators distinguish genuine from diabolical and pathological levitations.

Other Phenomena
The mystical tradition attests to still more unusual bodily, mystical phenomena. For example, Sts. Clement, Francis of Assisi, Anthony of Padua, Francis Xavier, Martin de Porres, Alphonsus Liguori, and others experienced *bilocation*, the apparently simultaneous presence of their physical bodies in two distinct places at the same time. Mystical theologians usually add that the physical body is present in the second location only by way of "representation."

The bodies of Sts. Philip Neri, Peter Alcantara, Anthony of Padua, and others likewise exhibited *agility*, the spontaneous transport of their bodies from one place to another, seemingly without going through the intervening space. Mystical commentators point to Habakkuk (Dn 14:33f.) and the deacon Philip (Acts 8:39) as canonical examples of this phenomenon.

Scripture also indicates that the risen Christ appeared to his disciples, presumably by passing through locked doors (Jn 19:20f.). Sts. Dominic and Raymond Penafort likewise exhibited this *penetration of matter* by which

316

their bodies apparently passed through another material object.

A few mystics suffered extreme or partial *bodily elongation* during ecstasy. The abbess of Sister Veronica Laparelli, for example, measured Veronica's bodily length both during and after ecstasy and testified to a difference of over ten inches.

Inedia, or absolute and prolonged fasting, appears in the lives of some saints, blesseds, and others. Blessed Angela de Foligno, for example, lived on communion and a bit of water for eight years; St. Lydwina, for twenty-eight years. Despite the long periods of almost total abstinence from food, these mystics did not lose weight. They also demonstrated remarkable activity, energy, and mental health.

Mystical *insomnia,* or the prolonged absence of sleep, is yet another unusual phenomenon. Perhaps from the rest obtained during ecstasies, many saints lived for extensive periods of time on very little sleep. For example, St. Peter Alcantara slept for approximately an hour a day for forty years.

Mystical aureoles or *luminous effluvia* may emanate from the mystic's body, especially during contemplation or ecstasy. For example, a halo or corona of radiant light came forth from the head, face, or body of Sts. Ignatius of Loyola, Francis de Paula, John Vianney, and others.

Tokens of mystical marriage appear commonly among women mystics. For example, St. Catherine of Siena received an invisible wedding ring of gold, pearls, and diamonds. Others, however, saw a vivid red line with lumps on her finger that exuded an exquisite perfume. A wound or a scar over the heart may indicate an exchange of hearts between Christ and the mystic. The heart itself may bear the marks of Christ's passion and crucifixion. After St. Teresa of Avila had been wounded in the heart by the seraph's dart, she accurately described to her confessor the five wounds of Christ now present, and later confirmed by autopsy.

Flames of love may express externally the mystic's inner love for God. The spiritual flame of love may produce such a burning sensation in the body, especially in the heart area, that clothing actually becomes scorched. For example, during the autopsy performed on Maria Villani, the doctor could not endure the intense heat and smoke coming from her stigmatized heart. Sts. Catherine of Genoa, Paul of the Cross, and Philip Neri likewise suffered during their lifetime from the physical heat generated by their spiritual love of God. The numerous references in Ignatius of Loyola's *Diary* to the presence of a consoling, physical heat indicate that he commonly experienced this phenomenon.

Almost the reverse of flames of love are the *incombustible bodies,* or *human salamander,* occurrences. The saints' living or dead bodies, or material things associated with them, either suffer no injury from fire or will not burn in any way. Attempts to kill some saints by placing them on top of pyres failed. Others could carry live coals or have them heaped on their heads. Evidence for this phenomenon abounds, especially in the lives of Sts. Polycarp, Francis of Paula, Peter Igneus, Dominic, and Catherine of Siena.

Bloody sweat and *tears* have also appeared, albeit rarely, in the mystical tradition. Perhaps in imitation of Christ's alleged bloody sweat, St. Lutgard, Blessed Christina, Magdalene Morice, and a few others supposedly sweated blood. The only reputed cases for the shedding of bloody tears are Rosa Andriani and Theresa Neumann.

On the other hand, *mystical tears* is a rather common phenomenon, especially among the Eastern Christian Fathers. To name but a few, Cassian, Isaac the Syrian, Symeon the New Theologian, and John Climacus shed

318

physical tears because of a penetrating mystical experience of their own personal sins, the sins of others, and of the earthly exile in this "valley of tears." According to them, abiding sorrow for sins requires a special gift of tears from the Holy Spirit.

These mystical tears may also flow from a God-given consolation. The profound mystical graces experienced by St. Ignatius of Loyola, for example, frequently manifested themselves exteriorly in tears. De Guibert writes: "It seems to me that no other saint, man or woman, has in practice given to these tears a place equal with that of Ignatius."[15]

Because of their holiness, many mystics possessed the gift of *hierognosis*, the ability to discern immediately any holy, blessed, or consecrated person, place, or thing from those that are not. Many likewise exhibited a remarkable ingenuity to *read hearts*, in the sense that only God can truly read the human heart. St. John Vianney, for example, instinctively knew the sins of others, even before they confessed them. Although some gifted persons are capable of "reading" others through their words, gestures, and body language, the mystical reading of hearts in the strict sense denotes a God-given knowledge of other persons' deepest secrets.

Empire over creatures means the mystic has powers over created things. The mystical tradition attests to the saints' participation in Christ's thaumaturgic abilities. Francis Xavier, for example, once calmed the sea. Philip Neri brought forth springs of water from a barren field. Francis of Assisi and Paul the Hermit had sovereignty over wild animals. Examples abound of the saints' miraculous cures.

Blessed Raymund of Capua and others testified that St. Catherine of Siena sometimes received communion by way of *eucharistic telekinesis*. The Host traveled on its own through the air from the altar or the priest's hands to her lips. St. John Vianney likewise attested to this phenomenon. Many other examples could be given.

Bodily incorruption is the final secondary mystical phenomenon to be discussed. Despite the absence of sealed coffins, embalming, desiccation, or saponification, the corpses of many saints remained immune to natural decomposition, in some cases for centuries. In fact, the corpse may bleed on a feast day or some other occasion after weeks, months, and years have passed. Preternatural fragrances may also cling to the corpse for long periods of time. The bodily heat may persist long after death. On occasion, the dead saint has blessed those in the vicinity of his corpse. Although incontestable evidence exists for the bodily incorruption of between twenty-two and forty-two canonized saints, many did not escape humanity's common lot.

A General Description of Charismatic Phenomena

St. Paul clearly expected the early Christians not only to be informed about but also to desire earnestly certain spiritual gifts (1 Cor 12:1; 14:1). In 1 Cor 12:8–10 and Rom 12:6–8, he lists some of the charismatic phenomena that were appearing in the Christian communities: the utterance of wisdom, the utterance of knowledge, faith, gifts of healing, working of miracles, prophecy, discernment of spirits, various kinds of tongues, the interpretation of tongues, service, teaching, exhortation, contribution, giving help, and acts of mercy. For Paul, each Christian received charismatic gifts as "manifestations of the Spirit for the common good" (1 Cor 12:7).[16]

God's eschatological Spirit appeared among the early Christians in this highly visible, tangible, dramatic way to demonstrate God's unconditional love toward his people and to edify, or build up, the community. Although many of these charismatic gifts seemingly died out rather early in the Church's life, contemporary charismatic, or neo-Pentecostal, movements possess them, emphasize their rebirth, and force a theological reevaluation of these unusual phenomena.

Prophecy

Because *prophecy* involves an intelligible speaking in the Spirit for the entire community's building up, encouragement, admonition, and consolation, Paul values it over every other charismatic gift, including speaking in tongues. He teaches: ". . . earnestly desire the spiritual gifts, especially that you may prophesy" (1 Cor 14:1). Clearly Paul yearns for all to receive the charismatic gifts; "even more" (v. 5), however, does he specifically want them to be given prophecy.

Prophecy frequently occurs as a word of revelation (vv. 6, 26, 30). In fact, Paul seems to consider them as almost synonyms (vv. 26–32). Dominated by Christ's Spirit, the prophet spoke words of revelation in a way paralleling the Old Testament prophets who directly spoke God's word to the people. In this sense, both prophets and apostles were agents of revelation in the early Church, although only the apostles could officially testify to the revelation they had witnessed in Christ's life, death, and resurrection.

The polymorphous quality of early and contemporary prophecy does not lend itself to an easy definition. It might involve predictions (Rv 1:3), designating someone for office (1 Tm 4:14), testifying to Christ (Rv 19:10), or a charismatic form of preaching that consoles, threatens, or edifies. Be it charismatic foretelling or forthtelling, however, intelligible speech in the Spirit is prophecy's hallmark.

As intelligible speech in the Spirit, prophecy often reveals some practical course of action for an individual or a community. It might be as banal as saying the right thing at the right time. This word of revelation, however, casts the light of Christ upon the details of daily Christian living. It might also include praying or

singing "with the mind" (1 Cor 14:15). By its power
and content, moreover, prophecy reveals the secrets of
persons' hearts; it may force even unbelievers to acknowledge God's presence in the community (v. 25).

Glossolalia

In 1 Cor 14, Paul contrasts mindless utterances, or *glossolalia,* with the highly valued intelligible speaking, or
prophecy. Pauline glossolalia, or *speaking in tongues,* involves speaking in a language unintelligible both to
speaker and hearer alike, unless one has received the
gift of interpretation. Irrational utterances, sounds, cries,
praises, and singing possessing a definite structure and
manifesting deep religious emotions constitute glossolalia. Perhaps it can be compared to the love language
between persons, a language that does not mean anything but which denotes their love, intimacy, and affection. Paul seems to understand it as angelic speech (1
Cor 13:1) or as a heavenly language of heavenly secrets
(1 Cor 14:2). Although somewhat difficult to describe,
once glossolalia is heard, it is not easily forgotten.

Paul gives both a negative and positive assessment of
this strange phenomenon. He emphasizes, for example,
that no one understands a person speaking in tongues
because the utterances are unintelligible (1 Cor 14:2,9).
Moreover, glossolalia leaves the mind unfruitful (v. 14).
Paul "would rather speak five words with my mind
. . . than ten thousand words in a tongue" (v. 19). The
speaker in tongues edifies only himself (v. 4) and
should ask for the gift of interpretation (v. 13). Unlike
prophecy, which stresses even for unbelievers God's
undeniable presence in the community, uncontrolled
glossolalia bears the signs of madness (v. 23). Because
of its tendency to disrupt community order, Paul demands that speaking in tongues be limited to "only two
or at most three, and each in turn" (v. 27). If the gift of
interpretation is absent in a community, glossolalia
must remain private (v. 28).

On the other hand, speaking in tongues is a form of prayer (vv. 2, 14). It transforms the person (v. 4). Paul himself spoke in tongues (v. 18), wanted all Christians to speak glossolalia (v. 5), considered it a sign for unbelievers (v. 22), and commanded: "Do not forbid speaking in tongues" (v. 39). When done with interpretation, moreover, it seems to be of equal value as prophecy, because interpreted glossolalia builds up the community (v. 5).

Speaking in "various kinds of tongues" (1 Cor 12:10) may also include talking in an intelligible foreign language that the speaker has neither learned nor understands. On Pentecost, the apostles received the gift of praising God in foreign languages, although exegetes dispute whether this involved charismatic tongues (Acts 2:2), charismatic hearing (Acts 2:8), or possibly both. It must be emphasized, in any case, that contemporary charismatics sometimes speak in foreign languages and sometimes in "angelic," or unintelligible, glossolalia.

Some contemporary commentators commonly reduce glossolalia to the frenzied, ecstatic speech found in many primitive oriental cults, to emotional disorder, to a sign of demonic possession, or to a rare gift from God. Although speaking in tongues can be frenzied, pathological, or demonic, it may also be a genuine God-given charism. For example, contemporary speaking in tongues frequently takes place in a quiet, peaceful setting. The speaker remains fully conscious, calm, and acknowledges the presence of others. Glossolalia is essentially prayer (1 Cor 14:2). Contemporary charismatics often experience deep, distractionless prayer and a renewed docility to the Holy Spirit. It is, moreover, a rather common, contemporary phenomenon.

Against certain contemporary charismatic overemphases, however, it is instructive to note that Paul rates prophecy the most desirable and glossolalia the least desirable charism. Because glossolalia can be induced in so many different ways, is it really necessary to see the authentic version as something directly caused by the Holy Spirit? Speaking in tongues seems to be an innate potential of the human psychological structure, a language and rhythm of the unconscious mind that reaches the surface mind when triggered either by the Holy Spirit, the devil, the self, or group dynamics.

Interpretation of Tongues

The *interpretation of tongues* is, of course, the complementary charism to glossolalia. Tongues and their interpretation are the two sides of the same charismatic coin. Although unnecessary, most often only one who speaks in tongues can interpret the tongues of others.

Interpretation transforms the private gift of tongues (1 Cor 14:4) into a public gift that serves the entire assembly (v. 5). As indicated above, Paul allows public glossolalia only when interpretation is present (v. 28). Perhaps this is the way Paul ensured that the community could control and constructively benefit from a potentially selfish and abused gift.

If glossolalia can be considered to be apophatic (without the mind) prayer, the interpreter intuits in faith the meaning of the human-divine relationship. Interpretation requires a faith instinct to sense what is taking place during this private prayer in order to transform it into public prayer. Neither rational discernment nor an exact translation, interpretation offers an insight into the charismatic speaker's unintelligible psychosomatic language. Perhaps it can be compared to a loving mother's penetrating interpretation of her babbling, retarded child's needs, desires, frustrations, fears, affections, joys, and loves.

Paul preached Christ crucified as "the wisdom of God" (1 Cor 1:24). For Paul, Christianity was a new wisdom that had little in common with pagan wisdom and rhetorical skills. Christian wisdom denotes the experiential participation in the whole mystery of redemption (1 Cor 2:6f.). In a sense, it is synonymous with revelation and grace. Illuminated by the Spirit of Christ, the mature Christian understands God's mysterious workings, especially in Christ crucified. Essentially practical, Christian wisdom transforms the Christian's entire way of thinking and acting.

The charism of *utterance of wisdom* flows from the above attitude. These words of wisdom stir others in the Christian community to a deeper understanding and appreciation of God's secret, salvific acts in the past, present, and future (Eph 1:17f.). This inspired preaching in the power of the Spirit reveals to others in a saving way the depths of Christian wisdom and knowledge. It may be simple, practical, earthy advice on how to live certain aspects of Christian life. By throwing light on what God has done, is doing, and will do for his people, it may be the right word at the right time that transforms daily Christian living.

The *utterance of knowledge* has much in common with words of wisdom. A charismatic world view that cannot coexist with unholiness, selfishness, and arrogance toward others (2 Cor 6:6) constitutes Christian knowledge. Christian oracular sayings issue from this world view. These inspired words bring insight into God's gifts, awaken love, and transform knowledge into acknowledgment. By their power and content, these God-given revelatory words benefit the community. Perhaps the saying, "there is no God but one" (1 Cor 8:4), with all its practical ramifications for Christian living and conduct, is an example of the utterance of knowledge charism.

Faith
The charism *faith* must be distinguished, but not separated from, the theological virtue of justifying faith, which embraces a person's entire relationship to God.

This gift enables the charismatic to trust God in specific circumstances against all odds. The person receives an unwavering conviction that God will act even in seemingly impossible conditions.

Faith bestows such a clear insight into God's specific will that the charismatic will risk everything to accomplish it. This gift also brings the unshakeable conviction that God is speaking and working through the charismatic's words and actions. Monica's persistent prayer for Augustine's conversion, Job's blessing of God even in his time of adversity, and Abraham's entrusting of his son to God are paradigms of charismatic faith.

Healings and Miracles

When Paul lists the gifts of *healings* among the charisms, he gives firsthand testimony that various cures occurred in the early Christian communities. Paul undoubtedly linked these cures with the ones performed by Jesus and the apostles and saw in them the signs of God's overall saving power. It is important to note, however, that this charism refers to the actual healings, and not to the healing power able to cause various cures.[17]

The numerous outbreaks of charismatic healings throughout the world give irrefutable evidence of this gift. Although the existence of authentic cures is beyond dispute, more work still needs to be done to determine how many cures are, in fact, permanent. Charismatics must also be reminded that God normally works through natural means, for example, modern medicine. For example, Paul advised Timothy to take wine for his medical problem (1 Tm 5:23). Moreover, the inability to cure or to be cured is not a sign of a lack of faith or a hidden sin, as some contemporary charismatics maintain. How many of the Church's very own saints suffered various illnesses until the day they died?

326

The *working of miracles* is yet another charismatic phenomenon attested to by Paul. The Christian community witnessed persons in their midst who had the ability to affect dramatically and for the better persons and perhaps even things. This display of divine power seems to have appeared most conspicuously in nature miracles and in exorcisms.[18] It remains clear that certain charismatics had the unusual power to impress and transform others by their words and actions.

Other Charisms

The *ability to distinguish between spirits* is the charismatic gift of discerning both an inspiration's source and its meaning for the Christian community. For example, despite the slave girl's true utterances, Paul discerned that a demon possessed her and exorcized it (Acts 16:17). Authentic Christian living demands the proper assessment, consideration, examination, and testing of both the source and the significance of various utterances in the community. 1 Corinthians 12:3 offers a rule of thumb for discerning: ". . . no one speaking by the Spirit of God ever says 'Jesus be cursed!' and no one can say 'Jesus is Lord' except by the Holy Spirit." Only those utterances that originate from God's Spirit and do not contradict the community's canon of scripture may be considered genuine.

Although unlisted by Paul, *slaying in the Spirit* commonly occurs in some contemporary charismatic circles. When prayed over or receiving the imposition of hands, a person may partially or totally lose consciousness. With the loss of ego control comes the experience of abandoning oneself to God's will with peace and joy. Slaying in the Spirit may produce radical conversions and fill the recipients with various charismatic gifts for the service of others. The Bible gives numerous examples of persons falling to the ground in fear, while the awe and reverence shown by Abraham, Moses, Peter, and others are perhaps biblical examples of this phenomenon.

327

Service (Rom 12:7) is a charism of serving that renders the presence of the Holy Spirit transparent to the community in the very act itself. The hospitality rendered to Paul by Stephanas and his family (1 Cor 16:15) is an example.

Teaching and *exhortation* (Rom 12:7-8) have close affinities with prophecy (1 Cor 14:6,26) and perhaps with utterances of wisdom and knowledge. Teaching denotes charismatic exegesis, or a novel insight into God's word. Exhortation denotes charismatic preaching, or applying the word of God creatively to the community situation.

Contribution, giving help, and *performing acts of mercy* (Rom 12:8) are essentially welfare service charisms. They involve the act of sharing one's food and possessions with the community or cheerfully giving financial assistance to the needy. Moreover, certain Christians took it upon themselves to care for and to protect widows, orphans, slaves, and strangers. Genuine sharing, caring, and taking the lead to find ways to alleviate misery and to meet people's basic needs reflect God's grace, the totally generous and unmerited sharing of his life and love.

If one examines 1 Corinthians 12:28-30 and Ephesians 4:11-12 (to give but a few examples), it becomes clear that Paul looks upon charismatic gifts, functions, and offices as gifts of the Spirit. The Holy Spirit offers proof of his presence by specific acts, works, and structures within the Christian community. The genuine charismatic should be aware of the incredible variety of ways in which the Spirit operates throughout the entire Body of Christ.

Concluding Reflections

What can be said theologically about secondary mystical and charismatic phenomena? First, most Christian mystics agree that *intellectual* visions, locutions, touches, tastes, and odors are intrinsically linked with God's self-communication. God's loving influx refracts itself throughout the mystic's spiritual dimensions to purify, illuminate, transform, and reintegrate these spiritual levels around infused contemplation. Although these authentic phenomena cannot be counterfeited by either the devil or the self, they must be carefully distinguished from the psychosomatic shocks they cause throughout the mystic's other dimensions. It can also be asked if these genuine phenomena ever occur in a pure state. Do they not almost always produce aftereffects from which they must be carefully discerned? For example, do intellectual visions ever occur without a concomitant imaginative vision?

Second, most of the remaining phenomena, when genuine, may be regarded as the echoes, reverberations, radiations, shocks, and percolation of infused contemplation into the total body-person. The Christian's psychosomatic structure assimilates and adjusts to God's self-communication to his deepest core through these phenomena. God purifies, illuminates, transforms, and reintegrates the entire body-person, moreover, by means of these psychosomatic phenomena. Therefore, commentators who emphasize only what begins and ends in the mystic's core are certainly wrong.[19] Grace's incarnational dimension requires the enfleshment of infused contemplation, its psychosomatic manifestation.

Still, in one sense, many secondary mystical and charismatic phenomena reveal God's intimate presence, but by way of the language of the Christian's own psychosomatic structure. If the scriptures are God's word in human words, genuine mystical and charismatic phenomena express infused contemplation in psychosomatic language. God's pure light, voice, touch, odor, and food refract themselves into the mystic's full body-person prism. Secondary mystical and charismatic phenomena not only reveal something more intimate and deeper, namely, infused contemplation, but they also express symbolically the way the Christian's inner mystical life reaches the surface mind. They should be compared, therefore, to the poetry, literature, music, paintings, and sculptures of the world's great artists.

Genuine secondary mystical and charismatic phenomena never occur alone. The mystic or charismatic normally experiences genuine, pathological, and diabolical phenomena during the course of his mystical ascent or charismatic life. These phenomena will reveal not only his God-induced psychosomatic integration, but also his brokenness and the presence of the demonic. Taken together, therefore, these phenomena manifest God's presence, the devil's presence, and the Christian's own healthy *and* pathological accommodations and resistances to both the divine and the demonic presence.

Furthermore, it is not surprising that some of these phenomena reflect the Christian's infantile dreams, inordinate desires, immature projections, and pathological hallucinations. Others, however, counter directly the Christian's physically, psychologically, and morally pernicious tendencies. Conversion, renewed energy, strength, courage, authority, and peace accompany them. They bestow insight, knowledge, and wisdom, while deepening faith, hope, and love.

The Christian mystics unanimously teach that genuine God-induced phenomena leave behind in their wake faith, hope, love, humility, and peace. The enhancement of life at all levels of the person's being attests to their authenticity. They both produce and flow from holiness.

On the other hand, self-induced phenomena eventually bring to light the hidden desires of the Christian's exhausted and starved psyche for disguised satisfaction. Causing no transformation, they leave him arid, straining, and uneasy. Demonically induced phenomena attempt to produce pride, self-satisfaction, bitterness, and anything else that diminishes genuine faith, hope, and love.

The pathological triggering of some of these phenomena in no way calls into question the possibility of authentic, that is, God-induced and life-enhancing, secondary mystical and charismatic phenomena. The mentally ill, for example, frequently express their madness through chaotic song, dance, paintings, and poetry. Does this fact negate or even call into question the genuine creative enterprise of healthy artists? It is no more surprising for both genuine and pathological phenomena to arise within the same person than for an authentic artist's creative genius to go awry occasionally.

Some earlier Catholic studies of secondary mystical phenomena definitely overemphasized their importance. Superstitious attitudes, uncritical hagiography, and a facile supernaturalism permeate even some contemporary Catholic circles. It must be stressed, however, that most of these phenomena have appeared in a highly pronounced form in noncanonized and even non-Christian mystics. Some canonized saints, moreover, exhibited none, or few, of them. Also, have past studies distinguished clearly enough between those phenomena that usually accompany infused contemplation and those that only rarely accompany it?

In addition, the Church had lived a deeply mystical life for centuries before some of these phenomena began appearing. Bodily incorruption, for example, was first noticed in Christianity in the fourth century; the stigmata and levitation, in the thirteenth. Most, if not all, of these phenomena find their counterparts in other religions. What mystical religions lack visions, locutions, raptures, revelations, and so on? The heat generated through kundalini yoga, for example, parallels the Christian phenomenon of flames of love. The fire walking phenomenon found throughout the world has affinities with Christian incombustible bodies. Under certain conditions (perhaps cult-induced hypnotic trance), the human body can withstand without injury the heat from large areas of white-hot rock.

Some contemporary charismatics likewise overemphasize the importance of certain charismatic phenomena. Yet Paul saw nothing uniquely Christian about charismatic phenomena. He knew of their frequent occurrence outside of the Christian communities, often in morally, psychologically, and physically destructive settings. Their highly ambiguous nature in the context of Paul's time must likewise be underscored.

Neither in Paul's time nor today do charismatic phenomena indicate a higher form of Christianity. The charismatic who possesses some of the more showy gifts is not a special Christian. "The distinctive mark of the Christian," writes James D. G. Dunn, "is experience of the Spirit as the life of Christ."[20] This indicates that extraordinary charismatic experiences have no necessary relationship to distinctively Christian experience.

That the *communal* experience of these gifts after the apostolic age, especially the more dramatic ones, almost always occurred in heretical splinter groups should give today's enthusiasts food for thought. Still, the great variety of charismatic movements today needs underscoring. Some reflect an attractive, balanced, genuine Christianity; others, a nearly pathological emotionalism. This is a time for penetrating discernment to purge the distortions from the movements and to encourage the good therein.

For example, both the Corinthian and some contemporary charismatic movements exhibit definite unacceptable tendencies. With their penchant for overemotionalism, some charismatics see in every emotional and psychological twitch an epiphany of the Holy Spirit. Is it true, as often claimed, that the Holy Spirit is always inspiring them directly to speak or to act in a certain way? Moreover, some charismatic spirituality focuses too exclusively upon the Spirit and neglects the Father and Christ crucified and risen.

In this distorted context, the more spectacular gifts, especially glossolalia, become the hallmark of the authentic Christian. With the emphasis upon signs, power, wonders, and dramatic evidence, some charismatics overlook "the more excellent way" of daily, humdrum, seemingly unspectacular love described in 1 Corinthians 13. They forget that Paul urged Christians to make love their aim (1 Cor 14:1) and discussed the charisms in the context of Christian love.

On occasion, some contemporary charismatics act as if they have a monopoly on the Holy Spirit and that only they know God's will. Often naive and antiintellectual, they resent critical and penetrating discernment, especially if theological in some form. Although distrustful of ecclesial authority and institutions, they blindly follow the charismatic guru of the hour and may even set up structures more rigid than those of any universal church. With their enthusiasm for the more showy charisms, have some groups ignored the social justice and welfare charisms of Romans 12:8? In their desire for a totally new and transformed church, elitism, disorder, arrogance, jealousy, and disobedience may instead prevail. Although Paul did not explicitly link the charisms with holiness, charismatic gifts attest to their authenticity *only* when the fruits of the Spirit are also present (Gal 5:22–23).

Yet this is only one, and not the most important, side of the charismatic story. Today's charismatic movements have brought much undeniable good to the Christian churches. Increased vigor, vitality, conversion, and renewal often result in and from them. Most importantly, significant numbers of Christians experience in charismatic groups for the first time a genuinely *com-*

333

munal Christianity. The reawakening of the experience of belonging to the Body of Christ as the people of God is perhaps the most significant benefit of the charismatic revival. Despite the obvious difficulties, these movements present many ecumenical opportunities because their membership and the gifts bestowed often transcend denominational lines.

Neo-Pentecostalism has given vast numbers of Christians a taste and facility for deep prayer. The charismatic often discovers a new and richer dimension to private and group prayer, liturgy, and the sacramental life. Prayer becomes not only a request for things from God, but also praise of God and rejoicing in his presence. The duty to pray is transformed into fidelity to the *life* of prayer.

The charismatic movements have also been communities of holiness and sanctification. Many charismatics become more loving, selfless, concerned for others, dedicated, and upright. Deeper Christian living and acting in peace and joy result. Charismatics often discover, moreover, that Christian ethics flows from an inner tasting of the Spirit's life and power, which facilitates and transcends obeying the ecclesial codes of morality.

With this in mind, it is clear why Rahner takes careful note of the ambiguous nature of charismatic experience and still contends that it may be "mysticism in ordinary dress" and a "mysticism of the masses."[21] For Rahner, genuine charismatic experiences intensify an ever-present, mostly anonymous, mystical experience that haunts every human heart. Charismatic experiences bring this basal experience more directly and explicitly into consciousness. "Through these phenomena," Rahner writes, "a man comes face to face in a particular way with his own transcendence."[22] When genuine, which is not always the case, they make a person "confront in a free and conscious manner the fact that his transcen-

334

dence is raised up by grace and ordered to the direct and immediate presence of God."[23]

Because of their uncommon psychological structure, or special kataphatic elements, Rahner maintains that genuine charismatic phenomena may play a greater role than mysticism in the strict sense in objectifying and attesting to the presence of the experience of grace in the Christian community. These events further challenge normal, daily Christian living; they make more evident the human need to surrender totally to God. Although they can concentrate and make more explicit the human person's often only anonymously experienced attraction to God, their unusual nature likewise contains the seeds for distorting and corrupting the genuine core experience of grace.

Rahner contends that authentic charismatic phenomena are neither the pure, unadulterated effects of the Holy Spirit nor only a psychological event. These phenomena can be the psychosomatic echoes, reverberations, or radiations of infused contemplation. As with secondary mystical phenomena, infused contemplation may awaken certain latent and dramatic psychological structures to express, intensify, and incarnate God's loving influx throughout various levels of the charismatic's being and thus affect the entire Christian community in the same way.

Therefore, the specific structure, conceptual framework, imagery, and actual utterances contain no intrinsic guarantees of being purely divine inspirations. They may *point to* and underscore the presence of the Holy Spirit, but only in a highly ambiguous psychosomatic language. Once again, it must be pointed out that mass suggestion, hyperemotionalism, psychosomatic techniques, and the demonic may likewise trigger them.

Still, right-wing Christians who discover the devil behind all charismatic phenomena must be reminded that genuine charismatics have Paul, the official contemporary Church, and many of the saints on their side. Paul considered charismatic phenomena in the Christian communities as expressions or dramatizations of God's grace. They were not intensified natural abilities; *God* spoke and acted through these phenomena. In fact, a genuine Christian community could not exist without these events, which disclosed the Spirit's transcendent otherness and the supernatural dimension of Christian living. Therefore, one must deny both scripture and many recent Church statements in support of these movements to impute demonic causes as the sole explanation of these phenomena. With the exception of glossolalia (although even here, a few canonized saints had this gift), many of the Church's canonized saints possessed charismatic gifts. The Church has always exhibited its charismatic structure in a variety of ways throughout the ages. Both mysticism in the strict sense and "mysticism in ordinary dress" can be found throughout the Christian tradition.

If the person is purified, healed, illuminated, and transformed by God's loving inflow, which is inextricably linked to Christ's life, death, and resurrection, his entire body-person ought to manifest this. Not only the person's spirit, but also his psychosomatic structure, can and should anticipate in some way the glory of the beatific vision and life in the risen body. The perfected Christian becomes connatural, not only with a God above all names and images, but also with the God whose human life, death, and resurrection are the seeds of the new creation, a creation from which matter cannot be removed.

In the context of a fully transformed, holy life, therefore, secondary mystical and charismatic phenomena anticipate the risen life and signify a God who has actually immersed himself in matter to have it participate in his own life. Even if some secondary mystical and

336

charismatic phenomena have a natural or parapsychological basis, cannot these be taken up into the eschatological life, just as Christ's corpse was? If yoga, drugs, pathology, and the demonic may tap human potential for a variety of reasons, why cannot infused contemplation energize this same potential in the service of authentic, incarnational Christianity? In short, is it really necessary to insist upon the miraculous nature of secondary mystical and charismatic phenomena, even when genuine, or to attribute them to demonic influence when they occur in non-Christian religions?

If some contemporary Christians see miracles everywhere, the neodocetic tendencies of our age have infected others. Technically speaking, docetism contends that Jesus Christ had only an apparent body and only appeared to suffer and die. Pastorally speaking, neodocetism implicitly or explicitly believes that true Christianity affects only the human spirit, that God works only in the depths of the soul and does not really change matter in any way. The reduction of Christ's bodily resurrection to the faith experience of the apostles, the eucharist to "transsignification," the ridiculing of relics, and so on, cannot be attributed solely to a reaction against crudely materialistic emphases in the past. The "scandal of matter" affects many contemporary Christians, even those purporting to have an incarnational spirituality.

A genuine incarnational outlook, on the other hand, sees in Christ's bodily resurrection the goal of the material world and the paradigm of the new creation. From this perspective, mystical and charismatic phenomena, even if sometimes miraculous, do not contradict the laws of nature, but fulfill them. If cosmogenesis is really Christogenesis, as Teilhard contends, these phenomena can be understood as the anticipations of the eschatological age wherein God will be All in all, even material creation.

In conclusion, a contemporary Christian should have the same attitude toward these unusual phenomena as the great saints themselves had: a *greater* concern for a life of naked faith, hope, and love; an emphasis upon conversion and transformation; a desire not to experience them; penetrating discernment; fear of being deceived; a knowledge that they may arise either from God, the devil, or the self; ignoring them whenever possible; respect for and participation in the Church's liturgical and sacramental life; valuing the life-enhancing quality of genuine mystical and charismatic phenomena; discovering in and through them the deeper gift of God's own self-communication; and finally, seeing them as the tokens of the risen life and the beatific vision in the age to come.

PSYCHEDELIC DRUG EXPERIENCES
Although the psychedelic drug fad has subsided considerably, some still experiment with these mind-altering drugs in the hope of confirming for themselves the extravagant claims made for their use by Aldous Huxley, Alan Watts, and Timothy Leary.[24] By imposing the richly mystical language of the East upon their psychedelic experiences, these authors have promised instant salvation, enlightenment, universal love, easy union with the Absolute, and escape from the problems of daily life.

Even if contemporary researchers in psychedelic drugs have more or less successfully refuted these claims, numerous scientists and scholars would agree with W. T. Stace's statement: "It is not a matter of its [the psychedelic experience] being *similar* to mystical experience; it is mystical experience."[25] Approximately seventeen years ago, moreover, two reputable drug researchers wrote: "At the present writing most of this controversy has not yet erupted into print; but the authors are amazed at the easy acquiescence of seminari-

338

ans and theologians to the claims of religious and mystical efficacy made for psychedelic drugs."[26]

There is much truth to this claim even today. Except for R. C. Zaehner's peppery denial of any relationship between Christian mystical experience and psychedelic drug experience and the balanced views of William Johnston on this issue,[27] very little Christian reflection has taken place. Perhaps Christian theologians have remained silent on this topic because they find Stace's thesis absurd and unworthy of an answer. Yet responsible researchers in this area and some scholars of mystical and religious phenomena agree with Stace. Furthermore, the statement made to this writer recently by an intelligent, seemingly authentic Christian seeker that he had "glimpsed the Divine Essence" by ingesting LSD still represents the view of some Christians and non-Christians with whom the author has had academic or pastoral contact.

Although most drug researchers make only tentative statements about psychedelic drug experiences, they seem to have reached a reasonable consensus on a number of points. First, they emphasize not only the great variety of psychedelic experiences, but also their varying *quality*.[28] The psychedelic experience ranges from: ". . . schizophrenic-like delusions to enhanced perception of visual relations; from paranoic withdrawal to expansive recognition of the living interrelatedness of all beings in everyday life; from chaotic anxieties to a liberating experience of 'union with God' which carries over into the commonplace."[29] This observation must be emphasized against those merely interested in "experiences" or altered states of consciousness, and not in their quality.

Even reputable researchers ready to grant a religious and mystical import to some psychedelic experiences under certain conditions distinguish sharply between personality-enhancing and personality-destroying experiences. The latter become especially pernicious when interpreted by the person as religious and mystical. Masters and Houston claim, for example, that "depersonalization is mistranslated into the Body of Bliss, empathy or pseudo-empathy becomes a Mystical Union, and spectacular visual effects are hailed as the Clear Light of the Void."[30] Instead of being genuine mystical experiences, therefore, psychedelic experiences often bring about psychosomatic depersonalization, ego dissolution, and flights from reality.[31] The destructive potential of psychedelic experiences, especially when hawked by today's gurus as religious, mystical, and the keys to the mysteries of the universe, must be underscored.

Furthermore, delusions and illusions frequently fill the psychedelic path. For instance, there is no guarantee that objective truth is involved merely because a psychedelic drug user *thinks* he is experiencing God, is loving, benevolent, and open to the cosmos. Pious desires and good will do not eliminate self-deception. As Masters and Houston write: "We, too, in the course of our research . . . have encountered numerous claims from our subjects and others to the effect that they have become more loving, more 'outgoing,' more 'related' to their fellow men, more altruistic. . . . Unfortunately, we find these claims . . . among the most dubious and self-delusive."[32]

These same researchers have also uncovered much "neurotic need," "wishful thinking," "self-deceit," "the delusion that one loves when one doesn't," and "spiritual hubris" among those making religious and mystical claims for their psychedelic experiences.[33] Even the late Aldous Huxley admitted after a drug experience toward the end of his life that "it was absolutely terrifying, showing that when *one thinks one's got beyond oneself, one hasn't* . . . inasmuch as one was worshipping oneself."[34] If the great masters of almost every mystical tradition insist upon the need for discernment of spirits, the same definitely holds for psychedelic experiences.

340

The second main point centers upon the person's predisposition, motivation, expectations, past history, present life situation, and the physical and psychological setting in which psychedelic drugs are ingested. These factors play a tremendous role in what happens during and results from any psychedelic drug session.[35] An authentic seeker who has prepared himself for a controlled drug session with a skilled therapist, for example, will obtain results far different from someone using these drugs alone or in a group devoted to amusement and escaping the realities of daily life.

Masters and Houston note, for example, that "the depth and intensity . . . were largely dependent upon what we have called the *preparation*, the readiness or need of the individual for a religious-type experience."[36] Another researcher maintains, moreover, that in the successful therapeutic use of psychedelic drugs, "the patient's value orientation changes in the direction of the therapist's."[37] To be sure, setting, preparation, and the spiritual father play a significant role also in the mystical life, as noted numerous times throughout this book.

The third point focuses upon the risk involved in taking these drugs. Emotionally borderline persons who take these drugs without professional supervision run the risk of suicide, psychosis, or irresponsible behavior. Indiscriminate drug use can lead to psychological dependence and mental and physical deterioration. The psychedelic drug faddist must not forget that even in religions that use these drugs in their religious ceremonies, they do so in a highly stable social context of long traditions with implicitly built-in safeguards. Still, with professional guidance and control, the relative safety of using these drugs for *therapeutic* purposes, especially when compared with other methods of psychiatric treatment, seems well established.[38]

Some researchers deny that psychedelic drugs improve self-integration in any significant way.[39] Others, however, underscore the psychotherapeutic benefit of properly used psychedelic drugs for certain emotional and mental disorders.[40] These drugs seem to take "depth soundings" in the psyche or amplify nodal points of psychic dysfunction. This facilitates the emergence of and the therapeutic working out of unconscious material from various levels of the psyche.

In this context, drugs frequently reduce a person's defensiveness, enhance creativity, melt away certain psychic blocks, rapidly eliminate neuroses, and even transform the person.[41] Some researchers also point out that "psychedelic psychotherapy tends to be more effective precisely when *religious-type* experiences of some profundity do occur."[42] However, the results are by no means automatic. As one researcher says: ". . . perhaps the hardest work comes after the experience when insights must be integrated . . . into the ongoing life of a person."[43]

The key question is whether psychedelic drugs can induce genuine, Christian mystical experiences. Masters and Houston say that some psychedelic experiences "are analogous in some way to religious and mystical experience. But religious analogues are still not religious experiences."[44] R. C. Zaehner also hits the mark when he states: "Of course, no one will probably deny that there are parallels between *some* aspects of religious mysticism . . . and some LSD experience."[45] Superficial similarities between some psychedelic drug experiences and some Christian mystical experiences do exist. Still, the burden of proof is on those who assert their identity.

W. T. Stace argues that: ". . . if the phenomenological descriptions of these two experiences [mystical and psychedelic] are indistinguishable . . . then it cannot be denied that if one is a genuine mystical experience the other is also."[46] Following up on Stace's work, W. Pahnke and W. Richards offer phenomenological categories to demonstrate the identity of mystical and psychedelic experience.[47] These categories are: undifferentiated unity, sense of objectivity and reality, transcendence of space and time, sense of the sacred, deeply felt positive mood, paradoxicality, alleged ineffability, transiency, and positive change in attitude or behavior.

The category of undifferentiated unity, however, does justice neither to a whole variety of mystical experiences nor to Christian differentiated unity. Some researchers' anti-Christian bias or uncritical acceptance of Stace's dogmatic philosophical abstraction, not an exact and critical phenomenology, is responsible for a reduction of mystical experience to undifferentiated unity.

The category of deeply felt positive moods is also inadequate. The mystical pains, sufferings, and death experienced during the dark nights contradict this category. Moreover, some Christian mystical experiences are not transient. This category fails to account for the existence of mystical *states*. The remaining categories could also be applied to nature, aesthetic, and athletic experiences. In addition, do these categories as a whole take into account the personality-enhancing or personality-destroying quality of differing psychedelic experiences? In short, these phenomenological categories are much too broad to be effective. At most, they bear superficial similarities to the characteristics of authentic Christian mysticism sketched out in the introductory chapter, but similarities do not make identities.

On the other hand, the nuanced study by Masters and Houston does present some evidence that psychedelic drugs may cause genuine religious experiences, although they emphasize that this occurs much less frequently than others would maintain.[48] They offer the following criteria for the authenticity of psychedelic religious experiences: encounter with the Other on the integral level; transformation of the self; and a process of phenomenological progression through a rather superfi-

343

cial, sensory level of experience, to a recollective-analytic and symbolic level, into the integral level.[49]

At the deepest level, moreover, "the subject experiences what he regards as a confrontation with the Ground of Being, God, Mysterium, Noumenon, Essence, or Fundamental Reality."[50] In their typically precise fashion, however, Masters and Houston qualify these remarks by adding: "We see no reason why this level and its effects could not be experienced in other than religious terms."[51]

The *stages* of psychedelic experience presented by Masters and Houston parallel in some ways the stages of classical Christian mystical ascent. But significant differences must be noted. First, these researchers, along with others, contend that the experience of unity in itself was more important to the drug user than the "object" with which he claimed union.[52] Communion with the self, nature, a chair, the universe, a flower, or God were of equal value. Christian mystics have unanimously underscored the importance, however, of discerning with what or whom they experience unity, for God alone suffices.

Second, although the psychedelic stages and some of their experiences may resemble the Christian mystical stages of increased purification, enlightenment, and eventual transformation, resemblances are not identities. The integral level and the transformation of the self described by researchers do not attain the profundity and the radicalness of Christian integrity and transformation. The integrity attained through Christian mystical prayer has been so profound in some cases that a Church with two thousand years of Christian experience has been willing to canonize these lives as models for other Christians to follow. The intensification of Christian faith, hope, and love has not resulted from psychedelic experiences. Neither have genuine spiritual fecundity, heroic virtue, constant self-sacrific-

344

ing love, peace, joy, and self-surrender even in the midst of severe adversity. When the lives of Aldous Huxley, Alan Watts, Timothy Leary, and those recorded by drug researchers are compared to the lives of the great Christian mystics, it is even more striking how paltry psychedelic transformation is when compared to Christian mystical transformation.

To be sure, psychedelic drugs under highly controlled circumstances may cause a certain degree of psychosomatic healing and transformation. In short, they can be used therapeutically. Still, they totally lack God's dark, silent, loving influx at the core of the person's being. Whereas infused contemplation works from the spirit outwards, psychedelic drugs work from the senses inwards. Genuine Christian mystical experiences always manifest or express a deeper life at work in the mystic's being.

To summarize, this author contends that most of the claims made for the mystical effects of psychedelic drugs are bogus. Most psychedelic experiences are nothing more than low-grade, destructive alterations of consciousness that diminish consciousness, integrity, and personality. They should be called what they are: regressive, and often pernicious, pseudo-mystical experiences.

From sufficient pastoral experience with psychedelic drug users and genuine Christian mystics, as well as from reading on psychedelic research and the Christian mystics, I would unhesitatingly say that the qualitative difference between the two is as great as that between God-induced phenomena and demonic or self-induced phenomena. It is true, however, that psychedelic drugs often leave their users, even indiscriminate ones, with a sense of transcendence.[53] But as one user who quit says so well: "Drugs can clear away the past, enhance the present; towards the secret garden, they can only point the way. Lacking the grit of discipline and insight, the

345

drug vision remains a sort of dream that cannot be brought into daily life. Old mists may be banished, that is true, but the alien chemical agents form another mist, maintaining the separation of the 'I' from the true experience of the infinite within us."[54]

Some psychedelic experiences undoubtedly have religious implications, however, and might be the catalyst for authentic religious conversion. If well-timed beatings or even being struck by a cannon ball (as in the case of St. Ignatius) can be the occasion for Zen enlightenment and Christian conversion,[55] perhaps drugs can be the same "trigger." They may function in the same way that alcohol can cause a person to sink into such misery that he is forced to rethink and do something about his life.

Some psychedelic experiences resemble genuine Christian mystical experiences in the same way that self-induced and demonically induced experiences likewise resemble them. Infused contemplation, the devil, the pathological self, and psychedelic drugs all have the ability to awaken deep levels of the psyche and to bring about secondary or charismatic mystical phenomena. But the same discernment that genuine Christian mystics have always used to differentiate God-induced phenomena from phenomena induced by other factors must be applied to psychedelic drug experiences.

The above sections have stressed that God must be distinguished from the psychosomatic "writings" he produces in the person's psychosomatic structure, although such writings will bear the authenticity of the divine hand. The self, the devil, and drugs may also produce a similar "writing"; this "writing," however, eventually betrays its true author. A handwriting expert can often uncover a faked signature and even say something about the writer's personality. The art of the discernment of spirits performs the same function.

Therefore, God's loving inflow will produce a variety of secondary effects at many levels of the person's being. Other causes may counterfeit these secondary effects, but never perfectly. The Christian mystics unanimously teach, however, that even God's beneficial side-effects should not be sought in and for themselves. The genuine Christian mystic seeks God, God alone, God for his own sake. Christian mysticism must never be reduced to a primitive form of psychotherapy, despite its frequent psychotherapeutic effects.

It cannot be overemphasized that an unrestricted love affair between God and the person, initiated by God, and bringing with it many secondary benefits, constitutes Christian mysticism. Unrestricted love, interpersonal relationships, the reference of the mystic to a totally transcendent, personal Other, total transformation, and spiritual fecundity are its hallmarks. These are simply not the hallmarks of psychedelic drug experiences.

THE DEMONIC

A careful reading of the New Testament indicates that Jesus partially understood himself as the one through whom Satan's definitive defeat would take place.[56] A major element of Jesus' mission consisted in doing battle with the forces of evil. He performed his exorcisms, therefore, as part of a dramatic struggle with demonic forces that reached its climax in Jesus' crucifixion and resurrection.

For the most part, Jesus' demonology coincided with that of his Jewish contemporaries. The Jews, however, considered the devils as individual, unorganized personal beings haphazardly bent on physical, psychological, and moral evil. Jesus held a unified view of individual and collective evil in the world. He saw Satan as the ruler and commander of a vast, but highly organized, army of demons. In short, evil for Jesus did not happen by chance. Various devils carried out and manifested the one will of Satan, whom Jesus encountered as a personal being of power. Evil for Jesus was a person, not a thing.

The Judaism of Jesus' day also taught nothing of the defeat of devils in the present. According to Jewish beliefs, God's definitive intervention at the end of the world would put an end to the powers of evil. On the other hand, Jesus saw in and through his exorcisms a victory over Satan's person and power and a revelation of the start of the time of salvation.

Although Jesus' redemptive death and resurrection decisively crushed Satan's power, only Christ's second coming at the end of the world would finally and definitively reveal this. Although defeated, the devils still possessed enough power to concentrate their attacks upon Jesus' Church and its members. For this ongoing battle against Satan and his minions, Jesus gave his disciples and the Church authority and power.

Almost every part of the New Testament teaches something about demonic "principalities and powers."[57] The all-pervasiveness of these teachings indicates just how central the belief in demonic forces was to the apostolic faith of the early Church. Even after a contemporary and intelligent demythologization, however, it still seems impossible to dismiss something so intimately a part of the Christian message as mere fictions, allegories, and myths of an earlier and more primitive age.

The New Testament depicts demons, principalities, powers, and spirits as subordinate to Satan, expressions of his power, and as the varied manifestations of a diffused, but highly unified, evil phenomenon. The New Testament, moreover, views them as nothing less than *personal* beings of intelligent will, might, and power. "It would be more exact to say," writes one exegete, "that their being is the being of an intelligent will which has power and aims at power; it is the being of a 'will-power' and also of a 'power-will.' "[58]

348

These beings of distortion, truncation, falsehood, ruin, annihilation, and death focus on a creation subservient to their alleged autonomy that wrestles against their original creatureliness. They wallow in self-aggrandizement, self-glorification, self-centeredness, and pseudo-autonomy. Only through the existence and power they receive from God, however, can they exert their energies against God. Yet they cannot escape their creaturehood; neither can they successfully set themselves up as the equal of God or Christ.

Their relationship to this world must also be emphasized, for no one and nothing is immune to their influence. As one exegete puts the matter: "They can occupy the human body, the human spirit, what we call 'nature,' and even the forms, bearers and situations of history. Even religions, including the Christian teaching, can become tools of their activity. Their spirit penetrates and overwhelms everything."[59]

Perhaps even more perniciously, they can affect even the general spiritual atmosphere, ambiance, or overall spiritual climate of groups, societies, nations, and various political, religious, and social movements. All too frequently, they are the "spirits" of the age, those hidden forces that establish the ambiance of interpretation, the implicit norms by which persons decide and judge, the unquestioned commonsense maxims by which people live and act. Their hidden nature, however, is their hallmark. "They take possession of the world and of men in such a way that they let these appear in their spirit. Withdrawing and concealing themselves, they reveal themselves through the world and existence, of which they have taken possession, and which they transcend in themselves."[60]

The New Testament underscores, of course, that Jesus' passion, death, and resurrection definitively defeated Satan. Jesus Christ, not Satan, is the Lord of this world and the entire universe. No Christian should consider

Christ and Satan as two equal forces, for Christ has bound the "strong man." In Christ, the love of God has decisively conquered the forces of evil, for "where sin increased, grace abounded all the more" (Rom 5:20).

Baptism into Christ's life, death, and resurrection frees the Christian from the domination of principalities and powers. Still, Christian life remains a war. The Christian must resist and fight Satan through faith, good works, truth, constant prayer, freedom from illusions, and a watchfulness based on the knowledge of the all-pervasiveness of demonic power and influence. Therefore, discernment of spirits remains essential to Christian living.

Of course, Satan tempts both coarsely and more subtly Christians from every walk of life. However, the mystical life seems to dramatize and make more explicit the Christian battle against the enemy of our human nature, the one who will do everything in his power to divert anyone from genuinely seeking, finding, and doing God's will. In addition, even a casual reading of the Christian mystics indicates a less hidden, more emphatic, and intensified confrontation with Satan by those who walk the mystical path.

St. John of the Cross is paradigmatic of the many Christian mystics who teach that Satan "establishes himself cautiously at the passageway from sense to spirit" (*LFL*, s. III, no. 64, p. 655). The devil makes his strongest stand at this point, because he cannot enter the person's innermost core. He will do everything he can to prevent the mystic from entering here to surrender to God's purifying, illuminating, transforming, and uniting self-communication.

To distract the mystic from this vital center, Satan may harass the person with bodily pain and a great variety of counterfeited secondary mystical phenomena. The

350

mystics unanimously teach that the evil one may make use of the person's lesser centers to concoct tricks, lies, illusions, delusions, and pseudo-mystical phenomena in general. St. John of the Cross also contends that Satan may occasionally touch the mystic's spirit in an unforgettably horrifying and painful way if the mystic ventures out from his inner sanctum because of the devil's distractions (*DN* II, chap. 23, no. 5, p. 383). However, demonic touches are a blessing in disguise. They make the mystic aware of the different levels of his being, force him even deeper into his own inner core, and teach him that this is the only genuinely holy vital center.

A contemporary neuropsychiatrist, Dr. Elmer Green of the Menninger Foundation in Kansas, has discovered one aspect of traditional Christian mystical teaching from his own empirical observations. He writes: "According to various warnings, the persistent explorer in these . . . realms . . . *brings himself to the attention of indigenous beings who, under normal circumstances, pay little attention to humans.* . . . They are of many natures and some are malicious, cruel and cunning, and use the emergence of the explorer out of his previously protective cocoon with its built-in barriers of mental and emotional substance as an opportunity to move, in reverse so to speak, into the personal subjectivity realm of the investigator. If he is not relatively free of personal dross, they can obsess him with various compulsions for their own amusement and in extreme cases can even disrupt the normally automatic functioning of the nervous system, by controlling the brain through the *chakras.* Many mental patients have made the claim of being controlled by subjective entities, *but the doctors in general regard these statements as part of the behavioral aberration, pure subconscious projections, and do not investigate further.*"[61]

This is a remarkable statement from a person free from a primitive, mythological world view. Green refuses to

351

reduce demonic forces to unconscious projections of subjective elements. He underscores the malicious activity of these "indigenous beings" that they carry out through the *chakras*, or centers of psychic energy, especially against unpurified inner explorers. It can be disputed, however, whether these "subjective entities" do ordinarily ignore humans. Ordinarily they influence all persons secretly, indirectly, and less dramatically. Once again, the mystical life makes their constant presence more visible and obvious.

The preceding chapters purposely omitted discussion of three demonically related phenomena so that they might be treated here: obsession, possession, and charismatic deliverance.

Obsession

In *obsession*, the devil stirs up especially violent and persistent temptations. He may harass the mystic by agitating the imagination, the passions, the emotions, and the external senses for long periods of time. Through repulsive, seductive, or perverted apparitions, sounds, and so on, the mystic is subjected to extraordinary fits of anger, hatred, lust, and despair. More crudely, the demon may touch, wound, punch, or embrace the mystic. The mystic may even be forced to utter words of blasphemy or to attempt suicide, although it seems the latter act is never carried out. The genuine Christian mystic remains conscious of his actions and refuses interior consent. On occasion, free will may be paralyzed, so sin does not come into question.

Julian of Norwich, for example, never consented to the blasphemies she involuntarily uttered. The devil applied to the face of St. Francis of Rome a decomposing corpse. St. Teresa of Avila and St. Catherine of Genoa likewise suffered from many repulsive forms of demonic obsession. St. Teresa of Avila was hurled down the convent steps by a demonic force and suffered

352

greatly during her long recovery. St. John Vianney and St. Alphonsus Rodriguez experienced the more seductive forms. The description by Joseph Surin, S.J., the exorcist at Loudun, of his own demonic obsessions is instructive: "The spirit unites himself with me without depriving me either of my consciousness or of my liberty. He is there as though it were another self. It is then as if I had two souls, one of which is deprived of the use of its bodily organs and remains, as it were, afar off, contemplating the other's actions. . . . I am simultaneously filled with joy and overwhelmed with a sadness that finds a vent in lamentations and cries according to the demon's caprice. . . . This stranger-soul, which seems to be mine, is penetrated with despair, as though by arrows, while the other, full of faith, despises these impressions. . . . If, at the invitation of one of these souls, I wish to make the sign of the Cross upon my lips, the other soul forcibly withdraws my arm."[62]

Possession

During *possession* the mystic loses consciousness. The devil seems to take the place of the mystic's own soul and exercises total dominion over the body. Although demonic obsessions occurred frequently in the lives of the great Christian mystics, possession rarely, if ever, did. *Some* commentators conclude from this that demonic possession is not a trial, but a punishment, and never takes place without some consent from the one possessed.[63] Others point out, however, that possession may be just as involuntary as an administered drug that deprives a person of the use of free will, but does not touch the deepest roots of the person's freedom.[64]

The possessed person often exhibits great restlessness, agitation, incredible strength, animal-like movements, violent and tormented behavior, and unusual noises. He may begin to speak in unknown tongues and show an extraordinary and sudden knowledge of many things. He may be able to reveal the sins of others, other secret things, and even future events. Listening to the gospel or the presence of holy objects cause him great pain. He is unable to call upon God, Christ, Mary, or the saints. When he regains his own consciousness, however, he cannot remember what has happened.

Possession is perhaps nothing more than the exceptionally dramatic manifestation of the demonic element that affects everyone in some way. It may also say nothing more about a person's sinfulness, holiness, and freedom than a naturally induced comatose condition would. Moreover, the devil never appears in a "pure" form. Possession requires the devil's intensification of a person's natural psychosomatic weaknesses, of his parapsychological quirks, and of his sensitivity to the social evils and pressures of his particular historical period. Possession cannot be sharply distinguished from illness; in fact, the latter may be either a symptom of the former or its point of entry.

Christians should both pray and make use of current medical knowledge to recover from *any* illness. Prayer, psychology, psychiatry, and parapsychology must likewise be brought to bear on cases of possession. The fact that in recent years the Church has rarely used the solemn rite of exorcism (a publicly performed exorcism by an authorized priest, vested and in church) may indicate the need to change the concrete form of the rite itself.

Charismatic Deliverance
The Church does permit the performance of private exorcisms even by the laity. *Charismatic deliverance* is a form of private exorcism currently being used by many in the charismatic ministry of healing. These healers prayerfully discern that incurable drug addiction, alcoholism, certain sexual compulsions, self-hatred, suicidal

354

tendencies, hatred of others, bitterness, resentment, and hostility may be linked to something more than organic, emotional, or other natural factors. Unsuccessful attempts to cure these people by natural means may indicate quasi-possession. If possession may be compared to an army that occupies an entire city, quasi-possession is like an army that has only certain portions of the city under its control.

The charismatic deliverer prays over and with the person so afflicted. He commands the spirits to leave and to injure neither the afflicted person nor any other person. The entire charismatic community may be present in prayer around the person to be delivered. This person is asked to repent of his sins. The person may experience during this prayer process the psychological vomiting of minor spirits, and finally the major one from his being. In short, the successful charismatic prayer process is experienced as deliverance. The healer reminds the person to integrate this experience into the rest of his life and to remain loyal to his conversion.

It is well to keep in mind, however, that of all the charismatic gifts of healing, this one is the most susceptible to abuse. Some bishops have explicitly forbidden the performance of charismatic deliverance, especially when done in large groups. Once again, prayer for an afflicted person is always good, but not always the specific ways and presuppositions through which it is done.

No one in Catholic circles until fairly recently questioned seriously the existence of Satan and the devils. For some contemporary Catholics, belief in personal, superhuman beings of evil is an outright embarrassment. They find it difficult enough to believe in the existence of God and Christ's divinity, let alone demons. Today's cultural ambiance links belief in devils with naiveté, superstition, outdated piety, mythology, and a history of cruelty and barbarism. Many would argue

355

that human beings and their institutions alone explain the evil in the world. Devils are nothing more than mythological personifications of individual and collective evil, projections of unconscious, psychologically destructive impulses that have attained a relative autonomy. Belief in devils, moreover, conveniently shifts the blame from evil's true source: the human heart and human institutions.

Paradoxically, however, the contemporary scientific, technological, and demythologizing ambiance has also contributed to an exaggerated, superstitious, and un-Christian belief in demons. The current interest in black magic, astrology, seances, spiritualism in general, Ouija boards, satanic worship, demonic possession, exorcisms, and poltergeist phenomena indicates a serious Christian pastoral problem. It also underscores an un-Christian fascination with the occult which, in many cases, is connected to a more than implicit and highly distorted belief in devils.

It must be pointed out, however, that belief in the existence of demons does not come primarily from divine revelation. In line with Thomas Aquinas, Karl Rahner contends that the experience of angels and devils is inherently human.[65] If personal, nonhuman beings that are not God can in principle be known through natural, empirical knowledge, why should they not be experienced, Rahner asks?

To be certain, neither superficial experience nor scientific knowledge attains the presence of angelic and demonic beings. But if angels and devils do belong to the one totality of the material and spiritual creation, they can be experienced and known naturally. Furthermore, if today's cultural horizon accepts the existence of intelligent life on other planets as a plausible hypothesis, why all the fuss about the existence of angels and devils? For Rahner, divine revelation confirms and interprets this human experience and knowledge of angels and devils by relating it directly to God and his salvific activity.

One contemporary author, Jules Toner, S.J., asks this key question: "Do Sacred Scripture, conciliar declarations, or the Church's ordinary teaching justify that belief in good or bad angels is a matter of Christian faith?"[66] After a brief, but highly perceptive, treatment of this question, he draws several conclusions. First, no serious and reputable theologian says that the existence of devils is definitely not a matter of faith. Second, the evidence indicates that the burden of proof rests squarely on those who question or deny the traditional belief in evil spirits. Third, the few authors who call the Church's teaching on this matter into question confuse the difference between legitimately demythologizing archaic modes of representing demonic existence and their activities and actually disproving their existence. Fourth, "there seems to be no foundation whatever," Toner writes, "for the broad statement often heard nowadays that contemporary scriptural and dogmatic theologians generally or mostly doubt or deny the existence of good and evil created personal spirits."[67]

To conclude this section, a few selected reflections on this issue must suffice. A contemporary Christian mystical spirituality must neither exaggerate nor water down the traditional Christian belief in demonic beings and their activity. Authentic Christian living demands nothing less than an integral Christian vision. Contemporary preaching must place demonology squarely in the overall context of God's victorious love for us in Christ that has freed us from Satan's dominion. It must likewise demythologize the pernicious historically and culturally conditioned ways of depicting the devils and their influence. The contemporary un-Christian fascination with the occult and superstitious practices must be nipped in the bud.

Demonology underscores the depth and seriousness of the human situation. A history of misused angelic freedom precedes and situates human freedom. Angelology in its various forms indicates that humanity belongs to a much wider community of salvation and damnation than first meets the eye. The traditional doctrine on devils also brings out the radicalness and depth of evil. The evil in the world transcends the capabilities of humanity and its entire history. Only the mercy and love of God in Christ could and can overcome this demonic refusal to live, grow, hope, and love that one discovers at the root of all creation. A genuine demythologizing should not sidestep the fact that personal beings of evil that intensify the human tendencies to chaos, destruction, sin, and death underlie the normal, natural course of history.

Christians must also be reminded that apart from God, only *his creatures* exist. Therefore, evil did not exist from the beginning; it has even temporal limits. God's freedom, goodness, and love, as well as the victory of his grace in Christ, circumscribe and embrace even the devils. Satan is not the equal of Christ in any way.

Although mystical theology should not lose sight of the possibility of demonic obsession during mystical ascent, the secret influence of the devils upon the interior movements of the human mind and heart must be underscored. A contemporary discernment of spirits must still confront the devil's ability to tempt, to deceive, to fabricate various mystical phenomena, and to lead the mystic subtly astray.

It must also be admitted that the classical Christian mystics tended to "privatize" the devil's operations. The biblical teachings on principalities and powers, however, also focus upon their tremendous cosmic and social influence. They have the ability to lead not only individuals astray, but also entire institutions, political organizations, and a variety of historical movements.

358

Those overly interested in secondary mystical phenomena and the more dramatic charismatic gifts must be reminded that these can all be induced demonically. As noted by the author of the *Cloud of Unknowing*, the devil, as well as God, has his contemplatives. In short, demonic, diabolical contemplation remains a possibility.

Finally, although the classical Christian mystics frequently depict the devils in a manner requiring demythologizing, their focus upon the battle with the forces of evil in the mystical life is still valid. Likewise, their stress upon the essential emptiness of satanic power in the light of God's purifying, illuminating, and transforming love given in Christ remains especially instructive for an integral, contemporary Christian mystical outlook.

Chapter Nine

Concluding Themes

By way of conclusion, I have selected two themes already mentioned briefly, but deserving a more extensive treatment. Both topics were chosen because of their special importance for a contemporary spirituality and mysticism, because of their significance for the future of the Christian mystical tradition, and because of my own current interests. First, the question of the relationship between mysticism and Christian perfection is an old theme in particular need of a contemporary exposition. The second topic, Christian mysticism and theology, has been undeservedly neglected in theological reflection.

THE RELATIONSHIP BETWEEN MYSTICISM AND CHRISTIAN PERFECTION

What Is "Perfection"?

Jesus demands that all Christians be perfect as their "heavenly Father is perfect" (Mt 5:48). The moral and religious maturity he enjoins, moreover, calls for a wholehearted love of God and neighbor (Mt 22:37–39). Therefore, the fullness of love constitutes Christian perfection.

Although most mystical theologians contend that Christian perfection consists primarily in affective charity toward God and secondarily in charity toward one's neighbor,[1] Karl Rahner has recently argued that love of neighbor *is* love of God.[2] In both cases, however, the

360

real issue centers upon integrating one's entire life into a love that implicitly and explicitly desires the greatest good for God himself, for one's neighbor, and for oneself.[3] But full Christian perfection, becoming Christ-like, requires both charity and those virtues that foster and are directed by it.

Mystical theologians agree that total Christian perfection is eschatological and that in this life one can always advance in love. For this reason, some speak of a "relative" perfection attainable during this earthly pilgrimage. For example, Joseph de Guibert says that the perfect Christian possesses "a certain stability in acting in a relatively perfect way."[4] He further distinguishes the "full and perfect charity, or heroic charity"[5] of the canonized saints from a "less full and resplendent perfection of charity"[6] of those who are more than "proficients" in the spiritual life.

The perfection of the canonized manifested itself, therefore, in outstanding and heroic virtues. Complete charity, great faith, perfect humility, total abandonment to God's will, habitual self-abnegation, ease in recollection, and extraordinary patience constituted their perfection. In addition, they came to enjoy freedom from sin and inordinate attachments, although faint traces of the latter were sometimes in evidence.

Furthermore, for de Guibert, even the relative perfection of those lacking heroic sanctity can be extraordinary.[7] These uncanonized saints cling to God with their love, live genuinely holy lives of self-abnegation, act virtuously and with ease even in difficult circumstances, and impeccably carry out the demands of their daily lives.

Some theologians contend that Christian perfection implies, as a minimum, immediate entry into heaven upon death without any purgatory.[8] For this life, on the other hand, it signifies that a person has become capable of "an ever more total self-commitment by ever deeper personal acts."[9] Having nearly overcome concupiscence completely, the person receives integrity, that is, the ability to gather the self together almost totally for any decision or act. The least sign of God's will and the slightest urgings of grace no longer encounter any conscious, preconscious, or unconscious resistance and disorder in the person because of his physiological, psychological, and personal wholeness and integration into the God of love.

Most mystical theologians agree, therefore, that the fullness of faith, hope, and love, as well as the accompanying virtues, constitute Christian perfection. They further agree that all Christians without exception are called to the full perfection of Christian life.

The Key Question
One of the most disputed questions among the different schools of spirituality centers, however, upon the precise relationship between this perfection and mysticism. The problem is whether Christian perfection is or is not attainable without infused contemplation. According to one view, a twofold unitive way exists. A person may attain the fullness of sanctity either by the common ascetical path, or by an extraordinary way that requires a special vocation. The proponents of this opinion maintain, therefore, that perfection does not necessarily require mystical graces. As one author writes: "There are very perfect persons to whom our Lord never gives such delights. . . . Not all the perfect are raised to perfect contemplation. . . . Many perfect men are canonised by the Church without there being in the process the slightest mention of infused contemplation."[10]

The second view underscores the one unitive way, the way of infused contemplation. Asceticism prepares the foundation for a later mystical phase that is the normal and necessary means for perfection, although not re-

362

quired in extraordinary cases. As one advocate of this position writes: "There are not two unitive ways. . . . There is only one . . . which by a docility to the Holy Ghost becomes more perfect day by day, leads to a closer mystic union."[11]

Most mystical commentators consider the controversy to concern the *means* to the fullness of Christian charity.[12] Relatively few authors contend that infused contemplation is an "essential element" of and constitutes in some way the state of perfection itself.[13]

The Twofold Path to Perfection

Joseph de Guibert has defended the two ways to full union with God with considerable skill and nuance.[14] Although he categorically denies that infused contemplation is required of all who attain perfection, his main thesis states: "The way of infused contemplation is not the only normal way to perfect love, although, apparently, generous souls do not ordinarily arrive at perfection unless God gives them some touches or brief participations in those graces which constitute strictly infused contemplation. Therefore souls can ascend to any degree of sanctity without habitually walking in the way of infused contemplation."[15]

Although de Guibert considers mystical prayer a "normal way" to sanctity, he holds for other normal ways to this goal. The purification required for great sanctity can come from means other than infused contemplation. He likewise denies that in every case mystical prayer is necessarily the most efficacious form of purification. Although mystical prayer may greatly aid a person along the path to perfect sanctity, de Guibert resolutely refuses to identify the states of infused prayer and perfection.

In one sense, however, "the way of infused contemplation is in itself a more excellent way, since it begets a greater conscious intimacy between God and man even while he is still on earth."[16] Nevertheless, mystical prayer produces no degree of perfection and sanctity that cannot be obtained through other means. De Guibert maintains that not all the canonized saints were mystics, although his main thesis underscores that perfection seems to require at least occasional "touches or brief participations" in infused prayer.[17]

The One Unitive Way

R. Garrigou-Lagrange strongly defends the one unitive way opinion.[18] On the basis of his readings of key figures in the Christian mystical tradition, he asserts that "the full perfection of charity in this life cannot exist without mystical contemplation."[19] One reaches the summit of Christian perfection only in and through infused contemplation; moreover, the fullness of Christian charity belongs to the mystical path. Mystical contemplation remains the most efficacious means to perfect charity, for it is a means united with the end. For Garrigou-Lagrange, therefore, infused contemplation takes place along with a high degree of love, and vice versa.

The seed of grace implanted at baptism establishes for all the call to perfection and, at least remotely, to infused contemplation. Just as a child naturally develops into an adult, grace will naturally flower into infused contemplation. The laws governing the growth of the divine seed demand that if grace follows its own inherent dynamism, infused contemplation will result as the perfection and crowning point of faith, hope, and especially love.

For want of certain conditions, however, grace may not reach its crowning point, the fullness of infused contemplation. Accidental circumstances and factors extrinsic to grace itself may thwart its normal development. Lack of proper direction, a hyperactive nature, grace received in an unfavorable atmosphere, too much study, or an ungrateful temperament that clings to imperfections may impede the growth of the divine seed.

It must be emphasized, however, that Garrigou-Lagrange does not consider these extrinsic factors as necessarily manifesting imperfections, lack of generosity, or sin on the person's part. These accidental circumstances may arise independently of the person's free will, just as a child may fail to develop physically in a normal way through no fault of his own. If the requisite conditions are present and the person cooperates with grace, the remote call to infused contemplation becomes a proximate call recognizable by the traditional signs. That many respond neither to the remote nor to the proximate vocation to mystical prayer explains why Jesus said many were called, but few chosen. For Garrigou-Lagrange, therefore, grace *of itself* should result in infused contemplation, but in fact, for reasons extrinsic to grace, frequently it does not.

Mysticism and the Canonized Saints
Concerning the exact relationship between Christian perfection and infused contemplation, several commentators underscore that neither the gospel nor the Church teaches the necessity of mystical prayer for perfection.[20] They endorse fully the view of Prosper Lambertini, who later became Pope Benedict XIV, that "many perfect souls are canonized although infused contemplation is not mentioned in the process (of inquiry into their lives)."[21] They further contend that even if it could definitely be proven that a person lacked infused contemplation, this would in no way be an obstacle to beatification.[22]

In short, many reputable theologians contend that it is possible to be a saint without at the same time being a mystic.[23] Oddly enough, however, many of these same authors attempt to show that *in fact* nearly all the saints were mystics or had at least received occasional mystical graces.[24]

The proponents of the counterposition argue that the gospel and the Church teach implicitly the necessity of infused contemplation to obtain Christian perfection. Since the Church canonizes only those who habitually practice heroic virtue, and since this is impossible without mystical contemplation, it follows that the Church canonizes only mystics.[25] All canonized saints had frequently experienced mystical union, therefore, except perhaps certain martyrs who received this gift only during their trials.[26]

The Church cannot and does not take infused contemplation into account during the beatification process, these theologians contend, because of the intimacy, interiority, and subjectivity of this phenomenon.[27] Beatification depends upon testimony, and the Church judges only from the evidence produced through testimony. Canon law states that the Church cannot judge internal matters. The only person capable of testifying to the purely internal phenomenon of mystical prayer is no longer living, that is, the person around whom the beatification question centers. Yet if the person possessed heroic virtue witnessed by others and later confirmed by miracles effected through his intercession, then he must have possessed infused contemplation.

Contemplation, the Active Life, and the Evangelical Counsels

J. V. Bainvel notes incorrectly that no attempt has ever been made to make the mystical life a special way to Christian perfection.[28] For example, the author of the *Cloud* speaks for a long-standing traditional opinion when he sharply distinguishes between those called to salvation and those called to perfection, and identifies the latter with the contemplative vocation (*PC*, chap. 16, p. 177).[29] To be sure, he deems "good" a life of love actively manifesting itself in corporal works of mercy, "better" a life comprising some meditation, but "best of all" the contemplative life (chap. 21, p. 76).

Only contemplative love can heal totally our human sinfulness. Moreover, the contemplative life begins in this life, but continues without end in heaven.

Despite the traditional view expressed by the author of the *Cloud*, the question still remains whether contemplation really is the only way to Christian perfection. Can any genuine Christian life be wholly contemplative or wholly active, as he too easily assumes?

Bainvel correctly states that the Church considers the life of the evangelical counsels, that is, poverty, chastity, and obedience, a special way of tending toward perfection.[30] In fact, Catholic theology has long considered the counsels to be the *better* means to Christian perfection. When St. Ignatius urged people to "praise highly religious life, virginity, and continence; and also marriage, but *not* as *highly* as the foregoing" (no. 356, my emphasis), he simply stated a long held Catholic view and anticipated the Council of Trent's official statement that it is "better and more blessed" to renounce marriage for the sake of the kingdom.[31] Only in the light of the Second Vatican Council has Catholic theology modified its approach to this issue.

Karl Rahner's Theology of the Counsels
Focusing upon the fifth and sixth chapters of Vatican II's *Dogmatic Constitution on the Church*, Karl Rahner makes much of the division of the material into two chapters.[32] The fifth focuses upon the universal vocation of all Christians to strive for perfection; the sixth, upon religious life as one of the ways to attain it. With his own creative nuances and contemporary transposition of the issue, Rahner defends both the universal call to perfection and the special function and value of the counsels.

He argues, for example, that all Christians are called to the fullness of love. But he also maintains that most Christians must accomplish this in and through their

367

secular professions and married lives. Catholic theology in general, he says, has overlooked the positive vocation to secular work and married life as a way to sanctity. He emphasizes that most Christians can and must become holy not only in worldly activity and marriage, but also can and must do so *through* them. All ways of life possess a radically saving, ecclesiological, and eschatological character. Moreover, for the majority of Christians, a secular vocation and marriage are the *better* means to perfection.

On the other hand, the evangelical counsels are a better means only relatively speaking, that is, only for those actually called to this way of life. Religious are not better or holier than married persons. When the vocation of one Christian is compared to the vocation of another Christian, it cannot be said that one is better than the other.

Still, Rahner considers the evangelical counsels a better means absolutely speaking because they objectify and manifest the gift and otherworldly character of faith and grace. Unlike marriage and secular activity, which make sense and retain their meaningfulness even without faith, the evangelical counsels do not. Because of their earthly significance and value, secular work and marriage do not dramatize as clearly (and may actually hide) the renunciation aspect of Christianity implicit in the baptismal vows. The counsels unambiguously symbolize the passion of Christ and that eventually everyone must renounce everything for the love of God. In short, they are a better means absolutely speaking because they directly manifest the eschatological situation of all Christians.

Rahner clearly holds the position that God calls all Christians to the fullness of charity in and through their various walks of life. However, his writings do not unequivocally answer the question concerning the relationship of mysticism to Christian perfection. That most Christians do not become mystics in the classical sense is obvious to him.[33] Since he equates perfection with the existential deepening of acts and calls this "the mystical factor in religion,"[34] he seems to propose the one unitive way to Christian perfection: that ascent to the fullness of love and mystical experience grow concomitantly.

Rahner criticizes past mystical theologies for their extrinsic views on grace and for focusing upon mysticism as God's intervention from outside the person.[35] For him, because of God's universal salvific will, God communicates himself to all persons, redeems them, and stamps their very being with an orientation toward a sharing in God's own life. This "supernatural existential," a modification of the person before justifying grace received sacramentally or extrasacramentally, signifies that every person's deepest and most pervasive *experience* is one of an orientation to God as the self-communicating mystery of his own life and love. The human person is essentially mystical because this basic orientation constitutes the most radical meaning of what the human person is, that is, a God-related entity. This relationship is always experienced, albeit often implicitly and anonymously. When this basal experience moves directly and explicitly into consciousness to dominate the center of consciousness in a nonconceptual way, this is mysticism in the strict sense.

For Rahner, everyday Christian faith, hope, and love always contain a mystical dimension, an experience of grace, no matter how hidden or implicit this experience may be. Moreover, the extraordinary experiences of the saints differ from normal Christian acts, not because they are mystical, but because they are unusual, yet natural, psychological manifestations. The saints' mystical experiences are, therefore, a deepening and intensification of their ordinary Christian life of grace, but are rooted in a natural, psychological substratum different

369

from daily Christian consciousness. Mystical experiences in the strict sense belong to the person's natural, psychological capability to "return-to-self," or to be self-present. This "return-to-self" concomitant in every act of knowledge and love is normally experienced only implicitly. When the implicitly experienced self-presence that contains a reference to God becomes explicitly experienced, one may speak about mysticism in the strict sense.

Moreover, mystical acts, although natural, may be of extreme significance for salvation, just as the natural acts of feeding the hungry and making free decisions have a salvific importance. Since they are also sporadically or habitually elevated by grace, they further help to anchor more deeply in the person his basic acts of faith, hope, and love.

Rahner contends that only psychology can decide whether these natural, but extraordinary, psychological phenomena must be present to render a person able to surrender totally to the mystery of life. If a person can attain the fullness of Christian wholeness without these unusual phenomena, then perfection is possible without infused contemplation. But if psychology shows these extraordinary phenomena to be intrinsic to the personal maturing process, even if they need not be cultivated "technically" or explicitly known, then mysticism and Christian perfection are intrinsically linked.

In view of the almost total lack of contemporary theological reflection upon this important problem, Rahner is especially to be commended for rethinking the issue in the light of his appealing theology of grace. Although he has not solved the issue, he has contributed to a contemporary transposition of the problem, introduced a new vocabulary, raised probing questions, and stressed the importance of this matter for Christian living. In addition, he is one of the few major contemporary theologians who focus upon the mystics and saints as a theological source and find in them a paradigm of every Christian's life of faith, hope, and love.

Concluding Reflections

In conclusion, it must be emphasized that no unanimity exists concerning the relationship between mysticism and full Christian maturity. The older Thomistic school, for example, tends to focus upon texts in the mystical writings that emphasize that all are called to infused contemplation as the normal crowning point of a life of fidelity to grace.[36] On the other hand, the Carmelite school stresses texts that underscore the opposite. The first school calls attention to what *should* happen in common Christian living; the second school to what *does* in *fact* take place. Furthermore, Rahner complicates the problem by making it essentially a psychological one. Perhaps Bainvel is correct when he states that not only is the problem not solved, the question has not even been properly raised, from either the view of principles or fact.[37]

Although visions, locutions, ecstasies, and other secondary mystical phenomena normally accompany infused contemplation, all commentators agree that Christian perfection does not require them.[38] All commentators likewise concur that infused contemplation usually provides the fastest and most effective means to perfection, that this way is most connatural with it. They further agree that full Christian maturity demands special graces at least occasionally, even if these graces are not recognized as such by the recipient. According to these commentators, the fullness of charity requires the passive purification of the senses and the spirit, although some maintain that exterior trials may replace mystical purgation in the strict sense.

If the integral person presented by St. John of the Cross is the norm, few Christians this side of death attain perfection. As described above,[39] the nights of the senses and the spirit must destroy all conscious, pre-conscious, and unconscious resistance to God's love and also enlarge the person's capacity to receive that love. Upon death, this person is so connatural with God that his soul is not wrested from him, but goes forth in loving ecstasy. The author of the *Cloud*, for example, also notes the ecstasy of the love experienced by some during their martyrdom (*PC*, chap. 9, p. 166).

If one takes seriously the claims made by numerous mystics about how resistant the human person is to God's grace, one must also ask whether mystical purification in the strict sense is required to overcome all traces of this resistance. Do exterior trials suffice for the requisite purification and for enlarging the person's capacity to receive God? Do Teilhard's "passivities of diminishment"[40] strike at the very roots of sin, kill the "old man," and bring forth a genuinely transformed person? Can the fully integral Christian be born without the purgatory on earth so vividly described by Catherine of Genoa?[41] Must God take immediate and direct action to purify, heal, and transform a person, if that person is to reach the integrity required for perfect charity? Whatever the case, if the integrity of the great saints is normative, few seem to attain it, be it through mystical purgation or through exterior trials.

The question can also be asked: did all canonized saints reach this level of Christian maturity before they died, or did some need purgatory, a purification process that some theologians identify with the very act of dying.[42] For example, is it possible that even St. Maximilian Kolbe, who gave up his life for another, still had areas of resistance to God's love in his unconscious, so that the death process itself was his definitive mystical purgation and passivity of diminishment?

Rahner's "mysticism of everyday life," Merton's "masked contemplation," and von Balthasar's "persevering through the grayness of every day in faith, hope, and love"[43] offer still another approach to the problem of mysticism and Christian perfection. These writers all emphasize the purification wrought by fidelity to the demands of daily living. Some people may attain an habitual, albeit implicit, union with God, even if they do not explicitly believe in God, by a total, loving, trusting self-surrender to the depths of life, even when their daily lives are collapsing. To be sure, mysticism in the strict sense requires the full consciousness of being grasped by God, that grace is not only working with us, but also operating alone and requiring only our consent.[44] Without reducing mysticism to religious experience, is there not need for a concept of mysticism in the broad sense wherein God's silent, mysterious, anonymous action remains unknown to the hidden contemplative?

The silent mystery of God's love that permeates each and every aspect of daily life calls all persons to total self-surrender, to that fullness of affective charity that constitutes Christian perfection. It seems possible that God communicates his purifying, illuminating, and transforming love not only through infused contemplation in the strict sense, but also through the hidden mysticism of daily life. Fidelity to the demands of a secular profession, radical love of one's spouse, ceaseless service of others, and the courageous and total acceptance of oneself and life may be the way the average person manifests his total surrender to God. But for the vast majority of persons, be they married, single, atheists, religious, or contemplatives in the strictest sense, perfection is eschatological: consummated only in *the* dark night of the senses and the spirit, *death itself.*

The problem of the relationship between mysticism and perfection could be clarified by a change of vocabulary. Does the word "perfection" of itself cause more confusion than necessary? Wholeness, integrity, maturity, au-

373

thenticity, and self-realization might be better words for the goal of human existence, especially if they remained anchored in a theory of cognitional and moral self-transcendence as firmly grounded as that of Bernard Lonergan.[45]

Finally, more work is needed to relate the stages of classical Christian mystical ascent, the deepening of existential acts, and the stages found in various contemporary life-cycle psychologies.[46] These psychologies stress the manifold transition periods in a person's life, usually associated with different age levels, and the concomitant psychological strengths and weaknesses during transition periods and different age levels. These psychologies have much to add to current studies on mysticism; they also have much to learn from the mystics.

CHRISTIAN MYSTICISM AND THEOLOGY

Now is the time to focus directly upon the significance of the classical Christian mystics for contemporary theology.[47] From the time of the apostles until approximately St. Thomas Aquinas, the greatest theologians were frequently mystics and saints. A number of reputable, contemporary theologians and thinkers have called attention to today's unhealthy divorce between mysticism and theology. In general, theologians of recent years have tended to overlook the Christian mystics and saints, despite their undeniable importance as a theological source. Although Jesus Christ must remain *the* most important source for contemporary theology, what Jesus Christ is by nature, the mystic and saint become by grace. Moreover, the great Christian mystics and saints amplify and make more explicit the basic experience of God that haunts every human heart.

To say that the biblical writings express the living faith of the Jewish and early Christian communities states the obvious. Not so obvious, however, is that the early

Christian community was able to bring forth through these writings a norm for all future Christianity because of its living, mystical faith in Jesus Christ. The Bible is essentially mystical literature; not to read it ultimately in that light is to miss "the one thing necessary" (Lk 10:42).

The Fathers of the Church carried on the mystical tradition begun in the scriptures, because they were men not only of great learning, but also of deep, mystical prayer and contemplation. Of course, the scriptures played a central role in their lives. They read them frequently; they also studied them by using the best secular tools of their day. Cultured, urbane, and learned, they could not help but be sensitive to the needs, religious questions, and aspirations of their contemporaries. They attempted, therefore, to transpose Christianity to meet the needs and aspirations of their pagan contemporaries. But they also extracted the best from their culture for Christianity.

The secret of the Fathers' success resides, however, not in their learning alone, but in the holiness and mystical wisdom that permeate their works. Their theology began and ended in mystical prayer. They wrote from what they had seen with the eyes of their spirit and loved from the depths of their hearts. Their theology flowed from their mysticism and their mysticism flowed from their theology. More importantly, their theology often led others to experience with lively faith and unction Christianity's great mysteries. The mystical and theological lives of many of the great Fathers of the Church are linked inextricably.

Much to the detriment of theology and the history of mysticism and spirituality, the reciprocal relationship between the living, mystical faith of the theologian and his theology gradually disintegrated. The mystic's world became increasingly private, subjective, psychological, and ascetic; that of the theologian, increasingly aca-

375

demic, professional, and "objective."[48] In fact, the divorce between mystical experience and the theology of the schools stamps much of the contemporary scene.

Theology has succumbed to the perennial temptation to sunder itself from mystical experience and living faith in favor of an overemphasized academic discipline. Piety and spirituality have also given in to the classic temptation of separating from critical self-interpretation and evaluation. That many contemporary theologians relegate the classical Christian saints and mystics to the realm of piety and spirituality, often pejorative terms in academic circles, and that many contemporary charismatics view theology or any hard thinking about the faith with great suspicion says much about the contemporary situation.

The questions that Christianity's mystics raise for theology visibly embarrass too many academic theologians. On the other hand, too many charismatics refuse to acknowledge that interpretation is intrinsic to experience, that the scriptures themselves contain much theological reflection upon certain experiences, persons, and events.[49] Have today's so-called spirituals grasped theology's legitimate place in Christian living, theology's mystical dimension, that theology itself can be a form of prayer? Faith seeking understanding can be worship with one's mind, a mystical surrender that heals and transforms the human mind with God's truth.

From the very beginning of Christianity, living faith and theological reflection have gone hand in hand. One could not survive without the other in the early days, nor can they survive without each other now. Perhaps the most hopeful sign for a reconciliation between mystical experience and theological reflection comes from the number of contemporary thinkers who view the current split between mystical experience and theological reflection as unacceptable.[50]

376

Perhaps no one has stated better the necessary unity in difference between the theologian's vital faith and his professional activity than Bernard Lonergan. He writes: "I believe a distinction is to be made between the spiritual life of a theologian and his professional activities; the former is religion in act; the latter is concerned with the interdependence of a religion and a culture. But the separation arises from the controversialist's need to claim total detachment. It arises from criteria of objectivity such as necessity and self-evidence that seem to imply that our minds should work with an automatic infallibility. It arises from an unawareness that the interpretation of texts and the investigation of history are *conditioned by the personal horizon* of the interpreter or the historian. It arises from an inadvertence to the dominant role of value judgments in much of theology as in much of human life."[51]

Therefore, Lonergan distinguishes between a theologian's spirituality and theological reflection. He refuses, however, to separate them. The theologian sees only as far as his personal horizon of faith allows him to see. Moreover, his living faith forms the matrix in which he interprets reality. It likewise forms the horizon in which his value judgments are made. In theology, as in the rest of human living, we ultimately know only what we love. And if in so much of human life, a person's values and grasp of truth change only if he changes his way of living, some theological breakthroughs occur only if the theologian's spiritual life changes or has been forced to change.

For Lonergan, human life should progress toward self-transcendence and authenticity by being faithful to the transcendental precepts: be attentive, be intelligent, be reasonable, be responsible, and be in love.[52] These transcendental precepts are not principles of logic nor extrinsic slogans of morality, but the very life and dynamism of the human spirit. As noted in Chapter 7, Lonergan calls them "the native spontaneities and inevitabilities of our consciousness."[53]

To be human means to have at the core of one's being a thrust toward being attentive, intelligent, reasonable, responsible, and in love. These precepts are lived by the human spirit before they are enunciated. To surrender totally to the human spirit's basic drives or demands is to become authentic, fulfilled, and fully human. To renege on any of these demands even slightly is to become inauthentic, unfulfilled, and less human.

More to the point, according to Lonergan, if the question of God is embedded in all our questioning, loving God fulfills the primordial orientation of our consciousness.[54] This love, as with all love, implies self-transcendence and self-surrender, "but being in love with God is being in love without limits or qualifications or conditions or reservations."[55] Being in love with God without reservations is our ultimate fulfillment, therefore, the gift of God's Spirit flooding and taking over the very ground of our being. Lonergan likewise views this unrestricted love as a transcultural constant and the inner core of all genuine religion that is disclosed in the variety of the great world religions.

This love poses serious threats, however, because "it dismantles and abolishes the horizon in which our knowing and choosing went on and sets up a new horizon in which the love of God will transvalue our knowing."[56] Unrestricted being in love with God provides the ultimate and essential source of all right living, right choosing, and right knowing. It likewise constitutes the basis for all religious, moral, and intellectual conversions.[57]

Only when this unrestricted love that occupies the core of the highest level of consciousness breaks forth, seizes the theologian, and converts him religiously, morally, and intellectually do we have "the efficacious ground for all self-transcendence."[58] These conversions transform the theologian, his living, values, horizon, and knowledge. The more he surrenders to the transcendental precepts, the more he surrenders to the basic dynamism of his being. In so doing, he must fully and consciously decide about his way of life, values, horizon, knowledge, and way of looking at reality.

Therefore, only when theologians allow themselves to be converted by the deepest aspirations of their spirits can the perfect marriage between living faith and theological reflection occur. When the Church's deepest thinkers are also its holiest members, then and only then will theology attain its authenticity.

William Johnston wryly writes that: "From the time of Thomas à Kempis better men than I have been attempting to convert the theologians—and they have been conspicuously unsuccessful. The theologians remain unregenerate."[59] Still, the future of theology depends upon the willingness of theologians to pay attention to their propensity or aversion for conversion. Today's theologian must be willing to ask himself how deeply his own theology flows out of an authentic mind and heart. Is he aware that his own "religion in act" conditions his own theological horizon? Is he prone to articulate only a faith tradition passed on in books, periodicals, and learned societies? Is he deeply aware that the living faith of the entire Church and especially that of his own heart are necessary sources for his theology?

This is not an harangue against academic theology nor an agreement with those who insist that interior, mystical, or charismatic experience is the *only* type of theology.[60] Rather, it underscores the mystical foundation without which theology cannot be itself. Theologians need not be saints, but they must be more aware of their need for conversion and how conversion plays a key role in their theology. They must also see the current chasm between mystical faith and scientific, critical reflection as a serious obstacle to both genuine mysticism and authentic theology. Even to admit this would be a step forward for theology.

This book's frequent reference to Karl Rahner indicates how boldly he has ventured to narrow the gap between mystical experience and theological reflection. In fact, many find Rahner's theology so satisfying precisely because of the critical rigor and the sense of God that permeate it. For Rahner, contemporary theology must explicate and make intelligible the fact that experiential reference to God as a holy, loving mystery is at least implicit in and the supporting ground of even the simplest task of Christian life, carried out in faith, hope, and love.[61] In this way, Rahner expressly links theology to the heart of all mystical experience. Deservedly he has been called *doctor mysticus*, a "mystical Doctor" of the twentieth-century Church.

What Rahner recently wrote in one of his volumes can be said about his theology in general, namely: "The different essays in this volume . . . are intended to show how religious experiences of a spiritual or mystical kind can overflow and be transposed into the idioms of theological reflection. In this way the rift, all too common even today, between lived piety and abstract theology may be bridged."[62] Even the book's subtitle highlights the Rahnerian enterprise: *Experience of the Spirit: Source of Theology.* The exchange between experience and reflection remains crucial. The mystical dimension of living faith must infuse theology.

Urging the Church to "have the courage to return afresh to its own experience of spirituality and mysticism which was much more alive in earlier times,"[63] Rahner stands as one of the first theologians of this century to take seriously the mystics, the saints, and their writings as valid theological sources. For him, the mystics actually do theology when they speak about their mystical experiences.[64] Moreover, he contends that the writings of the mystics are a "literature of piety which forestalls theological reflection, which is more fundamentally spontaneous than the latter, wiser and more experienced than the wisdom of the learned . . . a creative prototype . . . [and] a subject of tomorrow's theology."[65] Contemporary theologians should take their cue from Rahner by using the writings of more mystics and saints as creative prototypes and as the subject for today's theology.

Unlike much contemporary theology, which occurs within an academic tradition that presupposes faith but does not necessarily reflect the theologian's own living faith, Rahner's theology begins from his own religious experiences. From this basis, he critically evaluates the community's living faith and also allows the latter to correct his own. Although many commentators stress that Rahner's pious and spiritual writings are the overflow or the application of his highly speculative theology, the reverse frequently stands closer to the truth.

His awesome mastery of the Christian tradition, his Jesuit priesthood, and his profound empathy with the problems of faith confronting the contemporary person have nourished Rahner's own spiritual life. Most revealing is Rahner's admission that much of his theology springs from wrestling with the theological problems arising from his own faith experiences of *The Spiritual Exercises* of St. Ignatius of Loyola and of "the forgiving encounter with God in the act of repentance."[66]

Rahner has experienced for himself and explicated every person's experiential orientation to a holy, forgiving, loving Mystery. For Rahner, theological method involves making explicit something already lived, experienced, and known. One aspect of Rahner's theology is to evoke, deepen, purify, and bring to light the often anonymous mystical experience of being referred to God as mystery, enlightened in our depths by God as revelation, and loved in our roots by God as love's immediacy.

Perhaps the most significant reason for focusing upon the important Christian mystics and saints as an indispensable source of theology is the depth and clarity of their experiences of God and the dramatic way in which they have lived the mysteries of the life, death, and resurrection of Jesus Christ. In brief, they reveal what we ought to discover in ourselves. We find in their lives a clarification and an elucidation of what happens always and everywhere to all on the way to Christian perfection in faith, hope, and love, where salvation in the Christian sense is attained.

Because many of the Christian mystics and saints created new modes of Christian living, theological reflection should not overlook them as important theological sources. They have made visible and liveable for countless Christians new gifts of God's Spirit. As those on the forefront of evolving Christianity, they should be viewed as creative exemplars in the history of holiness, in the *historical* living out of the imitation of Christ.

Rahner has not only emphasized a development of dogma in the Church resulting from the historical assimilation of God's saving truth; he has also stressed the historical development of Christian holiness from the historical appropriation of God's saving, transforming self-communication as love, life, and truth.[67] Therefore, the Christian mystics and saints are not just models for Christian imitation. They show experimentally and explicitly that it is possible to be a Christian in an historical variety of ways.

Precisely because the great Christian mystics and saints were haunted, purified, illuminated, and transformed by Love in such a way as to become that Love by participation—the very Love that does the same for all Christians, albeit in a more hidden way—they are the obvious focal points for any serious theology. They are the truly Christian geniuses whose lives manifest the full blossoming of Christian existence. Their theology is a living theology, therefore, a theology written in their spirit and flesh. Prayer, adoration, discipline, integration, the horrors of the dark nights of purification, and self-surrender to the loving, forgiving, yet mysterious God gave birth to this enfleshed theology.

Moreover, the mystics have made the astonishing claim that they have the answer to life; their lives make that claim credible. Renouncing all, they claim to have found all. By cutting through their brokenness and sinfulness, they have discovered what it means to be an authentic human being. To be a saint and a mystic is to know explicitly and with full assurance that God is in love with us and that we are all secretly in love with each other.

The saints and mystics uncover what all of us are from the very depths of our being: a mystery related to the mystery of divine love and to each other. The questions that we live and that never go away—"What does it all mean?" and "Who am I?"—and the Christian answer of being unconditionally loved by a God of love and the need to love others become pellucid in the lives of the Christian saints and mystics. By listening to them, we actually listen more closely to our own depths. What they have lived, experienced, and manifested in their persons applies to us all. They are the true depth psychologists, who hear and see more clearly and explicitly what is in every human heart. Their lives are exemplars of genuine self-appropriation, self-transcendence, and authenticity. It is no wonder that Rahner insists that "the devout Christian of the future will either be a 'mystic,' one who has 'experienced' something, or he will cease to be anything at all."[68]

Notes

CHAPTER ONE

1. Dionysius the Areopagite, *Mystical Theology and the Celestial Hierarchies,* trans. by the editors of the Shrine of Wisdom (Surrey, England: The Shrine of Wisdom, 1965), chap. 1, p. 9.

2. Louis Bouyer, Cong. Orat., " 'Mysticism': An Essay on the History of the Word," in *Mystery and Mysticism: A Symposium* (London: Blackfriars, 1956), p. 136.

3. Quoted by William Ralph Inge, *Christian Mysticism* (New York: Scribner's, 1899), p. 335.

4. Ibid.

5. St. Teresa of Avila, *The Book of Her Life,* in *The Collected Works of St. Teresa of Avila* I, trans. Kieran Kavanaugh, O.C.D., & Otilio Rodriguez, O.C.D. (Washington, D.C.: Institute of Carmelite Studies, 1976), chap. 10, no. 1, p. 74.

6. St. John of the Cross, *The Spiritual Canticle,* in *The Collected Works of St. John of the Cross,* trans. Kieran Kavanaugh, O.C.D., & Otilio Rodriguez, O.C.D. (Washington, D.C.: Institute of Carmelite Studies, 1964), stanza 27, no. 5, p. 518.

7. William Johnston, S.J., *The Inner Eye of Love* (San Francisco: Harper & Row, 1978), p. 20.

8. Ibid., p. 31.

9. Quoted by William Ralph Inge, *Mysticism in Religion* (Westport, Conn.: Greenwood Press, 1976), p. 25. Also see: Rufus Jones, *Studies in Mystical Religion* (London: Macmillan, 1909), p. xv.

10. Ben-Ami Scharfstein, *Mystical Experience* (Baltimore: Penguin Books, 1973), p. 1.

11. Robert Ellwood, *Mysticism and Religion* (Englewood Cliffs, N.J.: Prentice-Hall, 1980), p. xi.

12. Walter T. Stace, *The Teachings of the Mystics* (New York: New American Library, 1960), p. 23. Frits Staal, in *Exploring Mysticism* (Berkeley: University of California Press, 1975, pp. 165, 190–99), also seems to hold this position.

13. Ellwood, *Mysticism and Religion*, p. xi.

14. Geoffrey Parrinder, *Mysticism in the World's Religions* (New York: Oxford University Press, 1976), p. 15.

15. Evelyn Underhill, *Mysticism* (New York: Dutton, 1961), pp. 76, 81–82.

16. Ibid., pp. 81–94.

17. Underhill's point offers the best reason for rejecting Robert Ellwood's position (*Mysticism and Religion*, pp. xi–xii), which includes shamans and occultists in the list of genuine mystics. Much more attention must be given to Karl Rahner's distinction between genuine mystical experiences and parapsychological phenomena with only a relative connection to mysticism. See his: "Mystical Experience and Mystical Theology," *Theological Investigations* 17 (New York: Crossroad, 1981), pp. 94f. (Volumes of the *Theological Investigations* will henceforth be cited as *TI*, followed by the appropriate volume number.)

18. Underhill, *Mysticism*, p. 85.

19. See: Harvey Cox, *Turning East* (New York: Simon & Schuster, 1977), esp. pp. 129–45.

20. Augustin Poulain, S.J., *The Graces of Interior Prayer* (Westminster, Vt.: Celtic Cross Books, 1978), pp. 54–99.

21. On this topic, see: Karl Rahner, "The 'Spiritual Senses' according to Origen," and "The Doctrine of the 'Spiritual Senses' in the Middle Ages," *TI* 16, pp. 81–103; 104–34.

22. Stace, *The Teachings of the Mystics*, p. 20.

23. Karl Barth, *The Epistle to the Romans* (New York: Oxford University Press, 1968), pp. 109–10.

24. See: Evelyn Underhill, "Mysticism in the Bible," in *The Mystics of the Church* (New York: Schocken Books, 1964), pp. 29–51; William Ralph Inge, "The Mystical Element in the Bible," in *Christian Mysticism*, pp. 39–74; F. Vandenbroucke, O.S.B., "Die Ursprünglichkeit der biblischen Mystik," in *Gott in Welt. Festgabe für Karl Rahner I*, hrsg. H. Vorgrimler (Freiburg im Breisgau: Herder, 1964), pp. 463–91; L. Cerfaux, "St. Paul's Mysticism," in *Mystery and Mysticism*, pp. 33–46. For a discussion of the thorny problem concerning the first-hand experiences of significant biblical figures and the biblical formulation of these experiences, see: Gerald O'Collins, *Fundamental Theology* (Ramsey, N.J.: Paulist Press, 1981), pp. 53–113.

25. "Dogmatic Constitution on Divine Revelation," in *The Documents of Vatican II*, ed. Walter M. Abbott, S.J. (New York: America Press, 1966), no. 16, p. 122.

26. Gershom Scholem, in *Major Trends in Jewish Mysticism* (New York: Schocken, 1954, pp. 6–7), writes: "It would be absurd to call Moses, the man of God, a mystic, or to apply this term to the Prophets, on the strength of their immediate religious experience." With other commentators, I disagree with Scholem's tacit acceptance of undifferentiated unity as the hallmark of all mysticism.

27. See: Rudolph Otto, *The Idea of the Holy* (New York: Oxford University Press, 1958).

28. On this point, see: Claus Westermann, *The Praise of God in the Psalms* (Richmond, Va.: John Knox Press, 1965).

29. See: Karl Rahner, S.J., "Dogmatic Reflections on the Knowledge and Self-Consciousness of Christ," *TI* 5, pp. 193–215.

30. See: Joachim Jeremias, *New Testament Theology* (New York: Scribner's, 1971), pp. 61–68; James D.G. Dunn, *Christology in the Making* (Philadelphia: Westminster Press, 1980), pp. 22–33; Bruce Vawter, *This Man Jesus* (Garden City, N.Y.: Doubleday, 1973), pp. 135–39.

31. See: Hans Küng, *On Being a Christian* (Garden City, N.Y: Doubleday, 1976), pp. 119–49; Gerhard Lohfink, *The Gospels:*

God's Word in Human Words (Chicago, Ill.: Franciscan Herald Press, 1972), pp. 50–52.

32. See: 1 Cor 6:11; 12:4f.; 2 Cor 1:21–22; 13:14.

33. Karl Rahner, S.J., & Herbert Vorgrimler, "Mysticism," in *Dictionary of Theology* (New York: Crossroad, 1981), p. 326 (hereafter cited as *DTh*).

CHAPTER TWO

1. Karl Rahner, S.J., ed., *The Teachings of the Catholic Church* (New York: Alba House, 1966), no. 156, p. 99.

2. See: Aldous Huxley, *Grey Eminence* (New York: Harper & Row, 1941), pp. 94–97, 101–2. Also see: Jean Baruzi, *Saint Jean de la Croix et le problème de l'expérience mystique* (Paris: Alcan, 1931), p. 498.

3. See: Victorino Osende, *Pathways of Love* (St. Louis: Herder, 1958), pp. 83–88.

4. H.O. Evennett, *The Spirit of the Counter-Reformation,* ed. John Bossy (Cambridge: Cambridge University Press, 1968), p. 45, my emphasis.

5. See: A. Astráin, *Historia de la Companía de Jesús en la Asistencia de España I* (Madrid, 1902), pp. 369f. Also see: P. Dudon, *Saint Ignace de Loyola* (Paris, 1934), Appendix, "Critique et apologistes des Exercises."

6. See: Joseph de Guibert, S.J., *The Jesuits: Their Doctrine and Practice* (Chicago: Institute of Jesuit Sources, 1964), esp. chaps. 2, 3.

7. See: Agehananda Bharati, *The Light at the Center* (Santa Barbara, Calif.: Ross-Erikson, 1976), pp. 48–86; Walter T. Stace, *The Teachings of the Mystics* (New York: New American Library, 1960), esp. chaps. 1, 6.

8. A. Mottola, trans., *The Spiritual Exercises of St. Ignatius of Loyola* (Garden City, N.Y.: Doubleday, 1964). Standard marginal numbers appear in the main text.

9. John Roothaan, S.J., *The Method of Meditation* (New York, 1855). For a contemporary truncation of Ignatian prayer, see:

Paul Suave, *Petals of Prayer* (Locust Valley, N.Y.: Living Flame Press, 1974), pp. 40–46.

10. For an excellent treatment on how to give the *Exercises* in this manner, see: Gilles Cusson, S.J., *Conduis moi sur le chemin d'éternité* (Montreal: Bellarmin, 1973).

11. William Young, S.J., trans., *Letters of St. Ignatius of Loyola* (Chicago: Loyola University Press, 1959), p. 8 and passim.

12. See: Karl Rahner, S.J., "The Ignatian Mysticism of Joy in the World," *TI* 3, pp. 277–93.

13. William J. Young, S.J., trans., *St. Ignatius' Own Story* (Chicago: Loyola University Press, 1956), no. 30, pp. 23–24.

14. For a careful discussion of this point, see: de Guibert, *The Jesuits*, pp. 122–32.

15. For a detailed exposition of the three times to make the election, see: Harvey Egan, S.J., *The Spiritual Exercises and the Ignatian Mystical Horizon* (St. Louis: Institute of Jesuit Resources, 1976), chap. 6.

16. Karl Rahner, S.J., "Comments by Karl Rahner on Questions Raised by Avery Dulles," in *Ignatius of Loyola: His Personality and Spiritual Heritage 1556–1956*, ed. Friedrich Wulf, S.J. (St. Louis: Institute of Jesuit Sources, 1977), p. 291, my emphasis.

17. See: Hugo Rahner, S.J., *Ignatius the Theologian* (New York: Herder & Herder, 1968), esp. chap. 1.

18. No. 209 states that the application of the senses *may* be dropped during the third week and no. 226 indicates that this is true in the fourth week. I would contend that the dynamics of the *Exercises* and the content for these two weeks make almost every exercise in the third and fourth week an application of the senses, or at least deep and simple prayer.

19. For an excellent discussion of the "spiritual senses," see: H. Rahner, *Ignatius the Theologian*, chap. 5; K. Rahner, *TI* 16, chaps. 6, 7.

20. See: John Ryan, trans., *The Confessions of St. Augustine* (Garden City, N.Y.: Doubleday, 1960), Book 10, chap. 6, pp. 233–34.

388

21. For the theological metaphysics behind this position, see: Karl Rahner, S.J., "Revelation," *Encyclopedia of Theology. The Concise Sacramentum Mundi* (New York: Seabury Press, 1975), pp. 1460–66 (hereafter cited as *EOT*).

22. Examples of such a God-given consolation which utterly convinces its recipients of its divine origin abound in the Christian mystical tradition. William of St. Thierry, in *The Golden Epistle* (Spencer, Mass.: Cistercian Publications, 1971, p. 97), describes a consolation so elevated that "it even transforms the man into a resemblance of ultimate reality" and imparts the gift to discern "the difference between the clean and the unclean." Walter Hilton, in *The Scale of Perfection* (St. Meinrad, Ind.: Abbey, 1975, p. 116), knows of a "supreme consolation" that makes all Christian virtues easy. The *Philokalia* (*Writings from the Philokalia on Prayer of the Heart*, trans. E. Kadloubovsky & G. Palmer, London: Faber, 1951, p. 242) insists that the experience of deep, interior grace is essential before one can discern deeply.

23. Karl Rahner, S.J., *Visions and Prophecies* (New York: Herder & Herder, 1964), p. 14., n. 12.

24. Ibid.

25. Claudio Naranjo & Robert Ornstein, *On the Psychology of Meditation* (New York: Viking Press, 1972), p. 21.

26. Ibid., p. 48.

27. K. Rahner, "The Ignatian Mysticism of Joy in the World."

28. Bede Griffiths, O.S.B., *Return to the Center* (Springfield, Ill.: Templegate, 1977), p. 78.

29. See: Harvey D. Egan, S.J., *The Spiritual Exercises and the Ignatian Mystical Horizon*, pp. 113–15, for a treatment of Ignatius' mediator mysticism.

30. For an excellent theology of mediatorship, see: Karl Rahner, S.J., "The Church of the Saints," *TI* 3, pp. 91–104; "Why and How Can We Venerate the Saints?," *TI* 8, pp. 3–23; "One Mediator and Many Mediations," *TI* 9, pp. 169–84.

31. William Young, S.J., trans., *The Spiritual Journal of Saint Ignatius*, in *Woodstock Letters* 87:3 (July 1958), p. 211.

32. Perhaps nos. 63, 64, 95, 102, 135, 147, 148, etc., make more sense from a trinitarian perspective.

33. Morton T. Kelsey, *The Other Side of Silence* (New York: Paulist Press, 1976), p. 138. For the points made in the following paragraph, see p. 130. For another approach to the use of spontaneous images, see: Ira Progoff, *The Practice of Process Meditation* (New York: Dialogue House, 1980); *At A Journal Workshop* (New York: Dialogue House, 1975).

34. For an excellent blending of Eastern and Western prayer techniques, see: Anthony de Mello, S.J., *Sadhana. A Way to God. Christian Exercises in Eastern Form* (St. Louis: Institute of Jesuit Sources, 1978).

35. On this point, see: de Guibert, *The Jesuits*, pp. 57–58.

36. On this point, see: H. Rahner, "The Spirit and the Church," in *Ignatius the Theologian*, pp. 214–38.

37. Jerome Nadal, quoted by H. Rahner, ibid., p. 217.

38. Ibid., p. 218.

39. For an excellent treatment of this issue, see: John W. O'Malley, S.J., "The Fourth Vow in Its Ignatian Context," *Studies in the Spirituality of Jesuits* 15:1 (January 1983), pp. 36–37.

40. Ibid.

41. See: Raymond Schwager, *Das dramatische Kirchenverständnis bei Ignatius von Loyola* (Zürich-Einsiedeln-Köln: Benziger, 1970), esp. p. 152.

42. Ibid., pp. 136–52.

43. Juan Alonso de Polanco, S.J., quoted by H. Rahner, *Ignatius the Theologian*, p. 221.

44. Jerome Nadal, S.J., quoted by H. Rahner, *Ignatius the Theologian*, p. 237.

45. William J. Young, S.J., trans., *St. Ignatius' Own Story*, no. 29, p. 23.

46. Erich Neumann, "Mystical Man," *Eranos Jahrbuch* 30 (1968), pp. 386–87.

47. See: O'Malley, "The Fourth Vow," pp. 43–45.

48. See, for example: Jose Magaña, S.J., *A Strategy for Liberation. Notes for Orienting the Exercises towards Utopia* (Jersey City, N.J.: Program to Adapt the Spiritual Exercises, 1974).

49. See: John C. Futrell, S.J., *Making an Apostolic Community of Love* (St. Louis: Institute of Jesuit Sources, 1970); "Communal Discernment," *Studies in the Spirituality of Jesuits* (November 1972), pp. 159–94; "Ignatian Discernment," *Studies in the Spirituality of Jesuits* (April 1970), pp. 47–88; Jules J. Toner, S.J., "The Deliberation that Started the Jesuits. A Commentary on the *Deliberatio primorum Patrum*. Newly Translated with a Historical Introduction," *Studies in the Spirituality of Jesuits* (June 1974), pp. 179–216; "A Method of Communal Discernment of God's Will," *Studies in the Spirituality of Jesuits* (September 1971), pp. 121–52; Ladislas Orsy, S.J., "Towards a Theological Evaluation of Communal Discernment," *Studies in the Spirituality of Jesuits* (October 1973), pp. 139–88.

CHAPTER THREE

1. William Johnston, S.J., ed., *The Cloud of Unknowing and the Book of Privy Counselling* (Garden City, N.Y.: Doubleday, 1973). I shall refer to this one volume as the *Cloud*, since the two works are easily understood together. *Counselling* can be viewed, moreover, as the more mature rewriting of the *Cloud*. Chapter and page numbers in the main text refer to this volume. References to *Counselling* in the main text are given as *PC*, followed by the chapter and page numbers.

2. In the introduction to his translation of *The Cloud of Unknowing* (New York: Dell, 1957), Ira Progoff seemingly misses the *Cloud*'s solidly intellectual basis. For a nuanced critique of many of Progoff's views on the *Cloud*, see: William Johnston, S.J., *The Mysticism of the Cloud of Unknowing* (New York: Desclée, 1967).

3. Karl Rahner, S.J., ("Mystical Experience and Mystical Theology," *TI* 17, p. 95) argues that, psychologically speaking, mystical experiences differ from normal conscious activities only in the order of nature. From this it follows that one can train oneself to have them. The *Cloud* stands in contradiction to this position.

4. See, for example: Edward Rosenfeld, *The Book of Highs. 250 Methods for Altering Your Consciousness without Drugs* (New York: Quadrangle, 1973).

5. I can find nothing in Transcendental Meditation which indicates that its main dynamism is love. Nescience is the key to TM, although it may be practiced in love. The Maharishi carries over into TM practice, moreover, the monism he attributes to certain passages of the Bhagavad Gita.

6. For what may be the best single-volume work on what contemporary Christian prayer can creatively be, see: Anthony de Mello, S.J., *Sadhana* (St. Louis: Institute of Jesuit Sources, 1978). For a critique of de Mello on certain points, see: Harvey D. Egan, S.J., "Prayer and Contemplation as Orthopraxis," *Proceedings of the Catholic Theological Society of America* 35 (1980), pp. 102–12.

7. For a reduction of mysticism to the ecstatic, see: Agehananda Bharati, *The Light at the Center* (Santa Barbara, Calif.: Ross-Erikson, 1976), and Andrew Greeley, *Ecstasy. A Way of Knowing* (Englewood Cliffs, N.J.: Prentice-Hall, 1974). Evelyn Underhill, in *Mysticism* (New York: Dutton, 1961, p. vii) writes: "No responsible student now identifies the mystic and the ecstatic."

8. For an example of a commentator who reduces all mysticism to the experience of undifferentiated unity, see: Walter T. Stace, *The Teachings of the Mystics* (New York: New American Library, 1960), p. 21.

9. For an excellent treatment of "spiritual fecundity," see: Underhill, *Mysticism*, pp. 431–37.

10. Quoted by Johnston, *The Mysticism of the Cloud of Unknowing*, pp. 122–23.

11. See: William James, *The Varieties of Religious Experience* (New York: New American Library, 1958), pp. 268–69, 317.

12. See: Henri de Lubac, S.J., *The Religion of Teilhard de Chardin* (Garden City, N.Y.: Doubleday, 1968), pp. 263–64.

13. Ira Progoff, *The Cloud of Unknowing*, p. 24.

14. See: Violet S. De Laszlo, ed., *The Basic Writings of C. G. Jung* (New York: The Modern Library, 1959), esp. pp. 292–96.

15. See: Peter Moore, "Mystical Experience, Mystical Doctrine, Mystical Technique," in *Mysticism and Philosophical Analysis*, ed. Steven T. Katz (New York: Oxford University Press, 1978), pp. 101–31; Steven T. Katz, ed., *Mysticism and Religious Traditions* (New York: Oxford University Press, 1983).

16. Ibid., p. 114.

17. See: William Johnston, S.J., *The Mysticism of the Cloud of Unknowing*, p. 17. For an excellent treatment of the relationship of Christ's humanity to apophatic mysticism, see his: *The Still Point. Reflections on Zen and Christian Mysticism* (San Francisco: Harper & Row, 1970), pp. 151–70.

18. Morton T. Kelsey, in *The Other Side of Silence* (New York: Paulist Press, 1976), makes such a strong case for prayer by way of images that he never grasps the value of the apophatic tradition for higher Christian mystical prayer. Ronald Knox, in *Enthusiasm* (New York: Oxford University Press, 1961, pp. 579, 582), seems to consider apophatic mysticism un-Christian.

19. See: Anne Marie Schimmel, *Mystical Dimensions of Islam* (Chapel Hill: University of North Carolina Press, 1975); Robert S. Ellwood, Jr., *Mysticism and Religion* (Englewood Cliffs, N.J.: Prentice-Hall, 1980); Geoffrey Parrinder, *Mysticism in the World's Religions* (New York: Oxford University Press, 1976).

CHAPTER FOUR

1. E. Allison Peers, trans. and ed., *The Autobiography of St. Teresa of Avila* (Garden City, N.Y.: Doubleday, 1960). Henceforth referred to as *AB*, followed by the chapter and page number from this work.

2. Quoted by E. Allison Peers, trans. and ed., *Interior Castle* (Garden City, N.Y.: Doubleday, 1961), p. 9. Henceforth abbreviated as *IC*, followed by the mansion number, the chapter in the particular mansion, and the page number from this volume.

3. See: *AB*, chap, 10, p. 123; *IC*, m. 1, chap. 2, p. 36.

4. E. Allison Peers, trans. and ed., *The Way of Perfection* (Gar-

den City, N.Y.: Doubleday, 1964). Henceforth abbreviated as *WP,* followed by chapter and page number from this volume.

5. See: Walter T. Stace, *The Teachings of the Mystics* (New York: New American Library, 1960), pp. 174–78, esp. p. 175.

6. Karl Rahner, S.J., "Teresa of Avila: Doctor of the Church," in *Opportunities for Faith* (New York: Seabury Press, 1970), p. 123.

7. Otilio Rodriguez, O.C.D., & Kieran Kavanaugh, O.C.D., trans. and ed., *Meditations of the Song of Songs. The Collected Works of St. Teresa of Avila,* vol. 2 (Washington, D.C.: Institute of Carmelite Studies, 1980). Henceforth abbreviated as *SS,* followed by the chapter and page number in this volume.

8. Francisco de Osuna, *The Third Spiritual Alphabet,* trans. Mary E. Giles (Ramsey, N.J.: Paulist Press, 1982). Also see: *WP,* chap. 26, pp. 173–78; chap. 28, pp. 183–90; chap. 29, pp. 190–95.

9. See: *IC,* m. 4, chap. 3, pp. 85–94.

10. See: *AB,* chap. 23, p. 221, and chap. 14, p. 148.

11. See: *IC,* m. 4, chap. 2, pp. 80–85; *AB,* chap. 15, pp. 154–63.

12. See: *AB,* chap. 32, pp. 300–3.

13. See: *IC,* m. 6, chap. 7, pp. 171–78; *AB,* chap. 22, pp. 209–19.

14. See: *IC,* m. 6, chap. 8, pp. 178–84; chap. 9, pp. 185–93.

15. See: *AB,* chap. 27, p. 250.

16. See: *IC,* m. 7, chaps. 1–4, pp. 206–33.

17. Quoted by E. Allison Peers, *AB,* p. 20.

18. See: *SS,* chap. 7, pp. 259–60.

19. See: *WP,* chap. 39, p. 259. Also see on this point, *Spiritual Exercises,* no. 77.

20. See: *AB,* chap. 38, p. 362; chap. 40, p. 391; *IC,* m. 6, chap. 8, p. 183; chap. 9, p. 189.

21. See: *AB,* chap. 5, pp. 84–85; chap. 10, p. 123; *IC,* m. 5, chap. 1, pp. 100–1; *WP,* chap. 3, p. 47; chap. 5, p. 63.

22. See: *SS,* chap. 6, p. 253.

23. See: *WP,* chap. 1, pp. 36–39; chap. 3, p. 50.

24. See: *AB,* chap. 40, p. 388.

25. See: *AB,* chap. 30, pp. 281–82.

26. For some of these points, see: *The Collected Works of St. Teresa of Avila,* vol. 1, pp. 6–19.

27. For an exposition of this contemporary thesis, see: Stace, *The Teachings of the Mystics,* esp. pp. 124–200; Erich Neumann, "Mystical Man," *Eranos Jahrbuch* 30 (1968), pp. 386–87.

28. When I say "many affinities," I do not want to exaggerate the influence of Ignatian spirituality upon Teresa. St. John of the Cross, the Franciscan, Francisco de Osuna, several Dominicans, and many others also had a great role to play.

29. For one example, see: Maharishi Mahesh Yogi, *Transcendental Meditation* (New York: Signet, 1963), esp. pp. 273, 283.

30. For proponents of this thesis, see: Stace, *The Teachings of the Mystics,* pp. 14, 21; Agehananda Bharati, *The Light at the Center* (Santa Barbara, Calif.: Ross-Erikson, 1976). Bharati strips mysticism down to a "zero-experience" totally lacking in noetic, moral, and religious significance.

31. See: Stace, *The Teachings of the Mystics,* pp. 10, 21; Friedrich Heiler, "The History of Religions as a Preparation for the Cooperation of Religions," in *The History of Religions: Essays in Methodology,* ed. M. Eliade & J. Kitagawa (Chicago: University of Chicago Press, 1959), pp. 142–53. See: Peter Moore, "Recent Studies of Mysticism: A Critical Survey," *Religion* 3:2 (Autumn 1973), p. 150.

32. Steven Katz, "Language, Epistemology, and Mysticism," in *Mysticism and Philosophical Analysis,* ed. Steven T. Katz (New York: Oxford University Press, 1978), pp. 22–74.

33. Stace, *The Teachings of the Mystics,* pp. 17, 185, passim. Also see his: *Mysticism and Philosophy* (New York: Macmillan, 1960), pp. 47–55.

34. See: Peter Moore, "Mystical Experience, Mystical Doctrine, Mystical Technique," in *Mysticism and Philosophical Analysis*, ed. Steven T. Katz, p. 119; R. Crookall, *The Interpretation of Cosmic and Mystical Experience* (London, 1961); Karl Rahner, S.J., "The Ignatian Mysticism of Joy in the World," *TI* 3, p. 279.

35. See: Bharati, *The Light at the Center*; Andrew Greeley, *Ecstasy. A Way of Knowing* (Englewood Cliffs, N.J.: Prentice-Hall, 1974).

36. See: Abraham Maslow, *Towards a Psychology of Being* (Princeton, N.J.: Van Nostrand, 1962); John White, ed., *The Highest State of Consciousness* (Garden City, N.Y.: Doubleday, 1972), pp. vii–xvii.

37. Evelyn Underhill, *Mysticism* (New York: Dutton, 1961), p. vii. See also: Gershom Scholem, *Major Trends in Jewish Mysticism* (New York: Schocken, 1954), p. 5.

38. For a nuanced presentation of some of the problems involved on this issue, see: Martin Tripole, S.J., "A Church for the Poor and the World: At Issue with Moltmann's Ecclesiology," *Theological Studies* 42:4 (December 1981), pp. 645–59.

39. See: Harvey Cox, *Turning East* (New York: Simon & Schuster, 1977). As we shall show later, however, this Eastern turn does have much positive value for Christianity.

40. Karl Rahner, S.J., *Visions and Prophecies* (New York: Herder & Herder, 1964), p. 14, n. 12.

41. On this point, see: Augustin Poulain, S.J., *The Graces of Interior Prayer* (Westminster, Vt.: Celtic Cross Books, 1978), esp. pp. 635–37.

42. For an excellent discussion of the "spiritual senses," see: Hugo Rahner, S.J., *Ignatius the Theologian* (New York: Herder & Herder, 1968), chap. 5; Karl Rahner, S.J., *TI* 16, chaps. 6, 7.

43. K. Rahner, "Teresa of Avila," p. 125.

44. See: Harvey D. Egan, S.J., "Rahner's Mystical Theology," in *Theology and Discovery. Essays in Honor of Karl Rahner, S.J.*, ed. William J. Kelly, S.J. (Milwaukee: Marquette University Press, 1980), pp. 139–58, esp. 150–51.

45. Karl Rahner, S.J., "Teresa of Avila," pp. 124–25.

46. It is not my intention to dissociate the resurrection from the cross. For an excellent presentation of their intrinsic unity, see: Karl Rahner, S.J., *Foundation of Christian Faith* (New York: Seabury Press, 1978), esp. pp. 228–93. In my view, Sebastian Moore, in *The Crucified Jesus Is No Stranger* (New York: Seabury Press, 1977), places far too much emphasis upon the cross and neglects its essential relationship to Jesus' bodily resurrection.

47. For a good treatment of narrative theology, see: John Navone, S.J., & Thomas Cooper, *Tellers of the Word* (New York: Le Jacq, 1981).

48. See: Segundo Galilea, "Liberation as the Encounter with Politics and Contemplation," in *Understanding Mysticism,* ed. Richard Woods, O.P. (Garden City, N.Y.: Doubleday, 1980), pp. 529–40.

49. See: Bernard Lonergan, S.J., *Method in Theology* (New York: Seabury Press, 1979), esp. index, p. 375, "conversion"; Robert Doran, S.J., *Subject and Psyche: Ricoeur, Jung, and the Search for Foundations* (Washington, D.C.: University Press of America, 1977); Walter E. Conn, ed., *Conversion: Perspectives on Personal and Social Transformation* (Staten Island, N.Y.: Alba House, 1978).

CHAPTER FIVE

1. *The Collected Works of St. John of the Cross,* trans. Kieran Kavanagh, O.C.D. & Otilio Rodriguez, O.C.D. (Washington, D.C.: Institute of Carmelite Studies, 1976), p. 67.

2. See especially: Georges Morel, *Le Sens de L'existence selon S. Jean de la Croix,* 3 vols. (Paris: Aubier, 1960–61); Jean Baruzi, *Saint Jean de la Croix et le Problème de L'expérience Mystique* (Paris: Felix Alcan, 1931). For didactic purposes, I have used the outline for reading St. John of the Cross suggested by Morel in vol. 1, pp. 182–83.

3. See: *The Collected Works of St. John of the Cross,* pp. 68–73; 295–97; 408–9; 577–78.

4. *The Ascent of Mount Carmel,* henceforth abbreviated as

AMC, followed by book number, chapter, section number, and page in the above translation.

5. *The Spiritual Canticle,* henceforth abbreviated as *SC,* followed by the stanza, section number, and page in the above translation.

6. *The Living Flame of Love,* henceforth abbreviated as *LFL,* followed by the stanza, section number, and page in the above translation.

7. See: "Sayings of Light and Love," *The Collected Works,* p. 667.

8. William James, *The Varieties of Religious Experience* (New York: New American Library, 1959), esp. pp. 292–94.

9. *AMC,* I, chaps. 1–12, pp. 73–101.

10. *AMC,* I, chaps. 13–15, pp. 101–6.

11. *The Dark Night (=DN),* I, chaps. 8–14, pp. 311–29.

12. *AMC,* II, chaps. 1–5, pp. 107–18.

13. *AMC,* II, chaps. 7–32, pp. 121–213.

14. *AMC,* II, chaps. 18, 22, 30, pp. 160–63; 178–87; 208–10.

15. *AMC,* III, chaps. 1–15, pp. 213–37.

16. *AMC,* III, chaps. 16–45, pp. 237–92.

17. *DN,* II, chaps. 1–3, pp. 329–34.

18. For the night as a trial, see: *DN,* II, chaps. 4–8, pp. 334–45. For the night as a way, see: *DN,* II, chap. 16, pp. 363–68; chaps. 18–20, pp. 371–78. For the night as a result, see: *DN,* II, chaps. 9–13, pp. 346–61; chaps. 23–24, pp. 382–89.

19. See: *SC,* ss. 1–11, pp. 416–53. It cannot be overemphasized how important it is to read and ponder John's poetry and not only to read the commentary.

20. See: *SC,* ss. 12–26, pp. 453–516.

21. See: *SC,* ss. 27–40, pp. 517–65.

22. See Joseph de Guibert, S.J., *The Jesuits: Their Doctrine and Practice* (Chicago: Institute of Jesuit Sources, 1964), pp. 50–59, esp. pp. 55–56.

23. *LFL,* pp. 578–649.

24. See: Friedrich von Hügel, *The Mystical Element of Religion,* vol. 1 (Westminster, Md.: Christian Classics, 1961), p. 25; Ronald A. Knox, *Enthusiasm* (New York: Oxford University Press, 1961), pp. 579, 582.

25. Dom Roger Hudleston, O.S.B., ed., *The Spiritual Letters of Dom John Chapman, O.S.B.* (London: Sheed & Ward, 1935), p. 269. He later revised his thinking about John and preferred him to Teresa.

26. See: Steven T. Katz, "Language, Epistemology, and Mysticism," *Mysticism and Philosophical Analysis,* ed. Steven T. Katz (New York: Oxford University Press, 1978), p. 57.

27. For an excellent treatment of the role of Jesus Christ in the works of St. John of the Cross, see: Morel, *Le Sens,* vol. 2, chap. 3. Also see: Sebastian Moore, *The Crucified Jesus Is No Stranger* (New York: Seabury Press, 1977). Moore's theology offers a novel way of reconciling apophatic mysticism with a Christianity bound to the person of Jesus Christ.

28. Walter T. Stace, *The Teachings of the Mystics* (New York: New American Library, 1960), pp. 185–86.

29. Agehananda Bharati, *The Light at the Center* (Santa Barbara, Calif.: Ross-Erikson, 1976), p. 101.

30. Andrew Greeley, *Ecstasy. A Way of Knowing* (Englewood Cliffs, N.J.: Prentice-Hall, 1974), pp. 71–72.

31. Arthur J. Deikman, "Deautomatization and the Mystic Experience," *Altered States of Consciousness,* ed. Charles T. Tart (Garden City, N.Y.: Doubleday, 1969), pp. 25–46.

32. Pierre Teilhard de Chardin, S.J., *The Divine Milieu* (New York: Harper & Row, 1960), pp. 80–83.

33. See: Medard Kehl & Werner Löser, eds., *The von Balthasar Reader* (New York: Crossroad, 1982), pp. 333–43.

34. Jacques Maritain, "The Natural Mystical Experience and the Void," *Understanding Mysticism,* ed. Richard Woods, O.P. (Garden City, N.Y.: Doubleday, 1980), pp. 496–97.

35. See: Michael Buckley, S.J., "Atheism and Contemplation," *Theological Studies* 40:4 (1979), p. 690.

36. *LFL*, s. I, no. 30, pp. 591–92.

37. This is a constant theme in Rahner's voluminous writings. For one example, see: Karl Rahner, *Foundations of Christian Faith* (New York: Seabury Press, 1978), pp. 116–32.

38. Evelyn Underhill, *Mysticism* (New York: Dutton, 1961), p. viii.

39. See: Richard Woods, *Mysterion. An Approach to Mystical Spirituality* (Chicago: Thomas More, 1981). Woods tends to value mysticism solely in terms of its personal and world-transforming effects.

40. For examples of this tendency, see: Erich Neumann, "Mystical Man," *Eranos Jahrbuch* 30 (1968), pp. 375–415; Carl Jung in his foreword to D.T. Suzuki's, *An Introduction to Zen Buddhism* (London: Rider, 1969), pp. 9–29; Erich Fromm, "Psychoanalysis and Zen Buddhism," *Zen Buddhism and Psychoanalysis* (New York: Harper, 1960), pp. 77–141.

41. See: *DN*, I, chap. 6, nos. 4–5, p. 308.

42. Hudleston, ed., *The Spiritual Letters of Dom John Chapman, O.S.B.*, p. 268.

43. For an excellent psychological analysis of the kataphatic and apophatic ways, see: Claudio Naranjo & Robert Ornstein, *On the Psychology of Meditation* (New York: Viking Press, 1972), esp. pp. 19–89.

44. See: "Common Misconceptions about Mysticism," in chap. 1 of this book.

45. For an excellent Catholic approach to the threefold Reformation formula, see: K. Rahner, *Foundations of Christian Faith*, pp. 359–66.

CHAPTER SIX

1. For an excellent treatment of this point, see: John F. Teahan, "A Dark and Empty Way: Thomas Merton and the Apophatic Tradition," *The Journal of Religion* 58:3 (July 1978), pp. 263–87.

2. See: Monica Furlong, *Merton: A Biography* (San Francisco: Harper & Row, 1980); and Elena Malits, *The Solitary Explorer:*

Thomas Merton's Transforming Journey (San Francisco: Harper & Row, 1980).

3. Walter T. Capps, *Hope against Hope: Moltmann to Merton in One Theological Decade* (Philadelphia: Fortress Press, 1976), p. xx.

4. Thomas Merton, *The Seven Storey Mountain (=SSM)* (New York: Harcourt, Brace, 1948), p. 169.

5. See: Malits, *The Solitary Explorer*, p. 128.

6. For a development of this point, see: ibid., pp. 139–56.

7. See: Thomas Merton, *Contemplative Prayer (=CP)* (Garden City, N.Y.: Doubleday, 1969). Also see his: *The Sign of Jonas (=SJ)* (Garden City, N.Y.: Doubleday, 1956), p. 187.

8. See Thomas P. McDonnell, ed., *A Thomas Merton Reader*, revised edition *(=TMR)* (Garden City, N.Y.: Doubleday, 1974), pp. 325, 328.

9. See: Thomas Merton, *William Blake, vol. X, Collected Essays* (Trappist, Ky.: Thomas Merton Collection, n.d.), p. 71.

10. See: Thomas Merton, *New Seeds of Contemplation (=NSC)* (New York: New Directions, 1961), p. 39. Also see: *CP*, p. 93.

11. Thomas Merton, "The Inner Experience," quoted by Raymond Bailey, *Thomas Merton on Mysticism* (Garden City, N.Y.: Doubleday, 1975), pp. 148–49. Also see: *CP*, pp. 91–92.

12. See: *CP*, pp. 29–30, 34, 90; *TMR*, pp. 326–27.

13. *TMR*, p. 433. See: Malits, *The Solitary Explorer*, chap. 6, pp. 120–38.

14. Thomas Merton, "The Inner Experience," quoted by Bailey, p. 152.

15. *CP*, p. 39.

16. See: *TMR*, pp. 326–27; "The Inner Experience," quoted by Bailey, pp. 152, 168.

17. *CP*, p. 89.

18. For the remarks that follow, see: *CP*, pp. 34, 36, 69, 96, 100, 105, 107–8; Furlong, *Merton: A Biography*, p. 197; Tho-

mas Merton, *Zen and the Birds of Appetite (=ZBA)* (New York: New Directions, 1968), p. 75.

19. *CP*, p. 97.

20. See: Teahan, "A Dark and Empty Way," pp. 267–69, 274; *TMR*, "Vision and Illusion," pp. 379–85.

21. Thomas Merton, *The Ascent to Truth (=AT)* (New York: Harcourt, Brace, 1951), p. 257.

22. *NSC*, pp. 134–35.

23. Thomas Merton, *Emblems of a Season of Fury* (New York: New Directions, 1963), p. 66.

24. See: *ZBA*, pp. 71–76; *TMR*, p. 515.

25. See: Abraham Maslow, *Towards a Psychology of Being* (Princeton, N.J.: Van Nostrand, 1962).

26. *ZBA*, pp. 71–72.

27. *ZBA*, p. 74.

28. For an excellent discussion on this point, see: Evelyn Underhill, *Mysticism* (New York: Dutton, 1961), pp. 418–31. For the distinction between a "mysticism of infinity" and a "mysticism of personality," see: Annemarie Schimmel, *Mystical Dimensions of Islam* (Chapel Hill: University of North Carolina Press, 1975), p. 5.

29. See chapter 4, "The Seventh Mansions," pp. 144–45; chap. 4, no. 16.

30. *ZBA*, p. 74. For a discussion of mysticism as a form of regression in the service of the ego, see: Arthur Deikman, "Deautomatization and the Mystic Experience," in *Altered States of Consciousness*, ed. Charles Tart, (Garden City, N.Y.: Doubleday, 1969), pp. 25–46. For some of the following views, see: John White, ed., *The Highest State of Consciousness* (Garden City, N.Y.: Doubleday, 1972), especially the essays by Raymond Prince, Charles Savage, Alexander Maven, and Kenneth Wapnick.

31. On this issue, see: Karl Rahner, *The Dynamic Element in the Church* (New York: Herder & Herder, 1964), pp. 94–95, n. 9.

32. See: *TMR*, pp. 328, 378; *SJ*, p. 152; "The White Pebble," *Sign* (July 1950), p. 27; *Mystics and Zen Masters (=MZM)* (New York: Dell, 1968), pp. 114–15; "The Inner Experience," quoted by Bailey, pp. 159–62.

33. See: *The Asian Journal of Thomas Merton*, edited from his original notebooks by Naomi Burton, Brother Patrick Hart, and James Laughlin *(=AJ)* (New York: New Dimensions, 1973), p. 325.

34. See: *CP*, p. 50.

35. "The Inner Experience," quoted by Bailey, p. 161.

36. *NSC*, p. 152.

37. See: *CP*, pp. 19, 42; *Contemplation in a World of Action (=CWA)* (Garden City, N.Y.: Image-Doubleday, 1971), pp. 100–1.

38. *CP*, p. 27.

39. See: *CP*, p. 54.

40. See: Carl Jung, *Memories, Dreams, and Reflections* (New York: Pantheon, 1963), pp. 176–78; *CP*, p. 85. For a fine treatment of how the monastic life neutralized the life-denying qualities of Merton's personality, see: Malits, *The Solitary Explorer*, pp. 151–53.

41. Thomas Merton, *Thoughts in Solitude (=TS)* (New York: Farrar, Straus & Giroux, 1976), p. 110; *CP*, p. 56. Also see: Monica Furlong, "His Solitude is His Being," *Merton: A Biography*, pp. 165–78.

42. See: *CP*, pp. 79, 86; Bailey, *Thomas Merton on Mysticism*, pp. 182–87.

43. *CWA*, p. 245.

44. *CP*, p. 24.

45. See: *ZBA*, pp. 27–28; *CP*, pp. 39, 103, 107–8; *MZM*, p. 168.

46. *CP*, p. 24.

47. See, for example: *ZBA*, pp. 121, 125; *MZM*, p. 283; *CP*, pp. 90, 94.

48. "First Christmas at Gethsemani," *Catholic World* 170 (December 1949), p. 30.

49. See: *ZBA*, p. 29; *CP*, p. 84; *TMR*, pp. 373–75; *Faith and Violence: Christian Teaching and Christian Practice (=FV)* (Notre Dame, Ind.: University of Notre Dame Press, 1968), p. 213; "The Inner Experience," quoted by Bailey, p. 157.

50. From his unpublished journals. See: Bailey, *Thomas Merton on Mysticism*, p. 114.

51. See: *CP*, pp. 28, 112; *TMR*, p. 373.

52. For an excellent treatment of Merton's views on silence, see: John F. Teahan, "The Place of Silence in Thomas Merton's Life and Thought," *The Journal of Religion* 61:4 (October 1981), pp. 364–83.

53. See: *CP*, pp. 52, 109; *FV*, p. 147; *The New Man (=NM)* (New York: Farrar, Straus & Giroux, 1978), pp. 142–43.

54. Thomas Merton, *Life and Holiness* (Garden City, N.Y.: Doubleday, 1964), p. 8.

55. See: *CP*, pp. 40, 55; *NSC*, pp. 51, 64; "The Contemplative Life," *Dublin Review* (Winter 1949), passim.

56. See: *TS*, p. 46; *NSC*, p. 22; *CP*, p. 23; *No Man is an Island (=NMI)* (New York: Dell, 1957), p. 95.

57. See: Thomas Merton, "Is Mysticism Normal?" *Commonweal* 51(1949–50), p. 98. *CP*, pp. 114–15; "The Inner Experience," quoted by Bailey pp. 137, 155.

58. On this point, see: Furlong, *Merton: A Biography*, p. 74.

59. See: *ZBA*, pp. 15–17.

60. See: *ZBA*, p. 207.

61. See: Malits, *The Solitary Explorer*, p. 168.

62. See: *AJ*, pp. 313, 342; Thomas Merton, "Christian Culture Needs Oriental Wisdom," *Catholic World* (May 1962), pp. 77–78.

63. Malits, *The Solitary Explorer*, pp. 113–19, esp. p. 113.

64. *AJ*, pp. 312–13.

65. See: *ZBA, MZM,* and *AJ;* Malits, *The Solitary Explorer,* pp. 104–13.

66. *ZBA,* pp. 60–61.

67. *ZBA,* p. 86.

68. See: *ZBA,* pp. 62, 68.

69. Thomas Merton, "The Zen Revival," *Continuum* (1964), p. 531.

70. For this quote, see: David Steindl-Rast, "Recollections of Thomas Merton's Last Days in the West," *Monastic Studies* (1969), p. 7. His deep experience of Jesus Christ during his Asian pilgrimage must also be emphasized in this context. See n. 33 above.

71. *ZBA,* p. 44.

72. *ZBA,* p. 34.

73. *ZBA,* p. 4. Also see: *MZM,* pp. 13–14.

74. On this point, see: *AJ,* pp. 309–10, 316, 322; *ZBA,* p. 43; Thomas Merton, *The Way of Chang Tzu* (New York: New Directions, 1965), p. 10.

75. *AJ,* p. 312.

76. On this point, see: *AJ,* p. vii; *CWA,* pp. 225–26; Thomas Merton, "Final Integration: Towards 'a Monastic Therapy,' " *Monastic Studies* (November 1968), p. 93.

77. Thomas Merton, *Conjectures of a Guilty Bystander* (=CGB) (Garden City, N.Y.: Doubleday, 1966), p. 21.

78. For these and the following remarks, see: Harvey D. Egan, S.J., "Christian Apophatic and Kataphatic Mysticisms," *Theological Studies* 39:3 (September 1978), esp. pp. 401–5.

79. Teahan, "A Dark and Empty Way," p. 284. Another author who has opened the treasures of Christian apophatic tradition to the English-speaking world is William Johnston, S.J. See especially his: *The Mysticism of the Cloud of Unknowing* (New York: Desclée, 1967); *Still Point* (San Francisco: Harper & Row, 1970); his edition of *The Cloud of Unknowing and the Book of Privy Counselling* (Garden City, N.Y.: Doubleday, 1973).

80. For one example, see: Aelred Graham, O.S.B., "Thomas Merton: A Modern Man in Reverse," *Atlantic Monthly* 72 (1953), p. 191.

81. See: William Callahan, S.J., "Noisy Contemplation," in *The Wind is Rising. Prayer for Active People,* ed. William Callahan, S.J., & Francine Cardman (Mt. Rainier, Md.: Quixote Center, 1978), pp. 34–37. After having first offered a few rather impractical suggestions on how to deepen the contemplative experience, Merton accepted the limitations that secular life puts on most people in search of richer prayer. He urged that they accept being "hidden contemplatives." On this point, see Bailey, *Thomas Merton on Mysticism,* pp. 154–55.

82. Ibid., p. 35.

83. Ibid., p. 37.

84. See: Karl Rahner, S.J., "Teresa of Avila: Doctor of the Church," in *Opportunities for Faith* (New York: Seabury Press, 1970), p. 123. For the following remarks concerning Rahner, see: Harvey D. Egan, S.J., "Rahner's Mystical Theology," in *Theology and Discovery. Essays in Honor of Karl Rahner, S.J.,* ed. William J. Kelly, S.J. (Milwaukee: Marquette University Press, 1980), pp. 139–58, esp. pp. 154–56.

85. Karl Rahner, *Visions and Prophecies* (New York: Herder & Herder, 1964), p. 14, n. 12.

86. For a few examples, see: Johnston, *The Still Point,* esp. pp. xiv, 28, 37; *The Inner Eye of Love* (San Francisco: Harper & Row, 1978), esp. pp. 20, 102, 131; *The Mirror Mind. Spirituality and Transformation* (San Francisco: Harper & Row, 1981), esp. p. 20; Richard Woods, O.P., *Mysterion. An Approach to Mystical Spirituality* (Chicago: Thomas More, 1981), esp. p. 364; Harvey D. Egan, S.J., *What Are They Saying About Mysticism?* (Ramsey, N.J.: Paulist Press, 1982), esp. chap. 9, "A Future Mystical Theology," pp. 109–16, which delineates the mystical theology of Bernard Lonergan, S.J., in terms of his emphasis upon human authenticity.

87. Gershom Scholem, in *Major Trends in Jewish Mysticism* (New York: Schocken, 1954, p. 5), likewise distinguishes the mystic from the ecstatic. This is also a point repeatedly made by Johnston. See also chap. 3, n. 7.

406

88. Yves Raguin, *The Depth of God* (St. Meinrad, Ind.: Abbey, 1975), p. 66.

89. Martin Buber, *Between Man and Man* (New York: Macmillan, 1972), p. 24.

90. See especially: R.C. Zaehner, "Standing on a Peak," *Concordant Discord* (London: Oxford University Press, 1970), pp. 302–22.

91. Ruysbroeck, *The Spiritual Espousals,* trans. Eric Colledge (London: Faber & Faber, 1952), book II, chap. 8, pp. 166–73.

92. See: Matthew 12:43–45.

93. See: Mircea Eliade, *Shamanism* (Princeton University Press, 1964), Bollingen Series 76; I.M. Lewis, *Ecstatic Religions* (Baltimore: Penguin, 1971); Carlos Castañeda, *The Teachings of Don Juan: A Yaqui Way of Knowledge* (New York: Ballantine, 1968).

94. Anthony de Mello, S.J., *Sadhana* (St. Louis: Institute of Jesuit Sources, 1978).

95. See: Johnston, *Silent Music. The Science of Meditation* (San Francisco: Harper & Row, 1974), p. 20; *The Mirror Mind,* p. 53.

96. See: Johnston, "Self Realization," *The Mirror Mind,* pp. 26–48. See esp. p. 48, n. 1.

97. See the various essays in: Tart, ed., *Altered States of Consciousness;* White, ed., *The Highest State of Consciousness.*

98. Carl Albrecht, *Psychologie des mystischen Bewusstseins* (Bremen, Germany: Schuenemann, 1951); *Das mystisches Erkennen* (Bremen, Germany: Schuenemann, 1958). Also see: Egan, *What Are They Saying about Mysticism?,* chap. 2, pp. 27–30.

99. Carl Albrecht, "Mystical Man," *Eranos Jahrbuch* 30 (1968), p. 404.

100. Johnston, *The Mirror Mind;* "Brainwave and Biofeedback," *Silent Music,* pp. 32–44.

101. See: *NSC,* pp. 86–88; *CGB,* pp. 222, 257; *Thoughts in Solitude* (New York: Farrar, Straus & Giroux, 1976), p. 22.

102. For excerpts from their correspondence, see: Furlong, *Merton: A Biography*, pp. 297–306, esp. pp. 300–1.

103. For a sample of the critiques of Suzuki, see: Johnston, *The Still Point*, pp. 1, 6, 15, 17, 18, 20–22, 52, 53, 58, 88, 95–96, 129, 171, 173, 184, 185.

104. Steven T. Katz, "Language, Epistemology, and Mysticism," *Mysticism and Philosophical Analysis*, ed. Steven T. Katz (New York: Oxford University Press, 1978), pp. 22–74, esp. pp. 26–27.

105. Zaehner, *Concordant Discord*, p. 436.

106. Ibid., p. 439.

107. See: Egan, *What Are They Saying about Mysticism?*, pp. 88–94.

108. For a positive evaluation of Eastern religions, see: William Johnston, S.J. and his works cited so far; Bede Griffiths, O.S.B., *Return to the Center* (Springfield, Ill.: Templegate, 1977); Karl Rahner, S.J., "Christianity and Non-Christian Religions," *TI* 5, pp. 115–134; Karl Rahner, S.J., "Observations on the Problem of the 'Anonymous Christian,'" *TI* 14, pp. 280–94.

109. Bailey, *Thomas Merton on Mysticism*, p. 12.

110. See: Malits, "Writing as Temperature," *The Solitary Explorer*, pp. 1–20.

CHAPTER SEVEN

1. Pierre Teilhard de Chardin, S.J., *Let Me Explain (=LME)*, ed. Jean-Pierre Dumoulin (New York: Harper & Row, 1970), p. 152.

2. Quoted by Henri de Lubac, S.J., *The Religion of Teilhard de Chardin* (Garden City, N.Y.: Doubleday, 1968), p. 16.

3. Ibid., p. 268.

4. Pierre Teilhard de Chardin, S.J., *Christianity and Evolution (=CE)* (New York: Harcourt Brace Jovanovich, 1971), p. 234.

5. See: Elena Malits, *The Solitary Explorer* (San Francisco: Harper & Row, 1980), esp. pp. 53–74.

6. Pierre Teilhard de Chardin, S.J., *Toward the Future (=TF)* (New York: Harcourt Brace Jovanovich, 1975), p. 16.

7. Pierre Teilhard de Chardin, S.J., *The Phenomenon of Man (=PM)* (New York: Harper & Row, 1959), pp. 284–85.

8. Quoted by de Lubac, *The Religion of Teilhard de Chardin,* p. 17.

9. Quoted by Thomas M. King, *Teilhard's Mysticism of Knowing* (New York: Seabury Press, 1982), p. 3.

10. Pierre Teilhard de Chardin, S.J., *Writings in Time of War (=WTW)* (New York: Harper & Row, 1968), p. 118.

11. Ibid., p. 119.

12. *CE,* p. 58.

13. *WTW,* p. 29.

14. Teilhard had said this about himself. Quoted by Ursula King, *Towards a New Mysticism. Teilhard de Chardin and Eastern Religions* (New York: Seabury Press, 1980), p. 112.

15. *WTW,* p. 29.

16. Henri de Lubac (*The Religion of Teilhard de Chardin,* p. 180) notes that Teilhard always specified what kind of pantheism he rejected, such as "common pantheism" or "humanitarian neo-pantheism." He had no difficulty, however, accepting "Christian pantheism" because it preserved the personal element which other pantheisms destroyed.

17. *WTW,* p. 32.

18. *WTW,* pp. 31–32.

19. *WTW,* p. 32.

20. Ibid.

21. Pierre Teilhard de Chardin, S.J., *How I Believe* (New York: Harper & Row, 1969), p. 3.

22. *PM,* p. 271.

23. Pierre Teilhard de Chardin, S.J., *The Divine Milieu (=DM),* (New York: Harper & Row, 1960), p. 106.

24. Quoted by T. M. King, *Teilhard's Mysticism of Knowing*, p. 69.

25. *WTW*, p. 136.

26. Pierre Teilhard de Chardin, S.J., *The Heart of the Matter* (=HM) (New York: Harcourt Brace Jovanovich, 1979), p. 94.

27. For example, see: *PM*, p. 31; *DM*, p. 46.

28. *DM*, p. 56.

29. See: de Lubac, "Creation, Cosmogenesis, Christogenesis," *The Religion of Teilhard de Chardin*, pp. 226–38, for an excellent treatment of Teilhard's views on creation and the traditional Christian doctrine of creation out of nothing.

30. Pierre Teilhard de Chardin, S.J., *Activation of Energy (=AE)* (New York: Harcourt Brace Jovanovich, 1963), p. 124.

31. *PM*, p. 65.

32. Pierre Teilhard de Chardin, S.J., *Human Energy (=HE)* (New York: Harcourt Brace Jovanovich, 1969), p. 72.

33. Pierre Teilhard de Chardin, S.J., *The Future of Man (=FM)* (New York: Harper & Row, 1964), p. 221; *Science and Christ* (=SC) (New York: Harper & Row, 1968), p. 94; *Man's Place in Nature (=MPN)* (New York: Harper & Row, 1966), pp. 36, 120; *PM*, p. 183; *HE*, pp. 23–24.

34. *SC*, p. 13.

35. *DM*, p. 59.

36. Quoted by T. M. King, *Teilhard's Mysticism of Knowing*, p. 57.

37. *AE*, p. 38.

38. *HM*, p. 47.

39. *PM*, p. 224.

40. *HM*, p. 78. Also see: *WTW*, pp. 266, 274, 275.

41. *DM*, p. 46, n. 1.

42. Quoted by U. King, *Towards a New Mysticism*, p. 115.

43. *HE*, p. 147.

44. Pierre Teilhard de Chardin, S.J., *The Making of the Mind (=MM)* (New York: Harper & Row, 1965), p. 207.

45. *DM,* pp. 76–77.

46. *DM,* p. 92.

47. *TF,* p. 117.

48. *AE,* p. 248.

49. For examples of Teilhard's views on death, see: *DM,* pp. 82, 89; *Hymn of the Universe (=HU)* (New York: Harper & Row, 1965), p. 31.

50. *HE,* preface.

51. *DM,* p. 102.

52. *DM,* p. 104.

53. *MM,* p. 149.

54. Quoted by T. M. King, *Teilhard's Mysticism of Knowing,* p. 136.

55. *DM,* pp. 133–34.

56. *WTW,* p. 246.

57. Pierre Teilhard de Chardin, S.J., *Letters from a Traveller (=LT)* (New York: Harper & Row, 1962), p. 73.

58. *LT,* pp. 99–100.

59. *SC,* p. 104.

60. *SC,* p. 106

61. *LT,* p. 216.

62. Pierre Teilhard de Chardin, S.J., *Lettres intimes (=Li)* (Paris: Aubier-Montaigne, 1972), p. 251.

63. *WTW,* p. 29.

64. T. M. King, *Teilhard's Mysticism of Knowing,* p. 84.

65. *DM,* p. 166.

66. For an excellent discussion of this point, see: U. King, *Towards a New Mysticism,* esp. pp. 138f., 197f.

67. Quoted by U. King, p. 176.

68. Ibid., p. 205.

69. For the remarks that follow, see: Ibid., esp. pp. 14, 96, 135, 145, 148, 190, 222–23.

70. Ibid., p. 222.

71. *Li*, p. 273.

72. *DM*, p. 118.

73. Quoted by U. King, *Towards a New Mysticism*, p. 48.

74. *SC*, p. 112; Pierre Teilhard de Chardin, S.J., *Lettres familières de Pierre Teilhard de Chardin, mon ami 1948–1955 (=Lf)* (Paris: Le Centurion, 1976), p. 186. On this point, see U. King, *Towards a New Mysticism*, pp. 192–218. For some of the following remarks, see esp. pp. 136, 155, 158, 165, 202, 213.

75. Quoted by U. King, *Towards a New Mysticism*, p. 158.

76. Ibid., pp. 202–3.

77. *FM*, p. 34.

78. Quoted by Christopher Mooney, S.J., *Teilhard de Chardin and the Mystery of Christ* (Garden City, N.Y.: Doubleday, 1968), p. 190.

79. *WTW*, pp. 39–40.

80. Ibid., p. 49.

81. On this point, see: Mooney, *Teilhard de Chardin and the Mystery of Christ*, pp. 95–111.

82. Pierre Teilhard de Chardin, S.J., "The Mass of the World," in *Hymn of the Universe* (New York: Harper & Row, 1965), pp. 19–37.

83. *DM*, p. 125.

84. Quoted by U. King, *Towards a New Mysticism*, p. 181.

85. *DM*, p. 117.

86. *HE*, p. 72.

87. *HM*, p. 41.

88. *AE,* p. 381.

89. *Li,* p. 309.

90. *SC,* p. 77.

91. U. King, *Towards a New Mysticism,* p. 205.

92. *DM,* p. 144.

93. *HM,* p. 15.

94. On Teilhard's triadic synthesis, see: King, *Teilhard's Mysticism of Knowing,* pp. 76–83, esp. pp. 78–79.

95. For an example of this view, see: Walter T. Stace, *The Teachings of the Mystics* (New York: New American Library, 1960), esp. pp. 14, 21, 23, 127, passim.

96. R. C. Zaehner, *Mysticism Sacred and Profane* (New York: Oxford University Press, 1961), p. 168.

97. Evelyn Underhill, *Mysticism* (New York: Dutton, 1961), pp. 192–93.

98. See: Yves Raguin, *The Depth of God* (St. Meinrad, Ind.: Abbey, 1975), p. 66; Martin Buber, *Between Man and Man* (New York: Macmillan, 1972), p. 24.

99. Quoted by U. King, *Towards a New Mysticism,* p. 98.

100. For an example of this nostalgic view, see: Bede Griffiths, O.S.B., *Return to the Center* (Springfield, Ill.: Templegate, 1977).

101. Friedrich Heiler, "The History of Religions as a Preparation for the Cooperation of Religions," in *The History of Religions: Essays in Methodology,* ed. M. Eliade & J. Kitagawa (Chicago: University of Chicago Press, 1959), pp. 142–53.

102. For a strong counterpoint to this common core view, see: R. C. Zaehner, *Concordant Discord* (London: Oxford University Press, 1970). For an example of one Catholic theologian who distinguishes East from West as sharply as Teilhard, see: Medard Kehl & Werner Löser, eds., *The von Balthasar Reader* (New York: Crossroad, 1982), pp. 333–43.

103. See: T. M. King, *Teilhard's Mysticism of Knowing,* pp. 137–42.

104. Aelred of Rievaulx, *On Spiritual Friendship* (Washington, D.C.: Cistercian Publications/Consortium Press, 1974), p. 112.

105. Bernard Lonergan, S.J., *Method in Theology* (New York: Seabury Press, 1979), p. 105. One criticism of Teilhard is his alleged blurring of the distinction between scientific and philosophical methodology. For a nuanced presentation of this point, see: Joseph Donceel, S.J., "Teilhard de Chardin: Scientist or Philosopher?," *International Philosophical Quarterly* 5 (1965), pp. 248–66.

106. Ibid., p. 113.

107. Ibid., p. 18.

108. Karl Rahner, S.J., *On the Theology of Death* (New York: Herder & Herder, 1961), p. 66. Also see his: "Christology within an Evolutionary View of the World," *TI* 5, pp. 157–92.

109. E. Récéjac, quoted by Underhill, *Mysticism*, p. 82.

110. *DM*, p. 78.

111. Griffiths, *Return to the Center*, p. 138.

112. Neumann, "Mystical Man," p. 388 (my emphasis).

113. For a fine treatment of this point, see: Underhill, *Mysticism*, pp. 421–38.

114. Ibid., p. 423.

115. For an excellent treatment of Teilhard on this point, see Mooney, *Teilhard de Chardin and the Mystery of Christ*, pp. 131–55.

116. Ibid., p. 211.

117. Ibid., p. 144.

118. Walter M. Abbott, S.J., ed., "Declaration on the Relationship of the Church to Non-Christian Religions," no. 2, in *The Documents of Vatican II* (New York: America Press, 1966), p. 662.

119. See: Karl Rahner, S.J., "Observations on the Problem of the 'Anonymous Christian,'" *TI* 14, pp. 280–94.

120. See: Egan, *What Are They Saying About Mysticism?*, pp. 64–75.

121. See: William Johnston, S.J., *Christian Zen* (New York: Harper & Row, 1971), p. 1.

122. U. King, *Towards a New Mysticism,* p. 212.

CHAPTER EIGHT

1. For the following remarks, see: Evelyn Underhill, *Mysticism* (New York: Dutton, 1961), pp. 358–79; Joseph de Guibert, S.J., *The Theology of the Spiritual Life* (New York: Sheed & Ward, 1953), pp. 353–55; A. Farges, *Mystical Phenomena* (London: Burns Oates & Washington, 1926), pp. 443–513; A. Royo, O.P., & J. Aumann, O.P., *The Theology of Christian Perfection* (Dubuque, Iowa: Priory Press, 1962), pp. 617–75.

2. See chap. 3, n. 7.

3. See: Karl Rahner, *Visions and Prophecies* (New York: Herder & Herder, 1964), pp. 86–88.

4. See chap. 5, pp. 182–83.

5. William J. Young, S.J., trans., *The Spiritual Journal of Saint Ignatius,* May 11–28 entries, in *Woodstock Letters* 87:3 (July 1958), pp. 247–50.

6. Ibid., May 22, p. 249.

7. See: Underhill, *Mysticism,* pp. 277–78.

8. Ibid., pp. 80, 241, 278, 293–96.

9. Quoted by Claudio Naranjo & Robert Ornstein, *On the Psychology of Meditation* (New York: Viking Press, 1972), pp. 126–27. Square brackets found in text.

10. Many theologians prefer to say that public revelation closed with the death of the last apostle. For a contemporary approach to this question, see: Karl Rahner, *Inspiration in the Bible* (New York: Herder & Herder, 1961).

11. Rahner, *Visions and Prophecies,* pp. 60, 82, 103.

12. Ibid., pp. 67f.

13. John K. Ryan, trans., *The Confessions of St. Augustine* (Garden City, N.Y.: Doubleday, 1960), book 10, chap. 6, pp. 233–34.

14. See chap. 3, "Mystical Discernment," pp. 98–101.

15. Joseph de Guibert, *The Jesuits: Their Doctrine and Practice* (Chicago: Institute of Jesuit Sources, 1964), pp. 62–64.

16. For a detailed exposition of this topic, see: James D. G. Dunn, *Jesus and the Spirit* (Philadelphia: Westminster Press, 1975); George T. Montague, S.M., *The Holy Spirit: Growth of a Biblical Tradition* (New York: Paulist Press, 1976).

17. On this point, see: Dunn, *Jesus and the Spirit*, p. 211.

18. Ibid., p. 210.

19. This seems to be the position of R. Garrigou-Lagrange, *Christian Perfection and Contemplation* (St. Louis: Herder, 1937), p. 458.

20. Dunn, *Jesus and the Spirit*, p. 323.

21. Karl Rahner, "Religious Enthusiasm and the Experience of Grace," *TI* 16, pp. 42, 47. For the following points by Rahner, see pp. 35–51.

22. Ibid., p. 44.

23. Ibid.

24. See: Aldous Huxley, *The Doors of Perception* (New York: Harper & Row, 1954); Alan Watts, *The Joyous Cosmology* (New York: Vintage, 1962); Timothy Leary, *The Politics of Ecstasy* (New York: Putnam's, 1968). For a fine treatment of "Psychedelic Drugs in the Twentieth Century," see: Lester Grinspoon & James B. Bakalar, *Psychedelic Drugs Reconsidered* (New York: Basic Books, 1979), pp. 56–88.

25. Quoted by Houston Smith, in "Do Drugs Have Religious Import?," *The Journal of Philosophy* 18 (1964), pp. 523–24. See also: G. Ray Gordan, "LSD and Mystical Experiences," in *The Highest States of Consciousness*, ed. John White (Garden City, N.Y.: Doubleday, 1972), pp. 278–94.

26. R. E. L. Masters & Jean Houston, *The Varieties of Psychedelic Experience* (New York: Dell, 1966), p. 323, n. 1.

27. R. C. Zaehner, *Zen, Drugs, and Mysticism* (New York: Vintage, 1974); *Mysticism Sacred and Profane* (New York: Oxford University Press, 1961); William Johnston, S.J., *The Still Point*

(San Francisco: Harper & Row, 1970), esp. pp. 143–50; *Silent Music* (New York: Harper & Row, 1974).

28. Masters & Houston, *Varieties*, p. 308; Stanislav Grof, *Realms of the Unconscious* (New York: Dutton, 1976), p. 16. Also see: Masters & Houston, "The Experimental Induction," *The Highest States of Consciousness*, ed. John White, p. 308.

29. Gordan, "LSD and Mystical Experiences," p. 288.

30. Masters & Houston, *Varieties*, p. 260.

31. Ibid., pp. 259, 305; Gordan, "LSD and Mystical Experiences," p. 286.

32. Masters & Houston, *Varieties*, p. 123.

33. Ibid., pp. 122–26, 259.

34. Quoted by Zaehner, *Zen, Drugs, and Mysticism*, pp. 108–9.

35. Masters & Houston, *Varieties*, p. 307; Grof, *Realms of the Unconscious*, pp. 14, 219–22; Walter Pahnke, "Drugs and Mysticism,' *The Highest States of Consciousness*, ed. John White, p. 273; Robert E. Mogar, "Current Status and Future Trends in Psychedelic (LSD) Research," *Altered States of Consciousness*, ed. Charles T. Tart (Garden City, N.Y.: Doubleday, 1969), pp. 392, 397.

36. Masters & Houston, "The Experimental Induction," p. 320.

37. Mogar, "Current Status and Future Trends in Psychedelic (LSD) Research," p. 400.

38. Grof, *Realms of the Unconscious*, p. 203; Masters & Houston, *Varieties*, p. 134; Gordan, "LSD and Mystical Experiences," p. 280.

39. Anthony Campbell, *Seven States of Consciousness* (New York: Harper & Row, 1974), p. 126.

40. Masters & Houston, *Varieties*, pp. 85, 187; "The Experimental Induction," pp. 308–9; Mogar, "Current Status and Future Trends," pp. 402–3; Gordan, "LSD and Mystical Experiences," p. 294.

41. Masters & Houston, "The Experimental Induction," pp. 304, 308–9; Grof, *Realms of the Unconscious*, pp. 20, 32, 216;

Mogar, "Current Status and Future Trends," p. 402; Masters & Houston, *Varieties,* p. 187.

42. Masters & Houston, "The Experimental Induction," p. 304.

43. Walter N. Pahnke & William Richards, "Implications of LSD and Experimental Mysticism," *Altered States,* ed. Charles T. Tart, p. 429.

44. Masters & Houston, *Varieties,* p. 258. See also pp. 261, 265.

45. R. C. Zaehner, *Zen, Drugs, and Mysticism,* p. 109.

46. W. T. Stace, *Mysticism and Philosophy* (New York: Macmillan, 1960), pp. 29–30.

47. Pahnke & Richards, "Implications of LSD," pp. 411–17.

48. Masters & Houston, *Varieties,* p. 257.

49. Ibid., p. 267. For a similar description of psychedelic phenomena, see: Grof, *Realms of the Unconscious,* pp. 158–205. Also worth noting is: Frank Lake, *Clinical Theology* (London: Darton, Longman & Todd, 1966).

50. Masters & Houston, *Varieties,* p. 148.

51. Ibid.

52. Mogar, "Current Status and Future Trends," p. 406.

53. B. Grom, "Die Jesus Bewegung," *Stimmen der Zeit* 9 (1972), p. 192; Gordan, "LSD and Mystical Experiences," p. 281.

54. Peter Matthiessen, "A Reporter at Large: The Snow Leopard I.," *New Yorker* (March 27, 1978), pp. 57–58.

55. Heinrich Dumoulin, S.J., *A History of Zen Buddhism* (Boston: Beacon Press, 1963), pp. 101, 109, 118–120; William Young, S.J., trans., *St. Ignatius' Own Story* (Chicago: Loyola University Press, 1956), pp. 7–12.

56. For a discussion of this point and some of the following, see: Joachim Jeremias, *New Testament Theology* (New York: Scribner's, 1971), pp. 85–96.

418

57. See: Heinrich Schlier, *Principalities and Powers in the New Testament* (New York: Herder & Herder, 1961).

58. Ibid., p. 20.

59. Ibid., pp. 28–29.

60. Ibid., p. 67.

61. Quoted by Johnston, *Silent Music*, pp. 98–99.

62. Quoted by Poulain, *Interior Prayer*, p. 438. See pp. 436–54 for an excellent treatment of demonic obsession.

63. See: Poulain, *Interior Prayer*, pp. 428–29.

64. See: Karl Rahner, S.J., "Possession," *EOT*, p. 1258.

65. See: Karl Rahner, S.J., "Demonology," and "Angels," *EOT*, pp. 4, 7, 333. For the next points made by Rahner, see also: Karl Rahner & Herbert Vorgrimler, "Angel," "Angelology," "Devil," "Devils, Demons," "Possession," *DTh*, pp. 10–12, 123–24, 389–98.

66. Jules Toner, S.J., *A Commentary on Saint Ignatius' Rules for the Discernment of Spirits* (St. Louis: Institute of Jesuit Sources, 1982), pp. 201–2. For some of the points which follow, see pp. 260–70.

67. Ibid., p. 270.

CHAPTER NINE

1. See: R. Garrigou-Lagrange, O.P., *Christian Perfection and Contemplation* (St. Louis: Herder, 1937), pp. 129, 135–39; Joseph de Guibert, S.J., *The Theology of the Spiritual Life* (New York: Sheed & Ward), pp. 289, 299.

2. On this point, see: Karl Rahner, S.J., "Reflections on the Unity of the Love of Neighbour and the Love of God," *TI* 6, pp. 231–49.

3. See: de Guibert, *Spiritual Life*, p. 289.

4. Ibid., p. 284.

5. Ibid.

6. Ibid.

7. Ibid., pp. 285–86. On this point, also see: Garrigou-Lagrange, *Christian Perfection,* p. 6.

8. Garrigou-Lagrange, *Christian Perfection,* p. 46.

9. Karl Rahner, S.J., "Reflections on the Problem of the Gradual Ascent to Christian Perfection," *TI* 3, pp. 3–23.

10. Quoted by J. V. Bainvel in his introduction to: A. Poulain, S.J., *The Graces of Interior Prayer* (Westminster, Vt.: Celtic Cross Books, 1978), p. lxxiv.

11. Garrigou-Lagrange, *Christian Perfection,* p. 160.

12. On this point, see: J. V. Bainvel, in Poulain, *Interior Prayer,* pp. liv, lxxiv, lxxxiv; de Guibert, *Spiritual Life,* p. 344; Garrigou-Lagrange, *Christian Perfection,* p. 147; A. Royo, O.P., & J. Aumann, O.P., *The Theology of Christian Perfection* (Dubuque, Iowa: Priory Press, 1962), p. 176.

13. For proponents of this position, see: A. Saudreau, *The Degrees of the Spiritual Life* (New York: Benziger, 1907); J. Arintero, O.P., *The Mystical Evolution in the Development and Vitality of the Church* (New York: Herder, 1949). On this point, see the perceptive remarks of: de Guibert, *Spiritual Life,* p. 286.

14. De Guibert, *Spiritual Life,* pp. 287–91, 340–52. Another proponent of this view is: A. Farges, *Mystical Phenomena* (London: Burns Oates & Washington, 1926), pp. 299–314.

15. De Guibert, *Spiritual Life,* p. 346.

16. Ibid.

17. Ibid. J. V. Bainvel (Poulain, *Interior Prayer,* p. liv) agrees with de Guibert on this point. He argues that persons experiencing contemplation are not always the most perfect (p. lxxiv). Both Bainvel (p. xci) and Royo & Aumann (*The Theology of Christian Perfection,* p. 194) concur that occasional mystical touches do not necessarily consitute a call to the mystical life.

18. Garrigou-Lagrange, *Christian Perfection,* pp. 23–44, 162, 175. For another proponent, see: Royo & Aumann, *The Theology of Christian Perfection,* pp. 178–96.

19. Garrigou-Lagrange, *Christian Perfection,* p. 175.

20. See: J. V. Bainvel, in Poulain, *Interior Prayer*, pp. lxxxix, lxxiii; Hans Urs von Balthasar, in M. Kehland & W. Löser, eds., *The von Balthasar Reader* (New York: Crossroad, 1982), pp. 333–34. Karl Rahner ("Reflections on the Problem of the Gradual Ascent to Christian Perfection," *TI* 3, p. 22) cautiously states that "the New Testament . . . does not give *explicit* expression to such an orientation towards mysticism" (my emphasis).

21. Quoted by de Guibert, *Spiritual Life*, p. 350.

22. Ibid. Also see: Farges, *Mystical Phenomena*, pp. 236, 243; Poulain, *Interior Prayer*, p. 524.

23. For a contemporary statement on this point, see: Kehland & Löser, eds., *The von Balthasar Reader*, p. 342.

24. See: de Guibert, *Spiritual Life*, p. 350; Poulain, *Interior Prayer*, p. 526.

25. See: Royo & Aumann, *The Theology of Christian Perfection*, p. 194.

26. Garrigou-Lagrange, *Christian Perfection*, p. 40. It is instructive to note that Garrigou-Lagrange quotes Poulain on this issue (p. 40, n. 42). Poulain says that: "Almost all." Garrigou-Lagrange says in the main text that: "All the canonized saints."

27. J. V. Bainvel (in Poulain, *Interior Prayer*, p. cii) quotes an entire letter from M. de la Taille, an advocate of the point under discussion.

28. J. V. Bainvel, in Poulain, *Interior Prayer*, p. lxxxix.

29. For an excellent discussion of the two lives in the Church, see: Dom C. Butler, *Western Mysticism* (London: Constable, 1926), pp. 227–42, 248–73, 277–87.

30. J. V. Bainvel, in Poulain, *Interior Prayer*, p. lxxxix.

31. Teresa of Avila, for example, held a view similar to Ignatius. She expressed surprise when she found great virtue in someone who was married. See: *AB*, chap. 13, p. 140; chap. 23, p. 222; chap. 31, p. 297; *IC*, m. 5, chap. 4, p. 118.

32. Karl Rahner, "On the Evangelical Counsels," *TI* 8, pp. 133–67. The remarks that follow come from this article.

33. Karl Rahner, "Reflections on the Problem of the Gradual Ascent to Christian Perfection," *TI* 3, p. 22.

34. Ibid., p. 23.

35. Karl Rahner, "Mystical Experience and Mystical Theology," *TI* 17, pp. 90–99. The following remarks in the main text are a summary of Rahner's position. Also see: Harvey D. Egan, S.J., "Rahner's Mystical Theology," in *Theology and Discovery. Essays in Honor of Karl Rahner, S.J.*, ed. William J. Kelly, S.J. (Milwaukee: Marquette University Press, 1980), pp. 139–58.

36. See: Royo & Aumann, *The Theology of Christian Perfection*, pp. 190–93. Farges, *Mystical Phenomena* (p. 299), on the other hand, underscores the rarity of mystical fruition. He denies that the life of grace develops into infused contemplation like an acorn becoming an oak. He says it is more like a block of marble becoming a statue (p. 300)!

37. J. V. Bainvel, in Poulain, *Interior Prayer*, p. lv.

38. Ibid., p. cvii; de Guibert, *Spiritual Life*, pp. 342–43.

39. *The Living Flame of Love*, s. I, no. 30, pp. 591–92.

40. See: Pierre Teilhard de Chardin, S.J., *The Divine Milieu* (New York: Harper & Row, 1960), pp. 80–83; chap. 7, "The Meaning of Human Activity and Passivity."

41. Catherine of Genoa, *Purgation and Purgatory* and *The Spiritual Dialogue* (Ramsey, N.J.: Paulist Press, 1979).

42. Karl Rahner & Herbert Vorgrimler, "Purgatory," *DTh*, pp. 426–27.

43. See chap. 6, n. 86, and "The Way of Ordinary and Hidden Contemplation," in *The von Balthasar Reader*, p. 342.

44. J. V. Bainvel, in Poulain, *Interior Prayer*, p. lxxxviii; Farges, *Mystical Phenomena*, p. 311. Garrigou-Lagrange (*Christian Perfection*, p. 162), leaves explicit consciousness out of his definition of mysticism in the strict sense.

45. Bernard Lonergan, *Method in Theology* (New York: Seabury Press, 1979).

46. See the works of E. Erikson, L Kohlberg, J. Fowler, and J.

Piaget. For a popular introduction to this approach, see: Gail Sheehy, *Passages: Predictable Crises in Adult Life* (New York: Dutton, 1976).

47. This section is a revision of my article, "The Christian Mystics and Today's Theological Horizon," *Listening* 17:3 (Autumn 1982), pp. 203–16.

48. See: Hans Urs von Balthasar, "Exerzitien und Theologie," *Orienterung* 12 (1948), p. 230; Théologie et Sainteté," *Dieu Vivant* 12 (1948), pp. 15–32; F. Vandenbroucke, "Le divorce entre theologie et mystique. Ses Origines," *Nouvelle Revue Theologique* 72 (1950), pp. 372–89.

49. See: Karl Rahner, S.J., "Theology in the New Testament," *TI* 5, pp. 23–41.

50. See: Eric Voegelin, "Gospel and Culture," *Jesus and Man's Hope*, ed. D. G. Miller & D. V. Hadidian (Pittsburgh: Pittsburgh Theological Seminary, 1971), p. 88; William Johnston, S.J., *The Inner Eye of Love*, esp. pp. 137, 219–27; Karl Rahner, S.J., *TI* 16, esp. chaps. 4, 5.

51. Bernard Lonergan, S.J., "Theology and Praxis," *Proceedings of the 32nd Annual CTSA* (June 15–18, 1977), p. 14 (my emphasis).

52. Lonergan, *Method in Theology*, esp. pp. 53, 231–32. Johnston (*Inner Eye* and *The Mirror Mind*) has shown how Lonergan's transcendental precepts can be used in the dialogue between Western and Eastern religions. For the importance of Lonergan for the future of mystical theology, see: Harvey D. Egan, S.J., "A Future Mystical Theology," *What Are They Saying about Mysticism?* (Ramsey, N.J.: Paulist Press, 1982), pp. 109–16.

53. Lonergan, *Method in Theology*, p. 18.

54. Ibid., p. 105.

55. Ibid., pp. 105–6.

56. Ibid., p. 106.

57. Ibid., pp. 52, 130, 267–70.

58. Ibid., p. 241.

423

59. Johnston, *Inner Eye*, p. 58.

60. St. Symeon, the New Theologian, seemingly held that only charismatic theology is genuine theology. See: George Maloney, S.J., *The Mystic of Fire and Love: St. Symeon, the New Theologian* (Denville, N.J.: Dimension Books, 1975).

61. Karl Rahner, S.J., "Transzendenzerfahrung aus Katholisch Dogmatischer Sicht," *Schriften zur Theologie* 13 (Zürich-Einsiedeln-Köln: Benziger, 1978), p. 210.

62. Karl Rahner, S.J., *TI* 16, p. 72, n. 12.

63. Ibid., p. x.

64. Karl Rahner, S.J., "Teresa of Avila: Doctor of the Church," in *Opportunities for Faith* (New York: Seabury Press, 1970), p. 123.

65. Karl Rahner, S.J., *The Dynamic Element in the Church* (New York: Herder & Herder, 1964), pp. 85–87.

66. Karl Rahner, S.J., *TI* 17, p. 97, n. 8; *TI* 16, p. x.

67. Karl Rahner, S.J., "The Church of the Saints," *TI* 3, esp. pp. 97–99.

68. Karl Rahner, S.J., "Christian Living Formerly and Today," *TI* 7, p. 15.

Index

James, William, 105, 172

Japanese mysticism, 280

Jaspers, Karl, 224

Jeremias, Joachim, 386n.30;
418n.56

Jesus-people movement, 93

John Climacus, Saint, 318

John of the Cross, Saint (1542–
1592), 4, 28, 29, 41, 151,
241, 254, 303, 309, 350,
351, 371, 384n.6; Doctor of
the Church, 165

Works: *Ascent of Mount Carmel
(AMC)*, 167–68, 170, 171,
172, 174, 175–76, 180, 184,
187–88, 202, 205, 211, 212,
213; *Dark Night (DN)*, 168,
170, 171, 172, 173, 178,
193, 202; *Living Flame of
Love (LFL)*, 167, 168, 171,
176, 200, 202, 205, 350;
Spiritual Canticle (SC), 167,
171, 193–95, 196, 199, 204,
205

Mysticism of John of the Cross

major theme of the Prologues,
167–73: *the dark night*, 167;
need for spiritual director,
167–68, 185–86, 202–4; *Ju-
daeo-Christian tradition*,
169; *scripture and Church*,
169–71; *nature of mystical
experience*, 171–73; *scholastic theology*, 172; *necessity of
language in mysticism*, 173

first phase of mystical ascent,
173–79: *apophatic character*,
174; *mortification of appetites*, 174–75

active night of the senses, 175–
76: *imitation of Christ*, 175–
76; *bridal mysticism*, 175–76

beginner's states, 176–77:

meditation, 176; *danger of
self-seeking pleasure*, 176–77

passive night of the senses, 177–
79: *from self-initiated meditation to God-given contemplation*, 177–79

second phase of mystical ascent,
179–93

active night of the spirit, 179–
89: *rejection of all understanding*, 179; *cloud of forgetting*, 179, 182; *pure naked
faith*, 179; *union of likeness
with God*, 179–80; *night of
the understanding*, 180; *from
meditation to contemplation*,
180–82; *imagination*, 180–
81; *fantasy*, 181; *sensory
meditation*, 181; *secondary
mystical phenomena*, 182–
83; *divine communications*,
183–84; *knowledge of naked
truths*, 184–85; *"formal locutions,"* 185–86; *supernatural communications and
Church*, 186; *night of the
memory*, 186; *night of the
will*, 187–89; *practice of virtues*, 188

state of proficients, 189: *like little children in the ways of
God*, 189

passive night of the spirit, 189–
93: *infused contemplation as
"mystical theology,"* 190;
*experiences of contemplatives
in the passive night*, 190–92

third phase of the mystical ascent, 193–204: *preliminary
remarks*, 193–95; *experience
of trinity*, 193–94; *wounds of
love*, 194–95

spiritual betrothal, 195–96

mystical marriage, 196–200:
total transformation into the

430

p. 358 = limits of evil

pp. 304-305 secondary phenomena ~ pp. 306-307

pp 367-378
Rahner's
theology of
the
Councils:
Theo Invest.
vol 3